From the provisional government of Kerensky in 1917 to the Cambodian transitional authorities in the early 1990s, interim governments provide a wide range of possibilities for political change and regime transition. Yet insufficient attention has been given to the role of interim regimes in democratic transitions – a serious shortcoming given the major impact these transitional authorities have wielded on the nature of the future political system: the degree of political openness in the democracy, including respect for human rights, the role of the bureaucracy in society, the position of the armed forces in the new political constellation, the country's future international standing, and the relationship between the economy and the government. *Between States* is the first book to systematically assess the broad implications interim governments have on the establishment of democratic regimes and on the existence of states. Based on historical and contemporary democratization experiences, the book presents four ideal types of interim government: opposition-led provisional governments, power-sharing interim governments, incumbent-led caretaker governments, and international interim governments mandated by the United Nations.

The first part of *Between States* explores the theoretical problems of each of these models from a broad comparative perspective. It uses historical and contemporary cases to present a wide spectrum of contexts for comparison. The second part provides extensive case studies, drawing on examples from Asia, South America, and Europe, which are intended to illustrate, appraise, amplify, and criticize the analysis in Part One.

Between states

CAMBRIDGE STUDIES IN COMPARATIVE POLITICS

General Editor
PETER LANGE Duke University

Associate Editors
ELLEN COMISSO University of California, San Diego
PETER HALL Harvard University
JOEL MIGDAL University of Washington
HELEN MILNER Columbia University
RONALD ROGOWSKI University of California, Los Angeles
SIDNEY TARROW Cornell University

OTHER BOOKS IN THE SERIES

Allan Kornberg and Harold D. Clarke *Citizens and Community: Political Support in a Representative Democracy*
David D. Laitin *Language Repertoires and State Construction in Africa*
Catherine Boone *Merchant Capital and the Roots of State Power in Senegal, 1930–1985*
Ellen Immergut *Health Politics: Interests and Institutions in Western Europe*
Sven Steinmo, Kathleen Thelan, and Frank Longstreth, eds. *Structuring Politics: Historical Institutionalism in Comparative Analysis*
Thomas Janoski and Alexander M. Hicks, eds. *The Comparative Political Economy of the Welfare State*
Paul Pierson *Dismantling the Welfare State: The Politics of Retrenchment in Britain and the United States*
Herbert Kitschelt *The Transformation of European Social Democracy*
Sidney Tarrow *Power in Movement: Social Protest, Reform, and Revolution*
Joel S. Migdal, Atul Kohli, and Vivienne Shue *State Power and Social Forces: Domination and Transformation in the Third World*
Roberto Franzosi *The Puzzle of Strikes: Class and State Strategies in Postwar Italy*
Theda Skocpol *Social Revolutions in the Modern World*
Marino Regini *Uncertain Boundaries: The Social and Political Construction of European Economies*
Ashutosh Varshney *Democracy, Development, and the Countryside: Urban-Rural Struggles in India*

Between states

Interim governments and democratic transitions

YOSSI SHAIN   JUAN J. LINZ
Tel-Aviv University   *Yale University*

With contributions from Lynn Berat,
Thomas C. Bruneau, H. E. Chehabi, Daniel V. Friedheim,
Paula Franklin Lytle, James W. McGuire,
Barnett R. Rubin, and Allison K. Stanger

CAMBRIDGE
UNIVERSITY PRESS

Published by the Press Syndicate of the University of Cambridge
The Pitt Building, Trumpington Street, Cambridge CB2 1RP
40 West 20th Street, New York, NY 10011-4211, USA
10 Stamford Road, Oakleigh, Melbourne 3166, Australia

First published 1995

Printed in the United States of America

Library of Congress Cataloging-in-Publication Data
Shain, Yossi, 1956–
Between states : interim governments and democratic transitions /
Yossi Shain, Jaun J. Linz ; with contributions from Thomas C.
Bruneau . . . [et al.].
p.   cm. – (Cambridge studies in comparative politics)
Includes index.
ISBN 0-521-47417-5. – ISBN 0-521-48498-7 (pbk.)
1. State, The.   2. Democracy.   3. State succession.   4. World
politics – 1945–   I. Linz, Jaun J. (Jaun José), 1926–
II. Title.   III. Series.
JC249.S47   1995
320′.01′1–dc20   94-39767
                                                          CIP

A catalog record for this book is available from the British Library.

ISBN 0-521-47417-5 Hardback
ISBN 0-521-48498-7 Paperback

For Nancy and Rocío

Contents

Preface

This book is the product of the authors' research and collaboration over many years. The project began, in a sense, in 1976 when Juan Linz presented a paper at the International Political Science Association in Edinburgh entitled "Time and Regime Change." In this paper Linz addressed the question whether political scientists can develop models of regime change that would include a time dimension. His attention to timing as a political factor led him to examine the impact of speed and deadlines for the process of holding first free elections. Linz returned to this theme in his subsequent research on the Spanish transition, where the timing factor was central to the strategy and success of Adolfo Suárez. This early examination produced the hypothesis that a regime transition led by an incumbent is more conducive to a democratic outcome than one led by opposition-led provisional government. In this early paper Linz also noted how crucial the commitment of the Portuguese army-led provisional government to hold free elections one year after the 1974 coup was in insuring a democratic exit after a protracted transition. A revised version of this early paper was published in 1986 in *Teoria Politica* under the title "Il fattore tempo nei mutamenti di regime."

In 1986, Linz introduced his paper to Yossi Shain, then a doctoral student of Linz at Yale. Intrigued by Linz's comments on timing in politics Shain explored the time factor in his works on the politics of exiles, and subsequently decided to probe the subject of interim governments in a more systematic manner. From 1989 to 1990, in the wake of the "third wave" of democratic transitions, the dramatic changes in Eastern Europe and the growing Soviet-American accord on regional conflicts, Shain began to elaborate on Linz's early writings and wrote the early version of Part One of this book. Troubled by the inability of employing domestic interim government arrangements in countries where accommodation between indigenous contestants seemed unattainable, Shain sought Lynn Berat's expertise on the role of the international interim government in Namibia. In a series of articles Shain and Berat explored the possibility of employing a modified Namibian model to other troubled spots, where the superpowers began their disengagement, and offered the model to Cambodia, Afghanistan, and South Africa. The UN Security Council subsequently followed their line of reasoning when it adopted a peace plan for Cambodia in August 1990.

In December 1990, Shain completed an elaborated version of the theoretical chapters and sent it to Linz who was then spending the year at the Wissenschaftskolleg zu Berlin. After several exchanges, they agreed to develop the manuscript into a book, and in the summer of 1991 a draft was circulated among scholars, some of whom participated in a panel on interim governments held at the 1991 American Political Science Association Meeting in Washington, D.C. A much shorter version of this conference paper was subsequently published in January 1992 by *The Journal of Democracy*. The 1991 version served as a point of departure for the case studies in Part Two.

Shain spent 1992 as an International Fulbright Fellow at Yale and as a Visiting Professor at Middlebury College. During this time, he and Linz expanded their theoretical essay and exchanged drafts with the contributors to the second part. The manuscript was submitted for review to Cambridge University Press in December 1992, and final revisions were made in the summer of 1993. Minor updating was made in August 1994.

While working on this project we have been pursuing other related issues. Juan Linz has continued his wide range exploration of regime transitions. He has completed a collective volume edited with Arturo Valenzuela entitled *The Failure of Presidential Democracy,* and he is now finishing a book with Alfred Stepan, *Problems of Democratic Transition and Consolidation*. Linz has also collaborated with Stepan and Gunther on the book, *Southern European Transitions in Comparative Perspective*.

Yossi Shain has been writing with Lynn Berat on the political, moral, and legal dimension of "evening the score" with the goblins of authoritarianism. His analysis of the subject as pertaining to the role of interim government was published with Lynn Berat in June 1993 in *Estudios Interdisciplinarios de America Latina y el Caribe* (EIAL). A paper by Berat and Shain on the transitional phase in South Africa is forthcoming in *Law and Social Inquiry*.

Obviously there are some overlaps among these projects, and probably some differences as they were completed in different points of time. Yet this book stands on its own, focusing on many problems almost ignored or only touched in the other works.

We wish to thank the authors of the second part for their contributions to the evolution of this project, particularly H. E. Chehabi for his close reading of the first part. We also wish to thank Alex Holzman, our editor at Cambridge University Press, and our copyeditor, Carolyn Viola-John. Yossi Shain also acknowledges the following colleagues for rendering their insightful comments and editorial assistance along the way. Lynn Berat has been an inspiring friend and a delightful coauthor. He also benefited from early discussions with Yitzhak Klein, and gained from Erez T. Yanuv's firsthand account on Cambodia's transition. At Middlebury College, Shain owes great thanks to Murray Dry, Michael Kraus, Russell Leng, and Ronald Liebowitz. The financial support of the Social Science Faculty at Tel Aviv University is gratefully acknowledged. We all are indebted to Tim Spears for suggesting the title *Between States*.

Contributors

LYNN BERAT is a visiting scholar at the Yale program on nonprofit organizations and a consultant to the Africa and Middle East program of the Ford Foundation. She is the author of *Walvis Bay: Decolonization and International Law,* as well as of numerous articles on African politics and law.

THOMAS C. BRUNEAU is chairman and professor of the Department of National Security Affairs, Naval Postgraduate School, Monterey, California. He joined the Naval Postgraduate School in 1987 after having taught in the Department of Political Science, McGill University, Montreal, Canada, since 1969. He has researched and written extensively on Portugal and Latin America, especially Brazil. His most recent book on Portugal (with Alex Macleod) is *Politics in Contemporary Portugal: Parties and the Consolidation of Democracy* (Boulder: Lynne Rienner Publishers, 1986). Since joining the Naval Postgraduate School he has focused on security policy in the United States and other countries. His most recent article on Portuguese security policy is "Defense Modernization and the Armed Forces in Portugal," *Portuguese Studies Review,* Fall/Winter 1991–92. During 1992–93, Professor Bruneau conducted research in Lisbon and Madrid on the topic of Portuguese and Spanish Defense Policies, which resulted in a series of reports and forthcoming articles. With support from the Luso-American Development Foundation, he and Dr. Mario Bacalhau conducted a national-level public opinion survey in the summer of 1993 on Portuguese attitudes and behavior concerning politics since the Revolution of April 25, 1974.

H. E. CHEHABI is a visiting Fellow at St. Antony's College, Oxford University. He is the author of *Iranian Politics and Religious Modernism: The Liberation Movement of Iran under the Shah and Khomeini* (Cornell University Press, 1990) and coeditor with Alfred Stepan of *Poli-*

tics, Democracy, and Society: Comparative Enquiries (Westview Press, 1995).

DANIEL V. FRIEDHEIM is finishing his dissertation "Democratic Transition through Regime Collapse: Elite Legitimacy and the Peaceful East German Revolution," which was supported by Yale University, the Social Science Research Council, and the Berlin Program at the Freie Universität. He has published articles and presented papers on aspects of democratization, civil society, and state sovereignity, as well as the East German, Portuguese, and Brazilian transitions.

JUAN J. LINZ is Sterling Professor of Political and Social Science at Yale University. He holds degrees in law, political science, and sociology and has contributed to books on authoritarianism, fascism, political parties, nationalism, religion, and politics. He is the author of *Crisis, Breakdown, and Reequilibration,* volume 1 of a four-volume work, *The Breakdown of Democratic Regimes,* which he coedited with Alfred Stepan, and of "Totalitarian and Authoritarian Regimes" in *Macropolitical Theory,* volume 3 of the *Handbook of Political Science,* edited by Fred L. Greenstein and Nelson W. Polsby. He is coauthor and editor, with Larry Diamond and S. M. Lipset, of *Democracy in Developing Countries* and coauthor and editor, with Arturo Valenzuela, of *The Failure of Presidential Democracy.* He has written extensively on the transition to democracy in Spain and is coauthoring with Alfred Stepan a book entitled *Problems of Democratic Transition and Consolidation: Southern Europe, South America, and Eastern Europe.* In 1987 he was awarded the Premio Príncipe de Asturias de Ciencias Sociales, and he holds honorary degrees from the Univeridad Autónoma de Madrid, Georgetown, Granada, and Marburg.

PAULA FRANKLIN LYTLE is assistant professor of political science at Lewis and Clark College. Her research has focused on mass mobilization at times of state crisis with emphasis on the symbolic and ritual dimensions of politics. She is currently working on a manuscript on the mobilization of the peasantry by the Communist party of Yugoslavia during World War Two.

JAMES W. MCGUIRE is assistant professor of government at Wesleyan University. He is the author of *Peronism Without Perón: Unions, Parties, and Democracy in Argentina* (Stanford University Press, forthcoming) and of several articles on Argentine politics. His current research involves quantitative analyses of the causes of Argentine strikes and qualitative analysis of growth, equity, and poverty reduction in East Asia and Latin America.

BARNETT R. RUBIN is associate professor of political science and director of the Center for the Study of Central Asia at Columbia University. He is also director of the Columbia Project on Political Order and Conflict in the Former Soviet Union, funded by the Carnegie Corporation, and acting director of the Center for Preventive Diplomacy at the Council on Foreign Relations, supported by the Twentieth Century Fund. He is the author of *The Fragmentation of Afghanistan: State Formation and Collapse in the International System* (New Haven: Yale University Press, 1995) and *From Buffer State to Failed State: The Failure of International Cooperation in Afghanistan* (New Haven: Yale University Press, in press). He has also published articles and reports on South and Central Asia, human rights, conflict resolution, and development.

YOSSI SHAIN teaches political science at Tel Aviv University. He is currently a Fellow at St. Antony's College, Oxford University. He is the author of *The Frontier of Loyalty: Political Exiles in the Age of the Nation-State* (winner of the Helen Dwight Reid Award of the American Political Science Association), and editor of *Governments-in-Exile in Contemporary World Politics*. He was an International Fulbright scholar at Yale University and held visiting appointments at Wesleyan University, Middlebury College, Yale, and The Fletcher School of Law and Diplomacy. He is currently writing a book on the role of diasporas in world affairs.

ALLISON K. STANGER is assistant professor of political science at Middlebury College. She has written articles on the international interests of democratizing elites, the impact of constitutional conflict on Yeltsin's foreign policy, and the constitutional leadership of Charles De-Gaulle and Boris Yeltsin. Stanger is presently working on a comparative study of the role of constitutional debates, forms and norms in attempted transitions from dictatorship to the rule of law in Poland, the Czech Republic, Slovakia, and Hungary.

PART ONE

Theory

Introduction

He who desires or attempts to reform the government of a state, and wishes
to have it accepted and capable of maintaining itself to the satisfaction of
everybody, must at least retain the semblance of the old forms; so that it
may seem to the people that there has been no change in the institutions,
even though they are entirely different from the old ones.[1]

Niccolò Machiavelli

The newly emerging regimes, democracies or otherwise, around the
world, including those of the breakaway republics of the former Soviet
Union, provide a wide range of vastly different possibilities for political
change and regime transitions. This range includes states that have been
challenged on either one or two fronts: the legitimacy of the political
entity itself and/or the nature of its regime.

First, there are states whose very existence, because of their multiethnic compositions and the crisis associated with political changes in nondemocratic regimes, failed to acquire or sustain de jure status over the
full territory to which they claim sovereignty. This fact has led to the
complete dissolution of the states, the partial breakup of constituent
entities within the former state, the emergence of new states, or the
subsuming of, or capitulation to, former state institutions. Examples of
the last two categories could be the way in which Yeltsin and Russia
absorbed the major institutions of Soviet power, and the way the former
German Democratic Republic was absorbed by the larger institutions of
the Federal Republic.

Second, when the status of the state as a political entity was either (1)
a nonissue – as was the case in Poland where the community is more or
less ethnically or religiously homogeneous; (2) overshadowed by the
illegitimacy of the old regime or by the revolutionary euphoria that followed its demise – as was the case in Czechoslovakia; or (3) was settled
peacefully because of the clear commitment of the outgoing regime to

democratization and minority rights – as in the case of Spain, the emphasis was on the removal of the old order to be replaced by a democratically elected government.

Regardless of these two challenges, the countries mentioned previously as well as others experienced a hiatus between the demise of the old regime and the establishment of the new order dominated by interim governments. Transitional authorities, whether the efficacy of the state is challenged or not, tend to promise democratic elections in order to move from a de facto to de jure status. But, in instances where the state's legitimacy is contested during the transition, as in the former USSR and former Yugoslavia, republic-level interim governments may use the same democratic pledge in order to sever ties with the larger political entity.

Indeed, the question of who governs between the start of a democratic transition and the assumption of power by a freely elected government has been a central one in many regime transitions around the world, from Latin America, to Eastern Europe, to Africa, and to the protracted and seemingly unresolvable conflicts in Afghanistan, Cambodia, and South Africa. In the last case, where the prospects for a peaceful democratic transition have long been in doubt, many political groups were vying for maximum control over the interim government that ruled South Africa in the months leading to its first universal elections in April 1994.[2] Whether, when, and how the conflicting objectives will be harmonized in interim governments will inevitably shape the future political development of these countries. The type of interim administration is crucial in determining the subsequent regime, and may affect whether ethnic and regional conflicts will interfere with the prospects for long-term stability.

Yet to date, insufficient theoretical attention has been given to the role of interim administrations (or provisional governments) in the development of democratic governments.[3] This is a serious shortcoming because most routes from dictatorship to political democracy or other forms of government are marked by different types of interim administrations that greatly affect the dynamics and outcomes of the transition process. Interim governments may influence the mere existence of the state: its constitutional framework, and the nature of the future political system – parliamentary, presidential, constitutional monarchy, *gouvernement d'Assemblée;* the degree of political openness in the future democracy, including respect for human rights and willingness to eradicate the legacies of the old regime; the nature of the economy; the role of bureaucracy, especially the position of the armed forces in society; and the country's future international posture and alliances. However, their obvious importance notwithstanding, all interim administrations are hindered insofar as they lack a democratic mandate until free and contested elections are held and a popularly mandated government assumes power.

Their lack of legitimacy is inherent in their self-labeling as "provisional" or "interim" which indicates their realization that their authority is transitional. Their title is, therefore, not just a label arbitrarily applied ex post facto.

This book analyzes the role that interim governments play in enhancing or impeding the democratic outcome in the transition from authoritarianism, including extreme cases that lead to the breakdown of the state. Through the prism of interim governments the book also attempts to develop theoretical issues at the center of national and international politics, such as the interplay between regime's legitimacy and the rule of law. For analytical purposes we introduce and explore four major models of interim governments (which in reality are quite flexible) and assess their impact on regime change. These models are (1) revolutionary provisional governments, which emerge after the fall of the *ancien régime* in internal revolution or a coup d'etat, or as a result of a war followed by external conquest and the ouster of the home regime; (2) power-sharing interim governments, in which an incumbent authoritarian government and the democratic opposition share executive power temporarily before elections; (3) incumbent caretaker governments, in which members of the outgoing elite manage the transition until the transfer of power to a democratically elected government, or alternatively, to another nondemocratic regime; and (4) international interim governments, in which the international community, through the aegis of the United Nations, directs and monitors the process of democratic change.

While this classification is, in a sense, formal, these models tend to exhibit certain dispositions with regard to governability, agenda-setting, and rule making, as well as toward a host of other critical issues concerning the security and stability of the nascent democracy and the integrity of the state. Thus the book will also appraise the bearing of interim administrations on the nature of a country's first democratic elections ("founding elections") and their timing, the constitution making process, the country's foreign relations, and the process of "evening the score" with dictatorial legacies and human rights abuses. Indeed, interim governments influence not only the timing, method, and parameters of the treatment of human rights abuses committed by predecessor regimes but also societal attitudes toward liberal-democratic ideas of justice and the rule of law. Ultimately, the behavior of interim governments may define how successful new regimes will be in minimizing violence by channeling dissent into legally accepted means of dispute resolution, establishing the accountability of the new governments and their organs, propounding a culture of human rights, fostering reconciliation rather than confrontation, and subordinating the military and security forces.

Finally the book examines the role of interim governments in transitions from multiethnic polities, especially where the issues of political integration and secession are intense and, thus, add a further degree of complexity. It must be remembered that in the case of republics succeeding a federated state, as in the former USSR and the former Yugoslavia, two stages of interim status could be identified. First, incumbent assemblies or institutions (Supreme Soviets in the USSR or League of Communists in Yugoslavia) were the highest government organs in the republics which called for freely contested elections; these elections were eventually held. Shortly after these elections, the newly elected assemblies declared themselves sovereign and, therefore, independent of the old center-dominated order. In some republics, presidential elections were set, but in most, the ascension of a president was determined by the republican assemblies. Second, after the state's dissolution had been launched by elected republic-level governments and independent statehood was announced, these transitional governments endeavored to establish effective control within their claimed territory. Their rule, though legitimated through popular elections at the republic level, may still be considered makeshift until they hold free elections within the newly established state.[4]

INTERIM GOVERNMENTS AND THEIR LEGITIMATING MYTHS

It is a truism among political scientists that any political regime, in order to endure and govern, requires that people believe that those who rule them have the right to do so, that they are not governing in their own selfish interest, and that they are entitled to use force to sustain order. Naturally, not everybody shares such beliefs, and in some societies the majority in fact reject the rulers' right, though not always boldly enough to articulate their reservations openly. Undoubtedly, dictatorial regimes vary in the degree of legitimacy (or illegitimacy) with which the population view them. Some of them enjoy considerable approval and support, which derive from the genuine popular belief in their right to govern, as well as from purely opportunistic grounds, material self-interest, apathy, or simply because there is no acceptable alternative. The claims of others are very weak, and their power is mostly dependent on the sheer exercise of the state's coercive apparatus. Those who reject the rulers' claim to legitimacy are likely to be ready, with differing degrees of intensity, to transfer the right to rule to the opposition, or to allow that right to any contestant who, according to certain procedures such as free elections, turns out to deserve it. These various scenarios are directly relevant to our problem: who shall govern in the hiatus between the beginning of a democratic transition and the assumption of power by a freely elected government?

The paths from dictatorship to democracy are numerous and diverse. Democratization may be instigated from within in two ways: (1) following the victory of a revolutionary elite that breaks (or claims to break) completely with the *ancien régime,* or (2) in a more peaceful consensual fashion where the authoritarian regime initiates, supports, and often plays an important role in the transition process. Democratization may also be the result of foreign intervention, in which the invading country dictates or monitors the installation of the democratic regime.[5] The important fact for our analysis is that in all transitions, whether internally or externally motivated and regardless of whether the legitimacy of the state is contested or not, the hiatus between the breakdown or abandonment of the old regime and the selection of a new government as a result of free and contested elections (or other nondemocratic forms) is dominated by an interim administration whose functions are of critical significance in determining the setting of what Alfred Stepan calls the "political society" in democratic transition: "the arena in which the polity specifically arranges itself for political contestation to gain control over public power and the state apparatus."[6]

The term "transition" in democratic regime change has come to denote an undefined period in the interval between "the launching of the process of dissolution of an authoritarian regime," at the outset, and "the installation of some form of democracy, or the return to some form of authoritarian rule, or the emergence of a revolutionary alternative" at the end.[7] Within this period of incremental changes and qualitative alteration of the old political regime, there exists a more defined interlude characterized by the rule of an interim government that has committed itself to hold free and competitive elections of one sort or another within a relatively short span of time.[8]

The interim government usually operates within a context of volatility and political vulnerability marked by uncertainty, anxiety, and high expectations concerning the future distribution of power and loyalties.[9] The nature and the action of the interim government are of enormous political moment. The degree of boldness and skill with which it makes certain policy decisions, and its willingness and ability to fashion an efficient succession (whether based on continuity or disjunction with the past), can help to determine whether or not the character and conduct of its successors will be democratic. Moreover, interim governments may affect the mere survival of the state by determining the type of its institutional structures, sequence of elections, as well as the state's national character.[10]

Of course, not all cases of authoritarian breakdown are followed by transition to a democratic system; dictatorial regimes are often replaced by other nondemocratic governments or may result in the establishment of new states that are governed undemocratically. Yet in our era, when the decline of communism and of military and bureaucratic authoritarianism has left democracy almost unchallenged as the supreme principle of political legitimacy, democratic rhetoric is on the lips of almost all those who are struggling to overthrow nondemocratic regimes.[11] And almost all nondemocratic regimes – including some of the most despotic – acknowledge the moral authority of the democratic principle by staging some semblance of elections and formally granting the vote to their citizens.[12]

That a government has declared itself provisional, interim, transitional (or uses other similar appellations) bespeaks a choice (or at least the appearance of a choice) not to translate its de facto control to a de jure power "because the legitimating myth it invokes in order to pretend to power involves the performance of certain principles and procedures which have not yet been completed."[13] Historically, the principles invoked to justify the rule of temporary governments have varied according to the legitimating myth of each era. Counterrevolutionaries who sought to reinstall a deposed monarchy declared themselves – upon seizing power – provisional government until the monarch's return.[14] For instance, in the Glorious Revolution of December 1688, after James II fled London for a week without appointing a regent, the king's loyalists, the Peers, formed a provisional government. They sought to save the kingdom, prevent the ascendence of William of Orange to the throne, and appease the Protestants by restoring the "Anglican Toryism" of the 1670s and 1680s. Regarding James as "their lawful God-given sovereign," they based their claim to rule as provisional government in the absence of a king "on their right as peers of the realm." The week-long rule of the provisional government was regarded by the British historian Robert Beddard as the most critical period of the Revolution.[15]

In our epoch, by contrast, self-declared interim governments usually pledge their allegiance to "democracy," an allegiance which is to be validated by free and fair elections. This book, therefore, focuses on cases in which the move from provisionality to de jure rule is tested in the fulfillment of the promise to hold free and contested elections to resolve the question of conditional and temporary legitimacy. Hence, a definition of an interim government, *qua* temporary government, assumes such a government's promise to facilitate the country's transition to a democratic political order in free and contested elections.[16] Today, as never before, it is ironic that in order to justify their nondemocratic conduct, even self-proclaimed interim authorities that captured power by ousting a democratically elected government or by intervening to thwart a democratic transition, feel compelled to promise democratic elections and resort to the rhetoric of human rights and the rule of law. In Algeria the military that intervened to halt the country's first democratic elections in January 1992 declared its interim rule to be a protection against the ascendance of the Islamic fundamentalists who would most certainly suspend democratic practices and civil liberties. The interim government promised "to prepare the society for true democratic practices."[17]

The question of democratic legitimacy, therefore, constitutes both a normative and a practical challenge to contemporary interim governments. Unlike caretaker governments in parliamentary democracies – that is, governments that lost their mandate in a vote of no-confidence or following their voluntary resignation but which "continue to act under a special commission given by the [democratic] law itself"[18] – interim governments in the transformation from authoritarianism to democracy have no politically defined rules to consult; they have no choice but to devise norms and regulations as they go. Sometimes these guidelines are inherited from the outgoing system. As long as those who hold power in the interim period do not organize themselves as a contending party and win a mandate in free and fair elections, they have no democratic legitimacy.[19] Interim governments comprised of incumbents, opposition, or a combination of the two may claim to represent the people, but without a clean electoral victory to back the claim up, it is bereft of democratic validity and subject to rejection.

In this book we will examine the way such governments try to complete – or frustrate – their declared agenda, which is to set the stage for the "founding elections" that are to launch the legitimate successor regime.[20] Yet it is not always clear which are the determining electoral acts that lead us from the old system to the new. In some countries, like Poland and Brazil, the lengthy sequence of elections "obscured a clear passage from the old system to the new in a decisive electoral act."[21] Moreover, electoral sequences are often dependent on the character of the interim government. In the case of provisional governments, for example, a democratic transition is not completed after the first elections which are intended only to elect a constituent assembly responsible for drafting a new constitution. The first elections must be followed by first regular elections to the legislative body whose vote of confidence will ultimately endow a government with democratic legitimacy. Indeed, in many instances electoral sequences depend upon constitution making or restoration and, in particular, on the determination of electoral law. The determination of the electoral sequence is especially critical when the legitimacy of the state (and not only of the regime) is contested, and where different levels of elections (regional or all-union) are held.[22]

In cases where the state legitimacy remains unchallenged, the success-ful holding of free national elections followed by the convening of a new parliament on whose confidence the government rests, and/or the inauguration of a new president, may be considered the end of the interim government. From then on, contests for power will proceed within gener-ally accepted democratic constraints; the question of institutional legiti-macy is, at least in principle, settled. Hence, even if future constitutional changes are contemplated, they will take place within the existing institu-tional framework and will not be perceived as a severing of normal democratic legitimacy.[23]

DEMOCRATIC LEGITIMACY AND THE RULE OF LAW

Democracy, which has constituted itself as the highest moral principle in justifying political power, is often equated in our time with the rule of law. Thus most regimes, including nondemocratic ones, "lay particular emphasis on the state's relationship to law."[24] They rule according to some legal norms, including rules of succession, a constitution, party statutes and military chains of command; these norms establish predict-ability over who can decide what. The power of some regimes is com-pletely unbound by such standards, and their lawless rule, almost by definition, may be considered illegitimate.[25] The frameworks that lend the regime its "legal" character are to some extent independent of its claim to legitimacy.

Undoubtedly, the central attribute of the modern impersonal state – the *Rechtsstaat* – is, as the name implies, the rule of law.[26] The essence of the *Rechtsstaat* is "to deprive arbitrium of its ultimate ground – the ability to get away with it."[27] In its positivist version the concept of a legal authority and of a legal order does not tell us anything about how rules should be enacted or who has the right to hold office, nor does it prescribe the precepts delimiting the scope of authority, that is, the range of commands based on established rules that can be issued. Legal-ity in its positivist form, therefore, does not require democracy but only the exclusion of arbitrary personal orders that go beyond the impersonal norms established according to some procedures and enacted as laws. These laws have come to replace "the potentially capricious appeal to transcendent norms," and are, in principle, "what free men would estab-lish by their own rationality."[28]

The positivist juristic position that rejects appeals to higher law like religious commands or natural law has been also in contention with the democratic dogma that laws should be enacted only with the consent of the governed – theoretically the political community, in practice by a majority or in exceptionally important rules by qualified majorities – by those holding office thanks to democratic procedures (i.e., elections) or by those deriving their authority from the duly elected.

Since "legality" has become the major trait of the modern impersonal state – its distinguishing mode of expression – it has also acquired an "ideological charge" of inborn legitimacy, as if an obvious affinity exists between legality and legitimacy.[29] Hence, as Giovanni Sartori has pointed out, in our epoch "legality" has emerged as a "trap word" often applied to any form of state organization with no value qualification of its legitimacy.[30] This reality enabled many despotic regimes in this century to obscure their lack of intrinsically valid claims to rule in justifying the use of arbitrary power, or to portray their de facto lawlessness as the highest form of lawfulness by underscoring the sanctity of procedural rules as if they validate their commands as authentic legitimacy.[31] The fact that state legality has created for itself what Carl Schmitt called "a political surplus value . . . 'a value that breeds surplus value'[32] has enabled totalitarian regimes to disregard legality and at the same time pretend to establish "total" lawfulness. As Hannah Arendt has pointed out, totalitarian "defiance of all, even its own positive law implies that it believes it can do without any *consensus juris* whatever, and still not resign itself to the tyrannical state of lawlessness, arbitrariness, and fear. It can do without the *consensus juris* because it promises to release the fulfillment of law from all action and will of man; and it promises justice on earth because it claims to make mankind itself the embodiment of the law."[33]

Indeed, the judicial licensing of lawlessness and terror in treating potential and plausible enemies, helped totalitarian regimes to ensure an unrefutable legal coherence.[34] During the Third Reich it was law professors at German universities that "provided a philosophical cloak for the Nazis' arbitrary acts and crimes, which would otherwise have been clearly recognized as unlawful."[35] They introduced the "teleological method" of judicial interpretation which essentially applauded all evils carried out by Nazis as "supremely just."[36] Yet even the Nazis did not enact the "final solution" in statute. In the words of the Israeli Supreme Court that rejected Adolf Eichmann's appeal of his conviction for the commission of crimes against humanity, the German restraint in formally legalizing the final solution "was not, . . . because of the Nazis' respect for legal orders, which they presumably refused to breach, but because they were highly concerned with covering up their actions under the veil of darkness, and [their desire] not to unveil them to the enlightened civilization – what also demonstrates their self-awareness that they are committing crimes."[37]

Undoubtedly, many of the crimes committed by highly oppressive states are not in accordance with their own legal systems and those ordering them have no legal right to do so. Thus, in principle, to resist those orders would not only have been moral but also legal without the need to question the legitimacy of the regime.

Under the Soviet-type post-totalitarian states, the attendant legalization of the polity intended to supplement the vacuum created by the erosion in the socialist creed. As much as this pledge to legality was no more than a facade, it also laid the foundation for a new "game" between governments and opposition, with significant bearing on the degree and method of state executed coercion. In reality, the fact that the post-totalitarian states were signatories of international human rights agreements, like the 1975 Helsinki Accords, and ritualized legality as a tool for domestic and external legitimation, affected the behavior of governments and oppositions toward each other. While the dissidents invoked positive legalism to discredit the government for violating its own constitutional guarantees, the government employed other articles of the law to scold dissidents' criminal activities.[38] This dynamic successfully reduced the brutality of arbitrary power. Václav Havel, in his fine appraisal of "legality" under post-totalitarian systems, has shown how the state's rhetorical adherence to human rights and legality for international propaganda and domestic routinization could be turned against it by its opponents: "I have frequently witnessed policemen, prosecutors or judges – if they were dealing with an experienced Chartist or a courageous lawyer, and if they were exposed to public attention (as individuals with a name, no longer protected by the anonymity of the apparatus) – suddenly and anxiously begin to take particular care that no cracks appear in the ritual. This does not alter the fact that a despotic power is hiding behind that ritual, but the very existence of the officials' anxiety necessarily regulates, limits and slows down the operation of that despotism."[39]

In the military authoritarian regimes of Latin America, by contrast, the emphasis on legality "has certain features in common with the return to democracy and which may be associated with a certain liberalization of political practices. [It] signifies that political power of the [regime] is embedded purely and simply within an institutional framework which is presumed to be legitimate."[40] Moreover, for military regimes, in particular, adherence to legality is critical in fostering the habits of professionalism and discipline among subordinates and superiors. Thus when they support illegal repression military regimes may blemish the army as an institution since "no military institution could emerge unscathed when the implicit message sent down the chain of command is 'go, kidnap and torture, and we'll overlook the looting'."[41] Indeed, the desire to unmask the fictional legality created in the name of democracy was a prime motivation behind the postdemocratization campaign for "truth telling" in the countries of the Southern Cone of Latin America. The efforts to reveal the truth about state terrorism and human rights violations in Argentina, Chile, Uruguay, and Brazil exposed how military regimes that "were obsessed with legality . . . dressed arbitrary violence with a veneer of legal respectability."[42]

No doubt, the surplus value of legality also explains, at least in part, the readiness of people to follow orders given according to the legality of the existing system even when they do not believe that the political regime is the most preferable and feel that it should be replaced by another based on different principles. To be more concrete, a military or police officer who favors transition to a democratic system is still likely to obey legally given legal orders, even in the absence of such a system.

The fact that legitimate rule became associated with formal legality, irrespective of the nature of the regime, has much to do, at least intellectually, with the reluctance of jurists and social scientists at the turn of the twentieth century, like Paul Laband, to grant intrinsic validity to any system of rule or political procedures, such as democratic elections. This failure is manifested most prominently in Max Weber's concept of legal-rational legitimacy which does not distinguish in terms of ethical norms or values between a regime based on voluntary submission and a regime based on imposition. Weber denies that elections are inherently legitimate legal means of altering an order, since "it is very common for the will of the minority to attain a formal majority and for the majority to submit. In this case majority rule is mere illusion."[43]

Weber's analysis of a purely formal basis of legality was applied to parliamentary democracy just as to other forms of domination with no ethical differentiation. As Wolfgang Mommsen has pointed out, Weber considered parliamentary democracy only as a convenient mechanism for selecting leadership, with no immanent ethical norms outlawing other procedures of leadership selections. "He therefore did not take into account the standard of any 'substantive principles of legitimacy.' Rather, he laid the accent on purely formal legality. Only in the background do we have the idea that democracy was *rebus sic stantibus* the most appropriate means of keeping bureaucratization in check. But Weber *never* consciously took the path of establishing a *value*-rational basis for democracy. . . . For Weber, democracy was just . . . a '*purely* expedient' system."[44]

Weber's formal legality was first criticized by the famous Weimar jurist Carl Schmitt, who in the 1920s argued that the school of legal positivism with its ethical neutrality had undermined the validity of the democratic parliamentary-legislative state and provided the theoretical foundation to justify legal revolutions. Ellen Kennedy has written that according to Schmitt, "the value-free perspective of German legal positivism, which separated the law from political and moral inquiry, was no longer capable of formulating questions about the legitimacy of the state and political power or a concept of justice that was relevant to the relationship of power and authority in the state."[45] Indeed, as John Finn has maintained, Schmitt's assault on legal formalism and his "friend/foe" distinction could have provided the intellectual vindication for outlawing disloyal opposition in democracies.[46] However, Schmitt's theoretical defense of the total state and his record as a Nazi supporter, despite recent attempts to exonerate him, cast a shadow on his designation as "the theorist of democratic legitimacy."[47] Only today, as liberal democracy has become the only acceptable form of the *Rechtsstaat,* and as the holding of democratic elections has acquired the status of a natural right, can one see an indisputable overlap between Weber's type of legal-rational authority and democratic regimes as we define them.[48]

BACKWARD AND FORWARD LEGALITY

The issue of regime change is tied to the question of regime legitimacy and state legality. Specifically, to what extent do transitional governments use existing legal systems, or choose to ignore or abrogate them, before they hold the first democratic elections? Although regime transition usually begins as a response to a crisis of legitimacy (in the normative sense as well as in terms of regime's performance), or as a result of a breach in the loyalty of the armed forces to the rulers (even if both happened to be part of the military), or both, state legality can serve to ensure continuity until the moment when the representatives of the new regime (or of new state) can take over the reins. Legality may ensure the continuity of the state's normal administrative functions – such as keeping order, collecting taxes, running the courts, and so on – if indeed the state itself remains intact. Thus during the interregnum the regents should be able to govern in accord with the existing legally given orders until (and if) the new regime decides to modify the normative system. Moreover, if a genuine transition to democracy is intended the interim government should annul the rules of the previous order that are incompatible with the freedoms required to conduct competitive elections. It should legalize freedoms of association for parties and of assembly, and provide enough time for campaigning, including fair access to the media.

The likelihood of benefiting from old-state legality in democratic transition is contingent upon the degree of legitimacy and effective control of the outgoing regime and the state institutions, how legality itself was used (especially how much incumbents have digressed in terms of human rights violation even from their own repressive laws), as well as the type and potency of the transitional government. Giuseppe Di Palma has rightly argued that democratic transition is more likely to be orderly and peaceful if the outgoing regime and the democratic opposition display a clear appreciation that state institutions of "legal-rational aspirations" (such as the armed forces, judiciary, and civil services) can and should serve democracy. Such may be the case when "past constitutional traditions construed the state as the impersonal carrier of specified public functions, indeed duties, in the continuous determination, allocation, and delivery of collective goods. Though the traditions may have been cast originally in an autocratic mold, though they may have assigned civil society and public opinion a narrow legal space, though they may have elevated the state and its armed forces to the role of arbiters of 'unnatural' societal conflict, they are still traditions anchored to notions of professionalism, legalism, impartiality, continuity of service, and institutional autonomy from partisan politics – that is, to notions that, whether myth or substance, are central to democracy."[49]

Indeed, many authoritarian or post-totalitarian regimes, which during their ascendence to power have employed extrajudicial (sometimes massive) repression, succeeded over time in consolidating themselves in a *Rechtsstaat*-like fashion. Their laws are enacted formally and publicly, only binding after enactment and not retroactively, and have to be applied by a relatively independent judiciary. Such a judiciary can serve even to protect the rights of individuals against the government. The decisions of the government will have to be in accordance with the enacted laws and, if the decisions are arbitrary according to those laws, they may be reversed by the courts. Authoritarian regimes may, therefore, approximate the standards of a democratic state of law, except in highly political matters. This is the case in particular where the bureaucracy exercises much of the power and where a significant part of the elite is recruited from the legal profession.

As long as such regimes do not digress greatly from their formal legalistic bind and refrain from practicing brutal and lawless repression (that will render them criminals), the likelihood that old-legality may serve to promote a peaceful transition is higher. Yet when the incumbent regime has been undermined to the point that it has no effective power over the decisions of the transitional government, and when state institutions of repressive nature have lost any perceived legitimacy in the eyes of the opposition and the public at large, the chances of clinging to old-state legality are reduced dramatically.

The last point can be best illustrated in the democratic transitions in Argentina where during the military rule the formal *Rechtsstaat* was violated unremittingly and systematically by a large segment of the army ("as-government" as well "as-institution"), which perpetrated the heinous crimes of the "dirty war."[50] This fact left no room for an "opposition compromise with the legality of the authoritarian regime."[51] In Chile, by contrast, Pinochet was able to hold firm to his insistence on leading a transition via his own devised constitution, despite his grisly human rights record. Pinochet exploited Chileans' "overblown sense of legalism"[52] while retaining a strong hold over the army. He also enjoyed substantial popular approval among large segments of the society.

All in all, in any regime transition there are legal norms which are directly linked with the legitimating principles of the outgoing system. These principles are often abrogated de jure or de facto, not only by a revolutionary provisional government, but in some cases by the outgoing regime itself. The breakdowns of democratic regimes, for example, have been on many occasions the outcome of "legal revolutions" by antidemocratic forces. The most famous example of this trend is, of course, the collapse of the Weimar Republic and Hitler's *Machtergreifung* by means of the infamous Article 48. Even more common dynamics of democratic collapse are "executive coups" by democratically elected leaders who exploit the institutional mechanism designed for emergency situations.[53] Such clinging to formal legalism may be also invoked shamelessly in military coups by plotters with no elected mandate. Such was the case in Haiti on September 30, 1991, when the first elected President, the Reverend Jean-Bertrand Aristide was deposed in a military coup. After removing the president, the coup leaders forced the Haitian legislature at gun point to name a Haitian supreme court justice as provisional president – as the Haitian constitution of 1987 requires in the absence of an elected president. They then declared elections to restore democracy within ninety days, again as stipulated by the constitution. Father Aristide would be barred from the election under the constitutional provision preventing a president from succeeding himself.[54]

Yet just as democratic legalism may be exploited to destroy democracies from within, authoritarian constitutionalism may be turned against dictatorships and may serve as a spring board for democratization, either by the incumbent regime or its democratic opponents. The most celebrated example of well-intentioned use of an existing legal framework is the Spanish Law for Political Reform introduced by the Suárez government in Spain (1976). Similarly, one can look to the changes in the definition of the vanguard role of communist parties in Eastern Europe which voted themselves out of power fully within the old legal framework. So too in South Africa, members of the Cape Town Parliament that excluded blacks voted themselves out of office shortly after the leaders of the parties of South Africa Transitional Executive Council, or TEC, endorsed a transitional constitution that combined provisions for majority rule with those safeguarding minority rights.[55]

In transitions to democracy interim governments may benefit from legality because they can demand, at least in principle, the obedience of those who have identified with the outgoing regime, primarily the police, the armed forces, and the judiciary (whatever their attitudes toward the transition process and future democracy might be). This process of "legal takeover" may facilitate a peaceful and orderly transfer of power – provided, of course, that the interim administration intends to allow those who have been democratically elected to assume power. One must keep in mind, however, that the legal process may be manipulated to impede the full transfer of power to elected leaders. This happened in Chile where Pinochet exploited his own constitution to ensure himself an advantageous position when democratic elections were finally held in 1989. Yet even in the case of Chile, Pinochet's adherence to his pseudoliberal constitution ultimately facilitated his legal removal (see Chapter 3).

Moreover, one should not mistake the importance of retaining the legality of normal state structures and institutions during a transition to democracy with the licensing of incumbents' use of state assets to secure for themselves future political gains. This has been one of the most daunting problems of post-Communist societies, where for decades ruling parties were state parties with total monopoly. They were endowed with resources, through taxation and coercive contributions (which properly belonged to the state), and sought to appropriate them to successor reformed parties. In reality, such state monopolistic parties should be dissolved and their property and resources transferred to the state; yet those who hold positions of power in government should not lose civil or political rights or be prevented from organizing and campaigning as political contestants. In the Spanish transition (1976–77), the Movimiento, the official single party, was dissolved, its legal monopoly was abrogated and its properties were transferred to the state.

Moreover, just as an incumbent should not confuse the benefits of state legality with the utilization of state assets during a democratic transition, so also a provisional government of the opposition must not translate its duty to abrogate coercive legality with a mandate to eradicate more or less customary bureaucracies. According to Richard Pipes, one of the gravest errors of the Russian provisional government of Lvov and Kerensky was the hasty dissolution of the old provincial bureaucracy, which was accustomed to submitting to central authority and in fact welcomed the new regime, before it could be replaced by a new one of its own creation. "The result was instant nationwide anarchy: anarchy that the new government liked to blame on the old regime but that was, in fact, largely of its own doing."[56]

It is, therefore, important to discern why and to what extent interim governments use existing legal systems or choose to ignore or abrogate them before they hold the first democratic elections. Two general options are evident. First, interim governments can use the tactic of "backward legality, forward legitimacy" as a mechanism to ensure a transition to democracy, which may or may not entail the dissolution of the old state. This path is most common in cases where a caretaker administration of the incumbent regime, or a surrogate heir, initiates or leads the transition. It also exists in cases where an interim arrangement vests joint executive power prior to the first elections in elements of the incumbent and the opposition.[57] Second, revolutionary provisional governments comprised of the opposition that overthrew the *ancien régime* tend to discard the old legal system and rule, at least initially, by decree. They reject the advantage of legality of an authority based on preexisting normative framework, even when the old legal order continues to command respect. Certainly, even provisional governments may adhere, irregularly, to notions of old legality to promote their goals via the state apparatus.

In general, the range of options available for transitional leaders who employ old legality also depends on what is possible and still in accordance with the existing constitution and legal norms. This last point is especially crucial in recognizing the ability of breakaway political units in federal systems to establish independence from the center, as happened in the former USSR and Yugoslavia. The former Soviet Republics, for instance, used their existing republican constitutions, which mirrored the former all-Union State constitution, in order to legitimize the transfer of sovereignty from Moscow to the republics. Once sovereignty was attained, the interim leaders were able to determine the timing and nature of the first elections, which were all hailed as democratic (even though in many of them there were no independent parties).

Furthermore, the fact that regime transition is closely tied to the viability of the old legality may have important implications for the issue of evening the score with those in the outgoing regime believed to be responsible for human rights violations and other political and social crimes. The treatment of such crimes, which has become one of the most daunting tasks of many new democracies, is greatly affected by the nature of the interim government which plays a crucial role in facilitating or impeding suitable resolutions. Such solutions may include the outgoing regime's promulgated amnesty to its opponents or to itself (the latter as a preemptive mechanism from future liabilities and trials), the use of the old legality by the opposition to even the score with their predecessors, or the abrogating of the state legality by a provisional government that resorts to extreme means, by decree, to revenge the old order.

The relevance of legality and democratic legitimacy for interim administrations in both facilitating or obstructing a regime change was best demonstrated in the Soviet Union during the last phase of the Communist era, when the notion of "constitutionality" was invoked loosely by Gorbachev and his critics alike to legitimate their actions. In the former Soviet Union it was the changing view of legality, and not only the changes in the legal code itself, that allowed the reform process to take root both in Moscow and in the republics. Under Gorbachev, changes were always backed by laws and the Soviet constitution, and decrees were only used in what were declared to be extraordinary or emergency situations. Yet Gorbachev's creation in 1989 of a new system of legislative representation signaled a watershed in how legal norms could be used by the state. The overwhelming promulgation of new laws and decrees by the USSR Supreme Soviet (1989–91) and by the president during the same period obscured the Soviet constitution and undermined its command. It prompted some union republics to launch their own independent constitutional path (in accordance with the USSR constitution) that disputed further the all-Union document.[58]

Moreover, despite the predetermined composition of the all-Union legislature, the new system allowed for popularly elected government. And while opposition political parties were yet to be legalized, the presence of outside interests, along with a whole new institutional bureaucracy, created, in effect, de facto opposition parties. This de facto opposition insured some form of transition both at the all-Union level and in the constituent republics, which had also created the new legislative bodies. On the all-Union level, one can interpret Gorbachev's choice to limit democratic elections to the Congress of People's Deputies (March 1989) in two ways: first, there are some who argue that Gorbachev was following a well-designed plan of transition, in which certain democratic rights needed to be circumscribed in order to fend off extreme conservative challenges from within the incumbent regime, who, of course, were resistant to change. This view also argues that Gorbachev was balancing these pressures from the right with great demands for accelerated reforms from Boris Yeltsin and those who felt the pace of democratization was too slow. Others, however, argue that Gorbachev's half-hearted attempt at reforming the political system was more intended to increase his own power and ability to act independently than to establish a fully democratic process.[59]

Whatever Gorbachev's real intentions, his partial democratization of the all-Union electoral process took on a life of its own and led to the eventual disintegration of the Soviet state. By using legality as he did, Gorbachev demonstrated to local leaders the "legal elasticity" of the Soviet constitution. At one extreme, during the totalitarian period, the all-Union constitution required the population to act in a rigid and lawful manner while it also enabled the regime to act in near lawlessness. During the era of perestroika, however, the same constitution enabled

local leaders and eventually the entire population to accelerate democratic reform and the movement toward republican sovereignty by pointing to constitutional rights and guarantees.

The interplay between legality and legitimacy in the breakdown of the
Soviet Union reached its climax during the dramatic events of the August
1991 coup and in the ensuing months that led to the USSR's final demise.
Both the coup plotters and the democratic victors reached for Soviet
"constitutionality" to reinforce their bid to power. The communist con-
spirators declared President Gorbachev to be crippled, "thus putting
Yanayev as vice-president in charge and so [were] able to establish
'legally' a State Committee of Emergency." When Boris Yeltsin and his
loyalists finally prevailed, they restored Gorbachev's presidency "both
to ensure continuity of state power and to give constitutional legitimacy
to their own de facto exercise of that power." As Martin Malia pointed
out, "Admittedly, Soviet 'constitutionality' is not worth a great deal
because it derives from the Party, not the people. Still this fig leaf of
legitimacy was useful, both domestically and internationally, in the heat
of the crisis."[60] But Gorbachev's mere legality soon became his greatest
liability as Yeltsin was quick to assert his own legitimacy as the democratically elected president of the Russian Republic (June 1991) while
criticizing Gorbachev's unwillingness to put himself to the test of popular
elections and accusing him of resting his legitimacy solely on the discredited existing legal order. Yeltsin, who had used Gorbachev as an interim
"legal" figure, ultimately forced Gorbachev to abolish the Soviet Union
in a legal and orderly fashion and to surrender all state powers to Russia.
Robert Sharlet, a scholar of Soviet constitutionalism who has examined
the tenacious clinging of all players in the Soviet drama to some form of
constitutionality has written: "Paradoxically, the Constitution reached
the zenith of its symbolic life as the USSR approached the nadir of
its existence."[61]

Altogether, it must be clear that once a new democratic government or
assembly is elected, it should have the power to enact a new constitutional framework or restore an old constitution congruent with the democratic principles, and it must reserve the right to abrogate the authoritarian normative system. Certainly, democratic transition is not complete
and cannot be consolidated if such congruence is restricted. An interim
government of incumbents may try to rig the legal system so that elected
officials cannot easily change it, sometimes establishing barriers meant to
prevent such officials from exerting authority over various nonelected
power centers. Revolutionary provisional governments of the opposition
might try to do much the same thing by demanding preelection concessions from other contending parties on certain principles that the elected
constituent assembly will be forbidden to change.

The question of who governs in the interim period and the way they use their power is, therefore, crucial to the outcome of democratic transitions and thus will be the focus of this book. Based on historical and recent democratization experiences, four ideal types of interim government are analytically discernible: opposition-led provisional governments, power-sharing interim governments, incumbent-led caretaker governments, and international interim government by the United Nations. Part One explores the theoretical problems of each of these models from a broad comparative perspective. It uses as illustrations historical and contemporary cases that present a wide spectrum of contexts for comparison. Part Two provides extensive case studies that are intended to illustrate, appraise, amplify, and criticize the analysis in Part One. These essays, written by country specialists, are presented in accordance with the theoretical design of Part One.

CONTENTS

Part One is divided into six chapters. Chapters 1 through 4 explore the four interim government prototypes mentioned previously. Chapter 5 analyzes the bearing of the interim government's design on the timing and nature of first democratic elections and on the efficacy of the state. In Chapter 6 we present our conclusions.

Chapter 1 focuses on opposition-led provisional governments. It distinguishes between the objectives and challenges facing revolutionary, democratically leaning, and postwar provisional governments. Its main contention is that revolutionary provisional governments are usually inadequate in leading to national reconciliation and democratic rule. This has been the tendency even in countries where the issue of national division has not been pivotal. Leaders of revolutionary provisional governments, tend to assume that they are legitimate even though they have not been democratically elected. They are inclined to compromise their initial promise to hold democratic elections in favor of other revolutionary – social, economic, or religious – agendas. When democratically leaning elements are part of a revolutionary provisional government, they face the danger of being outmaneuvered by nondemocratic forces who exploit the vacuum created by dissolution of the old authoritarian fabric and employ competing centers of power to obstruct a democratic outcome. Today, however, when holding democratic elections is almost an indispensable ritual in justifying authority and securing international legitimacy, revolutionary provisional governments are less likely to evade elections, but are still inclined to manipulate them to their advantage.

Chapter 2 examines the dynamics of interim power-sharing governments between elements opposing the authoritarian regime and elements of the regime itself. Such arrangements may be the product of genuine accommodation and compromise, although they are more often the result of political expediency. The viability of such temporary coalitions is contingent upon the relative strength of the regime and the zealousness of the opposition. The temporary partnership imparts a degree of legitimacy both on the opposition and the government. However, such mutual recognition may be only tactical, serving the interests of a weakened incumbent or an unorganized and weary opposition. Indeed the sine qua non of power-sharing governments is the balance between the degeneration of the outgoing government and the maturation and growth of other contestants for power. This balance will also determine whether and when coalition partners may be treated as criminals.

Chapter 3 explores regime transitions conducted by caretaker governments of reformist incumbents or their heirs. It argues that if incumbents have not been completely discredited in the eyes of the opposition and the public at large, have displayed a genuine commitment to democratize, and have dissociated themselves from the brutality of the past, they have great potential for averting chaos. If the caretaker government declares elections in a realistic date while retaining solid positions of power, and if the legal system has not been compromised in the oppressive arbitrary rule and is still serviceable to the interim government, this model is more likely to produce a democratic outcome. It may be preferable to an opposition-led provisional government of self-proclaimed democrats who might be tempted to broaden their agenda beyond the holding of free elections. Yet, when elements of the incumbent serving as caretaker authorities retain strong positions of power and are able to manipulate the legal system they may hold newly democratic regimes hostage.

Chapter 4, written by Yossi Shain and Lynn Berat, analyzes possible interim solutions in countries where long-standing political, ethnic, religious, or racial divisions are so deeply ingrained that the opposition, because of profound mistrust, finds incumbent-led caretaker administrations to be repugnant. In such cases the legitimacy of the state itself may be challenged. Such pandemic mistrust was found, for example, among the contending parties in Cambodia and cast a pall on the possibility of achieving a successful interim power-sharing arrangement. South Africa escaped such a predicament only after F. W. de Klerk and Nelson Mandela agreed on the formation of a multiparty Transitional Executive Council (representing most of the political parties and institutions that sat down to negotiate a settlement) to pave the way for universal free elections in April 1994. Obviously, under such circumstances the rise to power of a revolutionary provisional government of the opposition is neither desirable nor conducive to democratic regime change. In order to avoid the pitfalls associated with these three types of interim government, the authors propose the "international interim government" model based on the transition to democracy in Namibia. In this model the international community, through the agency of the United Nations, monitors and directs the process of change. In 1990 the authors offered this model for Cambodia, before it was adopted by the UN. Now when the UN has committed the largest and most ambitious peacekeeping force to ensure stability and democratic regime change in Cambodia, known as UN Transitional Authority in Cambodia (Untac), Shain and Berat reevaluate the efficacy of the international interim government arrangement.

Chapter 5, examines the role of interim governments in setting the conditions under which political competition will proceed as such governments move from provisionality to de jure legitimacy. It demonstrates how crucial is the interim government's choice of the timing and the form of first elections in ensuring a democratic outcome. The choice of elections and their timing are most critical when the legitimacy and/or efficacy of the state is undermined, and when different elections are called by center- and republic-level authorities. Thus the chapter also highlights how problems of "stateness" place certain constraints on interim governments, and how interim governments, in turn, affect the viability of the multinational state.

To underscore the variation in the performance of provisional governments Part Two presents two case studies of revolutionary replacement, in Portugal and Iran. Both demonstrate how exits from provisionality are contingent on the character of the *ancien régime,* the nature of its opposition, and the viability of the state apparatus.

H. E. Chehabi analyzes the failure of the Bazargan provisional government in Iran to carry a democratic transition. He stresses the nature of the *ancien régime* and the state as indicators for the exit from provisionality. The sultanistic traits of the Shah's rule de facto erased the distinction between the regime and state and left little room for a functioning *Rechtsstaat.* Consequently when the Iranian revolution erupted, it generated the disintegration of the state apparatus. Thus, despite democratic leanings of the Mehdi Bazargan's provisional government, the devaluation of state powers and the elimination of old legality ushered the Islamic forces of Khomeini on the road to power.

Thomas C. Bruneau examines how the Portuguese "revolution" resulted in a democracy despite the fact that radical elements with strong Marxist-revolutionary leanings dominated five of the six provisional governments that ruled the country between April 25, 1974, and June 1976. Moderate elements finally prevailed because of the rapid emergence of political parties, the initial promise of the Armed Forces Movement

(MFA) to hold elections to a Constituent Assembly within one year of the 1974 coup, the professionalism of the armed forces maintained notwithstanding its division into competing centers of power, the promulgation of a constitution that stipulated that Portugal would be democratic, even though on other critical matters it restricted the power of the electorate, and, finally, the force of international pressure.

In an attempt to underscore the gravity and symmetry of power-sharing in resolving issues of legality, legitimacy, and past abuses, Daniel V. Friedheim examines the sudden collapse of the German Democratic Republic in the Fall of 1989. As East Germany went through a process of accelerating regime collapse in 1989 and 1990, three separate governments oversaw its democratic transition. Communist hard-liner Honecker was deposed in mid-October by liberalizing Communist Krenz, who opened the Berlin Wall overnight then lost control of his own party. He was succeeded in December by reform Communist Premier Modrow, who formed a consciously interim caretaker government to oversee democratization. When Modrow, too, lost control of the situation in January, he had to share power with Round Table opposition groups in another interim arrangement. This third transition government held the free elections in March that produced a clear mandate for German reunification.

The legacy of this succession of ever weaker governments was the unexpectedly rapid pace of reunification and the widest-ranging purge of the old nomenklatura and secret police informers of the East European transitions to democracy. The mutual weakness of collapsing governments faced with one of the region's weakest oppositions fueled ever more ambitious reunification proposals, from a "treaty community" to confederation to monetary union to full union by year-end. The large degree to which old regimes elites have been purged reflects the short-lived democratic East Germany's creation of an agency to open police files as well as opposition intellectuals' efforts to "even the score." The process of accelerating collapse, from October 1989 to March 1990, made the subsequent fast-track reunification and extensive purge possible.

In order to explore further the intricacies of the caretaker government model, James W. McGuire delves into the history of interim governments in Argentina with particular emphasis on the 1983 transition. After a period of repressive military rule (1976–82), Argentina lost a war with Britain and began a transition to democracy under an incumbent caretaker government led by Ret. Gen. Reynaldo Bignone. Military officers controlled this transition more closely than has previously been recognized. They apparently made a pact with a faction of the Peronist union leadership, exchanging immunity from future prosecution for a policy that would have given certain union leaders control of certain unions. Had the Peronists won the October 1983 presidential election, Argentina's transition might have been viewed as carefully staged and incumbent controlled, a transition on the Brazilian, Chilean, or Spanish model, and not as a case of "regime collapse" as in Greece or Portugal. Although the Peronists lost, the Argentine case shows that caretaker governments afford authoritarian elites special resources for controlling the transition process. A comparison of seven transitions in Latin America and Southern Europe suggests that greater authoritarian control of the transition results in higher initial stability but the initial quality of an emergent democracy is lower, particularly if the authoritarian actors controlling the transition are military rather than civilian. Argentina became an exception to this rule, but only because the Peronists unexpectedly lost to the Radicals in the 1983 presidential elections.

Barnett Rubin discusses the limitation of the international interim government solution in places where the state has virtually disintegrated. He offers a firsthand account of how an attempt by the international community to resolve the conflict in Afghanistan, by installing an interim government produced by UN mediation, ended in failure in April 1991. When President Najibullah announced his willingness to resign in favor of the interim government, he was overthrown by rebels in his own military and party who allied with ethnic kin in the former resistance. Instead of a Cold War-propelled ideological conflict, the war now turned into an ethnic conflict. The UN plan could not prevent this because it involved only mediation through the good offices of the Secretary General and did not involve UN peacekeeping or administrative forces as in Cambodia or Namibia. The UN had to rely on local military forces, but no plan reorganizing them for peacekeeping existed. The end of the Cold War and of the USSR also stopped the flow of aid that had united the main military organizations. As a result they began to reflect local social structure more than the global conflict, and thus fragmented along ethnic lines. Finally, Rubin argues that democracy is far from a hegemonic ideology in legitimating power. In Afghanistan Islam played this role, and the Islamic groups opposed political participation by the former ruling party which had engaged in anti-Islamic campaigns and acted as agents of the Soviet occupiers. These three factors (insufficiency of UN force, decreased leverage by the superpowers, and the weakness of democratic institutions and ideology) are common to many conflict areas throughout the world and will limit the effectiveness of international interim governments as a means to conflict resolution.

Paula Franklin Lytle demonstrates how the sequences of elections

in Yugoslavia, devised by republic-level governments, encouraged the
Yugoslav civil war. Indeed, the electoral transition from communism in
the case of Yugoslavia is noteworthy due to its punctuated nature. A
separate electoral process took place in each of the republics, which held
elections at different times through 1990. This pattern was largely dictated by the devolution of political decision making to the republic-level,
which had been taking place even before the death of Tito. The League
of Communists of Yugoslavia as a central institution collapsed in January
1990. Each republic-level transition is analyzed within our framework
examining the role of Communist party elites in each republic-level election. In addition, the nature of each election's rules and outcome was at
least partly the response to the elections in other republics, both in terms
of the writing of election rules and as a response to new leadership in
some of the republics. The punctuated nature of the transition complicated negotiations on the future shape of Yugoslavia, transforming the
debates from elite discussions to public formulations submitted to democratic tests. The timing and nature of the transitions thus contributed to
the ongoing destabilization and crisis of governability within Yugoslavia.

In the last chapter of Part Two, Allison Stanger examines the critical
role interim governments can play in recasting the outgoing order's international relations. Reviewing a wide range of cases, her argument is two-
pronged. First, the type of interim government shapes the reformation of
the authoritarian state's international interests in critical ways. Provisional revolutionary governments were most likely to break abruptly
and radically with the external policies of the outgoing order. Interim
governments based on power-sharing arrangements, whether explicit or
implicit, are more likely to recast the state's external orientation in
more cautious fashion, the resultant policies embracing elements of both
continuity and change between past and present. Caretaker interim regimes, where the independent power of the military was often a factor,
were more likely to defer major policy decisions until after the first
elections had been successfully held. Second, interim governments which
renounce the external policies of the dying authoritarian order in such a
way that relations with other democracies are concurrently improved
seemed to be more likely to avoid authoritarian retrenchment and consolidate democracy. Similarly, interim governments which severed the international ties of the outgoing order in such a way that relations with the
West worsened were more likely to lose control of the transition and
find their democratic goals threatened by rising antidemocratic public
sentiment. What these patterns suggest, Stanger concludes, is that even
when the path to internal *ruptura* is foreclosed, external *ruptura* (in the
realm of the state's international obligations) that strengthens the nascent
democratic regime's ties to other democracies can enhance the prospects

for democratic consolidation. Finally, Stanger's analysis reveals the limits of systematic international relations theory, which she claims cannot fully account for the transformation of state interests that accompanies democratization. Her study provides a fertile ground to expand international relations theory.

1

Provisional governments: Revolutionaries and moderates

When a regime has been superseded in a revolutionary struggle (frequently violent) or a coup d'état, the new ruling elite claims to break completely with the old order. It usually declares itself a provisional government, thereby indicating its intention to lead a democratic transition via free elections within a short period of time. Many revolutionary provisional governments are the initial successors of personalized sultanistic regimes which leave little if any room for moderate opposition. Sultanistic systems lack recognized and reliable rules of political opposition or action, are uncommitted ideologically, have no institutionalized procedures for succession, and are dominated by personal ties and attributes. Despite their official fidelity to legality they tend to practice de facto a state of legal anomie within a system completely devoid of checks and balances.[1]

In the postwar era the lawlessness of many sultanistic regimes was augmented by international support provided to their rulers due to their role in the Cold War rivalry between the United States and the Soviet Union. In Latin America personalized sultanistic dictatorships were frequent and in more recent times included the family-based rule of the Somoza dynasty, the Duvaliers, particularly Baby Doc, Trujillo, and Batista. Postcolonial Africa also produced many such despotic and corrupt rulers who in their "megalomaniacal pursuit of wealth and power . . . plundered or squandered their nations' coffers, leaving their people to endure lives fraught with privation, fear and hopelessness."[2] Their excessive dictatorships vary from the booty of Zaire's Mobutu Sese Seko (whose personal wealth is estimated at 6 billion dollars), to the murderous Jean-Bedel Bokassa of the Central African Empire, to the horrific Idi Amin of Uganda. The rule of the Shah of Iran, Ferdinand Marcos in the Philippines and, in the opinion of some observers, General Stroessner in Paraguay, also had strong sultanistic components.

Sultanistic rule reduces the possibility of a negotiated settlement for a democratic transfer of power because of the lack of institutional channels for bargaining over transition rules and power sharing. The brutal suppression of the opposition by the incumbent elite reduces further the likelihood of forming a civilian-military union to launch and administer a political opening from above. Even when incumbent dictators are inclined to compromise and step down peacefully, they may still be inhibited by fear of prosecution for their abusive practices.[3] The opposition, in turn, tends to resort to a violent campaign, even when it is dominated by democratically oriented forces. As Lisa Anderson pointed out, "in flouting the legal systems which they themselves [created, such dictatorships] sow the seeds of intolerance and disrespect for law and reap the harvest of deviousness, extremism and illegality." Although they "often justify repressive policies by pointing to the irresponsible extremism of their opponents, in many respects [sultanistic] regimes face the opposition they deserve."[4]

Hence sultanistic rulers are likely to be overthrown by a revolution or a nonhierarchical coup. Their collapse is likely to create a vacuum as the state's institutions are often left entirely disabled, the country's capital stolen, and the nurturing of civil society and political parties becomes an extraordinary task. Yet even when civil society and parties do organize, the clientelistic system may continue to hold the polity hostage, and the security forces, previously loyal to the dictator, are most likely to retain some tutelage. If the dictator is removed by revolutionaries the struggle for power is likely to endure and to produce further abuses. And even if the transition is negotiated between opposition and the regime, the corrupt elements in society are apt to continue. When sultanistic regimes are overthrown in societies where minorities are particularly oppressed, a civil war may ensue with a strong drive for secession.

In reality, sultanistic regimes are usually replaced by another nondemocratic regime, sometimes with characteristics similar to their own, or by a revolutionary regime that attempts to create *ex novo* organized social forces, assuming power without allowing the development of competitive social and political forces and the relatively free competition of democratic rule. Though the revolutionary path is the most probable outcome of transition from sultanistic rule, as Richard Snyder has pointed out, less radical outcomes are possible if sultanistic dictators fail to penetrate military institutions and to sustain societal elite patronage networks.[5]

After seizing power and establishing themselves in complete discontinuity with their predecessors, revolutionary provisional governments are beset with multiple challenges. First, they tend to define themselves as "democratic," although they have no democratic legitimacy since the electorate has not yet had the opportunity offered by free elections to support or reject their claim to power. Second, they do not enjoy (in most cases) the advantages of old legality as do authorities based on the old normative framework, whatever their legitimacy for a significant segment of the population. Third, they usually rule by decree and, even if they wish to rely temporarily on old forms of legalism (where they existed) to avert a situation of anarchy or to further their own interests, the revolutionary fervor, the discrediting of the old state mechanisms, and the possible emergence of competing centers of power are likely to jeopardize such legal continuity. The total rejection of old forms of legality and/or the lack of any credible state institution raise critical questions regarding the provisional government's responsibility to honor public obligations and contracts made by their predecessors. This dilemma, already articulated in Aristotle's *Politics* (Book 3, chapter 3), has critical ramifications in the sphere of international affairs.

Moreover, once in power, provisional revolutionary governments are often loath to relinquish authority. The rulers may use more or less spontaneous mass demonstrations, popular-mobilization campaigns, or even staged plebiscites, as means of bolstering their legitimacy. They often make vague promises to hold free elections that are rarely held. They also enact constitutional reforms designed to enhance their power or they manipulate election results to ensure their own victory. In postrevolutionary Romania, the ascendence of the National Salvation Front (FSN) to power – a spurious popularly legitimated provisional government – can be attributed in part to the deep penetration of state and society by Ceauşescu's totalitarian-sultanistic regime. This self-proclaimed provisional government of disenchanted party apparatchiks, top *Securitate* officials, and some army generals, hijacked a spontaneous anti-Communist pro-Western revolution to catapult itself into power.[6] The Philippines' relative success in undergoing democratization in 1986 directly after sultanism, however, is unusual. It can be partly attributed to Marcos's failure to stymie institutional autonomy within the Army and in society.[7] Yet even in the Philippines where the revolutionary legitimacy of Corazon Aquino's provisional government did not conflict with the democratic requirements – since she was assumed to be the winner in Marcos's rigged elections – her opponents still attacked her government for refusing to hold new presidential elections immediately. They argued that "the self-proclaimed democrats had become tyrants."[8]

MARXIST LEANING REVOLUTIONARY PROVISIONAL GOVERNMENTS

With the end of the Second World War and the dismantling of Europe's overseas colonial empires, ideologies stressing some combination of nationalism, Marxist revolution, and the struggle against "fascism" (usually meaning right-wing dictatorships targeted by the revolutionaries as proxies of imperialist powers, primarily the United States) arose. These new ideologies opened the door for elites to exploit the notion that some kind of vaguely defined popular participation, rather than free and contested elections, was the essence of democratic government. A revolutionary provisional government emboldened by the heady wine of mass mobilization and apparent popular legitimacy might be tempted to use the interim period before the first elections to make major policy decisions by fiat, seeking to preempt the people's decision with decrees of its own. Such decisions are most likely to be neither wise nor popular; railroaded through with little forethought, they would threaten to alienate potential supporters and arouse active opposition. Moreover, the new rulers may be tempted to try to exclude whole social groups from the political process even if they are willing to play by the rules of the democratic game: the idea of "a democracy for the democrats only" has its charms. The new frustrations of governing (very often without experience), the problems generated by a sudden transition, the active opposition encountered, and the discovery that the people are not always unambiguously supportive of the new regime can cause so much exasperation that the idea of making big decisions before voting is allowed begins to appear highly compelling.

Famous examples of revolutionary provisional governments that failed to live up to their own democratic pledge include the National Liberation Front (FLN) that took power in Algeria after the termination of the French colonial rule in 1962; Fidel Castro's provisional administration that took power in Cuba after the removal of Batista; the Ethiopian Provisional Military Administrative Council (PAMC) that overthrew the monarchy of Haile Selassie, and the "social democratic" regime of the Nicaraguan Sandinistas. In Ethiopia, the PAMC, though initially proclaiming itself provisional "until the people elect their genuine representatives in truly democratic elections," soon invoked a Marxist-Leninist blueprint to justify its dictatorial rule. It withdrew from its earlier promise to hold elections and denounced as "anarchists" those who demanded full and unqualified liberties for all citizens.[9] Likewise, the provisional government that emerged in Nicaragua after the overthrow of Somoza's dictatorship in 1979 started as a national-unity coalition, known as the Governing Junta of National Reconstruction (JGRN). It comprised a broad array of anti-Somoza groups. Though initially its members pledged their commitment to "political pluralism" and a "mixed economy," the JGRN was from the outset subordinated to the National Directorate of the Sandinista National Liberation Front (FSLN), whose concept of democracy stressed "democratic performance" over democratic procedure and broad corporatistic participation over electoral institutions. The

National Directorate quickly prevailed over other coalition members who advocated representative government and constitutionalism, asserting instead that "electoral democracy [will] have to await the establishment of national institutions capable of defending the revolution."[10] In August 1980, the Directorate decided to postpone elections until 1985, stressing that, " 'for a Sandinista, for a revolutionary,' democracy means 'PARTICIPATION of the people' in the entire range of the nation's affairs."[11]

The revolutionary character of provisional governments is also manifested in the way they "even the score" with their predecessors. They tend to conduct summary trials which are often followed by quick execution of the old leaders. Although such actions may have a cathartic effect on the people, as was the case of Ceaucescus's execution, they often leave a suspicion of a cover-up contrived to conceal early collaboration between elements of the revolutionary core and the outgoing regime.[12] Moreover, by denying due process to the old leaders it is questionable whether a provisional government will restore it in the future. In Romania, despite some token trials of *Securitate* leaders, opposition activists alleged that a high proportion of secret policemen with shadowy pasts were simply absorbed into government agencies, the armed forces, and the revamped services.[13] Altogether, the summary trial and execution of Ceauşescu had enormous psychological effect in Africa where fear of prosecution by their opponents have led sultanistic dictators to desperately cling to their power.[14]

In Nicaragua, after the Sandinistas came to power in 1979, thousands of Nicaraguans who had been involved with the predecessor regime's National Guard, or who were thought to have engaged in counterrevolutionary activities, were summarily tried and imprisoned. In 1983 the Sandinistas formed the Popular Anti-Somozista Tribunals (TPAs), which prosecuted those suspected of counterrevolutionary behavior while downplaying the defendants' rights under the guise of purging those who seemed to pose an immediate danger to the revolution. Despite domestic and international criticism that the TPAs' system violated the "universal principle of equal justice," the Sandinistas insisted that it was a mechanism vital to the enforcement of the "principles of the revolution."[15]

Portugal stands as a unique example of a country where democracy emerged after a coup developed into a revolution and not as an outgrowth of the old regime; although it could as easily have "resulted in another authoritarian regime of the Left or the Right under either civil or military control."[16] The junior officers who toppled the Salazar-Caetano fifty-year-long dictatorship on April 25, 1974, realized that the eradication of the Estado Novo could be achieved only by terminating the colonial wars in Angola, Guinea-Bissau, and Mozambique. But four of the six provisional governments that followed the *putsch* were dominated by left-leaning military officers and civilians who attempted to implement their radical agenda rather than creating a government accountable to the people via elections. And indeed, in the first year of the revolution the policies of the provisional governments were overwhelmed by the program of the radical military and Communists. After the resignation of President Spinola in October 1974 it seemed as if a Marxist takeover was inescapable.[17] The Armed Forces Movement (MFA), controlled by Marxists and military leftists, adopted a revolutionary course of economic nationalization. It conducted a huge land seizure, purged many individuals associated with the *ancien régime,* introduced major changes in labor legislation, and attempted to control the media, all before the first free elections. Despite these revolutionary methods, the initial commitment of the MFA to hold elections for a constituent assembly one year after the coup and the insistence of the moderate forces within the MFA to implement this promise helped halt the process of radicalization. The holding of elections in April 1975 became dependent on a formal agreement between the MFA and the parties that set the guidelines for constitution drafting by the Constituent Assembly. Yet the provisional government was not dependent on the confidence of the elected assembly. It was only after the suppression of a left-wing armed revolt on November 25, 1975, that the road was opened for the moderates to sign a pact with the political parties, which they did in February 1976. Another key factor determining the eventual democratic result was the Western powers' threat of economic sanctions if there was a nondemocratic outcome.[18] Altogether, with the approval of the constitution the government needed the confidence of the elected assembly and the president; yet it also had to respect certain powers vested in the Council of the Revolution which continued to represent the armed forces until the 1982 constitutional reform.

Portugal's democratization, the first of the democratic transitions in Southern Europe in the 1970s, is in many respects the watershed that began the tide of the "third wave" of democratic revolutions that has swept the globe in the last decade. The triumph of the liberal-democratic principle over its rival ideologies, primarily Marxism-Leninism, and the pressing need to internationalize the state's economy forced many Communist and Third World countries to choose between democratization and political and economic collapse. This new situation made it more difficult, although by no means inconceivable, for provisional revolutionary elites to attenuate their initial democratic promise by appealing to other ideological commitments. Hence, even in the case of postrevolutionary Romania, where Ceauşescu's former allies exploited a power vacuum to stage a highly doubtful transition, it is important to recall that the FSN made some substantial concessions to the revived opposition parties. It accepted the opposition participation in the interim assembly, gave in to its pressure to negotiate an electoral law that had been simply decreed, and kept its promise to hold elections. Most importantly, the allegation of fraud in the May 1990 elections loomed heavily over the FSN's ability to function in the newly democratic world order.[19] Yet in October 1992, Romania held free elections and reelected President Ion Iliescu of the FSN.

THE WEAKNESS OF THE MODERATES

Until the 1980s many revolutionary provisional governments used their power to destroy old rivals under the label of an anticorruption cleansing campaign, thus preventing the emergence of competing parties, as happened in Castro's Cuba in 1959–60, and in Nicaragua in 1979. But even when provisional governments were initially well-intentioned in their desire to effect a democratic regime change, they were often unable to institute reforms that enjoyed widespread popularity because they could not unite opposing factions with conflicting desiderata, and as a result faced institutional paralysis. Most vulnerable are "true believers" in liberal democracy who, while in power, found themselves obliged to uphold the rights of extremists and refrain from suppressing their enemies in order to escape any association with authoritarianism. This syndrome, characterized by Crane Brinton as the "weakness of the moderates," was a major factor in the failure of Kerensky's provisional government to overcome the Bolsheviks' challenge.[20]

Kerensky's inability to unite the Russian support is an excellent example of a genuine provisional government whose failure to lead a democratic transition in Russia profoundly altered the course of this century. The coup d'état of the Duma in February 1917 brought to power the provisional government of Lvov and Kerensky. In its first months in office, the government moved, as promised, to transform Russia into a democratic polity based on liberal principles. The government passed laws to rectify the abuses of the old regime and to enhance freedom. As minister of justice, Kerensky did not allow mob lynching of ex-tsarist dignitaries. "He rescued high tsarist officials from certain death by having them taken into custody. Sometimes he personally snatched them from the hands of mobs bent on murder."[21] Yet, from the outset the provisional government enjoyed only conditional support of the Soviet of Workers, and in fact remained powerless within the system of dual power (*dvoevlastie*). "[I]n practice, the Soviet not only controlled the Provisional Government but legislated on its own. . . . [T]he government was not even allowed authority in the realm of military and foreign policy."[22] Most importantly, the provisional government's reluctance to suppress its Communist rivals, including the granting of "blanket amnesty" to terrorists and extreme radicals who openly declared their intention to overthrow it, ultimately led to its undoing.[23]

On the other hand, Max Weber, in his essay "Russia's Transition to Pseudodemocracy" denounced Kerensky's provisional government for failing to transform the old social order. Weber questioned the provisional government's commitment to a democratic social order, rather than its commitment to hold elections, and argued that the government's democratic pretense was only a token since it was dominated by bourgeois interests that supported the continuation of the war for their own selfish ends and had little regard for the concerns of the peasant majority movement that sought to expropriate land and renounce state debts.[24] Obviously, from the point of view of democratic theory, such emphasis on social policy is not sufficient to brand a provisional government as disingenuous in its stated intentions to hold free elections. In fact, it was the Bolsheviks who, after seizing power, sounded the death knell for democracy. They abrogated the constitution of the tsarist empire and the Kerensky regime, abolished the elected Russian Assembly, and established a "dictatorship of the proletariat." As Carl Schmitt has written, the October Revolution "was illegal from the standpoint of the established political norms, which were essentially based on the Western theory of a 'constituting power'."[25]

The lessons from Kerensky's failure to contain the Bolsheviks were put to use a year later by the German provisional government under the vigorous leadership of Friedrich Ebert. Ebert, proclaimed the "Weimar" republic, deflected a Soviet-style Bolshevik uprising, and rescued the democratic cause. Many would argue, though, that it was at a high price that laid the seeds for the republic's future problems.[26] In the case of revolutionary Germany "a line of constitutional legitimacy was preserved"[27] when in November 1918 the last imperial chancellor, Prince Max von Baden attempted to avert a chaotic situation by yielding power to Ebert, the leader of the moderate Social Democrats.[28] At its inception, Ebert's provisional government included the radical socialists. Yet Ebert himself remained faithful to the democratic constitutional path and did not vacillate in his efforts to bring the revolutionary forces under his control. His alliance with Gen. Wilhelm Groener, Chief of Staff of the *Reichswehr,* in quelling the revolutionary insurgency, and most importantly his use of the controversial *Freikorps,* discredited him in the eyes of his coalition partners who wanted a far-reaching social and economic revolution, rather than merely parliamentary elections. In December 1918, while the USPD of the far left resigned from the provisional government and a wing of it joined with other radicals to form the German Communist Party (KPD), and while many others took to the streets to demonstrate and strike, Ebert stuck to his resolve to hold elections to a constituent National Assembly that duly took place in January 1919.[29]

As H. E. Chehabi has pointed out, democratically leaning provisional governments are often caught between their promise to serve in a transitional capacity, with no authority to undertake major projects or make major decisions before elections are held, and the popular expectations and pressures that they will right all wrongs and deliver immediate improvements.[30] In the case of Kerensky's Russia, as Hough and Fainsod observed, the leaders of the provisional government "thought that their major mandate was limited to the calling of a constitutional assembly . . . and that only the democratically elected institutions that would emerge under the new constitution could appropriately introduce major policy change. In principle, it was an admirable decision; in practice, the question was whether the population was in a mood to wait."[31]

Finally, moderates are often forced, due to an indiscriminate dictatorial repression, to ally with radical revolutionaries who later outmaneuver them "as stepping stones to state power."[32] The story of the Islamic Revolution in Iran highlights this conundrum of moderate leaders of provisional governments. Like Russia in 1917, the contest for power after the revolution in Iran was won by the radicals; the Islamic extremists won over the moderates by November 1979. Initially, Ayatollah Ruhollah Khomeini appointed the moderate Mehdi Bazargan as an interim prime minister and called on him "to form the provisional government independently of your connections to a political party or to any other group, so that you can arrange for the administration of the country, organize a referendum concerning the establishment of an Islamic Republic, call a constitutional assembly composed of the people's elected representatives to ratify the constitution of the new political system, and organize parliamentary elections based on the new constitution."[33] Officially endorsing Bazargan, Khomeini also encouraged a parallel government of revolutionary committees, courts, and guard. Hence, Bazargan's provisional government, though it did not include clerics, was de facto subordinated to a Revolutionary Council dominated by clerics. Bazargan himself remained committed to his vision of a "democratic Islamic Republic," but he had no power to bring under his government's control the revolutionary tribunals that convicted and shot those considered affiliated with the Shah. Bazargan's followers among the middle class and the intelligentsia failed to read the handwriting on the wall when Khomeini persistently excluded any reference to democracy. Bazargan finally succumbed to the terror and manipulation of the Islamic forces and, on November 4, 1979, after the takeover of the American Embassy, his government collapsed in a clerics' coup known as "The Second Islamic Revolution."[34]

POSTWAR PROVISIONAL GOVERNMENTS:
THE CASE OF DE GAULLE

In contrast to the previous two categories where indigenous opposition brought about the revolution, most post-World War II transitions to democracy were launched after an external conquest by democratic countries that induced democratization. The Western powers restored deposed governments-in-exile that moved to renew their prewar legitimacy by elections or allowed the establishment of provisional governments without prewar democratic mandates that soon held free elections.[35] Due largely to the international conjuncture which represented the victory of the Western forces of democracy over the Axis powers, these postwar provisional governments were less likely to interrupt or prevent the holding of democratic elections. Moreover, since both the politics and the society of the occupied countries were heavily subservient to the democratic agenda of the Western powers, postwar provisional governments were less susceptible, although by no means immune, to attempts by revolutionaries to seize power and to sabotage the process of democratization. As Carl Friedrich pointed out, the policy of the Allies was directed "not toward 'imposing democracy,' but toward imposing restraints upon those elements in the population . . . which would prevent democracy from becoming established or, if established, would undermine and eventually destroy it."[36]

The most famous example of underground and exiled forces seizing control as provisional government, in contrast to the restoration in power of exiled governments, is de Gaulle's Provisional Government of the French Republic which governed France after its liberation in 1944. When, in June 1940, de Gaulle established the Free French in London, after Pétain had asked for an armistice, he clearly stood in revolt against the legal government of France, which initially was also legitimate for many Frenchmen. Indeed, until 1942 only a few renowned politicians and high French officials joined de Gaulle. The vast majority of the corps and officers of the French Army (including those who opposed the armsitice before it was signed) and all the French ambassadors remained loyal to the state. They followed France's old bureaucratic custom of serving "every regime with the same discipline and the same readiness."[37] Moreover, when de Gaulle first appealed to the British cabinet, to authorize the BBC to allow him to communicate by radio with France, he was rejected on the ground that Pétain's new government was legally constituted and had diplomatic relations with Britain.[38] But Churchill, who was absent from the cabinet meeting, reversed the decision. He had no use for legalistic formulae and saw in de Gaulle a man who could inspire the French to resist the occupation.[39]

The Free French gradually evolved into an embryonic state abroad, and ultimately the British and the United States succumbed to de Gaulle's pressure and reversed their initial plan to assume supreme authority in the liberated zones. It was General Eisenhower's headquarters that eventually helped de Gaulle's Provisional Government of Algiers to become the "sole legitimate authority inside France" from the day of the Allied landings. Eisenhower announced that "control of civil administration had been handed over to the French authorities."[40]

The obstacles facing postwar provisional governments in leading a democratic regime change are similar to the concerns confronting provisional elites that assumed power in a revolutionary struggle without such foreign intervention. They must contend with the legacies of the occupation and its proxies, deal with the issue of collaboration and trials, resettle refugees, work toward generating national solidarity and establishing the foundation for a cohesive military force, enforce law and order and eliminate multiple power bases, determine future international alliances, and reconstruct the political and economic systems. Setting the French economy on a liberal rather than a socialist course was one of de Gaulle's most important decisions. His support of Pleven, his minister of foreign trade who advocated capitalist economy, defeated the left-leaning economic direction advocated by provisional finance minister, Mendès-France.[41]

Impatience with the tedium of complying with democratic norms and legal procedures of provisional governments is particularly intense after a war, when the impetus for evening the score with collaborators and those responsible for the institutionalization of authoritarianism is particularly acute. In postwar Europe some of the political purges of provisional governments were affected by the presence of the Allied forces. Thus Italy's *defascistization* after the liberation of Rome in June 1944 was initiated by the Combined Chiefs of Staff (CCS) of the Allied Military Government of Occupied Territories (AMGOT), which ordered "the removal of fascists from the government and all positions of responsibility."[42] In France, however, where de Gaulle's Provisional Government regained sovereignty in 1945, "there was no outside pressure for a purge."[43]

After de Gaulle reconstituted his Algiers Committee as the French Provisional Government inside France, one of his most difficult challenges was to bring the treatment of those alleged to be Vichy collaborators under his control and end the unauthorized settlement of accounts that had claimed the lives of thousands in the months following the Normandy landings. In those times of emotional ferment, de Gaulle acknowledged that ordinary legal procedures were ill-equipped to deal with and punish collaborators, though he feared that the purge might "furnish occasion for disorders that might escape governmental control and trigger revolutionary situations."[44] Accordingly, de Gaulle created by decree the High Court (*Haute-Cour*) to judge top-level Vichy political officials, the Law Courts for crimes of collaboration, and the Magistrates Courts for lesser cases.[45] The publicized trials of Marshal Pétain, Laval, and Darnand, chief of the detested Vichy Militia, were not representative. According to de Gaulle's memoirs, 10,842 Frenchmen were put to death as collaborators without regular trial, and 779 more were executed after condemnation in court. Some historians have estimated that the first number was, in fact, much higher.[46] In addition to the risks of arbitrary justice many judges and public prosecutors were men who had themselves pledged allegiance to Pétain. There were, indeed, hundreds of thousands of other officials, important and petty, who had served under Vichy including many policemen with highly dubious records who were, without any serious inquiry into their past activities, absorbed into the new bureaucracy. De Gaulle did not dispense completely with the old legality. Even at the height of the purge, he refused to strip Vichy soldiers of their laurels for their fight against the Allies, and he vindicated those who were not considered part of the collaborationist apparatus: "These people, though misguided, . . . after all 'fought for France'."[47]

PROVISIONAL GOVERNMENTS AND INTERNATIONAL LAW

According to contemporary international law, aspirants who adopt the characterization "provisional government" may be recognized as such as long as they exercise effective administration within a defined territory. A government may recognize a new ruling elite as a "provisional government" regardless if this government itself embraces (or rejects) the title. A recognizing government may extend such recognition in order to encourage or pressure the new elite "to provide for procedures assessing the desires of the population in accordance with peremptory norms of international law."[48]

In reality, a new ruling elite may proclaim itself to be a provisional government without exercising effective control inside a territory and sometimes while in exile. Many exiled or underground aspirants who struggled to overthrow a colonial rule, occupying regimes, or indigenous governments may declare themselves provisional governments as an indication of being "authentic representatives" of their people. The Korean Provisional Government in exile in Shanghai, which considered itself the legitimate successor to the defunct Yi Dynasty, played an historical role in filling the governmental vacuum created by the Japanese occupation of Korea from 1910 to 1945.[49] Similarly, at the height of the Algerian struggle to abolish French colonial rule, members of the Algerian revolutionary elite in exile in Morocco declared on September 19, 1958, the formation of the Algerian Republic and proclaimed themselves to be its provisional government (GRPA).[50] More recently, on February 10, 1989, just shortly before the completion of the Soviet withdrawal from Afghanistan, an alliance of the seven opposition parties of the Afghan Mujahidin based in Pakistan, in a challenge to the Soviet-backed government of Najibullah, declared itself the "interim government" of Afghanistan. Claiming control over the vast majority of Afghan territory, the provisional government rejected the title of government-in-exile and proclaimed its intention to move inside Afghanistan and hold elections within six months.[51] Altogether, all these contending aspirants, whether they are located inside or outside the state territory, have made rhetorical commitments to a republican polity and democratic principles.

The title "provisional government" may be exploited by foreign powers that wish to install puppet regimes, under the guise of democratization, in their controlled occupied zones. A prime example was Stalin's creation of the so-called Lublin Committee, which was launched to undermine the legal Polish government-in-exile in London. It received diplomatic recognition and was held as a political trump card for Stalin's postwar aspiration in Poland. Finally, the most recent Iraqi ploy to install a so-called provisional government in occupied Kuwait in early August 1990 (just a few days before Saddam Hussein announced the annexation of Kuwait), was intended in part to legitimate Iraqi control over Kuwaiti assets, and to hide and justify, under the notion of territorial integrity, plans of permanent control.[52]

2

The power-sharing model

Revolutionary and postwar provisional governments must be distinguished from interim authorities which are the product of ad hoc coalitions between the democratic opposition and the outgoing regime and from incumbent administrations (or their heirs) which have declared themselves caretaker until a democratically elected government can take charge. In general, interim governments based on power-sharing coalitions are more likely to be initiated when the period prior to their formation is not overshadowed by large-scale violence, and when the opposition is not controlled by a revolutionary elite or ideology. Such conditions permit both the opposition leaders and the incumbent elite to go beyond retribution toward accommodation. Transitional moderation, however, may only reflect tentative political calculation, and it is reasonable to expect outbursts of zeal for evening the score after the first democratic elections.

For analytical purposes one must distinguish between interim governments based on a power-sharing formula and negotiated "pacts." The two differ in their objectives and scope. The term "pact" in the literature on regime transition refers to a wide set of negotiated compromises among competing elites with long-term goals of accommodating conflicts and institutionalizing the distribution of power in key aspects of state and society. Such compromises may be obtained within a power-sharing government as well as in situations where incumbent caretaker governments lead the transition. Pacts are unlikely to develop under a revolutionary provisional government. Power-sharing interim governments, in contrast, are in principle short-term political arrangements between incumbent and opposition, focusing primarily – though not exclusively – on determining the rules of and the time for the founding elections. In other words the parties making up the temporary government have come to no formal agreement that the distribution of power is permanent or legitimate, though the incumbent and occasionally the opposition may wish it to be so.[1]

The negotiations leading to the formation of a power-sharing interim government as well as the actual function of such a government impart a degree of legitimacy on the opposition without totally discrediting the outgoing administration. In theory, power-sharing helps reconcile the "us" and the "them";[2] it reduces the incumbent's fear of losing everything in the transition even as it assuages the democratic opposition's anxiety that the incumbents may somehow try to halt or rig the transition process and the elections. In practice, however, such reconciliation may be temporary and occur only because of the immediate political calculations of the time; the reconciliation may be altered if and when the full democratic process unfolds and elements of the incumbent regime are outmaneuvered politically and legally.

Indeed, in such cases, there may be delayed reaction on the issue of evening the score with members of the outgoing regime. Yet it must be remembered that even though it is authoritarian, the outgoing regime is not necessarily more villainous than some segments of the opposition, which may now resort to the rhetoric of democracy although in the past they violated such values.[3] This problem is particularly complex in cases of abrupt transitions from post-totalitarian rule or in less developed societies where the initial distinction between the outgoing regime and the "democratic" forces is to a large extent misleading.

The sine qua non of power-sharing governments is a balance between the degeneration of the outgoing government and the maturation and growth of other contenders for power. This balance has a powerful impact on whether and when, if ever, those controlling the new democracy will seek retribution from those responsible for the old order. Thus a critical issue facing the democratic opposition is, therefore, whether "the old guard [should] be treated as potential coalition partners or as criminals."[4]

Power-sharing interim governments are generally formed when the incumbents, though their authority is severely weakened, remain strong enough to exercise control. They agree to share executive power, if not in hopes of actually stemming the tide, at least in expectation of retaining some positions of power in the future democracy. The Polish transition shows how such expectations on the part of the incumbent can meet with disappointment. In April 1989 roundtable talks between the government of Gen. Wojciech Jaruzelski and Lech Walesa's Solidarity ended with the former agreeing to end the Communist monopoly over political power and acknowledge the legitimacy of the opposition in return for a long-term pact guaranteeing that the incumbents would retain executive power following quasidemocratic elections. Yet the Communists' humiliating defeat in the June 1989 elections discredited the early agreements and forced Jaruzelski to accept the formation of Tadeusz Mazowiecki's Solidarity-led government. To appease the Soviet Union, men from the outgoing regime were allocated key ministerial positions, including the Ministries of Interior, Defense, and Foreign Economic Relations. Gen. Jaruzelski, who was elected president as part of the negotiated deal, was eventually compelled to assent to direct presidential elections earlier than originally planned.[5]

The two-year transitional period during which ex-Communists dominated the lower house of the Parliament and participated in government left an indelible mark on Poland's developing democracy, with particular ramifications for its ability to confront its past. Most controversial has been the Mazowiecki transitional government's policy of "burying the past and exacting no retribution from individuals for the abuses of communism, [including even] the endemic criminality of the Communist-run secret police."[6] Although this policy may have helped in averting a revolutionary situation, some have maintained that in the long run it has "contributed to the breakdown of law and order" by allowing the former police apparatus to destroy compromising evidence of its past activities and thus left "a legacy of mistrust in the new police and security institutions, as well as in the new political elite. This policy also created a sense of moral ambiguity and raised doubts about the Solidarity government's political will to enforce justice."[7] It was only after the first free parliamentary elections in 1991 that the notion of evening the score began to be muted and the idea of reassessing the 1989 Round Table agreement and Mazowiecki's "ruling off" policy began to gather momentum. However, as Anna Sabbat-Swidlicka of Radio Free Europe has pointed out, "It is a matter for political debate whether the damage would have been more or less serious if the purge had been conducted immediately after the collapse of communism. It is unlikely to make the UOP's [the Polish State Security Office] problems any easier, torn as the office is between the need to establish its credibility as a loyal and dependable guardian of state security and pressure to maintain its operational efficiency."[8]

REGIME COLLAPSE AND TRANSITIONS

Sometimes power-sharing coalitions materialize only after the old regime collapses. In such cases, the opposition's unpreparedness for power and the danger of chaos may combine to produce a short-lived coalition whose mission is to avert violent upheavals, ensure the peaceful exit of the old elite, allow parties time to organize and campaign, and take care of various details of transition.[9] The demise of East Germany as well as Czechoslovakia's "Velvet Revolution" provide the best examples of power-sharing situations where the incumbent "had been weakened to the point of dependence on the opposition to avert its complete obliteration and to protect it from uncontrolled acts of retribution by the population."[10]

The abrupt disintegration of the Communist government in Czechoslovakia forced its leaders to yield their monopoly of power and accept, on December 10, 1989, a minority role in the Government of National Understanding. The goal of the temporary government was to set the date of free elections and maintain law and order until their realization. Those communists who still held power, like the federal prime minister Marian Călfa and the interim Slovak prime minister Milan Čič, "had made it quite clear that they would diligently carry out the orders of Civic Forum and [its Slovak counterpart, Public Against Violence] VPN."[11] In late December, Václav Havel was elected interim President by the outgoing Parliament and parliamentary elections were held on June 1990.[12] To a large extent, members of the outgoing Communist regime in Czechoslovakia were spared the fate reserved for dictatorships deposed by popular revolutions, largely because of the deep commitment of opposition leaders like Václav Havel to human rights and their "profound belief that a future secured by violence . . . would be fatally stigmatized by the very means used to secure it."[13]

Notwithstanding the atypical restraint of the opposition during the revolutions in East Germany and Czechoslovakia, these "collapsed transitions," as Nicolai Hansteen has shown, had far-reaching implications for the issue of evening the score with their loathed politicians, bureaucrats, and, in particular, secret police.[14] As noted in the introduction to this book, a democratic transition has much to gain if both the outgoing regime and the democratic opposition appreciate the role of state institutions of "legal-rational aspiration." This may be the case when "past constitutional traditions construed the state as the impersonal carrier of specified public functions, indeed duties, in the continuous determination, allocation, and delivery of collective goods. Though the traditions may have been cast originally in an autocratic mold, though they may have assigned civil society and public opinion and narrow legal space, though they may have elevated the state and its armed forces to the role of arbiters of 'unnatural' societal conflict, they are still traditions anchored to notions of professionalism, legalism, impartiality, continuity of service, and institutional autonomy from partisan politics – that is, to notions that, whether myth or substance, are central to democracy."[15]

Yet, when the incumbent has been undermined to the point that it has no effective powers over the decisions of the interim government and when state institutions have lost any perceived legitimacy in the eyes of the opposition and the public at large, the prospect for a transition via the old state-legality weakens, and attempts to salvage the role of the old state institutions, especially those representing the repressive nature of the regime, are highly improbable. Indeed, the collapse of the outgoing regime, even when it is still part of the interim arrangement, is likely to arouse popular demand for prompt cleansing. The challenge to the incumbent elements within the interim government under such circumstances is two-pronged. First, how can the old state institutions be reformed within a democratic framework so that a sufficient level of popular legitimacy can be secured? Second, when reform rather than elimination of the distrusted institutions becomes untenable in the public's view, how can the old institutions be modified without provoking a backlash from the army, the police, or the secret services, all of which have vested interests in the old order and are fearful of retribution? The latter question becomes further complicated when one tries to discern the strength of the links between incumbent leaders and discredited repressive institutions.

In East Germany, the Communists, despite their organizational advantages, were crippled by the forced pace of political change that culminated in the fall of the Berlin Wall on November 9, 1989. Egon Krenz, a party apparatchik who broke with Erich Honecker in October 1989 and offered limited reform in an attempt to forestall revolutionary chaos, failed to respond to the demand for political participation. On November 7–8, under immense popular pressure, the GDR Communists yielded their monopoly to reformer Hans Modrow who took it upon himself to prepare the country for free elections in May 1990. Yet, because the caretaker administration was led by a totally disgraced political party, Modrow's government could hardly rule. Its immobility was further accentuated by two major events. First, on November 28, Chancellor Kohl of West Germany called for reunification of the two Germanies, a subject which then dominated East German politics to the almost total exclusion of the issue of democratic transition. Second, there was the revelation in early December 1989 of widespread corruption on the part of the Communist party leaders and public realization that the State Security Service (Stasi) remained untouched. The two events rendered East Germany ungovernable and left the Communists "at the mercy of the revolution."[16]

Czechoslovakia's collapsed transition followed in the footsteps of East Germany's. The abrupt disintegration of Czechoslovakia's Communist government forced its leaders to yield their monopoly on power and accept, on December 10, 1989, a minority role in the Government of National Understanding. The goal of the temporary government under Marian Čalfa was to set a date for free elections and maintain law and order until that time.[17]

In both the GDR and Czechoslovakia, incumbent elements sought to transform the secret police (the Stasi and StB respectively) in eleventh hour efforts to make them part of the new state system. When the attempts failed because the secret police were so reviled, the caretaker administrations were left without effective means of enforcing order. In the GDR, beginning in January 1990, leading opposition groups backed by thousands of demonstrators were so enraged by Modrow's proposals to reform the security services that they forced an early adjournment of the weekly Round Table talks. Modrow's interim government, the opposition charged, was using every available tool to strengthen its power in the transition; they demanded that the government abandon its plan to preserve and rename the security force. In response, Modrow created a power-sharing "government of national responsibility," jettisoned his plan to reform the security police, and agreed with the opposition to move the elections up to March 18.[18]

As the reform process began in Czechoslovakia, newspaper articles reported that security agents and collaborators were burning thousands of secret police files in the forests and were, moreover, preparing for a violent coup d'etat.[19] Despite the insistence of security police officials that they were complying with the governmental reforms, it was clear that police agents considered such reforms antithetical to their interests. Hence, it is no surprise that the masses insisted that the StB had no role in the future democratic society.

These urgent popular demands placed the heirs to the incumbents in a difficult position. To continue the transition, they were dependent upon as broad a political consensus as possible. The ex-Communist East Germans could not endure a political exodus from the coalition government, just as the former Communist Czechs could not chance disrupted Round Table negotiations. In both cases, remaining in power meant bowing to the popular opposition's calls for the dismantling of the secret police. At the same time, however, the outgoing Communists' ability to constrain the interim governments had clearly diminished. In both countries, the ties between the Communist parties and the secret police had been severed as the police forces were subordinated to parliament. In addition, the collapse of the Communist regimes facilitated the interim governments' decision to yield to the popular opposition without exposing themselves to the risk of a Communist coup supported by the secret police, the Communist elite, or the army. Czech Interior Minister Sacher announced in a speech to the Federal Assembly in late January 1990 that "it is time to put the citizen's mind at peace and secure safety."[20] In late January, therefore, the Călfa government followed within days the example of the GDR and ordered the dismantling of the so-called Intelligence Services as well as the remaining state security components. As in Berlin, security headquarters in Prague were emptied and secret police agents were told to stay home. Their weapons would be confiscated. No longer were the Stasi or the StB to be reorganized under a new democratic banner; they would instead, at least officially, cease to exist as state institutions.[21]

The abrupt collapse of the Stasi and the StB and the early revelation of the astonishing contents of secret police files had not only a dramatic effect on the first democratic elections but also far reaching implications for the manner in which both Czechoslovakia and Germany have confronted their past. In Czechoslovakia, in particular, the security service's files held politicians hostage before the first free elections in June 1990. Selective disclosures of alleged collaboration with the StB were used for political blackmail and may have had an impact on the results of the first elections.[22] While in Germany the absorption of the east by the west deflected the institutional crisis resulting from the demise of the old bureaucracy, in Czechoslovakia, however, where state and society were entirely penetrated by Communist rule, the move to purify the polity had overwhelming institutional and political ramifications, far beyond Germany's personal and societal tragedies of the betrayal of friends by friends and relatives by relatives.[23] Nonetheless, even in reunited Germany, the early opening of the files has essentially discredited a generation of potential democratic leadership from the east.

The formula of power-sharing may either slow or hasten the full process of democratization; the tempo of the transition will depend on the balance of power between reformist and conservative factions in the outgoing elite, the ability of opposition leaders to restrain the more radical elements within their own ranks, and the relative ease of reaching an agreement on a timetable for the transfer of power. Conditions outside the country can also affect a transition's pace. In Poland, Tadeusz Mazowiecki's interim coalition government benefited from the friendly new climate in Moscow. Still, high-speed change and summary rejection of the Polish Communists seemed imprudent in August 1989; ultimately, the cause of democracy benefited greatly from Solidarity's patience, and radical critics of delay were proven wrong.[24] In fact, Poland kept its semidemocratic power-sharing system much longer than all other Eastern European countries that followed in its footsteps. It was more than two years from the 1989 elections until the first free national parliamentary elections to the *Sejm* in late 1991, that is, before a full-scale democratization was achieved.[25]

RISKS AND OPPORTUNITIES

The residual legitimacy of the old regime and the power resources it still holds will determine the degree to which it will be able to maneuver and gain concessions from its opponents in a power-sharing coalition. The old guard may introduce weak reforms that fall short of complete democratization, or it may push the opposition to accept a formula that favors incumbents in important ways. Yet the incumbents' very decision to compromise their own legitimacy and approach the opposition betrays the weakness of their hold on power. On the other hand, the opposition's agreement to share power – thereby partially legitimating the incumbents – also demonstrates the opposition's relative weakness or its hesitation to assume power alone. This is in contradistinction with the first model presented, where the very fact of revolutionary severance permits the provisional government to portray itself as untainted by the old regime, however inaccurate this perception may be.

Machinations by incumbent elements within the interim coalition are likely to arouse strong opposition on the part of democrats who reject intermediate solutions; these latter will then demand a rapid – and perhaps imprudent – move toward free elections. This is particularly the case when there is a rapid disintegration of the old regime, and where quick democratic elections become the only legitimate route from the government's temporary status.

Power-sharing becomes a remote option when the outgoing elite, even when still in control, is directly implicated in violent suppression of the opposition, the perpetration of human rights violations, or in economic crimes and corruption. In such cases the democratic forces are more likely to prefer to shy away from a unity interim coalition, fearing to shoulder some of the incumbent's unpopularity. It may be argued, however, that in declining to share power the democratic forces risk alienating a segment within the outgoing regime that may feel threatened by future reprisals to the point of contemplating the use of repressive force. Lech Walesa's drive to form the Mazowiecki power-sharing – which was adopted against the consensus position of The Solidarity Citizens' Caucus in the Polish Parliament that resisted any shared "responsibility for Solving the problems THEY crafted,"[26] – proved vitally useful in averting a situation of perilous ungovernability.

Moreover, an opposition that refuses to share power may also lead to the opposition's marginalization. By declining to share power the democratic forces may miss an opportunity to further discredit the incumbent regime from within the interim government. Additionally, they risk missing a chance to take advantage of the state apparatus to better position themselves for elections or to schedule elections according to their own convenience. Finally, by rejecting an interim coalition the opposition may indirectly reinforce the legitimacy of a self-reformed incumbent and inadvertently assist in its electoral victory.

In Bulgaria, the reformed Communists (renamed the Bulgarian Socialist party), who ousted the seventy-eight-year-old dictator Todor Zhivkov in a November 1989 coup, won a parliamentary majority in June 1990. But despite their apparent conversion the Bulgarian coalition of the democratic forces, known as the Union of Democratic Forces (UDF), rejected in early 1990 a Communist party offer to share power in the months leading to the elections, calling it "a ploy to get the opposition to share responsibility for four decades of mismanagement." Instead the UDF decided to negotiate only from without, and was thus outmaneuvered by the Communists.[27] Allegations of irregularities, an opposition boycott of parliament, and a general strike that forced the Bulgarian Socialist government's resignation in November 1990 led to a delayed formation of a power-sharing administration.[28]

Power-sharing, therefore, involves opportunities and risks for incumbents and opposition elites alike. Timing, that is, the question of how long the power-sharing administration is in control before democratic legitimation is conferred, is of critical importance. Any delay of transition to fully democratic institutions may also delay the ability to move toward daring policies on the domestic and international fronts, or enable the old guard to manipulate the situation and win some undeserved privileges. In rapid transitions, in contrast, in which a near target date for elections has been set, incumbent elites may not have time to "recover" from the authoritarian stigma, giving oppositionists the upper hand. Therefore, one can observe the phenomenon of "power-sharing from without," in which opposition elites use their influence to limit the freedom of action of the incumbent regime, without joining in the government. This was the case in Hungary where the self-nullification of the Communist party resulted in the formation of a caretaker administration that was entirely dominated by the agenda of the democratic forums.

Yet even in such dramatic circumstances of national reconciliation as the Hungarian National Round Table, the incumbent did not waiver in its attempt to retain positions of power by manipulation. On November 26, 1989, the reform Communists marginally lost a referendum in their bid to call a "snap" presidential election before parliamentary balloting, an election which would have been likely to catch the opposition unprepared and would probably have ensured the election of a Communist as a head of state. The defeat in the referendum, followed by the historic compromise on the Hungarian electoral law, rendered the caretaker government of Németh purely ceremonial. The interim administration was "suspended without either coercive power or democratic legitimacy," while the opposition parties enjoyed the time before the March 1990 elections to focus their disputes "as much on each other as on the communists."[29]

Although the Hungarian interim administration was "suspended without either coercive power or democratic legitimacy,"[30] the sense of early and genuine Communist repentance, as manifested in the reburial of former Prime Minister Imre Nagy in June 1989, as well as a "gentlemen's agreement" during the Round Table negotiations between the political opposition and the reformed Communists to lay the past to rest, reinforced the spirit of reconciliation and diminished popular pursuit of retribution. Even though the calls for retribution were weaker in Hungary than in neighboring Czechoslovakia and economic recovery was given top priority, the Hungarian Parliament adopted the Zetenyi-Takacs law on November 4, 1991, which removed the statute of limitations for crimes of murder and high treason that could not be prosecuted earlier. Hungarian President Arpád Göncz refused to sign the bill and sent it to Hungary's Constitutional Court which deemed the law unconstitutional.[31]

A reversed version of "power-sharing from without" may occur when the incumbent leaders realize that their dictatorship cannot survive a deep political crisis. To forestall a total collapse, they may choose to transfer power to a broadly acceptable interim rule, which they hope to dominate, even if from without. The timing of such "voluntary" surrender of power is critical, and the incumbent's prospects of achieving its goals decrease in direct relation to the speed of its internal disintegration.

Greece's redemocratization in 1974 affords the neatest example of incumbents failing to achieve power-sharing from without. In Greece, the junta chiefs rapidly lost control in the aftermath of their ill-fated intervention against Cyprus. The mutiny of the hierarchial military against the military in government (which always represented only a faction within the armed forces) on July 22, 1974, forced Ioannides to yield to his senior officers' demand to surrender power to civilian rule. Although the military, acting as a state institution, initiated the self-dissolution of the dictatorship and the transfer of power to civilian leaders, it failed to salvage its eminent role in Greek politics.[32] The officers who entrusted the premiership of the interim government to Constantin Karamanlis hoped to secure for themselves key ministerial positions and a grant of immunity from prosecution for human rights violations. But against these expectations, Karamanlis, the Conservative leader, capitalized on his victorious homecoming after eleven years in self-exile and moved swiftly to strip the military of all positions of power. His harsh policies towards the junta resemble in many respects the unyielding posture of a provisional revolutionary government towards the *ancien régime*. Untarnished by the events that led to the downfall of the democratic system in April 1967, and acceptable to a wide spectrum of Greek political groups, Karamanlis was in a unique position to assume the role of transition manager. He exploited the division within the military command and overwhelmed them with his determination to conquer full civilian control and to return quickly to parliamentary rule. In his four months as interim premier Karamanlis reached a cease fire agreement with Turkey, released all political prisoners and granted amnesty for all political offenses (except those committed by the junta), arrested and charged with high treason the leaders of the 1967 coup, recognized all political parties (including the Communists), dissolved the Military Police, dismissed junta officials in the civil service, ended Greek participation in the military side of NATO, and stuck to his resolve to hold parliamentary elections on November 17, 1974.[33] Just a few weeks before the elections Karamanlis arrested the leaders of the April 1967 coup, charged them with high treason, and initiated criminal prosecutions against an additional twenty-nine army and police officers who were implicated in the killing of students during the uprising at Athens Polytechnic University in November 1973.

3

The caretaker government model

Caretaker governments are the product of transitions in which the outgoing authoritarian regime, or perhaps a new elite within the incumbent institutions, initiates a transition in the face of a growing economic deterioration, a severe rupture within the ruling elite, or a threat of opposition and even revolt. The incumbent may also realize that the regime does not fit into the dominant democratic *Zeitgeist* and that change is necessary, possible and may even be in the interest of the country. The likelihood of a regime-initiated transition is explainable, to a certain extent, in terms of Robert Dahl's famous formulation that a growing perception of the cost of repression, on the one side, and developing awareness that the cost of toleration of change may be low or diminishing, on the other side, adds the optimum conditions for such a regime-initiated transition.

Indeed, in some cases the old regime wishes to head off a potential crisis in good time; in other situations the outgoing administration does so under immediate pressure. In all cases the incumbent regime creates expectations which, if denied, can spur the very upheavals it wishes to avoid; hence the irony that regime-initiated transitions are less likely to go astray than opposition-led provisional governments.

We use the term "caretaker government" to refer to two characteristics. First, the temporal nature of the government and second, its limited functions. The temporal nature aspect means that there should be an end in view: the holding of elections on a specific date which in this case involve a change of the regime (not the election of a new parliament in the case of dissolution to produce a new government nor the formation of a new government coalition that would be able to gain a vote of confidence, as it is the case of caretaker governments in parliamentary democracies).

The limited function aspect of a caretaker government dictates that such a government in principle has no or only limited legitimacy to make any decisions of importance except those conducive to democratization.

In parliamentary democracies caretaker governments are expected to deal only with routine and the most urgent business. They are often called managing or administrative government *(de gestion)*. As we shall see "caretaker governments" in regime change might go beyond those limits in time and functions. Let us stress that not all "caretaker governments" in transitions refer to themselves that way, although many would accept this designation. Although the calling of elections to change the regime render them temporary, they may consider themselves normal governments in the framework of the old regime or the special rules enacted to govern the transition.

The option of an incumbent-led transition is less desirable when there are deep-seated historical divisions within society of a national, ethnic, religious, or cultural character. Indeed, transitions initiated by reformist incumbents, although advantageous in their potential for averting chaos in more or less ethnically homogeneous societies, nevertheless may be totally unacceptable in countries where historical cleavages are so deep that the very idea of the incumbents leading the transition is repugnant to the opposition. In such countries the initiation of a democratic transition by the incumbent, even if limited, may set in motion a sovereignty movement that may result in the disintegration of the state, as happened in the Soviet Union.

South Africa managed to escape this predicament only after a laborious transitional phase characterized by the specter of escalating violence and the killing of thousands while the country awaited its first fully democratic elections. The democratization process in South Africa provides a fascinating example of a two-stage, dual form transitional authority: first, by means of an incumbent serving as a caretaker administration, and second, by means of a power-sharing coalition in which the incumbent retains decisive control. The idea of a caretaker government leading the transition was rejected by the opposition, primarily the African National Congress (ANC). Because of its profound mistrust in F. W. de Klerk's administration, the ANC first demanded a form of provisional authority to be selected by a constituent assembly. Yet the ANC's developing appreciation of de Klerk's democratic sincerity and its leaders' recognition of the importance of sustaining a viable incumbent to avert a situation of state anarchy, especially in the face of secession threats in Natal province orchestrated by Zulu Inkatha leader Chief Mangosuthu Buthelezi, eventually secured the formation of a power-sharing arrangement that made an enduring settlement possible.

On September 13, 1993, after many months of tortuous negotiations, de Klerk's administration and Nelson Mandela's ANC agreed on establishing a multiparty Transitional Executive Council, or TEC. The agreement was ratified by South Africa's outgoing Parliament, from which blacks were excluded, which later enacted an enabling law providing for the formal creation of the TEC as "a parallel cabinet" or a "super-cabinet." The TEC's main objective was to pave the way for free and fair elections for a national government and a constitutional assembly by all South Africans in April 1994. The constituent assembly would then draw up a final constitution.[1]

In principle, it would seem that the opposition that has fought for the creation or the restoration of a democratic system would have a better claim to rule during the interim period than the nondemocratic incumbents who had either opposed the democracy or belatedly come to accept to play by the democratic rules. Yet if the incumbents make a good-faith commitment to abide by the electorate's decision, providing evidence that they do not intend to falsify the will of the people, there is little reason to question their right to act as a caretaker government. Their legal authority, though nonlegitimate from a democratic perspective and only de facto, offers an advantage insofar as the state apparatus is accustomed to obey its decisions, while it would be more likely to question those of a provisional government headed by the opposition. In Spain, "bringing the opposition to collaborate in a process of democratization within Francoist 'legality' was to be one of Suárez's greatest tasks and consequently greatest triumphs."[2]

The Spanish reformist prime minister Adolfo Suárez, in his address upon assuming the premiership in June 1976, clearly stated his position that until the first elections he intended to stay in power and guide the transition process within the constitutional framework, rather than turning over power to the representatives of the large number of opposition groups, whatever their prestige, visibility, and potential backing. Indeed, Suárez conducted the transition with limited cooperation and virtually no participation of the democratic opposition in his administration. Although he agreed to legalize the Communist party, he rejected outright the plan of the opposition camp – communists, socialists, Basque and Catalan nationalists, and a few liberals and Christian Democrats – to install a provisional government divorced from the old regime, and objected to their idea of forming interim autonomous governments in Catalonia and the Basque Country. Ex-post facto, the Spanish elections of June 1977 came to support Suárez's position, for he won a plurality that allowed him to form the first parliament-based democratic government, a position reconfirmed by the 1979 elections. At the same time, the first free elections proved that opposition leaders of undoubted prestige and personal appeal who possessed a great record in the struggle for democracy did not garner significant popular electoral support. There can be little question that some of those leaders would have occupied key positions in any provisional government. It is also true that it is the successful management of a complex model of transition from authoritarianism to democracy that has been described as *reforma pactada,* negotiated reform, and *ruptura pactada,* as a negotiated break (reflecting the perspective of both incumbents and the opposition in those terms) under the direction of Suárez that gave him the chance to obtain widespread support and attracted an electoral plurality to his party, the Unión de Centro Democrático (UCD) that included leaders of the former democratic opposition.

It can be argued, therefore, that a caretaker government of incumbents acting honestly or out of necessity might provide a better chance for a successful transition than power-sharing administrations or revolutionary provisional governments. This may seem paradoxical and counterintuitive, but a further examination can reveal its plausibility. The incumbents or the heirs of the authoritarian regime, as caretakers, lack democratic legitimacy. But, although they are weak, they still control the state apparatus, allowing them to assure public order – in part because the opposition fears that a challenge might endanger the transition by mobilizing the hardliners opposed to change or by alienating the army. The goals of such a caretaker government include the successful transfer of power to those elected by the people (itself hoping to emerge the victor), to maintain order in the meantime and to check involutionary tendencies, to guarantee the electoral process, and to accommodate the demands of the opposition without abdicating power. On some of these goals a tacit understanding or agreement develops with the opposition. The incumbent's staying in power as a caretaker government gives to those still reluctant to accept the change of regime a certain sense of security; those not opposed to the change feel that they will not be totally excluded from political life. In short, everyone is given time to adjust to the continuous cumulative changes with a minimum shock. In addition, the opposition has time to start organizing for the elections instead of concentrating on mass mobilizations and protest actions, or alternatively to begin facing the difficult task of sharing power with the caretaker government.

In South Korea, for example, after Chun Doo Hwan was forced by his party to resign the presidency of the ruling Democratic Justice Party (DJP) in June 1987 (though he remained as caretaker President until the democratic elections in February 1988), opposition leaders first wanted to have their own members as ministers in an interim government that would take charge in the period before the presidential elections. However, they refrained from pressing hard for a power-sharing arrangement, fearing that this would provoke the hardliners in the DJP, and thereby risk a reversal in Roh Tae Woo's (the DJP's choice as presidential candidate) democratic path.[3]

The option of incumbent as caretaker government is greatly enhanced in the absence of a rapid loss of power and a subsequent power vacuum.

This was the pattern in Spain, Brazil, Chile, Uruguay, South Korea, and Ortega's Nicaragua prior to the February 1990 elections. A critical factor in such situations is the belief of the opposition and the public at large in the incumbents' genuine intention; a view shaped greatly by the government's liberalization policies – the lifting of martial law, the affording of press freedom and the organization of parties, the granting of amnesty to political prisoners, and permitting the return of exiles – as well as the personal record of incumbent leaders on human rights.

The Spanish situation represents a case in which the incumbent heirs of the authoritarian regime led by Prime Minister Suárez, in their capacity as caretaker government, enjoyed a substantial degree of support from the public and the majority of the opposition who have trusted their democratic commitment. Most important was the fact that Suárez and his ministers had no incriminating record of human rights violations and no association with the horrors committed decades earlier. The brutalities of the civil war and its aftermath could have been attributed to members of both sides. A notion of shared guilt, societal exhaustion, the subsiding of atrocities under Franco from the 1940s onward, a forward-looking mentality, and a willingness to forgive made possible a consensus on the renunciation of revenge. In July 1976, shortly after assuming power as a prime minister, still according to Franco's constitutional laws, Suárez declared the goals of his interim government: "To submit to the decision of the nation the questions related to the constitutional reforms and to hold general elections before June 30, 1977."[4] He further announced the reform of legislation to assure the exercise of basic freedoms and declared a universal amnesty that launched the transition. In October 1977 the majority members of the first democratically elected parliament approved an amnesty law, thereby signaling that the legitimate representatives of the people had finally settled the past.[5]

Undoubtedly the reformers of a regime who were not guilty of massive human rights violations in the years before the transition are more likely to succeed in their role as a caretaker administration. Brazil's protracted transition is an unusual case where the incumbent initiated and carried out an investigation into its own crimes as part of a gradual and controlled plan to withdraw from power peacefully and on its own terms.[6] In South Korea, Roh Tae Woo of the DJP distanced himself from both the uncompromising policies of Chun Doo Hwan (who initially designated Roh as his successor) and more critically from direct association with the Kwangju massacre in which at least 200 student demonstrators were killed by soldiers loyal to Chun. Roh's interim administration acknowledged past abuses, exonerated its victims, and accepted "the spirit of democracy" in which the opposition had acted. Significantly, Roh did not grant Chun and the military immunity from future prosecution. After he was elected president on December 16, 1987, benefiting from the split between the two major opposition contenders Kim Young Sam and Kim Dae Jung, Roh swiftly initiated an inquiry of the Kwangju affair. In his inaugural speech on February 25, 1988, he declared: "The days when repressive force and torture in secret chambers were tolerated are over."[7]

Even though in some instances incumbent reformers do not have a pristine record on human rights, their infamy may be mitigated in situations where elements of the opposition itself have acquired a notorious reputation regarding human rights violations. In the case of Nicaragua, the Sandinistas' incriminating record was often superseded by the abuses of their opponents, the Contras. Americas Watch reports indicate that in the mid-1980s Sandinista security forces committed many human rights abuses but their behavior was considerably less brutal than that of their adversaries.[8]

A transition led by incumbents as caretaker becomes a remote option when the previous regime has disintegrated, when the incumbents cannot count on the loyalty of the armed forces, and mass mobilization or the guerrilla activity against the regime has undermined its authority in large parts of the country. The implication of the incumbent elite in criminal human rights violations or large-scale corruption further erodes its chances of successfully constituting a viable caretaker government and its attempt to lead a democratic transition is more likely to be viewed as a sham. In Argentina, for example, the junta that assumed a caretaker position in the aftermath of the Galtieri government's humiliating defeat in the Falklands/Malvinas conflict (April–June 1982) – a war which was initiated to defuse the growing opposition to the regime by uniting Argentines in an outburst of nationalism – was overwhelmed by the popular outcry regarding the *desaparecidos* (the Disappeared) and was virtually left with no escape route.

Though the army had forced Galtieri's resignation, the military branches remained so divided that they could not agree on his successor or a future course for the country. After the air force and the navy withdrew from the junta, the army established a military caretaker government, with retired general Reynaldo Bignone as president. Unable to unite the military behind him, Bignone was forced to remove the ban on political parties and called for elections before the end of 1983. Indeed, in July 1982, the time was ripe for the opposition to move decisively and assume a role in the government. For tactical reasons, however, the leaders of the Multipartidaria (multiparty) front, shunned power. They chose to play it safe by allowing the military to exhaust itself further as a political force and to use the time left before elections for reorganizing and campaigning. Bignone's caretaker government, however, was preoccupied with safeguarding the military's position in any future arrangement. It sought assurances on military supremacy in matters relating to external defense and internal security and concentrated its effort on securing immunity from investigations into the junta's corruption, domestic terrorist policies, and its disastrous economic policies, as well as the army's defeat in the Malvinas. Bignone's failure to entice the Multipartidaria into accepting these conditions prompted his caretaker government, in July 1983, to decree an amnesty for itself for human rights abuses. This act provoked a massive protest by human rights groups and a constitutional challenge by some parties. Even though Bignone reached an agreement with the Peronista party, the would-be victors in the free elections, that there would be no derogations,[9] the victory of the Radical presidential candidate, Alfonsín, sealed the military's fate. In fact, the exposure of the secret agreement between the military and the Peronistas caused great damage to the latter. Alfonsín skillfully exploited the issue in his campaign to discredit Italo Luder, the Peronista candidate who was indirectly stained by the link to the military.[10] When democracy finally returned to Argentina in October 1983, the new civilian government conducted investigations and trials against the leaders and high officials of the military, some of whom were tried and convicted for involvement in the campaign to exterminate the Argentine left. Altogether, it is still debatable whether the trials in Argentina were the inevitable outcome of the military's loss of control over the transition or the result of the junta's miscalculation in betting on the Peronista candidate. Mark Osiel, a student of Argentine politics, has argued that "It would not be an exaggeration to say that if Alfonsín had not been elected President, there would almost certainly have been no trial."[11]

AMNESTY LAWS AND THE SEARCH FOR TRUTH AND JUSTICE

Amnesty, characterized by a broad spectrum of political behavior, is a multifaceted instrument. It may eradicate old legacies, create new ones, or do both at the same time in varying degrees. There is, however, a distinction between the behavior of popularly elected governments and that of interim administrations. With regard to caretaker interim governments of the incumbents, such behavior runs the gamut from the last-minute self-amnesty of an incumbent in disarray that is unlikely to survive the transition as in Argentina, to moves to grant amnesty only to opponents in an effort to saddle them with all the blame as the Sandinistas did in Nicaragua. Between these two extremes, there are often instances of mutual amnesty as occurred in Brazil, Spain, and de facto in Uruguay.[12]

In the case of Nicaragua, the Arias Peace Plan armed the Sandinistas with the tool of amnesty which they manipulated until their final exit from power. The Sandinistas used amnesty as a political device which they employed to ensure that outside assistance to the Contras ceased. When such assistance was believed to have resumed, they halted amnesty. Moreover, the Sandinistas were certain that only the Contras were villainous and, therefore, took no steps to acknowledge the presence of abusive elements in their own midst. Their lack of repentance manifested itself in their inability to imagine that the elections of 1990 would sweep them from power and in their insistence that the voting would merely confirm their revolutionary rectitude.[13]

The case of Uruguay is particularly telling with regard to the subtleties of incumbent-initiated amnesties either of self or others. The Club Naval talks during the interim period not only precluded, de facto and not de jure, the trying of the Army for abuses but also attempted to prevent as Lawrence Weschler has pointed out, a period of official "truth telling."[14] Those talks, held in Montevideo in June–July 1984 between the military junta headed by General Medina and the opposition, enabled Uruguay's military to exit from power on its own terms and paved the way for the November 25 presidential elections. The talks, attended by the opposition Colorado Party and the left-wing Frente Amplio but boycotted by the Blancos whose leader, Wilson Ferreria, was still in prison, were marked by the military's promulgation of a series of institutional acts which sequentially eradicated much of the repressive apparatus it had established in previous institutional acts. On August 3, the talks concluded successfully, "though without any formal signed agreements. Whether or not there were any secret protocols was later to become a subject of intense controversy,"[15] especially with regard to the issue of amnesty for army officers associated with extreme brutality. Officially, no decisions were made on the subjects of immunity and amnesty either for prisoners held by the outgoing regime or members of the dictatorship implicated in human rights violations. The issues came to the fore only in early March 1985 once Colorado leader Sanguinetti took office as president after winning 41 percent of the vote. He signed a bill that, in essence, granted amnesty to all remaining political prisoners but excluded torturers and other military violators of human rights.[16] Though formally the army received immunity neither during the transition negotiations nor after the elected president assumed office, some have argued that the army, in fact, unofficially secured Sanguinetti's guarantees that its rank and file would be exempt from prosecution. According to Manuel

Flores Silva, a senator from the Colorado Party, although the Club Naval Pact "did not speak explicitly, or even implicitly, about what would happen with regard to the past, . . . the military had a right to assume that a peaceful transition would entail a peaceful working out of the past."[17] In fact, both the army and the ruling Colorado Party tacitly, if not specifically, agreed that the March 1985 presidential grant of amnesty to the imprisoned far-left Tupamaro guerrillas and other political prisoners, which did not address the issue of whether individual military officers would be charged and tried, would absolve the military as well; both sides apparently saw this as a means of establishing "moral equivalency"[18] even though most of the human rights abuses were perpetrated by the army against innocent civilians.[19]

THE DANGER OF "TUTELARY DEMOCRACY"

In countries where the outgoing authoritarian regime, now defining itself as a caretaker administration, remain strong, there is a greater likelihood that the incumbent will force concessions from the democratic opponents. Such blackmail, usually under the threat of political chaos and violence or a halt to the transition altogether, is bound to cast a shadow on the functioning of the new democracy.[20]

When the incumbents manage to dictate constitutional norms that predetermine the nature of the political system, democratic practices may be imperiled for years to come. This was the case in Pakistan, where in 1985 the late dictator President Muhammad Zia-ul Haq promulgated a constitution that made his office supreme over the parliament. This constitution provided the legal basis for President Ghulam Ishaq Khan's successful effort to force Prime Minister Benazir Bhutto out of office in August 1990.[21]

The ability to "coerce hostages" is most characteristic of strong military governments. Through negotiation with the democratic forces they manage to extricate themselves from government while securing for themselves future positions of power or prerogatives, even if from without. If they manage to evade a violent crisis in good time, secure the loyalty of the armed forces, and maintain their internal unity, military governments are more likely to succeed in acquiring the status of "democratic guardians," in ensuring the creation of a "tutelary democracy," which Adam Przeworski defines as "a regime which has competitive, formally democratic institutions, but in which the power apparatus, typically reduced by this time to the armed forces, retains the capacity to intervene to correct undesirable states of affairs."[22]

Chile's transition to democracy in March 1990, after seventeen years of strong dictatorial rule during which more than 2,000 Chileans were either killed or "disappeared," is the best example of such a tutelary democracy. Gen. Augusto Pinochet Ugarte succeeded in forcing the opposition into working within the 1980 constitutional framework, which upheld a long transition formula designed to guarantee his remaining in power. According to this design, a popular yes-no plebiscite scheduled for October 1988 was to allow Pinochet's bid to remain President through 1997; in the unlikely event of his defeat, he would still secure the position of army commander for another decade.[23] After an unexpected rebuff in the referendum, Pinochet remained in power as a caretaker president for an additional fourteen months. Eventually his own presidential candidate, Hernán Buchi, the Finance Minister who had earned a reputation as the mastermind behind Chile's economic recovery, lost the December 1989 elections to Patricio Aylwin. Even during this second interim period, Pinochet worked to predetermine the future by making key appointments that the elected government would be unable to change. Most critical for the issues of amnesty and evening the score was the fact that, in his last year in office, Pinochet packed the Supreme Court by appointing nine new justices to life terms, a move that virtually guaranteed that the court would resist judicial reforms and efforts to reopen human rights cases that had been amnestied by Pinochet in 1978. In August 1990 the Supreme Court unanimously upheld a 1978 statute protecting members of the security forces from prosecution for abuses. It determined that because the amnesty was granted prior to the enactment of the 1980 constitution, the court could not alter it.[24] In December 1990, in response to incriminating revelations by Aylwin's Commission of Truth and Reconciliation, Pinochet put the army on alert reminding the elected President who was in charge.[25]

Altogether, the impact of caretaker administrations on evening the score may only be able to be assessed long after democratic transitions have occurred. In the Spanish case, time was on the side of reconciliation. Yet, when military incumbents retain some tutelage, it is not always immediately clear what type of treatment – harsh or lenient, by democratic choice or in response to the remnants of authoritarian compulsion – will benefit the fledgling democracy. For example, strong military incumbents that retain their tutelage and inhibit trials through self-amnesty may seem, at first glance, to hinder the moral refurbishing of society. However, in the long run, their attempt to hide the truth behind a veil of self-amnesty may perpetuate popular suspicion and distrust, undermine their claim to be "the nation's *moral reserve*," and encourage unity among the democratic forces. Conversely, when dictatorial or military regimes collapse and the investigations and trials conducted by new democratic governments fail to meet popular expectations of justice as a result of governmental bowing to political expediency, nascent systems may lose both the public's initial enthusiasm for them and stable, working relations with the military.

In her analysis of the responses of new democracies to human rights violations in Latin America, Alexandra de Brito has observed that in Chile, where the people and the democratic parties were aware that the report produced by President Aylwin's investigatory committee could not lead to government-sponsored prosecution, their expectations were lower than those in Argentina. In reality, the reports became "the focus of political activity on the issue of human rights, [and contributed] to the healing process of the transition."[26] In Argentina, however, the fact that the crimes chronicled in the Nunca Más report were not adequately reflected in the trials sponsored by the government, shattered the expectation of "total justice," made the victims of repression feel betrayed, and aggravated political polarization which, in turn, reinvigorated the undemocratic voices within the army.[27]

In sum, as Adam Przeworski has argued, when transitions involve the "guarantee [of] future victories," one must question the use of the term democracy to describe the new system of rule. The essence of a democratic government lies in the principle "that no one can be certain that their interests will ultimately triumph"; "No one can wait to modify outcomes ex post"; and there should be "no group whose interests would predict outcomes with a near certainty."[28]

4

The international interim government model revisited

The three aforementioned models – provisional, power-sharing, and caretaker governments – have described situations in which oppositions or incumbents are vying for state power. In all these cases, regardless of the final outcome – democratic or nondemocratic – we have witnessed a hiatus or, at least, a diminution in hostilities which made possible the emergence of a new regime. In this section, we are concerned with cases where deep-seated historical rivalries are so profound, so violent, and so seemingly irresolvable that the construction of an interim regime with the potential for creating real long-term stability is minimal. This is so despite the fact that the contending factions by and large do not dispute the legitimacy of the state; they are not typically irredentists or secessionists though they may still contest the rights of certain groups to be included in the demos.

These conflicts are further exacerbated by the strong influence and sometimes actual physical presence of foreign powers which may view certain peaceful solutions as inimical to their interests. The political and socioeconomic rivalries among aspirants for power in these instances may be so intense that they preclude the possibility of the acceptance of an incumbent leading the transition as a caretaker, a complete victory of an opposition group that installs a provisional government, or the creation of power-sharing interim rule among the rivals for power. This impasse may be reinforced by the very high level of accumulation of weapons which are dispersed widely without any faction having a clear-cut ability to exert a monopoly over them. Thus, even if such interim arrangements do materialize, the prospects for democratization are poor as the victors in the electoral contest and their rivals may prove unable to shed their historic animosities in favor of a new-found spirit of cooperation. By retaining control over arms and sometimes territory, in defeat

This chapter was written by Yossi Shain and Lynn Berat.

an aspirant for power which hitherto has accepted the holding of elections may spoil the democratization process. Such was the case in Angola where the opposition Union for the Total Independence of Angola (UNITA) refused to accept the October 1992 democratic victory of the incumbent Popular Movement for the Liberation of Angola (MPLA) and engaged in a renewal of hostilities. Equally or even more dismal scenarios are now pandemic.

We have long argued that there is a fourth model of interim government, the "international interim government," that may alleviate such problematic circumstances when a subset of domestic and international conditions is present. Indeed, because it endeavors to ensure that there is a level playing field shared by all political parties, it may be the only way to ensure that there is a greatly reduced level of violence. While extremist groups, no doubt, would continue to rely on the use of force, the perception of equality in the contest for power might well induce other groups that previously would have considered using violence to channel their energies into electoral politics.

Yet this model is not a panacea for "failed states"[1] where no modern civil institutions remain functioning, where no contestant enjoys broad-based support, where main players are ideologically committed to a nondemocratic form of government, and where lawlessness, warlordism, and clientelism are pandemic.

Based on the experience of Namibia which resulted in successful democratic state creation, beginning in 1990, in a series of articles, we proposed the applicability of the international interim government model to the cases of Cambodia, Afghanistan, and, with substantial modifications, to South Africa.[2] Indeed, our line of reasoning was subsequently followed by the UN's transitional governing of Cambodia where the success of the model now seems likely. In Afghanistan, however, the collapse of the Soviet Union left the Najibullah government naked. It also encouraged the Mujahedeen forces to abandon even the thought of compromise, intensify the war, and jettison all pretensions of subscribing to democratic procedure that they had previously endorsed in an effort to satisfy their American patrons. In Part Two of this study, Barnett Rubin analyzes why this model has hitherto been unable to salvage Afghanistan.

In light of events in Namibia and Cambodia, which will be examined in detail in the next section, the following propositions for the applicability of the international interim government model are revealed.

First, UN involvement at the level of an international interim government is suitable only in places where the state has not failed and where state institutions have remained largely intact.

Second, the incumbent regime, although perhaps severely weakened, has not been totally delegitimated by other factions and exerts a high level of control over the means of violence and other state institutions of legal-rational aspiration.

Third, parties to the conflict are bound to foreign patrons who are united in their desire to end strife and are in a strong position to influence the behavior of rival leaders and factions.

Fourth, parties to the conflict are largely interested in accommodating each other democratically or otherwise, and, indeed, are encouraged to do so by their foreign patrons.

Fifth, although there may be extreme positions among rival factions, there is still a thread of communication that may be bolstered by the presence of a symbolic central authority figure who is respected by all members of other factions across the political spectrum and by the population at large.

INTERNATIONAL LEGITIMACY AND THE CHANGED ROLE OF THE UN

Before we move on to test the validity of these propositions, we must first examine why the UN is now uniquely positioned to assume the role of international interim government. The termination of the Cold War and the subsequent disintegration of the Soviet Union brought the end of superpower rivalries that had fueled regional conflicts around the globe. It also meant that the principle of democratic elections as the sine qua non of legitimate authority became paramount. Yet, superpower disengagement did not signal an end to such regional conflicts as they had already acquired sufficient momentum of their own. In fact, it may be argued that this disengagement fueled them further. The examples of Somalia, Angola, and Afghanistan are a powerful testament to the durability of historically based conflagrations.

However, the end of the Cold War did open the door to a new kind of international involvement conducted primarily under the aegis of the United Nations whose role shifted from that of peacekeeper to that of activist used to take over governing as free elections are organized while disarming opposing factions in the process. During the Cold War, universal acceptance of notions of international legality and morality were subsumed by the global struggle for political primacy. Many broadly interpreted and mutually incompatible legitimating principles were interchangeably invoked for purely tactical reasons without any order of prioritization by members of the UN to justify their international practices. The inconsistency with which member states relied upon the principles of self-determination, human rights, territorial integrity, and democracy made a mockery of the UN's moral authority and undermined the idea of a world governed by law.[3]

As the superpower rivalry abated, so, too, dissipated the polarization of the world into competing mythologies of state sovereignty, self-determination, human rights, and democracy. The last two are now widely recognized as being essential preconditions for the exercise of the other two. Today, governments are finding it more difficult than ever to claim that their domestic human rights practices are purely internal matters or to excuse their behavior on cultural or religious grounds. At the same time, since the holding of universal free and fair elections has become the test of legitimate rule, it is near incontrovertible that sovereignty is no longer associated primarily with effective control. The significance of this new reality is that self-determination can be internationally legitimated only through the vehicle of constitutional democracy which itself is now regarded as a precondition for stability. Within this international framework, the United Nations, under the leadership of the United States, has emerged as the primary organization fostering the new world democratic order.

The UN's changed role manifested itself first in the case of Namibia where the international interim government model was instrumental in securing the end of Namibia's long colonial ordeal and set a precedent for the ultimate resolution of other long-standing conflicts. Even though Namibia represented the creation of a new democratic state rather than a regime change within a preexisting one, we have long felt that the UN's experience there would be instructive for situations like that in Cambodia as indeed seems to have been the case.[4] Now that Cambodia has completed its interim phase on the road to democratic stability, it is time to reevaluate the efficacy of such an arrangement and reassess our earlier conclusions.

LESSONS FROM NAMIBIA

Substantial South African involvement in what was then known as South West Africa began in 1915 when South Africa occupied the German protectorate. After the war, according to the terms of Article 110 of the Treaty of Versailles, Germany renounced its sovereignty over its South West African protectorate in favor of the Allied and Associated Powers that placed the territory under the mandate system of the League of Nations. The Union of South Africa administered the territory on behalf of the British Empire as a class C mandate. At the end of World War II, the United Nations replaced the defunct League. All mandated territories were to come under the United Nations trusteeship system. Instead, South Africa sought to incorporate the territory, a suggestion the General Assembly rejected.[5] In 1966, after an ineffective string of resolutions urging submission to trusteeship, the General Assembly decided to revoke the mandate based upon its determination that South Africa's conduct amounted to a repudiation of the mandate agreement.

Throughout the 1970s, South Africa remained steadfast in its efforts to retain control of the territory, which in 1968 at the request of the South West Africa People's Organization (SWAPO), the major indigenous liberation movement, the General Assembly had changed to Namibia. International opposition also continued and in January 1976, the Security Council passed Resolution 385, which provided for United Nations supervised and controlled elections in Namibia by August 31. Then, in 1978, under the terms of Security Council Resolution 435, which envisaged the implementation of Resolution 385, South Africa agreed to administer the independence process leading to elections for a constituent assembly under the supervision of the United Nations Transitional Assistance Group (UNTAG). South Africa backed away from its commitment and it was not until 1988, after a combination of superpower collusion and internal economic and political pressures, that South Africa finally agreed to the implementation of the United Nations plan for Namibian independence. The date for the commencement of this third attempt at a UN-supervised transition was set for April 1, 1989.

According to Resolution 435, the United Nations Transitional Assistance Group (UNTAG), headed by UN Special Representative (SR) for Namibia Martti Ahtisaari, had the responsibility for supervising the independence process and certifying its fairness. The UN officials interpreted their authority restrictively, and consequently, various problems arose that threatened to subvert the transition process. Despite these problems, UNTAG members showed a level of commitment to their task that helped allay the fears of many Namibians and was a model for the international community.

The November election itself should serve as an inspiration to those struggling to achieve democracy elsewhere in the world. Minor incidences of violence and scattered attempts at interfering with the process did not deter the Namibian people from exercising their right to vote. Some 97 percent of the 700,000 registered voters participated. SWAPO received 57 percent of the vote and therefore gained 41 of the seventy-two seats in the new Constituent Assembly. SWAPO's main rival, the South African-sponsored Democratic Turnhalle Alliance, garnered twenty-one places, with the remainder going to five small parties. All parties accepted the results, which UN Special Representative Ahtisaari duly certified as free and fair.

The members of the Constituent Assembly met for the first time on November 21 and immediately began the task of drafting a constitution for the soon-to-be-independent state. Under the UN plan, a two-thirds majority was required for ratification. Eighty days later, that body adopted by consensus the new democratic constitution. The document provides for a multiparty system, fundamental freedoms, and an independent judiciary. The constitution may be amended only by a two-thirds majority. It came into force on March 21, 1990, the day of Namibian independence.

Thus, the Namibian experience yielded a type of transitional government which we have called the international interim government model. As we have suggested in our earlier works, it is especially appropriate in situations where the prospects for power-sharing are minimal because of historical and brutal rivalries and total mistrust among the indigenous contestants, as well as the deep involvement of foreign states, and where none of the contestants, in power or in opposition, can claim, or nearly claim, total victory. The international interim government model requires that:

1. Factions must be disarmed and, to avoid any dual authority problem between the authority in power and the United Nations, local police and military functions must be taken over by the UN. Those groups with arms must be willing to surrender them to an adequate UN peacekeeping force already in place by the time a period for transfer begins.
2. Political parties must be allowed to organize freely with no groups barred from taking part. The only exceptions would be those that refuse to disarm. Any unconditional exclusions of groups will prevent the emergence of a stable, democratic order.
3. A definite and relatively short timetable for elections must be devised. Enough time must be allowed before election day to enable the repatriation of exiles and refugees and the organization of parties. We have suggested a maximum of eighteen months.
4. Elections must be conducted and carefully monitored by UN officials.
5. A constitution must be drafted as soon as possible after the UN certifies the elections "free and fair."
6. A two-thirds majority must be required for ratification of any new constitution, as in the Namibian case, to ensure greater stability but to avoid complete domination by any single group.
7. The UN seat belonging to the country in transition must remain vacant during the interim period.
8. As in the Namibian case, once the new government takes power, the international interim authority must remain in the country for some mutually agreed upon time to serve as a stabilizing and moderating influence.

It must be pointed out, however, that a peaceful transition to democracy via this model is no guarantee that a democratic order will survive for the long duration. Yet, a well-designed international interim government arrangement may have a long-term impact in securing not only the creation of democratic institutions that may minimize violence but also in ameliorating structural and socioeconomic defects inherited from the previous regime; in Namibia a major problem remained the large debt left by the South African authorities which impeded the development of the economy. This may seem an excessive demand on the UN but in Namibia a more prudent approach would not have been exorbitantly priced, and might have helped to avert the current slide in the country's fortunes.[6] Indeed, there should have been an aid package tailored to the country's needs from the appropriate UN development agencies as the reward for playing by the rules of the international transition game. Ideally, the receipt of that aid package would have been contingent upon the new government's continued adherence both to internationally accepted standards of human rights and particularly, those human rights guarantees enshrined in the country's new democratic constitution.[7]

Despite these caveats, the international interim government model may still provide the only hopeful exit from domestic conflicts that constantly threaten to spill over into the international arena and endanger the recent movement toward international cooperation and democratization. Cambodia has been the test case for the creation of a more democratic and peaceful world order via the vehicle of the United Nations. The organization's failure there would not only have plunged the people of Cambodia and Southeast Asia into anarchy and renewed horror but also could have had a chilling effect on the UN's ability to lead the way in the creation of a supranational order.

LESSONS FROM CAMBODIA

The war in Cambodia between the Vietnamese and a Sino-Khmer alliance began with the reign of terror of the Khmer Rouge from 1975 to 1979 during which a million people perished; it was followed by eleven years of Vietnamese occupation. From 1989 to 1993, the Cambodian factions continued their fighting amidst UN-sponsored attempts to effect a peaceful settlement and democratic transition in the country. In Cambodia, the UN, in an unprecedented show of unity, devised and launched the largest, most expensive, and most ambitious transitional peacekeeping mission in its history. Its mission was designed in line with the eight points we offered for the Namibian model and its greatest challenge was to ensure that elections could be held free of intimidation by armed factions. The estimated cost of the UN involvement was $2–3 billion. The operation involved about 22,000 UN soldiers, police officers, and civilian administrators who took over the running of the country in preparation for the democratic elections which occurred in May 1993.

As early as 1989, with the withdrawal of the Vietnamese occupation forces and a dramatic change in the foreign policy of the Soviet Union, weary indigenous and international actors in the Cambodian quagmire embarked on a new path. They all realized that stability and a mediated solution required international involvement and guarantees. This new posture gained stature with the final demise of the USSR and the renewed role of the UN in international affairs as manifested in the Gulf War. International cooperation in Cambodia was also augmented by the realization of Asian governments that their economic potency might be threatened unless they took a more active role in putting an end to the Cambodian civil war. Thus, the stakes were high for regional powers to find a peaceful resolution of the conflict.

For the Vietnamese, it became clear that continued occupation of Cambodia obstructed their international acceptability and frustrated their access to global markets. The Chinese government, the Khmer Rouge's main backer since 1979, realized that shouldering Pol Pot and his men had become a liability in international corridors that hindered China's economic overtures to the West. The economic factor was also behind the Japanese shift from a traditional reticence to shoulder the weight of regional conflict. The growing belief in the international community and inside Japan that the country could no longer stand on the sidelines as post-World War II pacifism had dictated, led to the Japanese cosponsorship of the UN mission. Japan then embarked on the historic deployment of 600 Japanese soldiers in Cambodia even though Japan's peacekeeping law of April 1992 restricted Japanese troops to reconstruction efforts and prohibited them from entering any area of conflict. Japan also became the largest financial contributor to the UN peace operation and a Japanese diplomat, Yasushi Akashi, was chosen to oversee the UN mission.[8]

The first country to suggest a Namibia-type approach for Cambodia was Australia which recognized the hopelessness of negotiating a power-sharing four-party coalition government to rule Cambodia before elections could be held. Australia proposed an enhanced role for the UN in organizing and overseeing a cease-fire, a halt in foreign aid, and free elections. The settlement was to be achieved either by: (1) UN forces taking the place of the two rival Cambodian governments – the Vietnamese-backed de facto government of Hun Sen and the de jure internationally recognized exiled government of the Khmer Rouge (in coalition with Prince Norodom Sihanouk and the followers of the former Prime Minister Son Sann) – or (2) by UN officials working alongside a coalition of these groups.[9]

In October 1991, after two years of torturous negotiation, the government of Hun Sen and the three rival rebel factions signed a peace treaty in Paris brokered by the UN. They all agreed to establish "a system of liberal democracy, on the basis of pluralism."[10] The treaty also called on all factions to disarm and to place their troops in cantonments and to form political parties to compete in internationally supervised elections. The UN would rule Cambodia until the elections in concert with an indigenous power-sharing interim government, the Supreme National

Council (SNC) representing the major contending factions.[11] The SNC was supposed to have a veto over the delegating of authority to the UN but, in practice, the Council proved ineffective.

In order to achieve its goals, the UN Transitional Authority in Cambodia (UNtac) had to overcome myriad challenges: resolving problems of governability and bureaucratic functioning in an impaired state; resettling refugees; organizing and monitoring the rules for fair and free elections; instituting and enforcing legal norms that guarantee human rights, and, most critically, disarming the rival factions, especially the loathed Khmer Rouge. Even though they signed the Paris accords, the Khmer Rouge refused to lay down their arms, confine their troops to barracks, allow UNtac peacekeepers into their territorial zones, or abide by other terms of the peace agreement. In June 1992 the Khmer Rouge withdrew from the peace process and, in the months leading to the elections scheduled for May 1993, they intensified their violent campaign.

Yet, UNtac's forces were bound by rules forbidding the use of force unless their personnel came under fire. Their tasks were to be accomplished while pleasing the international players and patrons still striving to protect their interests in the Cambodian debacle. Despite these overwhelming challenges, UNtac persisted in its efforts to hold free elections. In the initial months between the signing of the Paris accords and the deployment of UNtac forces, Cambodia was at risk of, but did not descend into, lawlessness and anarchy.[12] Incumbent Hun Sen's weakened regime left a dangerous power vacuum throughout the country. As apprehension among state officials mounted, some of them began selling the country's assets and pocketing the money. In December 1991 and January 1992 some bureaucrats and soldiers were reportedly jockeying to get what they could in case they were removed from power upon the arrival of UNtac forces.[13]

UNtac's first mission was, therefore, to deploy its forces as quickly as possible and to maintain those Cambodian state institutions which remained intact.[14] This meant that Hun Sen's incumbent regime enjoyed a relative advantage. UNtac increased its presence in the spring of 1992 and thereafter orchestrated, with great difficulty, the resettlement of some 360,000 refugees living in border camps in Thailand, a mission which was completed only in April 1993. UNtac was also relatively successful in resettling many thousand fighters from the contending factions whose absorption threatened to overload the already stagnant economy. UNtac took control over the National Bank of Cambodia, normalized relations with financial institutions, cleared the country's debt to the IMF, and stabilized the ruined economy.[15]

The Paris accords designated the SNC as coruler of the country with UNtac which, in fact, was an attempt to combine the power-sharing model with the international interim government model in an effort to demonstrate that sovereignty lay in the hands of the Cambodian people. In theory, by agreeing to join the SNC coalition the three main factions – Hun Sen, the Khmer Rouge, and Prince Sihanouk – recognized each other as legitimate contenders in the upcoming elections. The selection of Prince Sihanouk, the noted "symbolic center" of the nation, as the head of the SNC was intended to relax tensions between Hun Sen and the Khmer Rouge.[16] In practice, however, the distrust was unbridgeable.

As the scheduled elections approached, violent exchanges among the factions intensified. The Khmer Rouge's insistence on expelling ethnic Vietnamese residing in Cambodia was a strong political tool since many Cambodians feared being culturally overwhelmed by the Vietnamese. In fact, all Cambodian politicians wishing to gain popularity stressed an anti-Vietnamese attitude. For their part, the Khmer Rouge made a concerted effort to foment Cambodian anti-Vietnamese xenophobia: "By ratcheting up the rhetoric against the *Yuon,* the pejorative term for Vietnamese, the Khmer Rouges [were] also looking to rekindle an ethnic war against Vietnamese in Cambodia,"[17] and thereby undermine UNtac's mission.

The Khmer Rouge also claimed that UNtac failed to assert its control over Hun Sen's forces. This argument, though largely a pretext for the Khmer Rouge's continued belligerence, had some truth in it. Fearing chaos, UNtac was reluctant to insist on the complete dissolution of the Phnom Penh administration and, subsequently, Hun Sen's communists, who renamed themselves the Cambodian People's Party, remained de facto rulers of much of the state apparatus. The advantages of incumbency were manifest mostly in the provinces where UNtac forces were outnumbered by the established local officialdom supported by the Hun Sen government forces.[18]

Yet, UNtac took pains not to appear to be partial to any of the factions. In late 1992 and early 1993, Hun Sen's men were accused by UN officials and the Sihanouk-Son Sann faction of terrorizing and intimidating supporters of Sihanouk's nationalist and anti-Communist party. Hun Sen emphatically denied the allegations and charged that, "while some of the attacks on political and government officials were banditry, others may have been the work of Khmer Rouge *provocateurs* seeking to lay the blame on Phnom Penh."[19] After it failed to bring the Khmer Rouge back into the peace process on November 30, 1992, the UN warned that unless they permitted UN supervision of their zones by January 31, 1993, the Khmer Rouge would be excluded from the elections. The UN also imposed an embargo on log exports from Khmer Rouge-controlled areas of Cambodia and pressured Thailand into ending its trade with the group.[20]

A major issue of contention among the factions was the nature of the electoral system and the controlling of the electorate. Regional domination was likely to affect voter registration and, therefore, election results. Yet, as elections neared, registration continued with great enthusiasm and even the Khmer Rouge, who already had withdrawn from the peace process, could not stop the process even in some areas under their control. Despite these overwhelming challenges, the international community remained committed financially, morally, and physically. For its part, UNtac ran a successful party registration drive and promoted human rights ideas and respect for the rule of law.[21] Its bureaucracy became so entrenched that in September 1992 it reportedly investigated whether a Phnom Penh shop was selling apple juice from Yugoslavia in violation of the trade embargo on the Balkan country.[22]

In the final month leading to the May 23–27 elections, the Khmer Rouge intensified their violent assaults on UNtac and murdered several UNtac team members in an attempt to block the arrival of additional election observers. Most alarmingly, the Khmer Rouge slaughtered many ethnic Vietnamese, crimes which prompted more than 20,000 Vietnamese to flee the country. The Khmer Rouge also launched a campaign of intimidation and terror against the parties standing in the election, and employed terrorism to frighten the 5 million registered voters away from the polling booths. Despite these actions, more than 95 percent of eligible voters registered, and twenty parties, including eight led by Cambodian Americans, vowed their commitment to liberal democracy.

The elections were held in a reasonably peaceful atmosphere. Voter turnout exceeded 90 percent in an overwhelming expression of lack of confidence in the Khmer Rouge. The UN then certified the election results free and fair. The royalist Party, Funcinpec, headed by Prince Norodom Ranariddh, a son of Norodom Sihanouk, garnered 58 of the 120 seats in the Constituent Assembly. The Cambodian People's Party, the political arm of Hun Sen's incumbent government, won fifty-one seats. Son Sann's faction, under the name Buddhist Liberal Democratic Party, gained ten seats. The Constituent Assembly then set the stage for the drafting and eventual adoption of a new constitution based on democratic principles as specified in the Paris accord. While the new constitution was being drafted, the two main parties agreed on a form of power-sharing interim government which was approved by the assembly. Prince Norodom Sihanouk's strong and widely revered leadership prevented any postelection disruptions by disenchanted Hun Sen backers and by the Khmer Rouge. He curtailed the secessionist movement led by one of his sons and induced the Khmer Rouge to cooperate with the new government.[23]

REASSESSING THE MODEL

The UN mission in Cambodia provided the only hope the country had for a democratic future. The Cambodians, paradoxically, may finally have benefited from the long-standing foreign involvement in their country as major international players now accept that continued involvement or simple disengagement may be more costly than peaceful, democratic UN-orchestrated change.

While it may be too early to draw comprehensive lessons from the Cambodian experience, nevertheless, some already are apparent. First, the UN must deploy its forces quickly after a resolution on a matter is adopted to reduce the uncertainty of state bureaucrats and to avert a situation of potential anarchy. Second, the UN must be prepared to step up pressure on member states that do not comply with Security Council-mandated embargoes on economic dealings with factions which refuse to disarm; Thailand was condemned for its continued trade with the Khmer Rouge. Third, though elections should not be held in an atmosphere of intimidation and fear, they also should not be postponed much beyond the original deadline of eighteen months so that the growing popular sentiments in favor of human rights and democracy will not yield to disillusionment. Finally, in large countries, it is impractical to assume that the UN will be able to control effectively all administrative and coercive apparatuses. Thus, the UN should not dispense entirely with the incumbent's powers over certain noncontroversial aspects of state administration and even parts of the state's coercive apparatus of "legal-rational aspiration." The UN's reliance on Hun Sen's forces, though contrary to the idea that all factions should be disarmed, proved essential in offsetting the Khmer Rouge's continued belligerence. It is important, however, in order to avoid UN favoritism toward the incumbent, that incumbent forces be fully controlled so that the intimidation of other contenders may be prevented. In other words, high-ranking UN officers should subordinate the state's coercive apparatus to their authority. This blending of UN military personnel with the state, by definition, will transform the UN into an enforcing rather than purely peacekeeping agency.

The international interim government model is not one that has been or is likely to be tried frequently. It should be used only in very specific cases in which our five principles of applicability are present in varying degrees and then it should follow as closely as possible the eight point strategy we have articulated. Most significantly, from the experience of Namibia and Cambodia, we see that a "failed state," to use Helman and Ratner's terminology, is unsuited to the model. In the absence of any form of predictable central authority and "normal" state institutions, and with the wide dispersion of the means of coercion away from the central government, it is unlikely that UN intervention will be more than an ad hoc humanitarian effort.

Therefore, the most important factor for the success of the model is the viability of the incumbent regime which has committed itself, because of domestic and international pressure, to effecting a democratic regime change via cooperation with its rivals. If such is the case, our original idea, followed by the UN, that all parties must be disarmed must be modified so that incumbent forces remain strong and intact but with close monitoring so that they do not intimidate rival contestants for power. The ultimate desideratum is gradually for the UN to work to combine all armed factions into a professional national army.

Unexpectedly, the viability of the incumbent may be ensured not only by the continued support of its own patron government but also by the patrons of the regime's enemies who have reached the conclusion that undermining the incumbent will render the state anarchic and make any enduring settlement impossible. This can be achieved only if there is a rapprochement among the rival international patrons who feel the stakes are high enough to warrant a solution. One may speculate that if the United States and Pakistan had thrown their support behind a democratic arrangement between Najibullah and the Mujahedeen forces after the collapse of the Soviet Union and had insisted that Najibullah be part of any settlement, their concerted efforts might have salvaged the Afghan state.

The realization by patron states that a strong incumbent, even an enemy one, is essential for stability may result in a peculiar situation whereby nondemocratic governments find themselves agreeing to settle their international disputes in other countries by democratic means.[24] Thus, it follows, as we have argued in our previous work, that "the United Nations may have a lesser role to play in situations where the conflict is primarily a struggle between domestic contestants for power who are not directly or entirely supported by foreign powers, and where the country was not under foreign occupation or domination for long years."[25]

Ultimately, international machinations notwithstanding, the domestic parties themselves must, for the most part, be desirous of reaching a settlement. At the same time, they must be willing to abandon their previous practices of completely delegitimating their opponents and be able to open and maintain channels of communication. If such behavior is to be sustained, major parties must become convinced that the gains to be had by the successful completion of the transition far outweigh the disadvantages. Extreme views that the process is but a zero sum game can be minimized by the presence of a respected central authority figure such as Cambodia's Prince Norodom Sihanouk.

5

The timing and nature of first democratic elections

Democracy calls for deep-going, value-oriented changes in the public mentality – it calls for time[1]

Karl Popper

FINDING THE RIGHT PACE

In the process of political change much depends on pacing. Sometimes small steps create an expectation of change in reasonable time, and the incremental process of change can sustain that expectation even though the change itself might be small. A paced process can reduce both the fears of those afraid of change and the impatience of those demanding immediate change. One of the most difficult tasks for politicians is to find the right pace for their actions, neither too fast nor too slow, and preferably one step ahead of the expectations of their opponents.

"What is the right pace?" is a central question in transitions to democracy. Giuseppe Di Palma, in his book *To Craft Democracies,* has made a strong argument (mostly on the basis of his excellent knowledge of the transitions in Southern Europe) in favor of swift democratization in all countries, regardless of the nature of the old regime, the political culture, or other sociopolitical dimensions of a country. He asserts that quick elections have the tendency "to curb chaos" and "even when variously thwarted, confined, manipulated, or just not in the cards, once they are called, elections can still energize and possibly protect democratization beyond the hopes or fears, and indeed beyond the understanding, of the principal actors."[2] Other scholars are more cautious.

Samuel Huntington, in his book *The Third Wave,* has maintained that speedy elections may hinder long-term democratic practices and stability in certain countries: those that lack modern bureaucratic institutions, suffer low economic development and poverty, or have long been deprived of societal and economic freedoms. Huntington is also skeptical about the possibility of quick democratization in polities where the dominant culture is hostile to liberal democracy; he recognizes, however, that cultures are dynamic and have a tendency to adapt.[3] Similarly, the distinguished historian Bernard Lewis does not deem Islam as inherently antithetical to the development of liberal democracy, though he cautions against the temptation in some U.S. sectors to press moderate Muslim autocracies to democratize quickly, because "[t]he pressure for premature democratization can fatally weaken such regimes and lead to their overthrow, not by democratic opposition but by other forces that then proceed to establish a more ferocious and determined dictatorship."[4] John Guradiano, a student of Russian and East European economic affairs, has argued that in post-Communist societies where generations of centralized economy had inhibited economic freedoms, speedy elections invited anarchy, lawlessness, and the return of authoritarianism. He advocates the "Chinese model of reform – authoritarian political rule coupled with increasing economic freedom" over the Russian model of establishing political democracy first.[5] Yet others have warned against accelerated elections in multiracial societies because they may foster a drift toward ethnic or social conflict. Tom Lodge, a scholar of African politics, observed that in Africa's poor countries – where in the aftermath of the Cold War the United States has exploited the reluctance of some old "friendly tyrants" to democratize swiftly to justify American disengagement – speedy elections may turn into "a life and death struggle."[6] Finally, in countries ravaged by years of civil war, where geographical regions are controlled by heavily armed factions, the holding of democratic elections (even those supervised by the UN) before disarmament may result in renewed hostilities by the losers, as happened in Angola. Thus the wave of political violence in Cambodia in early 1993 (just a few months prior to the scheduled internationally supervised elections) led the UN Transitional Authorities in Cambodia to consider their postponement.[7]

Notwithstanding these compelling arguments, both in favor of and against quick elections, we wish to draw attention to the importance of interim government in setting the timing for elections and in determining their form. Indeed, it is the threat of procrastination which often creates a pressure to associate the pace of change with the setting of a target date (or sometimes a deadline). Once the target date is set, the time between the initial steps toward the solution of the problem and its final resolution is delineated to some degree. Interim governments are charged with deciding the target schedule for holding first elections.

Whereas the announcement by an incumbent administration or by a provisional government of the opposition that they plan to hold free elections is in and of itself an important landmark in the transition to democracy, the naming of a specific target date for elections initiates new political dynamics and expectations. The setting of such a date, if perceived as fair by other contending groups and the public at large, is likely to enhance the possibility of a peaceful transition: it can moderate opposition demands, avert protests and rebellion that would arise with uncertainty about the intended pace of change, increase the pressure on the interim administration to speed liberalizing reforms, or encourage foreign supporters of the opposition to suspend military aid during the interregnum. For example, the Sandinista government's promise to hold elections in February 1990, a decision made under the auspices of the five peace-seeking presidents of Central America in February 1989, curtailed American support of their surrogate Contras, and accelerated political and social reforms inside Nicaragua.

Under power-sharing interim governments, including "from without," the election date and the electoral laws are often the product of earlier negotiations between the incumbents and the organized opposition. The question of timing tends to be more controversial under strong incumbents serving as caretaker governments or under revolutionary-leaning provisional governments. Particularly in the latter case, preelection procedures (including media access) are usually imposed by the revolutionary elite as they attempt to manipulate the election date to their own advantage. Yet, if the target date for first elections is perceived by the opposition as biased it may stir fierce reactions. Elections scheduled too far away in time or too early may foster a potentially dangerous frustration in the people and initiate a storm of protest. Speedy elections may give a disorganized opposition too little time to learn and prepare and may result in an accusation of fraud if the opposition is defeated. A delayed target date may give a revolutionary provisional government the chance to consolidate its hold on power without elections or raise the temptation of a strong incumbent to cancel elections altogether.

Postponed elections may also hinder the authority of democratically leaning provisional governments and may be used by extremists as a pretext to justify its violent overthrow. In Weimar Germany, for example, the resolve of Friedrich Ebert, the head of the Provisional Government, to hold speedy elections for the National Constituent Assembly curtailed the bid of radical socialists to effect a communist revolution.[8] By contrast, the "dilatoriness" of the Russian provisional government to organize elections for a National Assembly hastened its ouster by the Bolsheviks, who, upon seizing power in the name of the Soviets, argued "that only a Soviet government could ensure the convocation of a Constituent Assembly."[9]

Indeed, the surprising collapse of governments in Eastern Europe in 1989–90 has highlighted the importance of finding the best date for elections. Many opposition parties that had demanded free elections so fervently faced a serious dilemma: whether to delay elections in order to gain more time for organization or to expedite the process and thus prevent the recovery of unpopular incumbents.[10] Communist incumbents made the opposite calculation.

Scholars studying the transitions from communism have made an interesting attempt to correlate levels of social and political autonomy in Eastern European countries "with the ordering of transitional events and inversely with a ranking of the speed of the first stage of the transition." Yet, they themselves recognized that the ranking of civil societies along a continuum of "strength and weakness remains misspecified."[11] What remains clearer, however, is that the viability of the outgoing regime and the relative potency of the democratic opposition, which may take part (directly or from without) in the interim government, will determine who will have the upper hand in manipulating the timing, form, and outcome of the first elections.

The Polish government, which sought to curtail Solidarity's strong penetration of society, called for early elections while still in control over the country's communication sources and propaganda organs. "Believing that an early election would be to their advantage, the [Polish] government set the date for early June, barely one month after the end of the round table. The government surmised, not unreasonably, that Solidaność did not have the funds, the expertise, or the time needed to launch a sizable political campaign."[12] In Hungary, where the democratic opposition had used its outside influence to limit the freedom of action of the caretaker government of proreform Communists, the latter still attempted to secure their power by approving presidential elections before parliamentary balloting. Their narrow defeat in a snap referendum on November 26, 1989, thwarted the almost certain election of a reformist Communist, Imre Pozsgay, as head of state. In East Germany, the virtually powerless caretaker government of Hans Modrow was forced to bring the election forward to March 18, 1990, rather than the initially planned date of May 6, 1990.

By contrast, in the Balkan countries, Romania, Albania, and to a lesser degree Bulgaria, ex-Communists ran as strong caretakers or under the guise of democratic revolutionaries and managed to "steal" controversial first elections. Ultimately, however, their mandate was stained by the imposition of an election date that left little time for the newly emerging opposition groups to organize and campaign. The Romanian elections were set only four months after the bloody December 1989 revolution. As a result, the FSN's sweeping victory was labeled a fraud. In Albania, after almost half a century under the rule of Stalinist dictator Enver Hoxha and his loyal successor Ramiz Alia, the "reformed" Communists running as a caretaker government allowed only four months of limited campaign before they obtained an overwhelming victory in the April 1991 elections. In mid-January 1991, Genc Pollo, a spokesman for the main opposition Democratic Party, said: "There has been so much indoctrination and political intimidation, the Stalinist legacy is so strong, that we do not think there is enough time for us before the elections to develop an alternative frame of mind among the majority of the electorate. We are therefore avoiding being excessively optimistic that we can win."[13] Consequently, Albanian Communists eventually won the first elections on the support of the rural majority (many of whom did not realize it was possible to vote against the ruling party). Yet they fared disastrously among workers and professionals in the capital city. This discrepancy led to charges of fraud and provoked massive demonstrations and general strikes. On June 12, 1991, amid a crippling strike, the Communist government was forced to abdicate power. It gave way for an interim power-sharing government in which half of the twenty-four ministers were drawn from newly formed opposition parties and half from the Communists. The first free, multiparty elections were finally held in March 1992.

In countries with a firm democratic tradition that have experienced only a relatively short interlude of dictatorial rule, it may be wiser not to waste any time in calling elections, especially if the old democratic forces remain more or less intact. This was the case in Greece, where the seven years of military dictatorship were in many respects "a *régime d'exception,* not yet consolidated in its institutions and practices at the moment of its fall, and therefore with limited claims to legitimacy."[14] Constantin Karamanlis's resolve to hold elections only four months after the collapse of the junta enabled the country to confront democratically some of its critical concerns. The quick elections in November 1974 afforded the Greek interim government – which can be described as one bordering on the category of a democratically leaning provisional government – the mandate to deal effectively with the question of constitution (with or without a monarchy), to determine Greece's relations with the European community, and to decide how many junta appointees in the state apparatus would be purged. As interim prime minister, Karamanlis, whose government was representative of wide sectors of the population,[15] rejected advice from the right that Greece needed more time under an interim government and dismissed protests from the left that a quick election, catching it unprepared, was unfair.[16]

Altogether, under incumbent authoritarian regimes that have chosen the democratic path with no immediate threat to their rule, the opposition is less likely to have control over the setting of an election date. From the time that an incumbent caretaker announces the election date until the realization of the democratic process, the opposition finds it more difficult to mobilize wide sectors of the society against those who have made such a commitment to elections, and can therefore not work at overthrowing rulers who guaranteed society an expectation of change. The setting of the target date, combined with continuous steps in the direction of democratization, gives the caretaker interim government a conditional and temporary legitimacy until a new legitimate democratic order can be created. It allows the government under such conditions to enjoy both the "backward" legality derived from the past and the "forward" legitimation based on the expected democratic future.

Prime Minister Suárez, between his appointment in June 1976 and the elections on the 15th of June 1977, was a master in this process of pacing the changes which ultimately led Spain to democracy. Though the initial steps seemed too slow to the opposition, it gave the opponents of democratization a chance to adjust to a process that appeared more inevitable every day. Once the "Law for Political Reform" was passed by what was described as the harakiri of Franco's Cortes in October/November 1976 and approved by the referendum in December, the pace of change could accelerate, moving even ahead of the expectations of the opposition with a legalization of the Communist party in May 1977. It has been argued that the disbelief in the possibility of keeping the promise to hold elections one year after taking power contributed to a certain lack of preparation for those elections by the parties that had so long awaited them. At the same time, the need to get the lists of candidates ready by the deadline made it possible for Suárez to facilitate the UCD coalition, and allowed Calvo Sotelo, the manager of the campaign, to prepare the list of candidates to be presented to the electorate. Timing was essential to the process.

The Spanish example represents a situation of an incumbent-caretaker government that enjoyed firm control over the state apparatus and whose leaders set the date for elections in "good time." But the commitment to hold elections on a specific date is most critical in revolutionary situations since, as noted earlier, provisional governments formed by the revolutionary opposition have the greatest propensity to evade democracy. A provisional government controlled by revolutionaries might be tempted to consider itself a tutelary regime to prepare the society to make truly democratic choices, to "conscientizise" the society, to indoctrinate the people through the mass media, before allowing them to vote. But as the difficulties of that task are faced, the idea of postponing elections until the goals of the revolutionary provisional government are accomplished becomes increasingly appealing. First the date is delayed, and finally it is postponed sine die.

Thus, what was to be a democratic transition can end in a revolutionary dictatorship; it might achieve many valuable goals but certainly not the establishment of and consolidation of a pluralistic political democracy. A new dictatorship can emerge presumably to create in the future a better democracy. The pro tempore transition regime becomes permanent. A mixture of decisions by some of the components of the provisional government coalition taken from above and supporting actions from below, sometimes spontaneous and more often organized, serve to justify and create the new regime. The power vacuum created by the disintegration, breakdown, or overthrow of the authoritarian regime is thus filled by a new regime without the intervention of the electorate until the new rulers have created the conditions for their hegemony, either by the exclusion or the withdrawal of other political forces that do not feel the conditions for a free and open election exits.

Even without the dramatic scenarios that certainly existed in Cuba,[17] Iran, and perhaps Nicaragua, such developments leave a legacy of bitter opposition to the new regime since those changes will be difficult to reverse by the democratically elected representatives and governments and are not perceived to be a result of a democratic process. The revision of those measures, in some cases a constitutional revision, will be on the agenda for the new regime. Potentially, those actions have a constituent effect in the sense of identifying their beneficiaries with a new regime, but even that might be sometimes in doubt since the disruption of the society and the economy might make those victories hollow.

It is, therefore, essential in any transition from authoritarianism to democracy that the interim government operate within rules that have clearly defined time limits. There should be a prudent time span between the moment when the commitment to democracy is made and the holding of free elections, recognizing there are those who do not want any change (or only cosmetic reforms) as well as those who desire the overthrow of the regime. Unless there is a clear deadline for truly free elections to accomplish transferring power to the people and from them to the new regime and its government, the transition to political democracy remains in doubt. The danger in the absence of a fixed time limit for the rule of an interim government is in many respects analogous to risks involved in the absence of a fixed duration of emergency powers in a democracy, since the use of emergency rule in the guise of protecting a democracy, just as a self-legitimized interim government, may be prolonged and indefinite, thus abandoning its qualified democratic objective.[18]

In Portugal, it was only such a clear commitment made in April 1974 by the Movimento das Forças Armadas (MFA) to hold elections one year later (for an assembly which would draft a democratic constitution to be implemented the following fall) that gave the democratic parties the opportunity to demand and force an end to the provisional government of the military-political diarchy that emerged out of the "revolution by people." That commitment made it difficult to postpone the elections in order to carry out the revolutionary process, as some sectors of the MFA proposed; and even so, the parties were obliged by the pact between them and the MFA to agree to "diarchy" of parties and the MFA, and to a government not responsible before the newly elected constituent assembly. It was, however, the outcome of the 1975 elections that radically changed the balance of power. The MFA was no longer the only legitimate institution, and the democratic commitment of the majority of the Portuguese electorate became visible.

TYPES OF FIRST ELECTIONS

No less crucial than the timing of the first elections is the interim government's decision on the nature of these elections, because the procedure of choosing among alternative constitutional and electoral systems profoundly affects the stability of the polity and the quality of its democratic performance. As noted in the Introduction, it is not always clear which are the determining electoral acts that lead us from the old system to the new. Indeed, not all first elections are "founding elections," and in some countries the lengthy sequence of elections clouds the final passage from the old system to a democracy. In Brazil's long process of opening (*abertura*) one can count up to eight rounds of elections between 1974 to 1989 when the first direct presidential elections were held. In this case, the gubernatorial elections which gave to the opposition control of eleven governorships in the most populated states did not lead to the collapse of the regime. However, the diarchy that emerged between the democratically elected governors and the indirectly elected military president made the need for a transition to democracy more evident and contributed to a negotiated transition in which the legislature (after many years of military rule) voted for a civilian president. Moreover, in multinational polities characterized by an intense "stateness problem," the nature of the first elections, all-union or regional, may ultimately affect the viability of the state.[19]

The holding of free elections presupposes a definition of what offices are to be elected and of electoral law procedures. The first point is of central importance for the future development of the democratic regime. There are essentially three options. First, the holding of presidential elections which means that the winner will be legitimated to hold power for a fixed period of time and independently of the confidence of a congress. Second, the holding of parliamentary elections with the elected legislature being the source of the government executive by giving its confidence to a prime minister or to a cabinet. Third, the election of a constituent assembly to which the government will not be accountable.

This means that some form of interim government will continue until the enactment of the constitution and the holding of a new election of either a president or a parliament that would produce the government. Each of these options has important implications that Juan Linz has discussed elsewhere.

The determination of which institution is to be elected first – the parliament, the presidency, or the constituent assembly – is of major importance to the relationship between the legislative and the executive branches, the role of political parties, and the nature of political life in general. The decision on the first elections may preempt future constitutional development, particularly if presidential elections are to be held first.[20] If there is a popularly elected president, a constituent assembly or congress is much less able to make an option for a parliamentary system, because it has to deal with an elected figure unaccountable to the confidence of the legislature, and whose term in office is fixed and most likely to extend beyond the approval of the new constitution. The president may use his influence to prevent the approval of a parliamentary constitution, as Sarney did in Brazil. In contrast, if the interim government decides to hold parliamentary elections or elections to a constituent assembly first, the options about the form of democratic government remain open.

The option of holding elections for a constituent assembly to which the provisional government will not be accountable tends to prolong the interim situation, thereby delaying the full transition to a responsible, democratic administration. This is most probable in a revolutionary situation where the possibility of legal continuity gives way to the idea that there must be general elections to express the national will of the sovereign people; the guideline for such expression, instead of being directed by the old constitution, must be born anew.

When the previous regime has been demolished and a new one is about to be established, in many cases the first elections do not lead to a fully, democratically accountable government; instead, these first elections lead to a constituent assembly elected to prepare a new constitution. "Until the new constitution is adopted and its institutions established, all powers would be concentrated in the assembly's hand, since there is no other elected institution and no framework (like the constitution) under which to act."[21] This legalistic formulation may be true theoretically, in the sense that the constituent assembly, elected by popular vote, is the only democratically selected body, while the government derives its authority from its interim status. Yet this ignores the fact that the executive rests in the hands of the interim government, be it the successor of the previous authoritarian regime, a provisional government of the opposition, or a form of a power-sharing, and that the interim government will have control over the apparatus of the state's coercive powers. That government should, therefore, be able to implement its will and, even in the case of conflict with the constituent assembly, could turn to dissolve the latter *manu militari*.

Obviously the interim government is not a democratic government, strictly speaking, because it is not dependent on the vote of confidence of the assembly whose powers are limited to the drafting of the constitution. This institutional balance may ultimately depend on the show of force of one or the other side in case of conflict; that is, on the ability of either side to assert control over the armed forces and to mobilize popular support. Naturally, such a situation can be a source of instability. After the May 1993 Cambodian elections, in the face of a secessionist threat by Prince Norodom Chakrapong, the wayward son of Prince Norodom Sihanouk, Cambodia's newly elected National Assembly in its first act approved a nearly unanimous resolution that vested Prince Sihanouk with all powers necessary "to save the nation." Although United Nations' officials deemed the resolution to be "of dubious legality, since the National Assembly is responsible only for writing a constitution," they decided not to meddle in Sihanouk's return to power.[22]

If there is no reinstatement of a previous constitution, or the interim government has not established new laws enabling civil rights, it is conceivable that a revolutionary provisional government will preside alongside an elected assembly in which it has a majority to exercise unlimited powers. Such a scenario may produce a situation traditionally known as revolutionary convention government (or *gouvernement d'Assemblée*), since its powers are not limited by a constitutional and legal framework.[23]

The power vested in the national assembly during the transition period may be exploited by its elected members. First, assembly members may use the populist notion of "democracy by the people" to deplore the isolation of the executive from the public, keep the government weak and eventually seize power themselves. Second, since a convention government has no authority to dissolve the assembly, arranging a real separation between the executive and the legislature in the future may be impaired. Third, since the constitution is formulated by an assembly dominated by political parties, some of which may have a revolutionary ideology, the proposed document may reflect partisan political interests, sometimes at the expense of democratic-liberal principles.

Undoubtedly, the danger exists that a new democracy established with a majority, particularly a revolutionary one, might produce a constitution whose principles are in conflict with those we associate with liberal democracy. This is a risk we run when a society undergoes a constituent process during a crisis situation. However, as this is already the problem of an existing democracy, it is the role of democratic representatives to amend such a charter. The fact that constitutions cannot be easily revised without qualified majorities when such a partisan document is legislated tends to leave a difficult legacy for the consolidation of a new democracy.

The 1931 Spanish constitution made by the republican left-leaning majority that refused to negotiate with the minority on basic provisions, led to a permanent confrontation and demands from the right for constitutional revision. It laid the seeds for the polarization in the 1936 elections. The last point is less related to the question of interim governments, but it is at the heart of what may be considered a Jacobin majoritarian conception of democracy.

Thus, it is possible that a revolutionary elite that seizes power and presides over the executive (until the first regular legislative elections) alongside a hostile elected assembly will feel intimidated and operationally paralyzed. This, in turn, may lead to its resignation or to the point of contemplating a dictatorial takeover. In January 1946, shortly after his resignation from his post as Provisional President of postwar France, de Gaulle expressed his frustration with his subordination to the elected assembly in these words: "The exclusive regime of political parties has returned. I condemn it. But unless I use force to set up a dictatorship, which I do not desire, and which would doubtless come to a bad end, I have no means of preventing this experiment. So I must retire."[24] This quote from de Gaulle is a good example of the tensions that can be generated between a provisional government and the constituent assembly, particularly when two different conceptions of democratic legitimacy clash – the one of representative democracy and the other of a charismatic popular leader. Indeed, one sign of the genuine democratic commitment of a provisional government is its promise to submit its actions to the judgment of an elected assembly.

But the greatest danger of assembly rule arises when its members are selected in a nondemocratic procedure and eventually adopt a nondemocratic constitution – thus curtailing the process of transition at the outset. Such was the case in revolutionary Iran where Bazargan's provisional government was too weak to confront clerical pressure. It failed to fulfill its initial promise to convene a democratically elected constituent assembly and eventually paved the way for the formation of a nondemocratic "Assembly of Experts" dominated by the traditionalist provincial mullahs. This assembly adopted a constitution which "in effect became a dyarchy in which the democratic elements . . . coexisted with a 'religious leader' who had ultimate authority and was accountable to nobody."[25]

Finally, the holding of a parliamentary election first almost assures that the government, after the convening of the democratically elected parliament, will depend on its confidence. This is the difference between the development in Spain after the June 1977 parliamentary elections and the elections to the constituent assembly in Portugal in 1975.

SEQUENCE OF ELECTIONS AND THE QUESTION OF STATENESS

As previously noted, in multinational polities characterized by an intense stateness problem, the nature of the first elections, all-union or regional, may ultimately affect the viability of the state and its democratic character. Indeed, it is important to remember that only states can be democratized and that without a consensus about the boundaries of the state and the people who constitute its citizenry no democratic processes can work. Thus, democratic regime change that involves challenges to the legitimacy of the state poses a particular set of dilemmas to interim governments presiding over the transitional process. If the interim government is strong enough and clearly committed to abide by its promise to democratize, there is a strong prospect for holding statewide first elections from which a democratic body will emerge that will deal with the problems of stateness. If, however, the interim government is weak or undecided about the process of democratization, the question of regime change might be compounded with a problem of stateness. One of the possible outcomes that may ultimately ensue is the disintegration of the state with or without democratization of its component parts.

Confronted with challenges to the state from nationalist movements those in power have a variety of options. The first is an incumbent regime which presides over a caretaker government and asserts the legality of existing state institutions. The regime proceeds toward holding general elections that produce a democratically legitimated authority, be it a parliament or a president. In that case the democratically elected legislature or executive will have to deal with the challenges posed by nationalist, secessionist, or autonomist demands, generally by rewriting the old constitution, accepting the secession of components of the state, creating mechanisms for the representation of the different nationalities, redrawing the boundaries of the component units of the state, and so on.

Again, Spain is an excellent example of the multinational, multilingual societies that have made a transition to democracy. In this case it was first the caretaker government of Adolfo Suárez which guaranteed the holding of first democratic elections in June of 1977. Later, Suárez's already democratically elected government as well as the formation of the legislature charged with making the constitution of 1978 assured the integrity of the state and its consequent transformation into the quasifederal Estado de las Autonomías.

A similar policy could be pursued by an interim power-sharing government as eventually happened in South Africa. Yet in the case of power-sharing, especially when the incumbent has been greatly weakened, the participation of nationalists that challenge the integrity of the state is a source of more complex and difficult problems that may undermine the effort to combine democratization and reorganization of the state.

Second, a victorious revolutionary provisional government might proceed in the same way. Yet it often faces much more serious challenges by nationalists in the periphery who question both the interim regime and the integrity of the state. If, however, the revolutionary elite has already collaborated with secessionist forces in the struggle to overthrow the *ancien régime,* it may become itself the facilitator of secession. In Ethiopia the self-proclaimed democratic provisional government that in 1991 overthrew the Marxist-Leninist regime of Mengistu Haile Mariam (known in the Amharic language as the Derg) expedited the independence of Eritrea without putting the issue to a national vote. In fact, the Ethiopian transitional government has been dominated by former secessionists of the Tigrayan People's Liberation Front who prior to seizing power in Addis Ababa advanced the idea of Tigray's independence. Their support of Eritrean independence generated wide opposition among Ethiopian nationalists who are fearing the dissolution of the nation and the state. The provisional government's patronage of independent Eritrea alienated many former opponents of the Derg, some of whom went as far as declaring Mengistu to be "the only one who could save the country."[26]

Yet a different pattern is that of the federal state in which there is no central representative body directly elected by the people and where no decision was made in the transition to democracy to create such a body to deal with the challenges to statehood. This has been the case in Yugoslavia, where the central government, composed of representatives from the republics under a rotating chairmanship, was unable to concur on the possibility of democratizing the country by holding all-union elections to a constituent assembly. In consequence, democratization was attempted only at the level of the constituent republics of the federation. This dynamic encouraged the articulation of nationalist politics, the rejection of the Yugoslav state, and ultimately its disintegration.

Another somewhat similar situation developed in the Soviet Union where Gorbachev had been hesitant about a full democratization of the state. The procedure followed in the election to the Congress of People's Deputies (March 1989) – out of which the Supreme Soviet emerged and which, in turn, legitimated the authority of Gorbachev as president – was partially democratic. Notwithstanding the debate about whether Gorbachev intended to democratize the Soviet Union or not, the fact is that he decided to start the process of change by allowing a more competitive political process at the level of the republics to challenge the entrenched party oligarchy. In fact Gorbachev's government was not, strictly speaking an interim government between the post-totalitarian authoritarianism and democracy in the former USSR, since there was no clear plan to hold multiparty elections on a fixed date from which all power would derive rather than a share in power.

The holding of competitive elections to produce the legislatures of the Soviet republics created in each of them a more or less democratically legitimated authority, particularly in the case of the Baltic republics. Those elections focused on the issues of the different nationalities and their aspirations for independence. As a result the leadership of the newly democratized republics was able to challenge the authority of the union, the all-Union government, and Gorbachev himself, thereby accelerating the process of the Soviet Union's disintegration.[27] This demand obviously had even stronger basis in the case of the Baltic republics which had been annexed by force after the Hitler-Stalin pact. The Baltics claimed continuing statehood via their exiled institutions.[28] In this case the sequence of elections had a decisive impact on the survival of the USSR, the process of its breakdown, and the way in which the commonwealth of independent states would later be created and organized.[29]

There is no question in our mind that the interim period between the decision to hold elections and the emergence of a new democratically legitimated political system can be decisive for the future of a state challenged by nationalist demands. In the case of both Yugoslavia and the Soviet Union, it should be obvious that allowing more or less free elections in component parts of the state, like republics or territories, while retaining a central authority that is not democratically legitimated is a formula that might very well lead to the disintegration of the state, or to a very difficult and uncertain process of reconstruction. Among the nondemocratic countries in the world we think that Indonesia and maybe, in a not so remote future, China, may face such a problem.

The dilemma of statehood might also arise after the holding of first general democratic elections, but in that case it would be the responsibility of the democratically elected representatives to find solutions to the problem, and therefore the question is beyond our scope here. Whether the problem of secession will dominate newly democratized states may be determined in large part by the decision of interim governments to hold first elections according to the old constitutional framework or within a revised one. Following the old constitutional guidelines may be vital for speeding up first elections and deflecting pressing issues which the interim government is unprepared or reluctant to tackle. Yet the failure to reform the institutions may also exacerbate future conflicts between federal units and nationalities, as the experience of Czechoslovakia has shown.

To begin with, after the "Velvet Revolution" the relations between the Czech and Slovak coalition partners in the interim government were spoiled over the debate on renaming the state. The so-called hyphen war was heightened as Czech leaders refused to concede to Slovak's demand for greater autonomy. This failure to compromise, it was argued, facilitated the eventual breakup of the federation on January 1, 1993.[30] Moreover, the communist constitution, revised after the Prague Spring of 1968, was ultrafederal. Given the need for two-thirds majorities in each of the chambers of the federal parliament on constitutional issues, stalemated situations were constantly created. In addition, Václav Havel had not favored the idea of a statewide party so that in the first election his Civic Forum and its Slovak counterpart, the Public Against Violence, did not compete as a single or federated party.

The difficulties of reforming the Czechoslovak state by enacting a new, more viable constitution contributed further to the propagation of Slovak nationalism. The secessionist demands of Vladimir Mečiar's government were ultimately augmented by the readiness of Czech Prime Minister Václav Klaus to separate the state. Indeed, the decisions made in the interim period between the collapse of the Communist regime and the first free elections in June 1990, the definition of the body to which those elections would be held, and the rules by which that body would operate to a large extent determined the breakup of Czechoslovakia. Altogether, the fact that the leaderships of the Slovak and of the Czech republics were both democratically legitimated and that the boundaries between the republics more or less coincided with historic and ethnic boundaries made a peaceful divorce possible; although public opinion polls indicated continued support of Slovaks and Czechs for the maintenance of the common state.[31]

The absence of statehood makes democratization particularly difficult. The case of Hong Kong in this context is especially relevant since the authority over the Crown Colony is exercised by the governor general and the Westminster Parliament, and Chinese local representation is not fully democratic and has only an advisory role. Once the British government agreed with the People's Republic of China over the terms of return of Hong Kong to Chinese sovereignty, the decisions have to be made with the concurrence of the PRC, which is ready to veto any belated British attempt to democratize Hong Kong. In this case the interim situation is such that a non-fully democratic Hong Kong will be incorporated into the nondemocratic People's Republic, and the application of the concept of one country – two systems – and the future of Hong Kong as a Special Administrative Region makes a democratic future for Hong Kong highly problematic.

6

Conclusions

The reader at this point might ask what are the conclusions of our work that are relevant to the future of democracy in countries that have yet to undergo or complete a process of transition to democracy. It has not been our intention to make predictions but rather to draw the attention of scholars and politicians to the important questions of who governs in the interim period, with what authority, and how the governors use their power. We hope to have demonstrated how crucial interim governments are to the outcome of the transition and the character of the emergent polity.

Democracy is a way of governing a state, a political regime whose legitimacy stems primarily from the electoral procedure. The democratic procedure, as Robert Dahl reminds us, is not merely a process; it presumes the protection of specific rights – moral, legal, constitutional – that insures the procedure, including the freedoms of speech, press, and assembly, and the right to form opposition parties. Indeed, "that authoritarian rulers bend every effort to destroy all the institutions necessary to the democratic process demonstrates how fully aware they are that the democratic process is not 'merely formal' but would lead to structural transformation of their regimes."[1]

Undoubtedly there are, and probably always will be, nondemocratic systems with varying degrees of legitimacy that will be able to exercise effective control over people and territory. However, in a world in which alternative ideologies to procedural democracy have lost their appeal – due to the decline of nondemocratic monarchies, the defeat of fascism, the disintegration and crisis of communism, the loss of support by the Catholic church to any ideology of organic corporatist democracy, the failure of many military-social revolutionary regimes like that of Egypt's Nasser or Peru's SINAMOS, and the lack of any model like the self-management democracy of Yugoslavia – the holding of democratic elections has been elevated to an unprecedented new eminence. It is now the dominant formula for authenticating authority, contested only partially by religious fundamentalism, especially as it is found among Islamic groups in the Middle East.

Therefore, most of those who aspire to rule will either try to gain some form of democratic validity, if necessary even falsifying elections, or argue that they are preparing the country for democracy and hence under pressure to do so sooner or later. Those who are rejecting such a goal are subjected to growing pressures to give in to democratization. This new development does not mean that all nondemocratic regimes will lose whatever legitimacy they may now enjoy, and certainly not all of them will abandon power voluntarily.

Indeed, many of the situations discussed in this book do not lead to a fully democratic government nor do all those who promised elections by a fixed date or suggested a transition to democracy in broader terms intend to carry the process to its completion. Thus, it is important to distinguish a series of situations which do not result in democracy, as we have defined it, or do so only after a period of doubt about the legitimacy of the electoral process that confirms the heirs of the authoritarian regime in power.

First, incumbents try to guarantee themselves a permanent share in power by compelling the opposition to concede to partially free elections, or by protecting constitutionally a reserve domain not under the full control of the democratically elected government.

Second, a revolutionary provisional government that considers itself to have a popular mandate to make fundamental changes in the society preempts the people's decisions with decrees of its own. The postponement of elections, in principle, is temporary, but they are often delayed unrealistically or indefinitely.[2]

Third, interim governments (mostly of the incumbents) do not intend to abide by the outcome of the elections which they call, and void them if they turn out contrary to their wishes.[3]

Fourth, interim governments move to hold elections that can be defined as free, whatever local irregularities might exist, but with a time frame that makes it very difficult for an opposition to effectively contest the elections.[4]

In fact, some of these scenarios do not describe interim governments as we have defined them, because those in power have made no commitment to hold totally free elections by a realistic date and to abandon power should they be defeated. Altogether, in recent years leaders of interim governments have found it more difficult to depart from their initial pledge to hold democratic elections because alternative ideologies to democracy, which once shielded them, are no longer legitimate.

Our focus here was on that complex time span between regimes. We have primarily discussed interim governments in states where, despite the people's misgivings about the existing system of government and its legality, order had not disintegrated completely and even the opposition, especially after the incumbent committed itself to free elections, was ready to continue obeying the authorities' command over the state's bureaucratic machinery. As we have seen, a democratically leaning provisional government can make the mistake of disbanding the apparatus of the previous nondemocratic regime and consequently find itself defenseless against minority revolutionary movements. Such was the fate of Kerensky.

Thus, we have argued that one of the most important elements for ensuring a democratic outcome by any interim government is for the state to retain sufficient bureaucratic apparatus and minimal respect for the rule of law. When state institutions disintegrate and armed factions are dispersed as gangs without any faction having the ability to exert monopoly over them, any interim rule that may eventually emerge must begin by reconstructing the state. Yet, as Barnett Rubin has observed in Afghanistan where ethnic, linguistic, and religious factions are fighting a bloody war for control over the state, "building state power in an environment characterized by widespread military organization among the population requires a level of force (and other resources) the international community has been unwilling and perhaps unable to mobilize in more than a few cases."[5]

Our thesis about the importance of retaining an incumbent in a position of relative strength excluded culprit lawless regimes. This exclusion finds its theoretical underpinnings in the classic distinction between legality and legitimacy. As we pointed out, although the notion of the *Rechtsstaat* has often been confused with democratic legitimacy and was clearly hijacked by dictators to supplant their lack of intrinsically valid claim to rule, fidelity to basic bureaucratic legal norms, even of a repressive kind, is critical in preventing state collapse. Truly, legality, in and of itself, may sometimes even breed some legitimacy.

Lawless sultanistic regimes, however, are illegitimate by all definitions. Under such systems legality is compromised in oppressive, arbitrary rule and is not serviceable to the interim government (or the future government) because it does not respond to professional standards and criteria of recruitment. Nonetheless, in extreme cases, when only such despotic governments are still able to prevent the calamity of state disintegration and warworldism, the retention of a predatory incumbent showing some signs of change may be the only option.

In Zaire, where Mobutu's criminal state can no longer benefit from Western Cold War backing, the despot has responded to insurgent challenge by driving his country into the abyss of anarchy. Since 1990, when he declared his intention to launch a democratic transition, Mobutu has manipulated so-called interim governments with the intention to ensure his control. Indeed, his continuing rule, while his country of nearly 40 million people has lost even its most elementary institutions, has led some to conclude that the void likely to be created by his dislodging may be even more perilous than his staying in power. As Bill Berkeley has pointed out, "Mobutu has stoked the forces of anarchy to such a degree that he has made himself indispensable as a means of controlling them."[6]

The illegitimacy of a nondemocratic system almost always produces demands for regime transition. Such demands may become engulfed by challenges to the existence of the state or may, by themselves, propel the state's disintegration. Yet, the decomposition of states by secessionist movements following an ethnic civil war or as a result of a showdown between an authoritarian regime and a revolutionary popular movement tends to create conditions most unfavorable to the emergence of a stable interim government let alone conducive for a transition to democracy.

In the case of a civil war, in which one of the contenders has assumed control over part of the country and its power basis is the support of an ethnic, linguistic, cultural or religious population, the likely outcome is secession. However, as we know, secession is not an easy solution when people are intermingled, when cities are inhabited by one ethnic group and the countryside by another, or when indigenous peoples have dual allegiances. And even if secession is successful, we still would have the problem of an interim government of the new state as well as in the remnant of the old.

A different situation is that of a civil war in which the contenders, sometimes more than two, claim to represent the whole people and aspire to govern the entire state territory. Even if some contenders declare an intention to carry out democratic elections, it will be difficult to hold them if others are still dominating territory and population. The Khmer Rouge's failure to thwart Cambodia's free elections in May 1993 manifested itself most impressively in their inability to intimidate many Cambodians residing under their own territorial control from voting.

A civil war that ends in the total victory of one faction is not conducive to democratic reconstruction in which all, including those who have been fighting on the defeated side, will be allowed to participate. And even if a victorious contender allowed such participation, it is doubtful that opposition leaders would trust the process.

Should we, therefore, think that a civil war delays for a considerable period of time any hope for democracy? Not necessarily. Yet, a democratic outcome under such circumstances may require a specific subset of conditions that are difficult to attain: that all sides renounce the use of organized violence to resolve their conflict, that they control the armed forces in their respective sides, and that they agree to a whole series of steps to generate sufficient trust (including the willingness to compete openly under conditions of relative freedom and to abide by the election results).

To achieve these goals probably requires a complex set of interim agreements and institutions. In this case, the interregnum is especially fraught with dangers and difficulties, and the capacity of the interim government to maintain order and to control the situation is more critical than ever. An agreement to end a civil war without victory is unlikely as long as one of the contenders is hoping to prevail. Certainly, international pressures and assistance can help in such a process of negotiated peace, with the commitment to democracy as an end result.

In reality, in countries where warring factions have reached the point of exhaustion before they could agree on accommodating each other, the ability to break the impasse has often required outside intervention. Today, the United Nations is most likely to render its services if the contestants themselves agree on forming an interim government that will facilitate free elections. Thus, the signatories of the Cambodian peace accord, including the Khmer Rouge, agreed to create a liberal-democratic polity governed by the rule of law and subjected to the principle of periodic and genuine elections.[7] A more recent example is Liberia, where thirteen years of civil war has devastated the country, killing an estimated 150,000 people and displacing another 750,000 out of a population of 2.6 million. In the hope of soliciting UN backing, leading factions signed an accord on July 1993 that initiated a seven-month interim period that will end in the holding of democratic elections.[8]

We have already alluded to the complex problem of nationalism and democracy. To begin with, only a minority of states are strictly speaking nation-states. Many more are clearly multinational, although at times one of the nationalities might be hegemonic and claim that the country is a nation-state. The principle of national self-determination serves to question the legitimacy of those states. Thus, unless the consequent conflict is resolved either by secession, the creation of a new type of multinational state, or by the hegemony of one national group more or less accepted by the others, there are likely to remain forces who reject the idea of democratizing a state they consider illegitimate.

The question of stateness may take precedence to the question of democratization, even though the latter often surfaces first as a pretext for the former. Indeed, people might prefer to live under a nondemocratic state of their own nationality rather than accept a non-national state even if it is democratically inclusive. They might be ready to support a nondemocratic government to achieve the national goals rather than press for full democracy. Once the nationality conflict attains a certain level of intensity and violence, it is difficult to conceive an interim government with sufficient authority to facilitate an electoral process for all citizens irrespective of their identity.

One outcome may be an ethnic democracy, a democracy in which only those of a particular nationality are allowed to participate and choose between various political alternatives. Though that situation renders the system nondemocratic, it may be sustained as long as those excluded groups do not demand democratic participation in a vocal way. That is partly why for many years South Africa was considered one of the Western democracies; only the colored Capetowners and the Indians were allowed to participate democratically, blacks were not.

We have not delved into the complex problem of whether democratic procedures like plebiscites or referenda can effectively and democratically decide the questions derived from the principle of self-determination. The historical record on this is quite mixed, and there are good reasons to question the effectiveness of such devices in resolving problems in many parts of the world.

Our analysis did not focus on prospects for democratic consolidation, but rather on the layered legacies of the interregnum. With regard to the issue of "evening the score," we have seen that interim governments (by their actions or immobility) may perpetuate, aggravate, or reduce the likelihood of future human rights abuses. Their immense importance notwithstanding, they seldom bring an end to debate on this matter, and it is not always clear what type of interim government or which tactics are more conducive to achieving quality and tranquility for the new regime.

From a democratic standpoint, only evening of the score within the parameters of democratically enacted law may be considered legitimate. This is why summary justice by provisional revolutionary governments has the propensity to delay or destroy the future implementation of democratic procedures. Yet, in some instances, when moderate leaders of provisional governments are faced with more extreme opponents, their best hope is to take drastic actions – emergency or even harsh legal measures – to block the ascendancy of extremists lest such forces overwhelm them. Kerensky's demise was largely due to the fact that he was too timid in responding to the Bolsheviks' challenge. In instances of violent revolution, provisional governments may be required to yield somewhat to popular desires for revenge, but the task of those who are truly committed to democracy is replacing summary justice with real justice as quickly as possible. Altogether, the impact of interim administrations on evening the score may only be measurable long after democratic transitions have occurred.

Finally, the question has been raised whether all the attention to regime transitions is ultimately secondary since certain societies, by the nature of their cultures and religious convictions, do not fulfill the prerequisites that different theorists have suggested for a stable democracy. Indeed, the argument has been advanced that certain civilizations, cultures, and religions, primarily Confucianism and Islam, are not hospitable or may even be inherently hostile to democracy. It has also been argued that while Western science and technology, Western economic organization, capitalism and market economy are being diffused successfully into non-Western societies, the legal and political institutions are not. Those institutions are presumably diffused only by imposition, colonialism, or Western pressure, but not because people might value them.[9]

Although the complex debate on the cultural dimension of democracy is beyond the scope of this book, we believe that the argument of cultural or socioeconomic determinists – whether advanced by those who would like to see democracy or those advocating alternative revolutionary solutions or conservative authoritarianism – is too simplistic. It does not give enough attention to the diversity within cultures, downplays the struggle between moderates and extremists over cultural interpretations, and disregards the powerful pressures on authoritarian governments to establish democratic procedures in all societies regardless of cultures and levels of economic development.

Even more critically, we believe that the idea that certain civilizations are destined to clash and the so-called ancient hatreds are bound to erupt is risky. It may help dictators and inciting demagogues to cover their actions with nebulous notions of cultural relativism and to hide behind the impression of primordial compulsions. Susanne Hoeber Rudolph and Lloyd Rudolph (who have pointed to this tendency in Milosevic's Serbia and in India, where Hinduism has been hijacked by the fundamentalist Bharatyia Janata Party) have reversed the question "why old conflicts are flaring up anew" to ask "why traditionally harmonious mosaics have been shattered."[10]

In view of the process of change in Japan since the Meiji Restoration, in Korea, in Turkey, even in India, the idea of cultural relativism does not seem to fit the facts. It overlooks the possibility of selective borrowing and of cultural syncretism that characterized the contact between civilizations. Indeed, people outside the West may question some aspects of Western civilization – which Westerners themselves might do well in questioning – and denounce them while consciously or unconsciously accepting other aspects. The historian Bernard Lewis has argued, that the American popular culture and mores have penetrated Middle East societies so deeply that their appeal is "an object of fear and hatred among self-proclaimed custodians of pristine, authentic Islam."[11] In the international arena, the idea that human rights are shaded by culture is no longer admissible. In June 1993, the United Nations Secretary General, Boutros Boutros-Ghali, declared that when governments "become tormentors" of their peoples, "the international community must take over from the states that failed to fulfill their obligations."[12]

With regard to the question of culture and democracy we feel that it is important to distinguish between two aspects. One is whether certain cultural traditions will prevent the emergence of popular demands for democratization. Another is whether those traditions will prevent the consolidation of democracies and the persistence of liberal democratic institutions.

On the first question there is enough evidence that in societies whose cultures are presumably antithetical to procedural democracy, demands for democratization have risen and transitions have taken place or are in the process of taking place. At this point there is no doubt that, notwithstanding its Confucian culture, South Korea is a democracy, that it has held two free elections, that power has gone from one incumbent party to another, and that there is no immediate prospect of democratic breakdown. There can be also little doubt that in Taiwan the process of democratization is underway and pressures toward full democracy cannot be ignored. This means that two Confucian countries have not escaped the pressure of democratization and that one of them is well on the way to becoming a stable democracy.

The case of Cambodia, although still uncertain, reinforces our belief about the compatibility of pressures toward democratization and Confucianism. Indeed, the fact that China and Vietnam sponsored the Cambodian peace accord, which certified democratic elections as the only legitimate political rule, has indirectly questioned their own doubts about Western democracy.

As to Islamic societies, the cultural argument seems, at least empirically, somewhat stronger. To begin with, "of the forty-six sovereign states that make up the Islamic Conference, only one, the Turkish Republic, can be described as a democracy in Western terms, and even there the path to freedom has been beset by obstacles. Of the remainder, some have never tried democracy; others have tried it and failed; a few, more recently, have experimented with the idea of sharing, though not of relinquishing, power."[13] Moreover, although many Islamic groups in the Middle East have pressed revolutionary dictatorships and traditional autocracies for political reform and some have already shown their ability to conform to the democratic game, their democratic sincerity is broadly questioned. Indeed, it has been widely assumed (not without basis) that, once in power, Islamic fundamentalists will void the democratic process.

Despite these fears and notwithstanding the real tensions that exist between traditional Islam and Western societies, as many have observed, Islam is neither a monolithic religion nor by its very nature contrary to the evolution of democracy.[14]

In Pakistan, for example, none of the nondemocratic regimes has achieved stability. Although both authoritarians and democrats have manipulated to some extent the demand for a more Islamic republic, the democratic ideal has served to license the opposition to authoritarianism, and we find constant attempts to create a stable democracy. It is difficult to explain here why democracy has failed in Pakistan, but certainly political conflicts, power struggles, and constitutional issues have contributed in critical moments to the demise of democracy, much more than Islam.[15]

Like other religious traditions, Islam can be broadly interpreted and may be practiced under various political systems. Yet at present it is evident, as Salman Rushdie has written, that in "the struggle for the soul of Islam" fundamentalists are setting the agenda.[16] The strength and appeal of Islamic movements have much to do with the failure of Arab revolutionary regimes. These regimes which conquered power on the wave of Arab nationalism, espoused social revolutionary ideologies embedded in Western modernist and secularist ideals, vowed to defeat Western imperialism and to resurrect Arab unity. The charismatic leadership of Nasser and the revolutionary ideology of the Ba'th and the FLN captured the imagination of the masses who rallied their support around Pan-Arabism and its progressive commitments.

Yet the nationalists' inability to deliver on their socioeconomic promises and their crushing defeat in their wars against Israel eroded their legitimacy. They became plagued with corruption and have resorted to lawless repression of even moderate voices. The failure to tolerate or coopt secular and liberal opposition, in particular, has hindered the ability of regimes like Egypt's al-Sadat, Algeria's FLN or Tunisia's Bourguiba, to consider a process of extrication and step by step democratization when conditions were ripe: that is, when "Islamists were still politically marginal, the political discourse was predominantly secular, most elites were Western educated, governments were still able to control societies, the demographic bomb had not yet exploded, urbanization was still manageable and secular parties had not yet been discredited. But the regimes were too authoritarian to understand the urgency of such a shift, let alone to embrace it; the Soviet model was not yet invalidated; and the West was much less preoccupied with human rights and democracy."[17]

These failures compounded by the disillusionment with Arab unity and manifested most prominently in the Gulf War, have been the hothouse for the rise of religiously based opposition movements.[18] Inspired by Khomeini's revolutionary conquest in Iran, clerical leaders used the mosque with its relative autonomy to mobilize followers. In countries where economic distress and repression have been particularly marked, clerical forces succeeded in building parallel institutions that served to alleviate the misery of the needy and supplanted the vacuum created by immobile state bureaucracies. Thus, when fledgling regimes in Islamic countries moved under pressure to hold free elections, as in the case of Algeria, the Islamic forces were well positioned to capture the protest vote.

At the same time, one should not forget that in many Islamic societies there are meaningful pressures toward democratization among secularists and committed democrats. Martin Kramer has pointed out that many of the new democratic converts in the Arab world belong to the depleted ranks of Arab nationalists whose enthusiasm for pluralism and democratic elections is no more than veneer, a desparate attempt to stem the tide of Islam.[19] Yet, throughout the Islamic world there are also genuine democrats who have often been enticed by the democratic rhetoric of fundamentalists and have moved to form coalitions with them in the absence of other channels for expressing dissent. As Houchang Chehabi's essay in Part Two of this study shows, many Iranians hoped that the fall of the Shah would lead to democracy and that the clerical forces would not dispense with electoral legitimation. Those forces, however, established their rule by excluding those opposing their theocracy and moved to export their radicalized agenda throughout the Middle East.

Two questions remain. First, should fundamentalists capture power, will they ultimately be rejected just as other authoritarian or communist regimes were repudiated? Second, is some accommodation possible between democratic regimes and traditional Islam?

Some Middle East observers have criticized the West for turning the idea that political Islam is its prime enemy into "a self-fulfilling prophecy." They have condemned the United States in particular for compromising its pledge to support democratic governments wherever they may emerge by failing to castigate the cancellation of the democratic process in Algeria and Tunisia that prevented Islamic parties from assuming power after winning free elections. If politics had taken its natural course, so to speak, the argument goes, sooner or later fundamentalist governments would have run their course; they would have faced democratic opposition and would be forced to liberalize.[20]

A counterargument, however, rejects the idea of testing the Islamic alternative. It calls on the United States not to become a hostage of its own rhetorical commitment to democratic elections in places where the outcome is most likely to produce Islamic dictatorships.[21]

It is difficult for us to take a certain position on these difficult options. Yet, we would like to remind our readers of Schumpeter's formulation that democracy might not be very liberal, and that some countries will be far from liberal in matters like family law, contraception, abortion, secular education, and so on. Let us not forget that Ireland has for decades been considered a democracy and certainly its legal system (until recent changes) has been in agreement with the most conservative interpretation of Catholicism.

Thus, we can assume that in the present historical context the electorate in an Islamic country, for a variety of reasons, might not give its vote to liberal, Westernizing secularists and may instead be attracted to parties which want to establish Islamic societal hegemony. We can also assume that in a number of those Islamic countries, perhaps all of them with the exception of Turkey, there will be no American-style democracy separating church and state. Yet, we should not forget that in Western democracies the American model and the French Third Republic model were exceptions. In fact, in the cases of Spain and Portugal and in the French Revolution, the insistence by democrats on anticlerical policies and the separation of church and state led to unstable democracies.

Certainly, democracies do not have to be secular states. In many Western democracies, established churches or patterns of collaboration between church and state predominate. Not only is there an established church in the United Kingdom and in the Scandinavian monarchies, but intimate cooperation between state and church prevails in Germany as well. The German model has now been copied in Spain. Indeed, it is difficult to think of Israel as a secular state. Hence, we can imagine that Muslim voters in Muslim democracies will enact constitutions and laws which give a special status to Islam in their states. Those democracies will not be satisfactory for many liberals, but even the United States is not always to their contentment.

The central question about democracy is whether it is possible to articulate a critique of certain policies and change them if the majority of the population desires. Let us not forget that democracy is a procedure to make decisions in a society that has certain requirements of freedoms but that does not define the content of those decisions in many matters that affect people. However, when democracies are established their legacy cannot be easily undone.

We believe, therefore, that in times of regime crisis and transition the character and conduct of the interim government may determine whether the country reaches the stage when a general declaration of human rights is recognized and certain freedoms are assured that will enable the holding of free and fair elections.

Notes to Part One

Introduction

1 Niccolo Machiavelli, *The Prince and The Discourses* (New York: Modern Library, 1940), p. 182. We are indebted to Stephen Skowronek for this quote.
2 The African National Congress has insisted on the creation of a transitional government of blacks and whites, "with a limited life span, charged with the task of preparing the country for a democratic constitution and governing the country during this period." See *The New York Times,* August 2, 1992, p. 3.
3 An early treatment of the subject is provided in Juan J. Linz, "Il fattore tempo nei mutamenti di regime," *Teoria Politica* 2:1 (1986):3–47. For a Spanish translation, see *El factor tiempo en un cambio de régimen* (Mexico: Instituto de Estudios para la Transición Democratica, 1994). For additional elaboration, see Lynn Berat and Yossi Shain, "Interim Governments in Democratic Transition: Lessons from Namibia, Hope for South Africa?," *Conflict* 11:1 (1991):17–39. Another exception to the scholarly neglect would be Giuseppe Di Palma, *To Craft Democracies: An Essay on Democratic Transitions* (Berkeley: University of California Press, 1990).
4 It is difficult to know what exactly constitutes a declaration of independence. Various Soviet republics issued statements in 1990 asserting their sovereignty, or the supremacy of their own local laws over those of the Union. A few republics made no real statement of independence until after the August 1991 coup. At that time several of the republics that had already issued statements of sovereignty came out with new declarations of independence. In almost all of the republics the declarations originated in the Supreme Soviet.
5 See Alfred Stepan, "Paths Toward Democratization: Theoretical and Comparative Considerations," in Guillermo O'Donnell, Philippe C. Schmitter, and Laurence Whitehead, eds., *Transitions from Authoritarian Rule: Comparative Perspectives* (Baltimore, Md.: Johns Hopkins University Press, 1986), pp. 64–84.
6 See Alfred Stepan, *Rethinking Military Politics: Brazil and the Southern Cone* (Princeton, N.J.: Princeton University Press, 1988), p. 4.
7 Guillermo O'Donnell and Philippe C. Schmitter, *Transitions from Authoritarian Rule: Tentative Conclusions about Uncertain Democracies* (Baltimore, Md.: Johns Hopkins University Press), p. 6.
8 Ergun Özbudun proposes three tests of the competitiveness of elections: "universal adult suffrage; fairness of voting, as guaranteed by such procedures

as the secret ballot and open counting, as well as by the absence of a significant degree of electoral fraud, violence, or intimidation; and the right to
organize political parties. . . ." See Ergun Özbudun, "Review Article: Studies
on Comparative Elections," *Comparative Politics* 21 (January 1989):237–8.

9 The transfer of power and leadership in democratic and nondemocratic polities has been the subject of great interest to many scholars. One study of
presidential change in the United States portrays the eleven-week hiatus
between the presidential election and the inauguration that involves the transfer of power from one political party to the other as "traumatic transitions."
This period is characterized by the absence of "dynamic leadership" at a time
when the expiring administration must produce some of it most critical policies. See Frederick C. Mosher, W. David Clinton, and Daniel Lang, *Presidential Transitions and Foreign Affairs* (Baton Rouge: Louisiana State University
Press, 1987). For an interesting analysis of the role of interim administrations
in business organizations, see Katherine Farquhar, "Leadership in Limbo:
Organization Dynamics During Interim Administrations," *Public Administration Review* 51:3 (May/June 1991):202–10.

10 It has been argued, for example, that the breakup of the Czechoslovak federation was induced by the cold response of the Czech partners of the Czechoslovak interim government that ruled the country in the months following the
"velvet revolution" to Slovaks' insistence that the republic be hyphenated.
See Tony R. Judt, "Metamorphosis: The Democratic Revolution in Czechoslovakia," in Ivo Banac, ed., *Eastern Europe in Revolution* (Ithaca, N. Y.:
Cornell University Press, 1992), pp. 104–6; Mark Stolarik, "For Slovaks, a
Hyphen Means Recognition," *The New York Times,* letter to the editor, April
22, 1990.

11 Even in societies where other sources of legitimacy are acknowledged, such
as religious sanction or the socioeconomic nature of the regime, appeal to the
people in some form is rarely absent.

12 See Robert Dahl, "Governments and Political Oppositions," in Fred I.
Greenstein and Nelson W. Polsby, eds., *Handbook of Political Science,* vol.
3 (Reading, Mass.: Addison-Wesley, 1975), p. 120.

13 Myres McDougal and W. Michael Reisman, *International Law Essays: Supplement to International Law in Contemporary Perspective* (Mineola, N. Y.:
Foundation Press, 1981), pp. 526–7.

14 Ibid.

15 See Robert Beddard, *A Kingdom without a King: The Journal of the Provisional Government in the Revolution of 1688* (Oxford: Phaidon Press, 1988).

16 This definition of interim government is different from the theoretical designation of Latin American military-authoritarian regimes as temporary. The latter
is based on the ideological dilemma inherent in many authoritarian regimes
(as opposed to totalitarian rule). Because they lack a permanent justification
for their rule, authoritarian regimes must justify their practice of dictatorship
and repression in the present as necessary means to ensure democracy and
freedom in the future. Indeed, as O'Donnell and Schmitter pointed out, the
Achilles' heel of authoritarian regimes is that "they can justify themselves in
political terms only as transitional powers, while attempting to shift attention
to their immediate substantive accomplishments – typically, the achievement
of 'social peace' or economic development." (*Tentative Conclusions,* p. 15)
"Provisionality" in our work, however, begins with the explicit promise of
transitional regimes to hold free and contested election within a reasonable

frame of time – up to two years. Under this definition we can include military administrations that deposed democratically elected governments and promise to relinquish power to a freely elected government as soon as they "restore law and order," as well as incumbent democratic governments which, under the pretense of emergency situation, stretches their mandate promising to resume the democratic process via elections without delay. Naturally, in both instances the democratic intent of the interim government is highly questionable. In Turkey, where parliamentary democracy and interim military governments have alternated three times since 1960, "The overall trend . . . has been *not away but toward* democratic government." See Ergun Özbudun, "Turkey: Crises, Interruptions, and Reequilibrations," in Larry Diamond, Juan J. Linz, and Seymour Martin Lipset (eds.), *Politics in Developing Countries: Comparing Experiences with Democracy* (Boulder, Co.: Lynne Rienner, 1990), p. 199 (emphasis in the original).

17 See Youssef Ibrahim, "Interim Leaders in Algeria Stop Elections for Seats in Parliament," *The New York Times,* January 13, 1992, p. 1.

18 See Claude Klein, "The Powers of the Caretaker Government: Are they Really Unlimited," *Israel Law Review* 12 (July 1977):276. Yet even caretaker administrations in democracies suffer from depreciated legitimacy in terms of their perceived entitlement to execute major policy decisions.

19 An intermediate scenario of a temporary government enjoying partial – though highly questionable – democratic legitimacy, is exemplified in the case of the interim government of Pakistan that took office following the dismissal of Prime Minister Benazir Bhutto in August 1990. Bhutto's rival, Ghulam Mustafa Jatoi, was appointed as interim prime minister by the Pakistani President Ghulam Ishaq Khan who used a constitution written during the dictatorship of the late President Zia ul Haq to launch a "constitutional coup." With no parliamentary motion to support him, Khan declared Bhutto's ouster on national television. He charged her with "corruption and nepotism," appointed an interim government, and promised elections on October 24, 1990. Regardless of Bhutto's alleged criminal record, the fact that the military was implicated in Khan's act and stood behind his choice for an interim prime minister, cast a shadow on Khan's democratic intent and undermined the legitimacy of Pakistan's democracy. In the October elections Bhutto suffered a stunning defeat but refused to concede. See, *The Economist,* August 11 1990, p. 35; *Newsweek,* August 20, 1990, p. 47; *The New York Times,* August 15, 1990; *The Jerusalem Post,* October 26, 1990.

20 The term "founding elections" is borrowed from O'Donnell and Schmitter, *Transitions from Authoritarian Rule: Tentative Conclusions,* p. 61.

21 See Andrzej W. Tymowski, "The Unwanted Social Revolution: Poland in 1989," paper prepared for the 50th Anniversary Congress of the Polish Institute of Arts and Sciences of America, Yale University, June 18–20, 1992, p. 7. The Polish transition has suffered from the absence of a clear conclusion since various elections were stretched out over more than two years (June 1989, quasidemocratic parliamentary elections; May 1990, local elections; November 1990, presidential elections; October 1991, first free parliamentary elections). Even more complex is the case of Brazil, where a number of types of elections were held regularly under the military regime. In Brazil's long process of opening (*abertura*) one can count up to eight rounds of elections between 1974 to 1989 when the first direct presidential election was held.

22 See Juan J. Linz and Alfred Stepan, "Political Identities and Electoral Se-

quences: Spain, the Soviet Union, and Yugoslavia," *Daedalus* 121 (Spring 1992):123–39.
23 Our study concentrates on the role of contending elites in forming the transition process and determining the outcome in terms of regime configuration. We are aware that an elite based analysis may overlook some critical factors affecting the outcome of a transition, such as political culture and the depth of societal cleavages. Moreover, by regarding democracy as the most valued-legitimated (or less discredited) form of authority in our time we are not dismissing the possibility that in some societies democracy is ill-understood or even viewed as a threat to other concerns like stability, security, economic welfare, equality, and so on. Yet, by and large, "poor state performance may lead to crisis in confidence, but it is unlikely to lead to a legitimation crisis (a rejection of democracy). Citizens' evaluation of democracy is likely to decline only if democracy itself is perceived not to function as it should." See Frederick D. Welfare, "The Sources and Structure of Legitimation in Western Democracies: A Consolidated Model Tested with Time-Series Data in Six Countries Since World War II," *American Sociological Review* 54 (October 1989):685.
24 Gianfranco Poggi, *The State: Its Nature, Development and Prospects* (Stanford, Cal.: Stanford University Press, 1990), pp. 28–9.
25 See Samuel Decalo, *Psychoses of Power: African Personal Dictatorships* (Boulder, Co.: Westview Press, 1989); Lisa Anderson, "Lawless Government and Illegal Opposition: Reflections on the Middle East," *Journal of International Affairs* 40:2 (Winter/Spring 1987):219–33.
26 For an excellent discussion on the philosophical origin of the *Rechtsstaat*, see Steven B. Smith, *Hegel's Critique of Liberalism: Rights in Context* (Chicago, Ill.: University of Chicago Press, 1989), ch. 5.
27 Poggi, *The State*, p. 75.
28 Smith, *Hegel's Critique of Liberalism*, pp. 146–7.
29 See Poggi, *The State*, p. 29.
30 According to Sartori, the analytical jurisprudence of John Austin and the juridical positivism of Kelsen that interpret constitutions in a value free fashion, "undermine law as a safeguard of liberty." See Giovanni Sartori, *The Theory of Democracy Revisited* (Chatham, N.J.: Chatham House, 1987), pp. 322–3.
31 Gianfranco Poggi, *The Development of the Modern State: A Sociological Introduction* (Stanford, Cal.: Stanford University Press, 1978), p. 107.
32 See Carl Schmitt, "The Legal World Revolution," trans. by G. Ulmen, *Telos* 72 (Summer 1987):74.
33 See Hannah Arendt, *The Origins of Totalitarianism* (New York: Harcourt, Brace & World, Inc., 1966), p. 462 (italics in the original).
34 See Leslie Holmes, *Politics in the Communist World* (Oxford: Clarendon Press, 1986), p. 62.
35 See Ingo Müller, *Hitler's Justice: The Courts of the Third Reich* (Cambridge, Mass.: Harvard University Press, 1991), pp. 68–81.
36 Ibid., p. 81
37 Translated by the author from the Hebrew version, Israeli Supreme Court, p. 2074.
38 For an illuminating exchange between dissidents and the government in Czechoslovakia on the meaning of the laws, see the documents in H. Gordon Skilling, *Charter 77 and Human Rights in Czechoslovakia* (London: George

Allen & Unwin, 1981), pp. 209–13. On the importance of legality in defining the relations between the government and opposition in Poland, see Stefania Szlek Miller, "Poland," in Jack Donnelly and Rhoda E. Howard, eds., *International Handbook of Human Rights* (New York: Greenwood Press, 1987), p. 310.

39 Václav Havel, et al., *The Power of the Powerless: Citizens Against the State in Central-Eastern Europe* (Armonk, N. Y.: M.E. Sharpe, Inc., 1985), pp. 76–7.

40 Alain Rouquié, "Demilitarization and the Institutionalization of Military-dominated Polities in Latin America," in O'Donnell, Schmitter, and Whitehead, eds., *Transitions from Authoritarian Rule: Comparative Perspectives*, p. 117.

41 María José Moyano, "The 'Dirty War' in Argentina: Was it a War and How Dirty was It?" in Hans Werner Tobler and Peter Waldmann, eds., *Staatliche und parastaatliche Gewalt in Lateinamerika* (Frankfurt: Vervuert Verlag, 1991), p. 69.

42 See Alexandra de Brito, "A Comparative Study of Truth Telling in the Southern Cone: The Nunca Más Reports of Brazil, Argentina, and Uruguay and the Informe Rettig of Chile in the Transition from Military Rule to Democratic Rule," unpublished manuscript, Yale University, January 1992, p. 1, n. 3.

43 See Max Weber, "Legitimate Order and Types of Authority," reprinted in Talcott Parsons et al. eds., *Theories of Society: Foundation of Modern Sociological Theory* (New York: The Free Press, 1965), p. 233.

44 For an excellent discussion "On the Question of the Relationship between the Formal Legality and the Rational Legitimacy of Rule in Max Weber's Works," see Wolfgang J. Mommsen, *Max Weber and German Politics 1890–1920*, trans. Michael S. Steinberg (Chicago, Ill.: The University of Chicago Press, 1984), 448–53. The quote is from p. 452 (italics in the original).

45 See Ellen Kennedy, "Introduction: Carl Schmitt's *Parlamentarismus* in Its Historical Context," in Carl Schmitt, *The Crisis of Parliamentary Democracy*, trans. Ellen Kennedy (Cambridge, Mass.: The MIT Press, 1985), p. xxxv.

46 See John Finn, *Constitutions in Crisis: Political Violence and the Rule of Law* (Oxford: Oxford University Press, 1991), p. 172.

47 The best criticism of recent revisionist literature on Carl Schmitt, is Richard Wolin, "Carl Schmitt, Political Existentialism and the Total State," *Theory and Society* 19 (1990):389–416.

48 Weber's scholarly refusal to differentiate democratic from nondemocratic forms of government in terms of ethical norms or values is consistent with his scientific enterprise of bringing social sciences to share the value-free character of all modern science in order to justify its claim to provide knowledge. His account of the "fact-value" distinction remains the clearest expression of the value neutral approach to political science. In his "Science as a Vocation," Weber stated his position in these words: "To take a practical political stand is one thing, and to analyze political structures and party positions is another. When speaking in a political meeting about democracy, one does not hide one's personal standpoint; indeed, to come out clearly and take a stand is one's damned duty. . . . It would be an outrage, however, to use words in this fashion in a lecture or in a lecture-room. If, for instance, 'democracy' is under discussion, one considers its various forms, analyzes them in the way they function, determines what results from the conditions of life of one form as compared with the other. Then one confronts the form of democracy with

non-democratic forms of political order and endeavors to come to a position where the student may find the point from which, in terms of his ultimate ideals, he can take a stand." See *From Max Weber: Essays in Sociology,* trans. and ed. by H. H. Gerth and C. Wright Mills (New York: Oxford University Press, 1958), pp. 145–6.

While some critics have alleged that his failure to equate democracy, unequivocally, with his type of legal-rational legality unwittingly provided legitimacy to nondemocratic regimes, Weber's scholarly position should not be confused with his personal political inclinations, which generally supported liberal democracy. Since Weber, who died in 1920, did not live to see the horrors of totalitarianism, it is futile to speculate what his position might have been toward Nazism. Yet it should be remembered that Weber, like many of his contemporaries, considered the modern constitutional state and its civil liberties to be unquestioned and irreversible acquisitions of society.

49 Di Palma, *To Craft Democracies,* pp. 94–5.
50 The brutality of the "dirty war" can hardly be rationalized only as an overzealous reaction to the terrorism of the Montonero guerrillas. The seeds for illegal repression in Argentina were already planted during the 1966–73 military rule and were further legitimated under the constitutionally elected Peronist government (1973–6). However, more critically, from 1976 on the antisubversive campaign was designed not only to overcome the guerrillas but to transform the Argentine society as a whole. As María José Moyano has shown in her splendid analysis of the army's motivation in the "dirty war," the "war" was waged in an attempt to eradicate what the Argentine military elite long considered the "international conspiracy directed against the Argentine republic" by proponents of "Marxism, Zionism and Freemasonry: and its branches . . . of communist and socialist parties, guerrilla organizations, varieties of liberal democracy, progressive Catholicism, Protestantism, the media and all artistic manifestations." The country was divided into war "zones" correlated to a branch of the military which was granted specific jurisdiction to fight against the subversion. Each of the zone commanders was also responsible for the activities of a "Task Forces" (Grupos de Tareas or GTs) which were in charge of illegal repression with particular specialization. The military command ordered a "Blood Pact" commanding officers to take part personally in the assassination of prisoners, thereby implicating all levels of the chain of command in illegal repression. See Moyano, " 'The Dirty War' in Argentina," pp. 45–73.
51 See Gerardo L. Munck, "Democratizing Chile: The View From Across the Andes: Transitions from Authoritarian Rule in Comparative Perspective," paper delivered at the 1992 meeting of the American Political Science Association, Chicago, The Palmer House Hilton, September 3–6, 1992, p. 19.
52 See Carlos Viana, "Chile's Transition to Democracy: Legalism, Legitimacy and Elite Settlement in a Transition by Pact," unpublished paper, Yale University, Fall 1992.
53 In the latter instance, elected officials – typically in the guise of protecting the democratic order – assume emergency powers as a "temporary measure" to deal with internal "conspiracy," but fail to resume liberal-democratic practices thereby de facto turning a "constitutional dictatorship" into a tyranny. The dictatorial system that emerged in the Philippines after Marcos declared martial law in September 1972 is a case in point.

54 See *The New York Times,* November 29, 1991, p. 14.
55 See *The New York Times,* June 14, 1992, p. 8; and Bill Keller, "South African Parties Endorse Constitution Granting Rights to All," *The New York Times,* November 18, 1993, p. 1.
56 See Richard Pipes, *The Russian Revolution* (New York: Vintage Books, 1990), pp. 298 and 321–2.
57 Giuseppe Di Palma introduced the phrasing "backward" and "forward" legitimacy in "Founding Coalitions in Southern Europe: Legitimacy and Hegemony," *Government and Opposition* 15 (Spring 1980):170. He underscores the benefits of a democratic transformation from the authoritarian laws and institutions. In the words of Samuel Huntington, incumbents may invoke "backward legitimacy" to "reassure standpatter groups with symbolic concessions, following, a course of two steps forward, one step backward." In our discussion we utilize the phrase "backward legality forward legitimacy" to make a clearer distinction between authoritarian rule of law and democratic legitimacy, obtained only in free and fair elections. See Samuel P. Huntington, *The Third Wave: Democratization in the Late Twentiety Century* (Norman: University of Oklahoma Press, 1991), p. 141. See also Donald Share, "Transition to Democracy and Transition Through Transaction," *Comparative Political Studies* 19 (January 1987):529.
58 See Rober Sharlet, *Soviet Constitutional Crisis: From De-Stalinization to Disintegration* (Armonk, N. Y.: M.E. Sharpe, Inc., 1992), pp. 106–7. Article 72, Chapter 8 of Section 3 of the Soviet Constitution (Ninth Convocation, Oct. 7, 1977) stated that, "Each Union Republic shall retain the right freely to secede from the USSR."
59 See Russell Bova, "Political Dynamics of the Post-Communist Transition: A Comparative Perspective," *World Politics* 44 (October 1991):128–9.
60 Martin Malia, "The August Revolution," *The New York Review of Books,* September 26, 1991, p. 26.
61 See Sharlet, *Soviet Constitutional Crisis,* p. 115.

1. Provisional governments: Revolutionaries and moderates

1 The term *sultanism* is introduced by Max Weber as an extreme case of patrimonialism. See Max Weber, *Economy and Society: An Outline of Interpretive Sociology,* edited by Guenther Roth and Claus Wittich (Berkeley: University of California Press, 1978), vol. 1, pp. 231–2. Juan J. Linz elaborated on Weber's discussion in "Totalitarian and Authoritarian Regimes," in Nelson Polsby and Fred Greenstein, eds., *Handbook of Political Science,* vol. 3 (Reading, Mass.: Addison Wesley, 1975), p. 259. Also see Linz, "Types of Political Regimes and Respect for Human Rights: Historical and Cross-national Perspective," in Asbjørn Eide and Bern Hagtvet, eds., *Human Rights in Perspective: A Global Assessment* (Oxford: Blackwell, 1992): pp. 193–5. In a forthcoming book Linz is editing with H. E. Chehabi they analyze the different dimensions of sultanistic regimes; the social, political, economic, and geopolitical conditions for the emergence of such regimes; and the circumstances leading to their breakdown.
2 See Alan Cowell, "Mobutu's Zaire: Magic and Decay," *The New York Times Magazine,* April 5, 1992, p. 32.

3 See Jeff Goodwin and Theda Skocpol, "Explaining Revolutions in the Contemporary Third World," *Politics and Society* 17 (December 1989):500; and Michael Bratton and Nicolas van de Walle, "Regime Type and Political Transition in Africa," paper presented at the annual conference of the American Political Science Association, Chicago, September 3–6, 1992. p. 16.
4 Anderson "Lawless Government and Illegal Opposition: Reflections on the Middle East," 223 and 228.
5 See Richard Snyder, "Explaining Transitions from Neopatrimonial Dictatorships," *Comparative Politics* 24 (July 1992):379.
6 The debate concerning the Romanian revolution is far from over. However, to date most observers agree that Iliescu's rise to power and the FSN's hegemony are not manifestations of popular will but the result of the general confusion that followed the collapse of the old regime. Through its control over the country's only television station, the "spontaneously" created interim revolutionary government was able to conquer the minds of the Romanian people by manipulating televised images. From the outset (January 1990), Ion Iliescu maintained in a quasitotalitarian rhetoric that, "the Front equals the people," and refused to share power with the newly emerging parties. The democratic opposition contested the FSN's monopoly over policy-making during the interim period and the use made of intimidation and violence to derail the transition to a competitive system. It protested the forcing of a close target date for elections which left no time for the new parties to gather strength and experience. In May 1990 the FSN managed to win an astonishing 85 percent of the vote in Romania's first free elections since 1937. The opposition declared that the results were rigged. The charges of fraudulent elections compounded with the brutal suppression of antigovernment protesters shortly thereafter eroded the legitimacy of the new system. It reopened the sores of the December uprising and led to international condemnation and sanctions by Western democracies. See Vladimir Tismaneanu, *Reinventing Politics: Eastern Europe: From Stalin to Havel* (New York: Free Press, 1992), pp. 232–6.
7 See Snyder, "Explaining Transitions from Neopatrimonial Dictatorship," pp. 380–4.
8 See Mark R. Thompson, "Democracy after Sultanism: The Troubled Transition in the Philippines," in H. E. Chehabi and Alfred Stepan, eds., *Politics, Society and Democracy: Comparative Inquiries* (Boulder, Co.: Westview Press, 1994). Also see Giuseppe Di Palma, *To Craft Democracies: An Essay on Democratic Transitions* (Berkeley: California University Press, 1990), p. 84.
9 See Mulatu Wubneh and Yohannis Abate, *Ethiopia: Transition and Development in the Horn of Africa* (Boulder, Co.: Westview Press, 1988), pp. 45–55.
10 See John A. Booth, *The End and the Beginning: The Nicaraguan Revolution* (Boulder, Co.: Westview Press, 1985), p. 186.
11 Cited in Dennis Gilbert, *Sandinistas: The Party and the Revolution* (Oxford: Basil Blackwell, 1990), p. 35 (emphasis in the original).
12 See Richard Falk, *Human Rights and State Sovereignty* (New York: Holmes and Meier, 1981), p. 206.
13 See Lucian Mihai, "On the 'Trial of Communism' in Romania," paper presented at the conference on Justice in Times of Transition, Schloss Leopoldskron, Salzburg, Austria, March 7–10, 1992. In 1991, Helsinki Watch

reported that "[r]epression in Romania was so severe under Ceausescu that a civil society had no opportunity to develop. There was no human rights movement, no samizdat press. No groundwork had been laid for the development of democratic institutions. Thus, despite some progress, Romania is still experiencing significant human rights abuses." Cited in István Deák, "Survivors," *The New York Review of Books,* March 5, 1992, p. 51.

14 See Samuel Decalo, "Democracy in Africa: Toward the Twenty-First Century," in Tatu Vanhanen, ed., *Strategies of Democratization* (Washington, D.C.: Crane Russak, 1992), p. 133. Also see Bratton and Van de Walle, "Regime Types and Political Transitions in Africa," p. 16.

15 See John J. Moore, Jr., "Problems with Forgiveness: Granting Amnesty under the Arias Plan in Nicaragua and El Salvador," *Stanford Law Review* 43 (February 1991):746–51.

16 Thomas Bruneau, "Transitions from Authoritarian Regimes: The Contrasting Cases of Brazil and Portugal," in Fred Eidlin, ed., *Constitutional Democracy* (Boulder, Co.: Westview Press, 1983), p. 470.

17 In his resignation speech General Spinola attacked the left for trying to create "a new kind of slavery" in the name of a "false democracy." See *The Economist,* October 5, 1974, p. 16. See also Thomas Bruneau, *Politics and Nationhood: Post-Revolutionary Portugal* (New York: Prager Publishers, 1984).

18 On the democratic transition in Portugal, see Kenneth Maxwell, ed., "Portugal Ten Years After the Revolution," Research Institute on International Change, School of International and Public Affairs, Columbia University, New York, 1984.

19 See Daniel Nelson, "Romania," *Electoral Studies* 9 (December 1990):355–66. Out of the 253 seats in the interim assembly half were allocated to the FSN and the rest to the other 37 parties. Though this disproportional division anatagonized the opposition, the fact that the opposition was represented in the interim legislature helped "diluting any tendency towards a reassertion of one-party rule" (360).

20 Crane Brinton, *The Anatomy of Revolution* (New York: Vintage Books, 1965), pp. 137–8.

21 See Pipes, *The Russian Revolution,* p. 303.

22 Ibid., p. 323.

23 Ibid., pp. 298–9. Also see Lionel Kochan, *Russia in Revolution 1890–1918* (London: Weidenfeld and Nicolson, 1966), pp. 169–92.

24 See Max Weber "Russlands Übergang zur Scheindemokratie," in Max Weber, *Gesamtausgabe,* Vol. 1/15, Wolfgang J. Mommsen, ed., (Tübingen: Mohr-Siebeck, (1917) 1984), pp. 238–60. Also see a discussion in David Beetham, *Max Weber and the Theory of Modern Politics* (Oxford: Polity Press, 1985), pp. 198–202.

25 See Carl Schmitt, "The Legal World Revolution," *Telos* 72 (Summer 1987):78.

26 See Mary Fulbrook, *The Divided Nation: A History of Germany 1918–1990* (New York: Oxford University Press, 1992), p. 26.

27 See Gordon Smith, *Democracy in West Germany: Parties and Politics in the Federal Republic* (New York: Holmes and Meier, 1979), pp. 16–18.

28 It is important to remember that despite its rapid development as a capitalist country around the turn of the twentieth century, Germany did not evolve into a modern parliamentary democracy until 1918. Yet many Germans did not consider the disparity between limited democratic institutions and wide

freedoms in the economic sphere to be a source of illegitimacy. They rather boasted Germany's "special constitutionalism" and hailed the achievements of the *Rechtsstaat*. See Klaus von Beyme, "The Effects of Reunification on German Democracy: A Preliminary Evaluation of a Great Social Experiment," *Government and Opposition* 27 (Summer 1992):158.

29 See Fulbrook, *The Divided Nation*, pp. 22–8; Sebastian Haffner, *Failure of a Revolution: Germany 1918–1919,* trans. by Georg Rapp (London: Andre Deutsch, 1973); Arnold J. Zurcher, *The Experiment with Democracy in Central Europe: A Comparative Survey of the Operation of Democratic Government in Post-War Germany and in the Russian and Austro-Hungarian Succession States* (New York: Oxford University Press, 1933); John E. Finn, *Constitutions in Crisis: Political Violence and the Rule of Law* (New York: Oxford University Press, 1991), pp. 152–3.

30 H. E. Chehabi, *Iranian Politics and Religious Modernism: The Liberation Movement of Iran under the Shah and Khomeini* (Ithaca, N.Y.: Cornell University Press, 1990), pp. 257–8.

31 Jerry F. Hough and Merle Fainsod, *How the Soviet Union is Governed* (Cambridge, Mass.: Harvard University Press, 1979), p. 42.

32 See Snyder, "Explaining Transitions from Neopatrimonial Dictatorships," 383.

33 Cited in Chehabi, *Iranian Politics and Religious Modernism,* p. 254.

34 See Chehabi, pp. 253–7. Also see Said Amir Arjomand, *The Turban for the Crown: The Islamic Revolution in Iran* (New York: Oxford University Press, 1988), pp. 134–41. In a widely publicized interview with Oriana Fallaci, Bazargan reflected on his failure as the head of the provisional government, referring to himself as "a knife without a blade." See Oriana Fallaci, "Everybody Wants to be the Boss," *The New York Times Magazine,* October 28, 1979, p. 20.

35 These scenarios occurred when it became impossible for an incumbent collaborationist regime to stay in power. The provisional governments were usually selected (or at least approved), installed, and closely monitored by the democratic occupation force. In Austria, the postwar provisional government, headed by Karl Renner, coalition chancellor from 1918 to 1920, was an externally nominated interregnum.

36 Carl J. Friedrich, *Constitutional Government and Democracy: Theory and Practice in Europe and America,* revised ed. (Boston: Ginn and Co., 1950), p. 593.

37 See Paul-Marie de La Gorce, "The Collapse of the Traditional Military Order," in David Ralston, ed., *Soldiers and States: Civil Military Relations in Modern Europe* (Boston: D.C. Heath & Company, 1966), p. 199.

38 See Bernard Ledwidge, *De Gaulle* (London: Weidenfeld & Nicolson, 1982), p. 67.

39 Still, as de Gaulle recounts in his memoirs, the British colonels who were sent by the War Office to address French soldiers in England in the summer of 1940 alerted them that if they joined the Free French they "will be rebels against [their] government." See Charles de Gaulle, *War Memoirs, Vol. 1, The Call to Honour, 1940–1942,* trans. Jonathan Griffin (New York: Viking Press, 1955), p. 94. Also see Yossi Shain, *The Frontier of Loyalty: Political Exiles in the Age of the Nation-State* (Middletown, Conn.: Wesleyan University Press, 1989), pp. 116–17.

40 Ledwidge, *De Gaulle,* p. 183. This is in contradistinction to the Allied interim governments in Germany and Japan.

41 Ibid., pp. 195–6.

42 See Lamberto Mercuri, "Defascistization in Italy," paper presented at the conference on Transitions From Fascism to Democracy: Europe After World War II, University of Bergen, Chr. Michelsen Institute, Bergen, Norway, June 27–29, 1985, p. 2.

43 Michele Cointet-Labrousse, "Between Summary Justice and the Reconstruction of Legality By Decree: The Theory and Practice of French Purge Policy 1943–53," paper presented at the conference on Transitions From Fascism to Democracy: Europe After World War II, University of Bergen, Chr. Michelsen Institute, Bergen, Norway, June 27–29, 1985, p. 2.

44 Ibid., p. 10.

45 See Brian Crozier, *De Gaulle* (New York: Charles Scibner's Sons, 1973), pp. 368–9.

46 See Ledwidge, *De Gaulle,* p. 204.

47 See Alexander Werth, *De Gaulle* (London: Penguin Books, 1969), p. 190.

48 See M. S. McDougal and W. M. Reisman, *International Law Essays: A Supplement to International Law in Contemporary Perspective* (Mineola, N.Y.: The Foundation Press, Inc., 1981), p. 527.

49 See Hyun-Hee Lee, "A Study of the History of the Provisional Government of the Republic of Korea," an English summary of his Korean book, (Chimmundang, 1982).

50 It did, however, control and administer part of the territory. For a debate on the legal status of the Algerian Provisional Government, see Mohammed Bedjaoui, *Law and the Algerian Revolution* (Brussels, Belgium: Publication of the International Association of Democratic Lawyers, 1961), pp. 78 and 113.

51 See Barnett Rubin, "Afghanistan: Political Exiles in Search of a State," *Journal of Political Science* 18 (Spring 1990):83.

52 In his first statement, the Foreign Minister of the Kuwaiti puppet government, Walid Saud Abdullah, declared that, "countries that resort to punitive measures against the provisional free Kuwait government . . . should remember that they have interests and nationals in Kuwait. . . . These countries should also not expect us to act honorably at a time when they are conspiring against us . . . in an aggressive way . . . If these countries insist on aggression against Kuwait and Iraq, the Kuwaiti government will then reconsider the method of dealing with these countries." See *The New York Times,* August 6, 1990, p. 1.

2. The power-sharing model

1 On the nature of pacts, see O'Donnel and Schmitter, *Tentative Conclusions,* pp. 37–47; Di Palma, *To Craft Democracies,* pp. 86–90.

2 The concepts "them and "us" were used by Oleg G. Rumiantsev, "From Confrontation to Social Contract," *East European Politics and Societies* 5:1 (Winter 1991):113–26.

3 Under the 1991 Cambodian peace accord the Cambodians agreed to create a power-sharing indigenous council that would rule the country until the elections alongside the United Nations Transitional Authority. Among the factions that signed the treaty that promised the creation of a constitutional democracy were the infamous Khmer Rouge, the incumbent Hun Sen, many

of his cadres, defectors from the Khmer Rouge and notorious on their own right, and the royalist opposition led by one of Prince Sihanouk's sons, Prince Norodom Ranariddh, a one-time rebel ally of the Khmer Rouge.

4 Stephen Sestanovich, "The Hour of the Demagogue," *The National Interest* (Fall 1991):7.

5 See Paul Lewis, "Non-Competitive Elections and Regime Change: Poland 1989," *Parliamentary Affairs* 43 (January 1990):90–107; and Antoni Z. Kaminski and Joanna Kurczewska, "Letter From Poland," *Government and Opposition* 26 (Spring 1991):215–28.

6 Anna Sabbat-Swidlicka, "Problems of Poland's State Security Office," *RFE/ RL Research Report,* February 28, 1992, p. 15.

7 Ibid.

8 Ibid., p. 20.

9 David Stark and László Bruszt, "Negotiating the Institution of Democracy: Contingent Choices and Strategic Interactions in the Hungarian and Polish Transitions," Working Paper on Transitions from State Socialism, Cornell Project on Institutional Analysis, Center for International Studies, Cornell University, September 1990, p. 20.

10 See Judy Batt, *East Central Europe From Reform to Transformation* (New York: Council on Foreign Relations Press, 1991), p. 40. A shorter version of this essay appeared in "The End of Communist Rule in East-Central Europe: A Four-Country Comparison," *Government and Opposition* 26:3 (Summer 1991).

11 See Misha Glenny, *The Rebirth of History: Eastern Europe in the Age of Democracy* (London: Penguin Books, 1990), p. 24.

12 See Gordon Wightman, "Czechoslovakia," *Electoral Studies* 9 (December 1990):319–26.

13 See Václav Havel, et al., *The Power of the Powerless: Citizens against the State in Central-Eastern Europe* (Armonk, N. Y.: M.E. Sharpe, Inc., 1990), p. 71.

14 Nicolai Hansteen, "Challenging the Legacy of the Secret Police: The Case of Czechoslovakia and East Germany," unpublished paper, Middlebury College, December 11, 1991. Our analysis of the two cases follows Hansteen's.

15 Di Palma, *To Craft Democracies,* pp. 94–5.

16 See Sigrid Meuschel "The End of 'East German Socialism'," *Telos* 82 (Winter 1989/90):17–24.

17 See Wightman, "Czechoslovakia," 319–26.

18 Already, on December 4, 1989, when rumors circulated that secret police files had been burned, demonstrators stormed the Stasi building in Leipzig. In mid-January, with the impasse in the Round Table, the crowd took over the Stasi headquarters in Berlin and seized the files. See Daniel Friedheim, "Regime Collapse in Democratic Transition: The East German Revolution of 1989," paper delivered at the Eighth International Conference of Europeanists in Chicago, March 27–9, 1992.

19 See *The Los Angeles Times,* February 3, p. 1.

20 See *FBIS-EEU,* January 30, 1990, p. 15, cited in Hansteen.

21 Hansteen, p. 8.

22 See Hansteen; and Jan Obrman, "The Parliament Approves Screening of Deputies," *Report on Eastern Europe,* February 1, 1991, p. 5.

23 The so-called lustration law passed by the Czech and Slovak National Assembly in October 1991. It barred former party officials, members of the Commu-

nist militia, secret policemen, and their informers from serving in "leading posts" throughout the state sector (though not elected posts, such as the parliament) for a period of five years. See Václav Havel, "Paradise Lost," *The New York Review of Books,* April 9, 1992, pp 6–8; Jeri Laber, "Witch Hunt in Prague," *The New York Review of Books,* April 23, 1992, pp. 5–8. Also see Stephen Kinzer, "East Germans Face Their Accusers," *The New York Times Magazine,* April 12, 1992, p. 24.

24 Solidarity leaders' readiness to share governmental power with the outgoing regime according to the negotiated time table, even after the latter's embarrassing defeat in the partly free elections, was criticized by radicals who demanded an immediate and complete transfer of power to the non-Communists. See Batt, "The End of Communist Rule in East-Central Europe," 381–2. Timothy Garton Ash argued that the first power-sharing coalition in Poland "was strong enough to sustain, in its first six months, a remarkable degree of national consensus through the most radical and painful economic shock therapy that has yet been seen anywhere in the ex-Communist world: the so-called Balcerowicz Plan." See Timothy Garton Ash "Eastern Europe: Après le Déluge, Nous," *New York Review of Books,* August 16. 1990, p. 55.

25 Since the Polish lower house remained dominated by ex-Communists who had a reserved bloc of seats (until the first free parliamentary elections scheduled for October 1991) while the president had already been democratically elected, the question of who governs remained unsettled for an extended period of time. In June 1991 a major conflict took place between the two branches regarding the voting law for the legislature which would determine whether the president or the parliament is preeminent and whether voters should cast their ballots for political parties rather than for individual candidates. See John Tagliabue, "Walesa vs. Parliament: Voting System Is at Issue" *The New York Times,* June 25, 1991, p. 13.

26 Cited in Andrzej W. Tymowski, "East European Social Movements in the Transition to Democracy: A Comparative Study of Poland, Czechoslovakia, and the GDR," paper prepared for delivery at the 1990 Annual Meeting of the American Political Science Association, San Francisco, Aug. 30–Sept. 2, 1990, p. 26 (emphasis in the original).

27 These negotiations resulted in an agreement on election date (June 1990), much earlier than the opposition wanted, and a complex voting system, as well as on the size and functions of the future Grand National Assembly. See "Bulgaria Opposition Rebuffs Communists on Sharing Power," *The New York Times,* February 1, 1990, p. 14. Also see Stephen Ashley, "Bulgaria," *Electoral Studies* 9 (December 1990):312–18.

28 On December 20, 1990, the Bulgarian Grand National Assembly approved the formation of a power-sharing interim coalition, pending the holding of new elections in 1991. See *Keesing's Record of World Events,* November 1990, p. 37865, and December 1990, p. 37923.

29 Batt, "The End of Communist Rule in East-Central Europe," 383–4; also see László Bruszt, "1989: The Negotiated Revolution in Hungary," *Social Research* 57 (Summer 1990):365–87.

30 At the same time the opposition parties used the period before the March 1990 elections to focus their grievances "as much on each other as on the communists." See Batt, "The End of Communist Rule in East-Central Europe," 383–4; see also Bruszt, "1989: The Negotiated Revolution in Hungary," 365–87.

31 See Judith Pataki, "Dealing with Hungarian Communists' Crimes," *RFE/RL Research Report,* February 28, 1992, pp. 21–4; Judith Ingram, "Coming Trials That May Try the Hungarian Soul," *The New York Times,* November 13, 1991, p. 4; *The New York Times,* December 26, 1991, p. 9; *Financial Times,* March 4, 1992, p. 1.

32 For an excellent discussion on the differences between the military acting as an institution of the state as opposed to the regime, see Robert Fishman, "Rethinking State and Regime: Southern Europe's Transition to Democracy," *World Politics* 42:3 (April 1990):422–40.

33 See Harry J. Psomiades, "Greece: From the Colonels' Rule to Democracy" in John H. Herz, ed., *From Dictatorship to Democracy: Coping with the Legacies of Authoritarianism and Totalitarianism* (Westport, Conn.: Greenwood Press, 1982), pp. 251–73; Christos Lyrintzis, "Political Parties in Post-Junta Greece: A Case of Bureaucratic Clientelism," in Geoffrey Pridham, ed., *The New Mediterranean Democracies: Regime Transition in Spain, Greece, and Portugal* (London: Frank Cass, 1984).

3. The caretaker government model

1 The key purposes of the TEC are listed in Patric Laurence, "The Diehards & Dealmakers," *Africa Report,* November–December 1993, p. 14. For an elaborated account of the South African transitional phase, see Lynn Berat and Yossi Shain, "South Africa: Retribution or Truth Telling? Legacies of the Transitional Phase," *Law & Social Inquiry* (forthcoming).

2 See Paul Preston, *The Triumph of Democracy in Spain* (London: Methuen, 1986), p. 94.

3 See *The Economist,* July 18, 1987, p. 54.

4 See Declaración Política del Nuevo Gobierno, July 1976.

5 Suárez's amnesty, which polls indicated was supported by 67 percent of the population, excluded terrorists who caused physical injury to persons but included conscientious objectors and military personnel who had been charged with sedition, although the latter were prevented from returning to the fold. The amnesty also reinstated university professors who had been opponents of the regime. The subsequent amnesty granted by the parliament was extended to those who had committed political violence; this had particularly significant implications for Basque terrorists. See Alfonso Osorio, *Trayectoria Política de un Ministro de la Corona* (Barcelona: Planeta, 1980), pp. 156–61; see also Samuel H. Barnes, "Democratization in Contemporary Europe: A Spanish Lesson," paper presented at the 1990 Annual Meeting of the American Political Science Association, San Francisco, August 30 through September, 1990, p. 5; Fernando Rodrigo, "The Politics of Reconciliation in Spain's Transition to Democracy," paper presented at a conference on Justice in Times of Transition, Schloss Leopoldskron, Salzburg, Austria, March 7–10, 1992.

6 Alfred Stepan stresses the fact that the limited brutality in Brazil, where, unlike in Argentina, the army killings affected a tiny proportion of the population, was critical in ensuring the opposition's support of the 1979 "mutual amnesty." Stepan, *Rethinking Military Politics,* p. 64. The case of Brazil is theoretically difficult from the point of view of designating the interim period.

7 Cited in *The Economist,* February 27, 1988 p. 45.

8 See Gilbert, *Sandinistas: The Party and the Revolution* p. 166.
9 The agreement, known as "el pacto militar-sindical" promised the Peronista presidential candidate the support of the army in the elections in return for the immediate suspension of all investigations on the *desaparecidos*. See *Keesing's Record of World Events,* December 1983, p. 23555.
10 See David Rock, *Argentina 1516–1987: From Spanish Colonization to Alfonsin* (Berkeley: University of California Press, 1987), p. 383–9; Aldo C. Vacs, "Authoritarian Breakdown and Redemocratization in Argentina," in James M. Malloy and Mitchell A. Seligson, eds., *Authoritarians and Democrats: Regime Transition in Latin America,* (Pittsburgh, Pa.: University of Pittsburgh Press, 1987), pp. 28–31; and Ronaldo Munck, *Latin America: The Transition to Democracy* (London: Zed, 1989), pp. 103–5.
11 See Mark Osiel, "The Making of Human Rights Policy in Argentina: the Impact of Ideas and Interests on a Legal Conflict," *Journal of Latin American Studies* 18 (1986):143. In late December 1990, despite the fierce protests of many Argentinians, the Peronista President, Carlos Saul Menem, pardoned the military officers as part of his attempt to calm resentment within his armed forces. See "Argentine Frees Junta Strongmen," *International Herald Tribune,* December 31, 1990–January 1, 1991.
12 On the exceptional case of Uruguay, see note 19.
13 See Moore, "Problems with Forgiveness," 733–77.
14 See Lawrence Weschler, *A Miracle, A Universe: Settling Accounts with Torturers* (New York: Pantheon Books, 1990), p. 189.
15 Ibid., p. 158. See also, "Derechos Humanos: Seregni-Marchesano-Ferreira," *El Popular,* Montevideo, December 5, 1986, pp. 1–8 (from debate on Club Naval and subsequent political developments leading to amnesty from television program "Prioridad" of Dec. 3, 1986).
16 Weschler, p. 159.
17 Cited in ibid., p. 183.
18 Ibid., p. 188. A similar moral equivalency argument was made by Marcel Niedergang in "Sanguinetti: es normal haber amnistiado a los Militares," *Brecha,* Montevideo, November 9, 1985, p. 32. On the pact of the Club Naval, see also "Ferreira: El Pacto de Impunidad existe desde el Club Naval," *El Pais,* Montevideo, December 20, 1986; Stepan, *Rethinking Military Politics,* p. 69; Huntington, *The Third Wave,* p. 226. The best study on Uruguay's transition to democracy is Charles G. Gillespie, *Negotiating Democracy: Politicians and Generals in Uruguay* (Cambridge University Press, 1991).
19 In 1986, when the Tupamaros and other victims of military repression began to bring charges against police and military officers for abuses committed during the dictatorship (1973–85), the military grew intransigent and made it clear that officers would not answer court summonses. Then, the Colorados and a majority of the Blancos, the largest party in the legislature, passed an amnesty on December 22, 1986, just a day before the first of the military subpoenas was due. Their action prompted a successful opposition campaign to force a referendum on the amnesty. However, on April 16, 1989, with the threat of military unrest looming large, a majority of Uruguayans voted to reject the effort to overturn the amnesty. See *The New York Times,* April 17, 1989, p. 6.
20 On incumbents' attempts to extort sacrifices ("hostages") from the opposition, especially in the economic sphere, see Robert H. Bates, "The Economics of Transitions to Democracy," *PS* 24 (March 1991): 24–7.

21 See n. 16.
22 See Adam Przeworski, "Democracy as a Contingent Outcome of Conflicts," in Jon Elster and Rune Slagstad, eds., *Constitutionalism and Democracy* (Cambridge University Press, 1988), p. 61.
23 Indeed, the question of whether to take part in the plebiscite posed a serious dilemma for the Chilean opposition. Participation could have been interpreted as conferring legitimation on the authoritarian elections, or even the regime itself. See Jean Grugel, "Transitions From Authoritarian Rule: Lessons From Latin America," *Political Studies* 35 (1991):363–8.
24 See Pamela Constable and Arturo Valenzuela, "Chile's Return to Democracy," *Foreign Affairs* (Winter 1989/90):169–86; and Valenzuela and Constable, *Current History* 90 (February 1991):54–6.
25 See Nathaniel C. Nash, "Pinochet is 'My Franco,' Chile's Chief Says, Going His Own Way (Carefully)," *The New York Times,* April 30, 1992, p. 3.
26 See Alexandra de Brito, "A Comparative Study of Truth Telling in the Southern Cone: The Nunca Más Reports of Brazil, Argentina, and Uruguay, and the Informe Rettig of Chile in the Transition from Military Rule to Democratic Rule," unpublished manuscript, Yale University, January 1992, p. 49.
27 Ibid., pp. 47–9.
28 See Przeworski, "Democracy as a Contingent Outcome of Conflicts," p. 62.

4 The international interim government model revisited

1 This is in marked contradistinction to the argument made by Gerald B. Helman and Steven R. Ratner who perceive the possibility of a United Nations governing body in states that "have already failed." The two use Cambodia as an example of a failed state, one whose "governmental structures have been overwhelmed by circumstances." We feel that the authors mistakenly equated Cambodia with Bosnia, Liberia, and Somalia in terms of the potential for UN success as follows from our hypotheses. See Gerald B. Helman and Steven R. Ratner, "Saving Failed States," *Foreign Policy* 89 (Winter, 1992–93):3–21.
2 See Lynn Berat and Yossi Shain, "Democracy: The Namibia Model," *The Jerusalem Post,* November 27, 1990, p. 4; Berat and Shain, "Interim Governments in Democratic Transition: Lessons from Namibia, Hope for South Africa?," *Conflict* 11 (January–March 1991):17–40; For fuller discussions of the Namibian case, see Berat and Shain, "Provisional Governments in Democratization: The 'International Interim Government' Model and the Case of Namibia," *Coexistence* 29 (March 1992):19–40.
3 See Yossi Shain, "Governments-in-Exile and International Legitimation," in Yossi Shain, ed., *Governments-in-Exile in Contemporary World Politics* (New York: Routledge, 1991), pp. 219–37.
4 Helman and Ratner remind us correctly that although the UN's responsibilities with regard to Namibia derived from unique circumstances, that is, Namibia's status as a former League of Nations mandate, this should not preclude UN involvement in other conflicts where the historical antecedents are different. After all, as they note, the UN Charter calls upon the organization to achieve "international cooperation in solving international problems of an economic, social, cultural, or humanitarian character, and in promoting and encouraging respect for human rights." Helman and Ratner, "Saving Failed States," 12.

5 UN GAOR Res. 65(I), Dec. 14, 1946. For a discussion of South African behavior in Namibia, see Lynn Berat, *Walvis Bay: Decolonization and International Law* (New Haven: Yale University Press, 1990), pp. 47–89.

6 The Namibian government's inability to attract foreign investment, despite considerable efforts including the passage of liberal laws, is largely the result of a sordid colonial legacy. The colonial boundaries Namibia inherited mean that it is largely desert with a sparse population. Consequently it does not have a domestic market of a size appealing to foreign multinationals and also has an unenviable position between economically and infrastructurally more advanced South Africa and the declining nations of sub-Saharan Africa. While geography might be surmountable if the population were highly skilled, the complete lack of regard for African education by Namibia's erstwhile German and then South African overlords has created a population that is barely literate and numerate. The inability to expand the private sector has meant that the government has bloated the bureaucracy – with disastrous effects on efficiency – in an effort to create jobs. Indeed, it is estimated that 55 percent of all employment is in the public sector. Robert Rotberg, "Namibia: An African Success Story – So Far," *Christian Science Monitor,* July 29, 1992, p. 19.

7 See Republic of Namibia, Constitution, Act No. 1, (1990).

8 See *The Wall Street Journal,* December 4, 1991; *The New York Times,* October 4, 1992, Section E. p. 7, and January 10, 1993.

9 *The New York Times,* February 19, 1990.

10 Cited in Morton Halperin, "Guaranteeing Democracy," *Foreign Policy* 91 (Summer 1993):118.

11 *Christian Science Monitor,* October 18, 1991.

12 See W. Vistarini, Letter to the Editor, *Far Eastern Economic Review,* January 30, 1992, p. 5.

13 See Nate Thayer, "Plunder of the State," *Far Eastern Economic Review,* January 9, 1992, p. 11.

14 Charles Wallace, "Cambodia Wants U.N. to Deploy Forces," *Los Angeles Times,* January 14, 1992, p. 21.

15 *Far Eastern Economic Review,* October 15, 1992, p. 56; and *New York Times,* Jan. 31, 1993.

16 The term "symbolic center of the nation" is borrowed from Craig Hutchinson's "The Khmer Way of Exile: Lessons from Three Indochinese Wars," in Yossi Shain, ed., *Governments-in-Exile in Contemporary World Politics* (New York: Routledge, 1991).

17 See Editorial, *Far Eastern Economic Review,* September 10, 1992, p. 6.

18 See William Shawcross, "Cambodia: The UN's Biggest Gamble," *Time,* December 28, 1992, pp. 30–2.

19 See *Far Eastern Economic Review,* December 24–31, 1992, p. 11.

20 *Far Eastern Economic Review,* December 17, 1992, p. 26.

21 See, Shawcross, *Time,* December 28, 1992, p. 31.

22 *The Economist,* September 19, 1992, p. 40.

23 *The New York Times,* June 26, 1993.

24 China and Vietnam's sponsorship of the democratic transformation of Cambodia indirectly undermines the legitimacy of their domestic rule.

25 See Berat and Shain, "Interim Governments in Democratic Transition," 29.

5. The timing and nature of first democratic elections

1 Cited in Ernst Kux, "Revolution in Eastern Europe – Revolution in the West?" *Problems of Communism* (May–June 1991):9.
2 Di Palma, *To Craft Democracies*, p. 85.
3 Huntington, *The Third Wave*, chap. 6.
4 Bernard Lewis, "Islam and Liberal Democracy," *The Atlantic Monthly*, February 1993, p. 98.
5 See John R. Guardiano, "Why Political Democracy Hurts Russia's Economic Reform," *The New York Times*, Letters to the editor, December 12, 1992, p. 22.
6 Cited in *Reuters*, March 17, 1992.
7 See Philip Shenon, "Wave of Violence Threatens Elections in Cambodia," *The New York Times*, January 28, 1993, p. 8.
8 See Mary Fulbrook, *The Divided Nation: A History of Germany 1918–1990* (Oxford: Oxford University Press, 1992), pp. 24–8.
9 See Pipes, *The Russian Revolution*, p. 328.
10 See Serge Schmemann, "Learning to Walk," *The New York Times*, Week in Review, January 21, 1990, Section 4, p. 1.
11 See László Bruszt and David Stark, "Remaking the Political Field in Hungary: From Politics of Confrontation to the Politics of Competition," in Ivo Banac, ed., *Eastern Europe in Revolution* (Ithaca, N.Y.: Cornell University Press, 1992), p. 15.
12 See Barbara Heyns and Ireneusz Bialecki, "Solidarność: Reluctant Vanguard or Makeshift Coalition?," *APSR* 85:2 (June 1991):353.
13 Cited in Vladimir Tismaneanu, *Reinventing Politics: Eastern Europe From Stalin to Havel* (New York: Free Press, 1992), pp. 276–7.
14 Giuseppe Di Palma, "Founding Coalitions in Southern Europe: Legitimacy and Hegemony," *Government and Opposition* 15 (Spring 1980):176.
15 Of the thirty-one members of the Greek interim government twelve were former deputies of Mr. Karamanlis's old conservative party, five were from the Centre Union, seven were technocrats, and seven belonged to new political forces. Thirteen of them were imprisoned, three court-martialed and convicted, and three others exiled under the 1967–74 dictatorship. See *The Economist*, August 3, 1974, p. 26.
16 See *The Economist*, November 16, 1974, p. 43; see also Psomiades, "Greece: From the Colonels' Rule to Democracy," p. 258.
17 Castro's Cuba is a classic example of such a development. Castro's initial commitment to democracy was received with encouragement by his democratically leaning allies. They hoped to organize themselves into political parties and participate in Cuba's first democratic elections. On January 5, 1959, a Cuban provisional government headed by President Urrutia was declared. It was immediately recognized by the United States. During his victorious march into Havana on January 8, Castro stopped at the presidential palace to pay his respect to the new president. A day later he declared that the new regime would hold elections "in a space of fifteen months more or less." He warned against false revolutions which end in coup d'etat and vowed that "the provisional government would be short-lived" and would last only until a "genuinely democratic" government could be elected. Yet, in the following weeks Castro deliberately undermined the democratically bent

provisional government. He pushed its premier, Miro Cardona, to agree that there would be no elections for eighteen months during which the government would rule by decree, the most significant of which was the one which provided for the abolition of the political parties. On February 16, 1959, Castro assumed the post of prime minister. He then launched a forceful campaign to abolish the corruption of the old regime and sidetracked, indefinitely, from his initial commitment to hold elections. See Hugh Thomas, *Cuba: The Pursuit of Freedom*(New York: Harper & Row, 1971), pp. 1083–84.

18 See Clinton L. Rossiter, *Constitutional Dictatorship: Crisis Government in Modern Democracies* (Princeton, N.J.: Princeton University Press, 1948).

19 See Linz and Stepan, "Political Identities and Electoral Sequences: Spain, the Soviet Union, and Yugoslavia," 123–39.

20 For an elaborate discussion on the consequences of institutional choices for new democracies, see Juan J. Linz, "Democracy: Presidential or Parliamentary, Does it Make a Difference?," in Juan J. Linz and Arturo Valenzuela, eds., *The Failure of Presidential Democracy* (Baltimore, Md.: Johns Hopkins University Press, 1994), pp. 3–87. For a debate among Donald L. Horowitz, Seymor Martin Lipset, and Juan J. Linz on presidentialism/parliamentarism, see *Journal of Democracy* 1:4 (1990):73–91, as well as in Arend Lijphart, "Constitutional Choices for New Democracies," *Journal of Democracy* 2:1 (Winter 1991):72–84.

21 Claude Klein, "The Powers of the Caretaker Government," 277–8.

22 Following the Assembly's act, the secessionist threat collapsed and Cambodia's two major parties, the royalist Funcinpec under the leadership of another of Prince's Sihanouk's sons, Prince Ranariddh, and Hun Sen's incumbent-led party, The Cambodian People's Party, formed a power-sharing interim government with Prince Sihanouk as the head of state. That government with broad-based support in the assembly would rule Cambodia until the elected assembly drafted a constitution. See reports by Philip Shenon in *The New York Times,* June 15–June 17, 1993.

23 Ibid.

24 Cited in Ledwidge, *De Gaulle,* p. 208.

25 See Chehabi, *Iranian Politics and Religious Modernism,* p. 265. The first stage in installing the Islamic Republic was the abolishment of the monarchy decided in a "no choice" plebiscite on March 30 and 31, 1979. Finally in a rigged plebiscite (December 2–3) the constitution was approved by over 99 percent of the vote. Bazargan's provisional government was already out of office by the time of the November coup.

26 See John Sorenson, "Essence and Contingency in the Construction of Nationhood: Transformation of Identity in Ethiopia and Its Diasporas," *Diaspora* 2 (Fall 1992):201–28.

27 To this we have to add the provision in the Soviet constitution that granted the republics the right to secede, even though prior to 1990 nobody intended to respect that right. See note 49 in the Introduction.

28 See Romuald Misiunas, "Sovereignty without Government: Baltic Diplomatic and Consular Representation, 1940–1990," in Yossi Shain, ed., *Governments-in-Exile in Contemporary World Politics* (New York: Routledge, 1991), pp. 134–44.

29 See Juan J. Linz and Alfred Stepan, *Problems of Democratic Transition*

and Consolidation: Southern Europe, South America and Post-Communist Europe (Baltimore, Md.: Johns Hopkins University Press, forthcoming).

30 See Jan Obrman, "Havel Challenges Czech Historical Taboos," *RFE/RL Research Report,* June 11, 1993, p. 50.

31 See Jiri Pehe, "Czechoslovakia: Toward Dissolution," *RFE/RL Research Report,* January 1, 1993, p. 84.

6. Conclusions

1 Robert A. Dahl, *Democracy and its Critics* (New Haven, Conn.: Yale University Press, 1989), p. 175.

2 In some cases elections are held under nondemocratic conditions.

3 This was the case of Panama when in 1989 Guillermo Endara was prevented from assuming the presidency after Gen. Manuel Noriega rigged the elections. Similarly, in June 1993, the president of Nigeria, Gen. Ibrahim Badamasi Babangida, voided the results of his country's first democratic elections after ten years of military rule. In some cases the outgoing rulers, in view of the result of elections to municipal or regional bodies, as part of a democratization process, realize that they are likely to lose a national vote and move to halt the electoral process. In Algeria the Islamic Salvation Front was on the road to win a plurality of the electoral votes in the national elections in December 1991, but was stopped by a military coup. Such developments further undermine the legitimacy of the incumbent, provoke greater opposition and violence, and produce harsher repression.

4 This has been the situation in some former Communist countries, like Romania and Albania, where the pressures for democratization emerged very late and where the system had been totalitarian almost to the end.

5 See in Part Two.

6 See Bill Berkeley, "Zaire: An African Horror Story," *The Atlantic Monthly,* August 1993, p. 28.

7 Although in theory they could have agreed on some form of permanent power-sharing arrangement. See Morton H. Halperin, "Guaranteeing Democracy," *Foreign Policy* 91 (Summer 1993): 118.

8 See *The New York Times,* July 18, 1993.

9 The first argument was advanced by Samuel P. Huntington, in *The Third Wave,* where he admits that cultures are dynamic and have a tendency to adapt (see chap. 6). More recently, in his provocative essay "The Clash of Civilizations?," Huntington suggests that despite the fluidity of civilizations and the strong interaction among them their fundamental differences lead them to collide. See *Foreign Affairs* (Summer 1993):22–49.

10 See Susanne Hoeber Rudolph and Lloyd I. Rudolph, "Modern Hate: How Ancient Animosities Get Invented," *The New Republic,* March 22, 1993, pp. 24–9.

11 See Bernard Lewis, "Islam and Liberal Democracy," *The Atlantic Monthly,* February 1993, p. 91.

12 See *The New York Times,* June 15, 1993.

13 Lewis, "Islam and Liberal Democracy," p. 89.

14 See Rafiq Zakaria, *The Struggle Within Islam: The Conflict Between Religion and Politics* (London: Penguin Books, 1989).

15 For the latest round of constitutional crisis in Pakistan, see Edward A. Gar-

gan, "Pakistan Government Collapses: Elections are Called," *The New York Times,* July 19, 1993, p. 3.

16 See Salman Rushdie, "The Struggle for the Soul of Islam," *The New York Times,* July 11, 1993, Op-Ed.

17 Ghassan Salamé, "Islam and the West," *Foreign Policy* 90 (Spring 1993):30.

18 See Fouad Ajami, "The End of Arab Nationalism," *The New Republic,* August 12, 1991; Yossi Shain and Reuben Aharoni, "Players or Playing Cards: The Palestinian and the Gulf Crisis," *Journal of Political Science* 19 (Summer 1991):55–68; Roger Matthews, "A Voice for the Oppressed," *Financial Times,* July 15, 1993, p. 11.

19 See Martin Kramer, "Arab Nationalism: Mistaken Identity," *Daedalus* 122 (Summer 1993):201–2.

20 See Leon T. Hadar, "What Green Peril?," *Foreign Affairs* (Spring 1993):27–42. A similar view is presented by Ghassan Salamé in his "Islam and the West," p. 31.

21 See Judith Miller, "The Challenge of Radical Islam," *Foreign Affairs* (Spring 1993):43–56.

PART TWO

Case studies

7

The provisional government and the transition from monarchy to Islamic republic in Iran

H. E. CHEHABI

INTRODUCTION

After Ay.[1] Ruhollah Khomeini triumphantly returned to Iran on February 1, 1979, he appointed Mehdi Bazargan, an Islamist and veteran of the anti-Shah opposition, to form a "provisional government." Its tasks were to "govern the country, hold a referendum on the change of regime to an Islamic republic, call an elected constitutional assembly to ratify the new regime's constitution, and organize parliamentary elections on the basis of the new constitution."[2] The revolution had united large sectors of Iranian society against the Shah's dictatorship, and now a man with impeccable democratic credentials was chosen by the charismatic leader of the revolution to head an interim administration until permanent institutions based on popular suffrage were put in place; the choice seemed to augur well for a transition to democracy. But by the end of 1979, Iran had a quasitheocratic constitution, and by the summer of 1981, radical Islamists had gained a monopoly of power, eliminated all other political parties (with the exception of the Communist Tudeh party, which was tolerated until 1983), and unleashed a reign of terror whose violence was unprecedented in twentieth-century Iran.[3]

Bazargan's ill fated administration exemplifies the first type of interim government identified by Shain and Linz in their Introduction, the "provisional revolutionary government." This chapter begins by discussing why the crisis of the Shah's regime found its denouement in a provisional government rather than a "power-sharing interim coalition" or an "incumbent as caretaker administration." From there it proceeds to an analysis of the problems the provisional government faced during its nine-month tenure in office, before turning to the crucial issue of how the institutional framework of the Islamic republic was put in place.

THE TRANSITION FROM MONARCHY
TO ISLAMIC REPUBLIC

The by and large successful transitions to democracy in Southern Europe, Latin America, East Asia, and Eastern Europe stand in such sharp contrast to the revolutionary upheavals in Iran and Nicaragua that "transitions to democracy" and "revolutions" are usually treated as analytically quite distinct phenomena.[4] Scholars study either the one or the other; at most they briefly admit that not all breakdowns of authoritarian regimes lead to democracy (then concentrating on those that do), or that revolutions are perhaps not inevitable. Yet the profound socioeconomic changes that characterize revolutions as opposed to more peaceful regime changes should not lead us to overlook the simple fact that a revolution effects, *among other things*, a transition from one *political* regime to another, which is all that many of those who participate in the revolution want. Similarly, many actors in a transition to democracy prefer a revolutionary uprooting of the old order, but do not have their way for one reason or another.[5] A revolution thus constitutes a borderline case of regime transition, and it is therefore legitimate to ask why one type of interim government separates the two regimes rather than another. In Iran this question is even more legitimate than in the case of Nicaragua, for unlike the latter, Iran did not experience a guerilla war before the revolutionary takeover; until early 1978 the country was quiet and the Shah in full control. He had been on the throne since 1941, had assumed control of the government after a foreign-aided coup ousted the constitutional government of Mohammad Mossadegh in 1953, and had ruled in an increasingly autocratic fashion since 1963 while paying lip service to the liberal 1906 constitution.[6]

If "transition" be defined as the interval between "the launching of the process of dissolution of an authoritarian regime" and, in our case, "the emergence of a revolutionary alternative,"[7] Iran's transition from monarchy to Islamic republic started in 1977. It began with a liberalization initiated by the regime, like many others in the "third wave" of democratic transitions.[8] In late 1976 and early 1977, influenced by Jimmy Carter's election to the U.S. presidency, the Shah ordered an end to the torture of political prisoners, had his obedient parliament pass new human rights legislation, and freed some political prisoners. In March 1977, Iranian intellectuals, and later oppositional politicians, began responding by writing open letters to the Shah, criticizing his regime's corruption and repression. Throughout 1977 the opposition was led by intellectuals and liberal politicians who had been associated, or sympathized, with Mossadegh's reform movement. Although the Shah replaced his longtime prime minister, Amir-Abbas Hoveida, with the technocrat Jamshid Amuzegar in August 1977, he did not charge his new prime minister with holding free elections. At a time when the opposition was weak and dominated by liberals, an "incumbent caretaker administration" could have overseen a transition to democracy. Yet the Shah reaffirmed his commitment to the single party system he had established in 1975.

At the beginning of January 1978 the situation changed in Iran. Large sectors of the population were becoming mobilized against the regime after a highly insulting article against Ay. Khomeini had been planted in a daily newspaper by the regime. In the course of the year the dissident movement of 1977 gradually became a revolutionary mass movement,[9] over which Khomeini and his radical followers exercised far more influence than the secular politicians and intellectuals. Recognizing their weak social base, the latter allied themselves with Khomeini, in the hope that their loyalty to the revolution's charismatic leader would enable them to have a moderating influence on events.

The bloody clashes between demonstrators and security forces that increased in scope throughout 1978 radicalized the opposition movement. In August 1978 the new prime minister, Ja'far Sharif-Emami, legalized political parties, and the Shah promised free elections. The leaders of the liberal opposition would have liked to accept such an offer, but Khomeini was against it, arguing that the Shah's illegitimate and illegal regime lacked the capacity to organize elections, and that an electoral campaign would have dissipated revolutionary energies. Both Bazargan, leader of the Liberation Movement of Iran (LMI), a liberal Islamist party, and Karim Sanjabi, leader of the secular liberal National Front, went to Paris in October to try to induce Khomeini to be more flexible, but he did not change his mind.

In 1978 there was much talk about a coalition government to guide Iran out of its crisis. In the first half of the year this might have been possible, but the Shah did not offer it: as late as the fall of 1978 he called the National Front traitors beholden to Western interests who wanted to deliver Iran to the Communists. After the massacre of September 8, in which hundreds, were killed, a coalition government would have been much more difficult to set up. In December 1978 the Shah did indeed offer two Mossadeghists, Gholam-Hossein Sadiqi and Karim Sanjabi, the premiership, but under conditions they could not accept. Khomeini's intransigence, as well as certain structural characteristics of the Shah's regime, impeded power-sharing and made it difficult to set up a coalition government.

Since 1963, the Shah's rule displayed increasingly sultanistic tendencies. Robert Fishman has pointed out the different implications of regime-initiated as opposed to state-initiated transitions.[10] In a sultanistic regime such as the Shah's, regime and state are largely fused, as the personalization of power does not allow any state agencies, in particular the crucial armed forces, to maintain their autonomy.[11] Within the regime, the personalization of power in the hands of the Shah had three consequences. First, a coalition with the Shah himself was not acceptable to the opposition, because it would have amounted to little more than a cooptation by his regime, which would have cost the opposition politicians the little popular support they had. Second, the fact that the Shah was a hereditary monarch complicated matters. As longtime dictator, he was not credible as neutral arbiter, a function King Juan Carlos had performed in the Spanish transition,[12] and his personal fate was linked with that of the monarchy as such. Third, even assuming that these difficulties could have been overcome by the formation of a regency council (an option that was discussed), no moderate personalities independent of the ruler existed within the regime who could have acted as a bridge to moderate members of the opposition. In 1978 the only Iranian politician who remotely fit this role was Ali Amini, who had briefly been prime minister in the early 1960s, but the Shah mistrusted him up to the end. As for the army, its lack of autonomy and organizational weakness prevented it from launching a coup against the regime and forming an interim coalition government with members of the opposition; a Portuguese scenario was thus ruled out. Given that Iran had had no meaningful political life since 1953, and, causally related to this, given Ay. Khomeini's charismatic hold on the masses,[13] political society in Iran was overwhelmed by civil society, and by the end of 1978 the transition was society-led. A *ruptura* was inevitable; the only question was whether there could be an orderly transfer of power to the opposition, or whether the state would disintegrate sufficiently for the opposition to seize power.

An orderly transfer of power was attempted. In January 1979 the Shah named Shapur Bakhtiar, a leader of the National Front, prime minister, and then left the country for good. Bakhtiar was invested with this position by the old parliament. This procedural continuity provided Bakhtiar with "backward legitimacy" not with the population, for whom the new prime minister was as illegitimate as the ruler and the ruler's hand-picked parliament to whom he owed his job, but with the armed forces. These did indeed remain loyal to Bakhtiar, which gives his administration certain traits of a "power-sharing interim coalition" government. Had the revolutionaries accepted Bakhtiar as an interim head of government, some measure of legal continuity could have been maintained and chaos averted. For this reason, Bazargan, an old personal friend of Bakhtiar, tried to arrange for Bakhtiar to go to Paris, present his resignation to Khomeini, and be immediately reappointed by him. Khomeini seems to have accepted this, but in the last minute some hardline clerics prevailed on him to change his mind and to demand that Bakhtiar resign before receiving him. It made no sense for Bakhtiar to see Khomeini as a private citizen, and the deal fell through.[14] As the state literally disintegrated, Khomeini returned to Iran on February 1, and named Bazargan prime minister on February 5. After some fighting between military units and revolutionaries broke out on February 9, the armed forces declared their political neutrality two days later, and soon after Bakhtiar went into hiding and later to Paris, where he led an exile opposition group until he was assassinated, probably by agents of the regime, in 1991.

Two points emerge from this analysis. First, the Shah's unsuccessful liberalization confirms Juan Linz's insight about the importance of timing in transitions: delayed actions are likely to be belated actions.[15] When a caretaker administration was possible in 1977, the Shah merely changed prime ministers. When a coalition government was at least conceivable, he charged a caretaker administration with organizing elections. When he finally named an opposition politician prime minister, the state had disintegrated to such an extent that many ministers were not even allowed into their ministries by the employees. The most plausible explanation for these belated actions is that deep down the Shah did not want to democratize Iran, that at each juncture he reacted to pressure, while trying to preserve as much of his rule as possible: in 1977 his power, in 1978 his throne, and in 1979 his dynasty. However, the Shah's lack of commitment to democratization alone does not explain the eventual emergence of another nondemocratic regime, for an opposition committed to democracy might have wrested it from the Shah. Given Khomeini's 1971 blueprint for Islamic government[16] and his charismatic hold on the mobilized masses, one is tempted to consider the outcome of the transition a foregone conclusion, whatever the Shah's motives. But the hypothesis that there can be no democracy without democrats is falsified by the experience of many other nations, where democracy resulted not from a general commitment of people to democratic ideals, but simply from a need to structure political conflict in a way that was acceptable to the adversaries. Which is why timing is so crucial to Iran's transition: in 1977 the masses were not mobilized yet, and the liberal politicians still had the upper hand in the opposition. Popular enthusiasm might have been channelled into the electoral arena.

Second, both structural factors and human agency affect the likelihood that one or the other type of interim government will usher in the new regime. The sultanistic traits of the Shah's regime rendered a coalition government very unlikely, but in the end an orderly transfer of power was prevented by Khomeini's personal choice. The chaotic circumstances of the revolutionaries' seizure of power left Bazargan's administration with "confining conditions"[17] that made his task almost impossibly difficult.

"A KNIFE WITHOUT A BLADE"

Formation

Bazargan was in many ways an ideal choice for prime minister. As a pioneer of religious modernism in Iran, he had spent his adult life trying to awaken believers to their duties as citizens, while at the same time propagating an interpretation of Islam that in the political realm called for democracy. Jailed a number of times under the Shah, he had been elected chairman of the moderate opposition's umbrella organization, the Iranian Committee for the Defense of Freedom and Human Rights, during the liberalization of 1977–8. His prestige was high with both secular liberals and religious activists. His nomination was greeted with enthusiasm by the mobilized masses, but his legitimacy was to a large extent derivative. Bazargan admits this when, in response to critics who charge him with having facilitated the establishment of a nondemocratic regime, he states that it was Khomeini who named him prime minister, not he who appointed Khomeini leader of the revolution. A reluctant convert to Khomeini's revolutionary strategy of *guerre à outrance* against the Shah, he did not hide his gradualism after becoming prime minister. On February 9, he told an enthusiastic crowd at Teheran University: "don't expect me to act in the manner of [Khomeini] who . . . moves like a bulldozer, crushing rocks, roots, and stones in his path. I am a delicate passenger car and must ride on paved and smooth roads."[18]

To fill his cabinet, Bazargan had a very small pool of men to chose from. Ministers had to be untainted by any association with the Shah's regime, they had to be, if not practicing Muslims, at least favorably inclined to religion, and they had to have some technocratic skills to get the country going again. Bazargan chose mainly old associates from his party, the LMI, and a professional association he had founded, the Islamic Association of Engineers, but secular liberals were also represented. Their leader, Karim Sanjabi, became minister of foreign affairs.[19]

While the cabinet was to act as the executive branch until the institutionalization of a new regime, the "Council of the Revolution," which had been formed even before Khomeini's return and on which his clerical followers were in the majority, was to oversee its activities as a substitute for parliament. It was Bazargan's understanding that until a new constitution could come into force, the 1906 document should guide the provisional government, except for the provisions on the monarchy, which were transferred to Khomeini.[20]

From the outset, the provisional government was bedeviled by a dilemma. On the one hand, it was a "revolutionary" regime, formed at the height of the revolution's triumph as the focus of the revolutionaries' hopes and expectations. On the other hand, it inherited the old state apparatus, which had largely broken down during the strikes of the Shah's regime's final months. The prerevolutionary fusion of regime and state mentioned earlier meant that the delegitimation of the Shah's regime had also deprived the state of legitimacy; yet Bazargan and his friends needed that state to fulfill their tasks. They were ministers, but were called elitist when they acted accordingly.[21] To appease strikers and lure them back to work, the Shah's last prime ministers had offered huge pay raises to government employees. Its treasury empty, the provisional government was held to the promises made by its predecessors. Telephone, water, and electricity bills had not been settled for months. When the government attempted to make customers pay, it was criticized for not heeding the needs of the poor.[22]

The economic situation was catastrophic, as most industries had stood still for months. Many entrepreneurs and managers had fled abroad, often taking their liquid assets with them; many enterprises were, in fact, bankrupt. Bazargan's initial policy was to try to start economic activity again by inviting Iranians to return. An economic liberal as well as a political liberal, he resisted nationalizations.[23] But in the end Khomeini ordered all banks, insurance companies, and most large industrial enterprises nationalized, which was done in June and July. The only bright spot was Iran's oil industry, which under the able leadership of Hassan Nazih, who was appointed managing director of the National Iranian Oil Company, managed to resume the production and export of oil in spite of many foreign expatriates' departure from Iran.[24] But soon Nazih, who was also a long-standing human rights activist and chairman of the Iranian Bar Association, became the first victim of the hardliners.

In foreign affairs, the government followed Mossadegh's policy of negative equilibrium, which called for neutrality and equidistance from the two superpowers. It also wanted to maintain courteous relations with foreign countries (except Israel and South Africa), especially the United States. The Carter administration, having first supported the Shah, tried to come to terms with the provisional government, which it regarded as the lesser of two evils. This was a kiss of death, as at the same time the U.S. government tried to maintain a secret listening post close to the Soviet border without informing the government of its existence, and sent a number of CIA agents to Iran, some of whom briefed ministers.[25] Hardline revolutionaries, both on the left and in the Islamist camp, could now depict Bazargan's team as betraying the revolution's anti-imperialist thrust.

In addition to the existential contradiction discussed previously, two factors contributed most to the provisional government's ultimate demise: the multiplicity of power centers and clerical interference.

Multiple power centers

As the state apparatus, and in particular the security forces, disintegrated in late 1978, citizens more or less spontaneously set up parallel structures to provide for basic administrative and security needs. Activist clerics often played a leading role. When the provisional government found itself at the helm of the old state, they found that each state agency had a revolutionary equivalent, starting at the top: the Council of the Revolution fast became a counterpole to the cabinet; for instance it conducted relations with the United States without informing the foreign ministry.[26]

The first of these revolutionary organizations to appear were the revolutionary committees, the *komitehs*. In the last weeks of 1978 young people, mostly from the lower classes, had formed neighborhood committees to organize demonstrations, strikes, and resistance against the state, and also provide for security. In the course of the February clashes, a number of arsenals had been stormed, during which the revolutionaries had obtained weapons. After the revolutionaries' seizure of power, armed komiteh members took the law into their own hands. In the name of neutralizing counterrevolutionary activity, they arrested and harassed citizens, seized property, and sometimes even fought with each other, paying no heed to the provisional government's efforts to restore law and order. As the police force was gradually reorganized, the komitehs became a counterweight to it.

The second revolutionary organization, the revolutionary tribunals, sprouted under the leadership of clerical self-proclaimed judges. In January when leaders of the opposition negotiated with high ranking figures of the regime, such as members of parliament and army officers, in order to induce them to agree to a peaceful transfer of power, Khomeini had said that in Islam repentance was accepted until the last minute.[27] Reassured, many minor regime figures had stayed in Iran. But as soon as the revolutionaries had seized power, the komitehs began rounding up officials of the *ancien régime* and handing them over to the revolutionary tribunals. After a few weeks the tribunals extended their reach and began summarily sentencing men and women accused of moral and sexual offenses.[28] These tribunals worked independently of the ministry of justice and the country's judiciary. Lawyers and judges had been a key element in the anti-Shah coalition, and when the minister of justice, Asadollah Mobasheri, a respected lawyer associated with the National Front, in spite of repeated requests failed to bring the tribunals' activity under government control, he resigned in protest on June 20.

A third organization, whose importance grew only later, was the revolutionary guards, or *Pasdaran*. Even within the provisional government there were some, like Mostafa Chamran (defense minister after September 18) and Ebrahim Yazdi (foreign minister after April 16), who mistrusted the armed forces sufficiently to call for a parallel armed force loyal to the revolution. The formation of the Pasdaran was announced on May 5. Although Chamran and Yazdi tried to wield some influence among them, they soon lost control to hardliners, and the revolutionary guards began in fact competing with the army.

While the Council of the Revolution, the komitehs, the revolutionary tribunals, and the Pasdaran paralleled respectively the provisional government, the police, the judiciary, and the armed forces, in other state agencies ad hoc revolutionary or Islamic committees made life difficult for the officials named by the government. In Washington and Paris young militants who had appeared out of nowhere seized control of the Iranian embassies, prompting the minister of foreign affairs, Karim Sanjabi, to resign on April 16.[29] In the oil industry, Hassan Nazih's pragmatic management came under attack by all sorts of Islamic committees.[30] Finally, in many enterprises workers' councils were created, often by radical leftists, that disputed the provisional government's plans for relaunching the economy.[31] In Bazargan's own words, the provisional government was a "knife without a blade."

Clerical interference

In light of Khomeini's known blueprint for clerical government, the moderate politicians allied to him viewed his plans for the future with suspicion. When Sanjabi asked him in Paris about the future role of the clergy, he had answered that its role was to preach and teach, not to rule. Politicians who believed in Islam and had technical skills had to govern the country.[32] Bazargan himself had always been of an anticlerical bent, as he blamed the clergy's narrow-mindedness and obscurantism for the decline of Muslim societies. But even he concluded after meeting Khomeini in Paris in October 1978 that Khomeini "wanted everything except for the clergy to end up governing the country. Had he felt otherwise, I would not have accepted the post of prime minister."[33] Bazargan hoped that by accepting the position of prime minister, he would be able to influence the new regime from within.

As soon as Khomeini was back in Iran, he began undermining the work of the provisional government. On February 16 a number of military leaders were executed by revolutionary tribunals. When the government complained that the accused had not been tried in court, Khomeini retorted that they were not accused but were in fact guilty, and therefore needed no trials.[34] The komitehs, revolutionary tribunals, and Pasdaran cooperated with each other, although there was almost no coordination among them. Khomeini and the Council of the Revolution were caught between supporting the provisional government, which they needed for running the country, and backing the initiatives of the revolutionary organizations. When Khomeini appointed the provisional government, he proclaimed obedience to it a religious duty. But the initiatives of the revolutionary organizations, such as the execution of the chiefs of the Shah's secret police, SAVAK, or even the humiliation of rich members of the former establishment and the seizure of their property, were very popular among the grass roots that had brought down the Shah with their demonstrations and sacrifices. This led Khomeini and the Council of the Revolution increasingly to side with the hardline revolutionaries, also to limit the appeal of the radical left which competed with the radical Islamists for the favor of the masses and capitalized on the cabinet's unrevolutionary moderation.

Although a few clerics such as Ay. Hassan Qomi in Mashhad and Ays. Mohammad-Kazem Shariatmadari and Nasser Makarem Shirazi in Qum complained about the lawlessness engendered by the komitehs and revolutionary tribunals, most of the politically active clerics got involved. One disciple of Khomeini, Ay. Sadeq Khalkhali, became the head of the revolutionary tribunals, and takes pride in having personally ordered the execution of former prime minister Amir-Abbas Hoveida on April 7, against the strong objections of the government.

Khomeini's son-in-law, Ho. Shehabeddin Eshraqi, personally led the campaign to oust Hassan Nazih. The latter had incurred the particular wrath of the clergy by being the first member of the government publicly to speak out against the creeping Islamization of society, which was not government policy but was promoted by the revolutionary organizations. At the end of May 1979, the Iranian Bar Association held its conference in Teheran. Nazih gave a speech in which he stated that to find Islamic solutions to all of Iran's economic, political, and judicial problems was not only unnecessary but even impossible and disadvantageous.[35] Nazih went into hiding in September, and later left Iran for exile in Paris.

In their struggle against hardline clerics, the provisional government was handicapped by the weakness of the political parties on which it was based. In a transition to democracy, an interim government is legitimated by the assumption that the parties represented in it also represent significant sectors of the electorate and that it will generate the political space for parties to expand. In Iran the moderate parties, not strong to begin with, were further weakened by Khomeini, who insisted when he appointed Bazargan that the members of the cabinet desist from any partisan activity and run the government in a nonpartisan way. Thereupon the Liberation Movement of Iran ceased functioning, as most leaders were busy enough in their governmental posts. This applied less to the National Front, whose representation in the government constantly fell, but the important point to note is that moderate parties in Iran were very weak to begin with. It is impossible to say with certainty what backing they had in the population compared to radical leftists and Islamists, but their organizational weakness is beyond doubt. This was due partly to the moderates' somewhat elitist conception of politics, which was a legacy of Mossadegh's heyday in which only the middle class had been politically mobilized, and partly to long years of royal dictatorship, during which all opposition party activity had been severely repressed. The liberalization preceding the revolution had simply been too short, and also too eventful, to allow for the constitution of strong moderate parties.[36]

The moderates found themselves confronted with radical leftists who had honed their organizational skills in the underground, and radical Islamists who disposed of a preexisting organizational network, the mosques. However, the Shi'ite clergy is loosely organized, not all clerics approve of political activity, and among those who do not all are radical Islamists. For this reason five followers of Khomeini, all members of the Council of the Revolution, deemed the existing clerical networks insufficient and founded a new political party in February 1979. They were Ay. Abdolkarim Musavi Ardabili, and Hos. Javad Bahonar, Mohammad Beheshti, Ali Khameneh'i, and Ali-Akbar Hashemi Rafsanjani. They called their party the Islamic Republican Party (IRP), and deliberately announced its foundation after the old regime's demise, so as to underline that, unlike the LMI, it represented a complete break with the past. The party program called for the establishment of an Islamic order. It had tremendous financial resources at its disposal, Khomeini having authorized the channeling of part of the religious tithes paid to him into party coffers.[37] In the course of 1979 gangs of club-wielding militants loosely affiliated with the party began harassing secular groups and their press organs.

In order to improve coordination between the government and the Council of the Revolution, Bazargan proposed in July that the two interpenetrate. He and three other ministers joined the council, while six council members were invited to join the government as vice-ministers. Of the five founders of the IRP, Bahonar, Khameneh'i, and Hashemi Rafsanjani went to the ministries of education, defense, and interior, respectively, but the two others, Beheshti and Musavi Ardabili, refused to join the ministry of justice, where Bazargan wanted them to bring the activities of the revolutionary tribunals under government control. Finally, Ho. Mohammad-Reza Mahdavi Kani, who headed the komitehs but was not a party member, also joined the interior ministry. Nothing came of this attempt to improve coordination between the two bodies.

As if the opposition of the radical Islamists and leftists was not enough, two former associates of the LMI and National Front leadership joined the radicals in denouncing the insufficient revolutionary zeal of the provisional government. These were Abolhassan Banisadr, a politically quite liberal, but economically socialist Islamist who was personally very close to Khomeini, and Sadeq Qotbzadeh, who headed the radio and television organization. Banisadr crisscrossed the country giving talks in mosques in which he criticized government policy, while Qotbzadeh, despite his former links with the LMI, opened the airwaves more to the government's critics than to its defenders. As for the written press, it was remarkably free in 1979, at least until August. But here too, moderate politicians had neglected to set up newspapers to defend their position, and thus most of the press was against the government. By the summer of 1979 the provisional government was under attack by radical Islamists, leftists, Banisadr, and the mass media. Two clerical leaders favorably inclined to the provisional government, Ay. Morteza Motahhari and the very popular Ay. Mahmud Taleqani, both old personal friends of Bazargan, died in 1979, the first in a terrorist attack the second of a heart attack. This left the government without allies among the politically active clergy.

The growing gap between Khomeini and the IRP on one side, and the provisional government on the other, poses the question as to why Khomeini had asked Bazargan to head the interim administration in the first place. It later transpired that in early 1979 that part of the politicized clergy that wanted direct power, which I have elsewhere defined as "clerisy,"[38] felt unready to exercise it.[39] They needed Bazargan's and his friends' organizational and technical skills, and told Khomeini so. Bazargan, in turn, underestimated the clerisy's political acumen, a result of the contempt in which he holds the clergy generally. Taking the three IRP leaders into his cabinet only helped them gain governmental experience and self-confidence. When Bazargan was interviewed by Oriana Fallaci shortly before his fall, he told her that his biggest mistake had been to underestimate the danger of clerical interference:

If we in the [LMI] – namely we who believe in God and Islam but not in the clergy – had been more alert; if, instead of being distracted, we had behaved like a party, then this mess wouldn't have occurred. Yes, we could have prevented it. The fact is that we were so overwhelmed by the country's problems, by the urgency of getting it back in shape, by the need to prevent excesses, that we didn't realize we were missing the boat.[40]

Towards the end of the provisional government's tenure, the question of Iran's future political institutions overshadowed all other issues. It was here that the clerisy outwitted the democrats with the gravest consequences for Iran's future.

INSTITUTIONALIZING THE NEW ORDER

The new constitution

Preparing a new constitution and holding elections had been specified as the main task of the provisional government. First, a plebiscite was held on March 30 and 31 to ratify the abolition of the monarchy. Participation was high, and 98.2 percent of the electorate voted in favor of an Islamic republic. The exercise was not strictly speaking a democratic one in procedural terms, since a non-Islamic republic was no option and royalists could not campaign against the abolition of the monarchy, but what with society's remarkable unity and unanimity the outcome probably reflected public opinion fairly accurately. One reason was that the institutional content of the "Islamic republic" had not been specified. For many Iranians a republic in a country whose population was over 90 percent Muslim would be by definition an Islamic republic. Casting his vote, the prime minister said: "The Iranian republic will be Islamic and democratic," although Khomeini had refused the qualifier "democratic" as being "Western."[41] Giving the Islamic republic concrete form was the next task.

A number of Iranian lawyers had been preparing the draft of a constitution since early January 1979. On June 18, the government presented this text to the public. It was basically modeled after the French Fifth Republic, with an executive presidency elected by universal suffrage, but a unicameral, popularly elected parliament, a majority of whose members had to invest the prime minister in charge of running the government. The document was essentially a secular democratic one, although the preamble mentioned the Islamic character of the state. Khomeini was satisfied with it and wanted an early second plebiscite for the public to approve it.

However, the draft constitution did not meet with universal approval. Some religious circles complained that it was not Islamic enough, while secular forces considered it too deferential toward religion. Bazargan was on record for having promised the nation a constitutional assembly, and he made the fateful blunder of insisting that one be convened. There was some argument about its size, but in the end it was agreed not to have a full size constitutional assembly but only a smaller "Assembly of Experts" with seventy-three members to review the draft and make small changes.

Elections were held to this Assembly of Experts on August 3, and when the results were in, secular Iranians realized with horror that of the seventy-three members fifty-five were clerics. The National Front and

Ay. Shariatmadari had called for a boycott of the elections, but given the secular parties' insufficient implantation in the provinces, clerics, who were often the only locally known figures, would have been elected in many places anyway. Under the leadership of IRP-head Beheshti, the assembly changed the draft beyond recognition. The powers of the presidency were reduced and under the impetus of Banisadr, who had been the second largest vote getter in Teheran after Taleqani, the nationalization of foreign trade and a number of other socialist provisions were inserted in it. But most importantly, the assembly proceeded to graft a theocratic element on the draft.

Among the Shi'ite clergy, there had always been a strain of thought that considered all secular government illegitimate, and that therefore invested the clergy with political power as well.[42] A majority of the hierarchy had always opposed this view and made accommodations with secular rulers, but Khomeini revived the other theory, which became known as *velayat-e faqih,* "dominion of the jurisprudent."[43] His political ascendancy had popularized this concept among radical junior clerics, and the IRP pushed for it, although all other senior religious leaders in Iran, such as Ay. Shariatmadari, opposed it.[44] In September 1979 the assembly began debating *velayat-e faqih,* and by October it became clear that the assembly was creating a document that enshrined theocratic rule.[45] Thereupon Bazargan and a number of ministers went to Khomeini to ask him to dissolve the assembly, but he refused. The final draft of the constitution was presented to the public on November 14, after the provisional government's resignation. It vested supreme and unaccountable power in the person of a supreme religious leader, but maintained a popularly elected president and parliament without instituting a single party system: Iran became a diarchy. The constitution was full of internal contradictions,[46] the political consequences of which would become apparent as early as 1980.

The end of the provisional government

By the fall of 1979, Bazargan's position became ever more tenuous. He had offered his resignation to Khomeini several times, but the leader of the revolution had always refused to accept it, telling Bazargan that it was his religious duty to carry on. In late October Bazargan and his foreign minister Ebrahim Yazdi left for Algiers, to attend Algeria's national independence day celebrations. Worried about Soviet encroachments in neighboring Afghanistan, they had a meeting with the U.S. national security advisor, Zbigniew Brzezinski, who, among the members of the Carter administration, was most hostile to the Iranian revolution. A few days earlier, the Shah's odyssey through Egypt, Morocco,

Panama, and Mexico had ended when he was admitted to the United States for treatment of his terminal cancer. In protest against Bazargan's meeting with Brzezinski at a time when the Shah was in America,[47] young radicals stormed the U.S. embassy in Teheran and took the diplomats hostage.[48] Mortified, Bazargan tendered his resignation. This time Khomeini accepted.

The end of the transition

After the seizure of the hostages, Iranian politics reached a feverish pitch. The Council of the Revolution, in which Bazargan remained a member, took over governmental authority. On December 2 and 3, in a plebiscite again marred by many irregularities, the constitution was approved by over 99 percent of the electorate. Despite its publicly stated reservations, the LMI had called for a yes vote. On January 25, 1980, presidential elections were held. The IRP had to withdraw its candidate in the last minute because it turned out he was of Afghan origin, and so Abolhassan Banisadr won with about 75 percent of the vote. Ahmad Madani, a former defense minister in the provisional government and National Front leader, came second with over 2 million votes in spite of strong propaganda unleashed against him by the hostage takers, who claimed to have found evidence linking him with U.S. interests. All eight candidates in this election had their roots in Mossadegh's movement and were politically liberals. But in the parliamentary elections that followed in the spring, the Mossadeghists' insufficient attention to grass roots organization came to haunt them. Wherever they ran, LMI and National Front leaders did very well, despite IRP-dominated local authorities' attempts to rig the elections. Bazargan was a top voter getter in Teheran and Sanjabi came first in his native Kermanshah, which prompted the authorities to cancel the elections in that city.[49] But in the vast majority of constituencies no candidates had been proposed by the LMI, the National Front, or Banisadr's office. The result was a crushing victory of the IRP and nonaffiliated clerics who soon gravitated into its orbit. A number of secular leaders, including Madani, were prevented from taking their seats, and so the IRP had an even more comfortable majority.[50] This majority soon came into conflict with the president.

The constitution had diminished the powers of the presidency, but Banisadr refused to be a figure head. He considered himself the democratically chosen leader of Iran and he had Khomeini's confidence. The logic of a semipresidential system, with its dual sources of democratic legitimacy, came into play.[51] Also, the fact that presidential elections had been held before parliamentary elections, added to the visibility, and hence importance, of the presidency. Yet Banisadr's policies were constantly opposed by parliament and the IRP. *Cohabitation* did not work, and Banisadr became in fact leader of the opposition. Bazargan and his colleagues from the provisional government forgave the president his past insults and attacks and loyally (but critically) supported him. By the spring of 1981 conflict between Banisadr, to whom many leftist and liberal parties, both secular and Islamist, had gravitated, and the IRP escalated. Khomeini first tried to stay above the fray, but in the end sided with his fellow clerics. On June 21, parliament declared Banisadr "politically incompetent" and the next day, using the powers vested in him by the constitution, Khomeini deposed Iran's first president.[52] A few days earlier, Khomeini had charged the National Front with apostasy. Both Banisadr and Sanjabi went underground and later left the country.

In the summer of 1981 two explosions decimated the IRP leadership. On June 28, Beheshti was killed with more than seventy other figures. On August 30, Banisadr's successor, Ali Raja'i, and Prime Minister Javad Bahonar were killed in another explosion. But the regime survived the deaths of the president and the prime minister and began a campaign of terror to eliminate its opponents that only abated somewhat in 1982. Bazargan and a dwindling number of liberals remained in parliament, but were not allowed to run in subsequent elections. Unimpaired by any opposition, the government of the Islamic republic implemented its Islamizing policies beginning in 1981.

The end of the transition in Iran can be marked in two ways. The institutions of the new regime were in place by the spring of 1980, but the regime found its definitive form only in the summer of 1981, when after Banisadr's ouster the IRP dominated the entire government apparatus.

CONCLUSION

The provisional government survived for nine months against tremendous odds: opposition from the radical left and Islamists, armed autonomist stirrings among Iran's Kurds, Turkomans, and Arabs, and Iraqi provocations which were settled through diplomacy.[53] All the while Iranian society was shaken by a deep crisis of identity, which pitted Westernized Iranians against the non-Westernized majority of the population. As liberal Islamists, Bazargan and his colleagues from the LMI tried to bridge the societal gap, but Khomeini's charismatic hold on the people, and the energies set free by the revolution overwhelmed them. With the benefit of hindsight the tenure of the Bazargan administration exemplifies the "rule of the moderates" in Crane Brinton's revolutionary pattern.[54] The confining conditions of the revolution were simply too unfavorable for the provisional government to be the harbinger of democracy.

The institutional legacy of the transition period is ambiguous. The structure of government was tailor-made for Khomeini and thus did not survive his death on June 3, 1989. The constitution stipulated that the incumbent of the position of supreme leader be a man vested with the highest religious authority. But none of Khomeini's peers agreed with the principle of *velayat-e faqih,* which meant that there simply was no successor for him. Also, the coexistence of a president and a prime minister became increasingly unwieldy. Consequently the constitution was changed in the summer of 1989. The position of supreme leader was opened to clerics of lesser rank, and the position of prime minister was abolished thus strengthening the presidency.[55] President Khameneh'i, who had replaced Raja'i upon his assassination in 1981, became the new leader, while Hashemi Rafsanjani, who had already wielded great power as speaker of parliament, became president. Government was thereby somewhat streamlined.

Constitutional government does not imply liberal democracy, but it does imply the rule of law. This, the Islamic Republic has failed to uphold. The constitution does contain certain safeguards for due process and civil liberties, but they are routinely disregarded by the regime. Like the Shah before them, the Islamic republicans often do not respect their own legality, and corruption is more rampant than ever. Nonetheless, the existence of these safeguards has allowed dissidents around Bazargan to ground their opposition against the government in the constitution, which may be one reason they have been allowed to survive.

And yet, there is a major qualitative difference between the Shah's dictatorship and the regime that followed. Even though only a very narrow range of opinions is tolerated, political life is more open and pluralistic than before the revolution. In 1987 the IRP was dissolved after factional disputes within it became paralyzing, and since then Iran has had a no party system. The vigor of the parliament has been the most astonishing feature of the regime. Elections to it have been partially competitive, debates within it have been wide ranging and adversarial, and on a number of occasions the legislature has refused to bestow its vote of confidence on ministerial candidates. The press, for its part, is livelier and less deferential toward the government than under the Shah and often criticizes not only individual ministers but also the president. On the other hand, repression has been much harder, and human rights violations much more widespread than under the Shah. Iran's political regime is a very odd mixture of democratic, authoritarian, and totalitarian elements.

8

From revolution to democracy in Portugal: The roles and stages of the provisional governments

THOMAS C. BRUNEAU

INTRODUCTION

Portugal was the first of the current and continuing transitions from authoritarian to democratic regimes. It is particularly significant in this study as it is the only successful transition which also underwent a revolution, transforming not only political but also economic and social structures. In the terms of the editors, it was a revolutionary provisional government that emerged after the overthrow of the *ancien régime*. The overthrow, in the form of a military coup, led to a revolution in which radical elements were ascendent during five of the six provisional governments between April 25, 1974, and June 1976. Moderate elements finally prevailed, however, and a democratic regime was established that continues to manifest the structures and processes of its founding. Indeed, the patterns established and issues raised during the provisional governments continue to define politics until the present. My purpose here is to briefly describe the political chronology of the twenty-seven month period of the provisional governments and explain how the revolution resulted in a democratic regime. The review of patterns and issues will bring the discussion up to the present. The perspective taken will focus on the processes of the provisional governments which were both the results of and led to democracy in Portugal.[1]

BACKGROUND

On April 25, 1974, a group of approximately two hundred junior officers gathered together in the Armed Forces Movement (MFA) overthrew the government of Marcello Caetano, thereby bringing to an end the Estado Novo created by António de Oliveira Salazar in 1930 and overseen by him until his incapacitation in 1968. The Estado Novo was a model of the classic authoritarian regime which sought to maintain socioeconomic structures of the past through denying political representation to all but a small segment of the population. Much of the past was indeed conserved, and Portugal remained the most underdeveloped country in Western Europe. Undoubtedly the most significant characteristic of the past justifying the authoritarian regime was the colonial empire in Africa, South Asia, and Southeast Asia. The origins of the coup are found in the unwillingness or inability of the regime to find a political solution to the wars in the African colonies of Angola, Guinea-Bissau, and Mozambique, which had begun in 1961. Despite widespread disaffection from the regime, the coup was exclusively a military event with minimal bloodshed and virtually no involvement by civilians. There were no legal means to change the government, and the opposition was too weak and intimidated to exert any pressure for change. There was little violence in the coup as virtually nobody sought to defend the regime; the government had in fact lost legitimacy. When pushed it simply collapsed, and with it went the elaborate structure of political and social control which had largely obviated the need for repression. The MFA knew that the wars in Africa could not be won, they were tired of fighting, and they became convinced that the regime would never negotiate. The only solution was to overthrow the government. The junior officers who made the coup did not anticipate it at the time, but they made a break with the past in more than political structures and processes. They would have the opportunity to begin anew, to create a new regime, with a completely new basis of legitimacy. The problem was that they did not anticipate the total collapse of the government and were not prepared to replace it.[2] Political action during the following two years would be mainly about who were the actors and what kind of regime would they construct. The provisional governments were the results of the struggle for power and symbolized plateaus on the way to its construction.

To the extent that there was any blueprint for the MFA's view of Portugal in the future, it was their program broadcast to the nation on April 26 justifying the coup. In retrospect it turned out to be a crucial document since it committed the MFA to work towards a democratic regime. The brief document stated that Portugal was in crisis and attributed it to the wars in Africa. The prerequisite for any improvement in Portugal was a political solution to the wars. They indicated that the old regime would be dismembered, and immediate democratization and serious socioeconomic changes would be forthcoming. In destroying the old regime, the MFA promised expanded mobilization, pluralism, and reforms. They promised, in summary, what came to be known as the three Ds of Decolonization, Democratization, and Development.[3] The MFA explicitly linked democratization to decolonization to make the loss of the colonies more acceptable to a country which had held colonies for half a millenium, which the old regime had identified with Portugal's existence as an independent country, and upon which economic groups relied for cheap supplies and ready markets. They promised the convocation of a Constituent National Assembly, within twelve months, to be elected by direct and secret universal suffrage. In sum, the MFA overthrew the old regime and proclaimed that there would be fundamental changes in much that had characterized Portugal during the five decades of the Estado Novo.

The main political dynamic during 1974–5 was based on the political and military relationship between the MFA and General Antonio Spinola. The MFA made the coup but the two hundred junior officers were not cohesive and had slight confidence in their minimal political experience. In contrast to the case in much of Latin America, the Portuguese junior officers were operators with extensive experience in warfare, but no experience in politics. They thus asked General Spinola to form a Junta of National Salvation which included him as provisional president and two senior officers from each of the three services. General Spinola had been the military governor in Guinea-Bissau and through meetings with Marcello Caetano had tried to convince him to negotiate an end to the endless wars. When Caetano was not responsive, Spinola published in early 1974 his *Portugal and the Future* which opened up to discussion a topic that had been excluded from the agenda; that is, decolonization. Spinola was a charismatic general and was an obvious choice for the junior officers unsure of their support within the military let alone society in general. However, Spinola had previously demonstrated political aspirations, and increasingly symbolized an orientation that was not in sympathy with the rapidly changing environment in Portugal after the coup. This concerned in particular the extent and speed of decolonization, the structure of the economy, and the degree of popular mobilization. While the center of political dynamics would focus on Spinola and the MFA, the provisional governments symbolized both the status of political activity in Portugal and gradually provided the elements of a new democratic regime. It was the political struggle for power that determined the emergence of democracy, and the forum for political action became increasingly the provisional governments.

THE PROVISIONAL GOVERNMENTS, 1974–6

The First Provisional Government was formed in mid-May 1974 following extensive discussion among General Spinola and the Junta of National Salvation, whose Coordinating Committee represented the MFA, and the emerging political parties. The MFA Program did not provide for the formation of political parties, but rather permitted "political associations, possible embroyos of future political parties." In fact, there was an immediate burst of party formation, and within three months there were some fifty groups formed, mobilized, and competing with one another for power.[4] The formation and competition created a tremendous momentum of political involvement and radicalization, particularly since most were located on the left of the political spectrum. Within a year there would be twelve officially recognized major political parties. In this area, as in others, the MFA lost control of the situation.

It was agreed that in the provisional government General Spinola would be president and the prime minister would be Adelino Palma Carlos, a law professor and friend of Spinola. The remainder of the cabinet was composed of civil and military figures who represented the emerging political forces. The leaders of the previously clandestine Portuguese Communist Party (PCP), the newly formed Popular Democratic Party (PPD), and the newly formed Socialist Party (PS), respectively Alvaro Cunhal, Sa Carneiro, and Mario Soares, would be in the cabinet. In addition to the cabinet, a Council of State was created to act as a type of supreme legislative body to guarantee adherence to the MFA Program. It was composed of the seven-man Junta of National Salvation, the seven-man MFA Coordinating Committee, and seven individuals selected to meet Spinola's satisfaction. Governing was very difficult with this new and probably unworkable structure since it included elements seeking to dominate the others, and there were no agreed upon rules of the game. The demands of governing were also extremely onerous in the context of decolonization and pent up claims by labor. It must be remembered that virtually all of the old regime with its structures of repression and labor control had already disintegrated. The provisional government had to face extremely difficult problems with virtually no previous political or administrative background and no established structures.

As part of the struggle for power, elements in the MFA established a military command structure which greatly corroded Spinola's control (as president and thus commander in chief) of the armed forces. The Operational Command for the Continent (COPCON) was created ostensibly to maintain law and order, and was headed by the operational commander of the coup, Major Otelo Saraiva de Carvalho. At the same time President Spinola and Prime Minister Palma Carlos proposed that the Prime Minister's powers be expanded to better deal with the multiple crises, that elections to the Constituent Assembly be delayed until 1976, and presidential elections be held within three months. Assuming that Spinola would be elected president, he would greatly increase his powers in relationship to the MFA and the emerging political parties. The proposal was rejected and Palma Carlos resigned in July. He was replaced

by Army Colonel Vasco Goncalves, who was the most senior officer on
the MFA Coordinating Committee. "The real meaning of the Goncalves
selection was not that the MFA had 'shifted left,' but rather that the
MFA leaders had acted to preserve the revolutionary movement of
events against what they increasingly perceived as the reactionary intent
of a man who was only titularly their leader."[5] At the same time, key
members of the MFA, Majors Melo Antunes and Vitor Alves, also entered the cabinet. Thus the MFA was asserting its power following the
lapse of allowing their coup to be captured by Spinola and his associates.
Otelo commanded COPCON, Goncalves from the coordinating committee became prime minister, and Majors Antunes and Alves were in
the cabinet. The Second Provisional Government was thus both more
military-dominated than the first and much further to the left. This was
due to the clear emergence of the MFA and to the increasingly dominant
role of the PCP with the MFA in politics and society in general. The PCP
pursued a strategy of supporting the MFA and seeking to impose their
Marxist-Leninist ideology on the generally ingenuous junior officers. At
the same time, the PCP took increasing control of labor and much of the
media, and encouraged takeovers in industry and agriculture. The PCP
did not make the coup, but they played a central role in turning it into
a revolution.[6]

With continuing mobilization and dramatic developments in labor
within Portugal and decolonization in Africa, Spinola attempted to consolidate his power in September. He encouraged the center and right in
Portugal to manifest their support for him at a weekend demonstration to
be held in Lisbon on September 28. In the face of serious rumors from
the right and left, and popular mobilization, there was much concern with
violence. Finally, in a showdown between Spinola and Otelo, the rally
was aborted and Spinola resigned. He was replaced by General Francisco
da Costa Gomes who was Spinola's chief of staff but more in sympathy
with the MFA than had been his predecessor. Thus ended the Second
Provisional Government.

The next three provisional governments saw the same president, Costa
Gomes, and prime minister, Vasco Goncalves. The cabinets changed,
however, in line with the jockeying for power among the different emerging and consolidating groups and parties. As underlying themes were the
continuing deterioration in the economy, decolonization, polarization,
and a sense of likelihood of civil war with major divisions in the armed
forces. The MFA, which was also a group or movement (since it did not
represent all of the armed forces) sought to institutionalize itself and its
preeminent role in governing. Political parties were forming, and in this
and other areas, foreign actors became heavily involved.

The elections for the Constituent Assembly, which were promised within a year in the MFA Program, were almost called off. While the motivations and details remain unclear, Spinola was involved in an attempted coup on March 11, 1975. The coup was easily put down and Spinola and other plotters fled into exile. In reaction, and taking advantage of the opportunity created by the virtual elimination of the right, the military and civilian left ascended very rapidly. A self-proclaimed Revolutionary Council assumed full government control in replacing the Junta of National Salvation and Council of State and subsuming the MFA Coordinating Committee. It was formally responsible solely to the Assembly of the MFA. Recognizing the virtual control of the military, the six most prominent political parties were forced to sign a pact on April 11 which sought to institutionalize the role of the MFA to "guide" Portugal. This was definitely the ascent of the radicals. The immediate policies after the attempted coup reflected and promoted the radicalization encouraged by the PCP and groups to its left with a wave of nationalizations. The takeover of banks and insurance companies was extremely important as they owned much of the capital in other areas, including the media.

Despite the radical and chaotic conditions, and qualified by the terms of the pact with the MFA, elections for a constituent assembly were held on April 25. By all objective accounts, the elections were fair and honest. Twelve parties ran and the results were surprising to some as the PCP (13 percent) came in third after the PS (38 percent) and PPD (26 percent) but ahead of the Social Democratic Center party (CDS) (8 percent). The elections, however, resolved little as the political struggle was now increasingly between factions of the MFA with high involvement by the PCP and other political parties. The economy and society saw continuing radicalization with takeovers of businesses, landholdings, and the media. In this context of radicalization and drawing on his party's plurality in the election, Mário Soares issued an ultimatum to President Costa Gomes listing his conditions for the PS to remain in the Fourth Provisional Government. There was no response and the PS withdrew from the government followed shortly by the PPD of Sa Carneiro. It was thus obvious to all, including foreign observers, that the two parties which had led in the Constituent Assembly elections were not in government and if anyone governed, it was the Revolutionary Council. Prime Minister Vasco Goncalves formed a new government, the Fifth Provisional Government, which consisted exclusively of left-wing officers and civilians, though none affiliated to the major parties.

The "Hot Summer" as it was popularly called, saw a general deterioration and radicalization in politics, violence in the North of the country against the PCP, and threats of civil war. In this context, and due to the linking of domestic and international factors, there was a major shift within the MFA with moderate elements assuming control. They were led by Major Melo Antunes, and thus in a sense there was a return to the original planners of the coup. The shift resulted in the resignation of Prime Minister Vasco Goncalves on August 29 and the collapse of the largely stillborn Fifth Provisional Government.

In recognition of the seriously altered political situation, the next and last provisional government required longer to form and was composed of very different political actors. The cabinet reflected broadly the results of the April elections for the Constituent Assembly and included four members of the PS, two of the PPD, and one of the PCP. It also included five moderate officers including Melo Antunes and Vitor Alves. The prime minister was Admiral Pinheiro de Azevedo, who was regarded as sympathetic to the left but pragmatic and not associated with the PCP. The Sixth Provisional Government, however, did not see or cause immediate political stability. The overall political context remained the same with a high degree of political mobilization and divisions in the armed forces with tremendous problems of discipline. In late November the prime minister and most of the Constituent Assembly who were writing the constitution were blockaded in Sao Bento palace for more than a day by striking workers. The efforts by the provisional government and the moderates in the MFA to exert control finally sparked a coup attempt by the left in the military on November 25 which was quickly put down by troops under the command of General Ramalho Eanes. Just as the frustrated coup from the right on March 11 resulted in a movement to the left, the events of November 25 led to their loss of power and the beginning of a purge from the MFA and the armed forces more generally. The revolution had reached its apogee and was now tending to stabilize as political forces were sorted out and society became exhausted from mobilization and radicalization. The radically changed situation was recognized in a new pact on February 26, 1976, to replace the pact imposed on the parties less than one year earlier. According to the terms of the pact, the Revolutionary Council would continue its functions, though with lessened power, until at least the first constitutional revision after the completion of the first legislature of five years. The major parties agreed to support a military figure for the presidency in elections to be held in June. The parties, however, would choose the specific military candidates.

After almost a year of work during extremely turbulent times, the Constituent Assembly completed its work and the new constitution was proclaimed in April, and on April 25, in accord with the constitution, elections were held for the Assembly of the Republic. In these elections the PS won 35 percent, PPD 24 percent, CDS 16 percent, PCP 15 percent, with all other parties receiving a total of 6 percent. Obviously no party received a majority, and Mario Soares of the PS indicated his intentions to form a minority government. In the presidential elections on June 27 General Ramalho Eanes, supported by the PS, PPD, and CDS, won easily with 62 percent of the vote. In July Ramalho Eanes was inaugurated as Portugal's first president to be elected by free and universal suffrage. Later in the month, having been appointed Prime Minister, Mario Soares formed the First Constitutional Government composed largely of socialists, independents, and moderate military officers. In August Soares presented his legislative program to the Assembly of the Republic. In the twenty-seven months between the coup on April 25, 1974, and the formation of the PS government by Mario Soares, Portugal saw tremendous changes in virtually all areas. The colonial empire dissolved with Angola still torn by civil war through 1994. The economy was nationalized and an agrarian reform implemented in the southern half of the country. Unions and cooperatives were formed and assumed significant roles in negotiations. The armed forces diminished from 250,000 to somewhere around 100,000, and began to withdraw from politics. And the main elements of democracy were in place including a constitution, elections, political parties, interest groups, and guarantees of civil and political rights.

CAUSAL FACTORS IN THE TRANSITION FROM REVOLUTION TO DEMOCRACY

How was it possible for the revolutionary processes initiated by the coup in April 1974 to result in a democratic regime within two years? How was Portugal able to evolve from an authoritarian regime unwilling to innovate, to a coup and subsequent revolution, to democracy? The prospects in 1974 and 1975 were not promising. Indeed, at the time it was not obvious this would be the result, and there were Cassandras both within Portugal and abroad who predicted any series of outcomes ranging from a military government of the left, to the rise of right, to civil war. In my own analysis at the time I thought it most likely that democracy would result, and in what follows will utilize the categories I found useful then to explain the largely unanticipated and positive outcome. These categories deal mainly with political will and the actions of domestic and international actors who were committed to the establishment of democracy first in Portugal, and then elsewhere. They emphasize how political actors took advantage of opportunities, created them, and negotiated to achieve their desired outcome.

The most significant causal elements within this perspective leading to democracy after the six provisional governments between 1974 and 1976 are the following:

1. The rapid emergence of political parties, particularly those to the right of the Portuguese Communist Parties (PCP).
2. The initial promise of, and then stimulated commitment to, elections to determine who would govern. Elections, at least free elections, presupposed a democratic regime in formation.
3. The reconstitution of the armed forces, their professionalization, and gradual removal from power.
4. The formulation of a constitution through broad participation and its consolidation of the democratic format.
5. The heavy and welcomed involvement by a wide variety of foreign actors.

1. The Estado Novo was a nonparty state. The regime utilized a movement, the National Popular Action (ANP), and periodic elections of extremely limited suffrage and significance, to help legitimate its rule. When an opposition was allowed it was immediately prior to elections and political parties were not permitted. The regime was explicitly nondemocratic and conservative, and political parties were simply not allowed. Only the clandestine PCP existed in fact in Portugal prior to 1974, though the Socialist Party (PS) was founded in the Federal Republic of Germany in April 1973. At the time of the coup the general secretary of the PCP, Alvaro Cunhal, was in exile in Prague and the leader of the PS, Mario Soares, was in Bonn.

As noted above, the MFA did not provide for the formation of political parties in their program. Once the structures of the old regime began to disintegrate and the struggle for power began, parties formed very quickly and became the means for participating in politics. Each formation encouraged others, and a tremendous momentum of political involvement and radicalization was established. The MFA had no option but to recognize that they were forming and attempt to cooperate with those closest to its (evolving) ideology and goals. In sum, political parties emerged as main contenders in the political struggle. It should be noted, however, that not until the formation of the Sixth Provisional Government in September 1975 did political parties play an important role in the provisional governments. This followed the elections on April 25, 1975, and the resolution of extremely serious political crises causing the collapse of all prior provisional governments. The main importance of the political parties was that they increasingly provided the means or structures whereby political action could be channeled and elites chosen to wield power. They did not exist previously, were not encouraged by the MFA, but were founded by the new political elites in any case. And, they increasingly monopolized power.

2. The Program of the MFA promised elections to a Constituent Assembly within one year of the coup. These would be the first ever elections of universal suffrage and the secret vote in Portugal, and the

first meaningful elections since the 1920s. On the one hand, political parties mobilized in anticipation of the elections as though these elections would determine their participation in government. On the other hand, some political parties and other political actors attempted to achieve power in a manner which would eliminate the need for the elections and a constituent assembly. This was particularly the case with the PCP and parties to its left which sought to establish a regime in which the elections were not required in determining who would govern. Due to a number of processes to be explained below, the elections were held and the turnout was a massive 92 percent. In the elections the moderate parties did extremely well with the PS winning 38 percent and the Popular Democratic Party (PPD, later PSD) winning 26 percent. The PCP received 13 percent. These elections not only determined the distribution of seats for writing the new constitution but, through the massive turnout, also legitimated the idea of popular participation and democracy. These founding elections firmly established that a democratic regime was the only appropriate system for Portugal.

3. Following the coup the Portuguese Armed Forces began to disintegrate as a cohesive force. At that time they consisted of over 250,000 men and were overwhelmingly involved in fighting against guerrillas in Africa. The coup was made by junior officers who overthrew not only the regime, but also the highest level officers who were an integral part of the regime. Although placing General Spinola in as provisional president and head of the Junta of National Salvation, they ultimately competed with him for power. This resulted in a breakdown of discipline and the complete fracturing of the MFA, and the armed forces in general, into competing and armed movements. Sectors of the armed forces sided with General Spinola and others with a variety of military leaders such as Colonel Vasco Goncalves, and Majors Otelo Saraiva de Carvalho, Melo Antunes and Vitor Alves, to name only some of the most prominent leaders. It was the dynamics within the armed forces, increasingly in conjunction with the political parties, which largely determined the resolution of the crises of power in 1975. For a period in mid-1975 sectors sought to institutionalize the MFA in power and govern Portugal as a leftist military regime. The reconstitution of the armed forces and their gradual removal from power beginning in 1976 owed much to General Ramalho Eanes who led the counter movement to the attempted leftist coup in November 1975, became president in July 1976, and would be reelected for a second term until 1986. During the period of the provisional governments, however, the armed forces were divided and competing for power with and against other actors, including the political parties.[7] The importance of the dynamics within the armed forces center

on their splits, alignment with political parties, and subsequent rise of the moderates with a commitment to turn over governing to the political parties.

4. Following the elections on April 25, 1975, the Constituent Assembly began work on June 2 with a majority of representatives from the parties to the right of the PCP. The context, however, remained revolutionary with a high degree of popular mobilization and ongoing struggles among a wide variety of actors. At one phase the Assembly was barricaded by movements led by the more radical parties of the left. At times it appeared as though it would not be allowed to complete its work; at other times it seemed almost to be superseded by events in the streets. In that context, and with all parties defined further to the left due to the character of the deposed regime and strong competition from the so-called popular movements, the document they elaborated was very long (312 items), programmatic, emphasized participatory democracy, and sought to lead Portugal to a socialist economy and society. The Assembly was not only influenced by the context of the period and the political struggle, but also constrained by the two political pacts demanded by the MFA. The second pact, in February 1976, became part of the constitution and its most important element was the institutionalization of the Council of the Revolution. The Council's powers included exclusive jurisdiction in military affairs, it was a state council for the president of the republic, and also functioned as a constitutional court. The constitution, though programmatic and overly detailed, did stipulate that Portugal would be democratic and slowly helped legitimate this regime.

5. The Portuguese revolution became a major international event. It captured attention due to at least the following factors: It overthrew an archaic regime which had appeared to be solidly in power; it initiated the dismantling of an old colonial empire with implications for all of Southern Africa; it held implications for Spain and coalitions of parties to the left in France and Italy; it took a radical orientation with the apparent goal of hegemonic power by the PCP; and the political instability was of particular concern for a NATO country with defense facilities utilized in particular by the United States and Germany.

A very wide variety of international actors thus became involved in the resolution of the multiple crises in Portugal. These included states, particularly the United States and Germany, but also smaller countries like Austria, Holland, and Norway. International organizations, particularly NATO and the European Community, but the World Bank also became involved as did international political and union organizations such as the Socialist International, ICFTU, and the foundations of the West German political parties. These states and organizations cooperated with individuals and organizations in Portugal in seeking to establish a pluralist democracy. They competed with other Portuguese political actors and their foreign supporters who sought to establish other forms of governments and societies. The prodemocratic international actors (particularly the United States and the European Community) promised loans, provided that Portugal became a pluralist democracy. They (particularly the United States, Germany, and NATO) promised equipment and training to the military, provided the armed forces promoted democracy and removed themselves from power. They supported prodemocratic parties, unions, and other groups and associations, in their competition with those linked to the PCP and parties or movements to its left. International involvement in Portugal during the two years of the provisional government was extremely high. It supported the four other elements in promoting the emergence of democracy.

The importance of the international support is obvious in seeking to explain why there was such a low level of violence during the Portuguese revolution. The main likelihood of violence arose from the return of more than one-half million Portuguese from the former colonies. The country was already in recession in the mid-1970s, unemployment was high before the revolution and increased, and the "retornados" largely blamed the MFA and provisional governments for the loss of the colonies and thus their investment of time and earnings in the colonies. Then too, their numbers had a substantial impact on Portugal's resident population of approximately 9 million. Yet, with the exception of some sporatic bombings, violence was at a minimum. Following the experience of France after the independence of Algeria, much more violence and threats to democratic consolidation could have been expected.

The explanation is to be found partly in the creation of parties and movements whereby their grievances could be registered in politics. Of greater importance was the provision of funds and facilities by the United States, Canada, and countries of the European Community whereby the "retornados" were housed, fed, and then provided with support to (re)establish their lives in Portugal. It seems to be that their absorption is one of the unrecognized successes of the provisional governments and the international support.

These causal elements largely explain the emergence and subsequent consolidation of democracy during the six provisional governments between 1974 and 1976. They were both dynamic elements in the provisional governments and were affected by these governments. They resulted in a system which has evolved, while maintaining the general framework defined and elaborated by 1976.

EVOLUTION OF THE MAIN POLITICAL ELEMENTS
FROM THE PROVISIONAL GOVERNMENTS

Of the fifty political parties and movements that emerged shortly after April 25, 1974, and the twelve that ran in the elections one year later, only four have remained viable. They were joined briefly by the Democratic Renewal Party (PRD), associated with President Eanes, which saw its 18 percent of the vote in the 1985 elections drop to 5 percent two years later. In the 1987 elections, for example, the PSD received 50 percent of the vote, the PS 22 percent, PCP 12 percent, and CDS 4 percent. These four parties were central to formulating the constitution of 1976 in which political parties receive special and favored attention. The constitution sought to integrate, rather than fragment, the political parties. The extent and detail of the articles in the constitution, and of the legislation deriving from it, dealing with political parties is vast.[8] The roles of the parties have expanded in the intervening fifteen years, particularly with the revision of the constitution in 1982. In the elimination of the Council of the Revolution in the revision virtually all its powers were assumed by the political parties. The parties have expanded beyond the political arena, however, to expand their roles and involvement in the economy, media, and social movements. In terms of the functioning of the democratic regime, Portugal is clearly a multiparty democracy. The key issues now concern changing leadership in all but the governing PSD and the consolidation of bases of support in regions and social groups.[9]

The single most important defining characteristic of a democratic regime is the electoral process. Since the revolution Portugal has had extensive experience with elections, and there is no question but they are free and honest. Further, the elections determine who governs, and considering the central importance of the political parties, they also determine much more in economy and society. Since the elections for the Constituent Assembly in 1975, elections for the Assembly of the Republic have been held in 1976, 1979, 1980, 1983, 1985, 1987, and 1991. Presidential elections were held in 1976, 1980, 1986, and 1990. There are in addition elections for local governments. Abstention rates have tended to be approximately 25 percent. It is important to note that no party won a majority until 1987 when the PSD won 50.22 percent which gave it 148 seats in the 250-member Assembly. This of course explains the frequency of elections beyond the requirement of every four years. In the intervening eleven years virtually all combinations were attempted: the PS alone (1976–7), the PSD alone (1985–7, 1987–91, 1991–), the PS and CDS (1977–8), the PS and PSD (1983–5), the PSD and CDS (1979–83), and nonparty governments of presidential motivation (1978–9). There has been no government, however, since the Sixth Provisional Government in 1976, with PCP participation.

The predominance of the political parties and of elections reinforce the point that Portugal is indeed a consolidated democratic regime. The armed forces which made the coup and in 1975 tended to want to institutionalize their role, removed themselves from power in 1975 and 1976. Under President Eanes, who held the positions of commander in chief of the armed forces, president of the Council of the Revolution, and chief of the General Staff, the control of the military was gradually transferred to civilians. In fact, between 1974 and 1982 the armed forces were not to any significant degree controlled by the assembly or government. The watershed in asserting control was the constitutional revision of 1982 that eliminated the Council of the Revolution which still held exclusive powers in military issues. It also diminished the powers of the president, including the incumbent, President Eanes. It should be noted that none of the candidates for the presidency in 1985–6 were officers. When Mario Soares assumed the Presidency in 1986 he was the first civilian to hold the position since 1926. The revision was followed later in 1982 by the Law of National Defense and of the Armed Forces.[10] Following these major legislative changes control of the armed forces was supposed to be exercised by the Assembly and Government. The former through legislation on all areas of defense policy, including budgets, and the latter through the Ministry of Defense. However, as the most astute observer of defense matters in Portugal observed in a book published in 1988:

. . . the National Defence Law has not been implemented by the successive governments since 1982 . . . The organic law of the Defence Ministry, the legal instrument necessary to provide the ministry with an operative structure, has not yet been approved; some people even say that the Defence Ministry does not exist but "de jure." It should also be noted that the new provisions of the 1982 National Defence Law relating to the Chiefs of Staff have not been implemented so far, and consequently they still have practically the same powers as before. In reality, the coordination of foreign militry aid, representation abroad and in international organizations, definition of strategic options and procurement are all powers which still lie with the Chiefs of Staff, even if, for materiel purchases, the signature of the Prime Minister, who then delegates this sort of power to the Minister of Defence, is legally required.[11]

This situation is now changing substantially. In the context of political stability resulting from the PSD majority government in power since 1987 and the rapid economic and social modernization, military and political elites have consolidated civilian control and are restructuring the armed forces.[12] The Ministry of Defense now has real juridical standing and the minister, Fernando Nogueira, is the second most powerful figure in the government. The ministry has been structured to exercise effective control over most aspects regarding the armed forces. The General Staff has been restructured as well which reduced the powers of the services, increased the power of the chief, and consolidated the powers of the ministry. Through hearings and subsequent legislation the Assembly of the Republic has also defined its role, which is fairly substantial in terms of budgets and personnel issues. While the political role of the armed forces is being greatly diminished, however, it must be noted that their prestige remains high. After all, they did make the coup, were involved in a revolution which eliminated several archaic structures, and turned over power to civilian political parties. As part of the restructuring the armed forces have also been receiving new equipment, largely within terms of defense agreements with the United States and Germany – the former in trade for access to facilities in the Azores and the latter for access to the airbase at Beja.[13] The Portuguese armed forces thus have, or will soon receive, modern frigates, submarine patrol aircraft, F-16 interceptors, tanks, and missiles. They are still in the process of restructuring and modernization, but they have improved tremendously since the revolution. And, they are now out of politics.

Much has already been made of the constitution of 1976 and its subsequent revision.[14] The original document included extensive sections delineating "Portugal's transition to socialism," guaranteeing a large state sector and maintenance of the nationalized lands and industries, and included the Council of the Revolution. No sooner had it been proclaimed than the context changed and much of it became unacceptable to politically ascendent parties and sectors. In 1982, when it became legal to amend the constitution, a coalition of the PSD, CDS, and PS achieved the necessary two-thirds majority and agreed on a revision which focused mainly on the structures of power. The issue became defined as the distribution of powers between the president and the parliament, and the solution was to decrease the powers of the former and transfer them to the latter. The Council of the Revolution was eliminated, powers of the president diminished, and other structures were created to replace them or the power was simply tranferred to the Assembly and government. The 1982 revision did not focus on the social and economic sections as the PS was still concerned about losing support to the PCP on its left.[15]

By 1989 this was no longer a strong concern and the same coalition revised the constitution in July. The second revision allows for reprivatization of nationalized industries and eliminates all remaining references to the transition to socialism. Since it was proclaimed in 1976, the constitution had been a political issue in Portugal. While the PCP and other parties and movements of the left wanted to leave it intact to "guarantee the conquests of the revolution," all other parties and sectors wanted to revise it. They identified in the constitution many obstacles to overall development of the country. Today, following the revisions in 1982 and

1989, the constitution is no longer a political issue. This is not to say that all 300 or more articles are followed, let alone appropriate for stability and modernization, but they are not perceived as a serious problem.

Prior to the revolution Portugal was a member of EFTA, NATO, and had a defense agreement with the United States. Due to the colonies and the general character of the regime, however, it was somewhat isolated from the main streams of international affairs. In the revolution a very wide variety of foreign actors became involved in Portugal, and the trends established during the provisional governments have continued and increased. Portugal joined the European Community in January 1986, and her economy is very rapidly integrating into the larger Community. As part of the process Portugal receives very substantial assistance and attracts significant investments. Consequently, the real GDP growth between 1987 and 1990 was about 5 percent and all other economic indicators, including employment and inflation, were also positive. In the first semester of 1992, Portugal held the presidency of the Community. In 1988, Portugal joined the Western European Union. Prior to 1974, Portugal's membership in NATO was merely formal. During and after the revolution it was in effect on hold. Today, with the modernization and reconstitution of the armed forces, Portugal is more active in NATO and can play a larger role.[16] The relationship with the United States is also closer, though based heavily on the defense areas relating to the Azores and provision of equipment and training. In sum, Portugal is now fully integrated into a community of nations and can play an active external role that has not been possible earlier in this century.

CONCLUSION

The six provisional governments which came and went in Portugal between May 1974 and July 1976 were contemporary with the coup, revolution, and beginning of democracy. These governments were barometers of the overall situation of power in the country as Portugal saw the end of a conservative authoritarian regime, the rise of the MFA, the potential for a Marxist regime, and finally an elected civilian government based on political parties and a popularly elected president. The causal factors which resulted in the establishment of a democratic regime can be generalized as those concerning the political will and behavior of domestic and international actors. The main elements defining the period of the provisional governments, and their specific interaction, also provide continuity with the current political situation. Their evolution in the intervening seventeen years describe the consolidation of Portuguese democracy.

9

Accelerating collapse: The East German road from liberalization to power-sharing and its legacy

DANIEL V. FRIEDHEIM

Because the state-socialist regime collapsed so quickly, the East German democratic transition was short. It lasted only five months, from the fall of hard-liner Erich Honecker on October 18, 1989, to the founding elections on March 18, 1990. In this short period three separate transition governments ruled the German Democratic Republic (GDR): (1) a liberalizing Communist regime, (2) a democratizing caretaker government, and (3) a power-sharing interim government that oversaw free elections. The succession of progressively weaker regimes added up to a process best characterized as "accelerating collapse." The legacy of this dynamic regime collapse shows up in the rapid pace of German reunification under a short-lived democratic government, with monetary union on July 1 and formal unification on October 3. The legacy also shows up in the extensive "evening of scores" with old regime collaborators in Germany today.

FALL OF THE OLD REGIME: EXIT, VOICE, AND COLLAPSE

As in the rest of East Central Europe, a neo-Stalinist regime had been imposed in the GDR from abroad. Collectivization got off to a slow start but was more ruthlessly completed than elsewhere. Socialist Unity Party of Germany (SED) leader Honecker, General Secretary since 1971, along with twenty-four of twenty-seven Politburo members belonged to the generation that had founded the regime in 1949. Honecker and eight others belonged to the prewar German Communist Party (KPD). Only three members had joined the SED after 1949. After the Soviet Bloc's first popular uprising had been crushed with Soviet assistance on June 17, 1953, no reform Communist leader ever rose to power in the GDR. The tactic of "exporting" dissidents to the Federal Republic of Germany (FRG), proved particularly effective and helps explain why a Václav Havel could become an opposition leader in Czechoslovakia but an exiled Wolf Biermann could not in the GDR. An imposed "social pact" meant to increase the supply of consumer goods was doomed to fail because Germans in the GDR compared themselves to those in the FRG rather than to non-Germans further east.

By 1989, a backlog of 1.5 million permanent emigration requests had built up. Then, the reform Communist Hungarian regime opened its border with Austria on September 11, allowing 15,000 vacationing East Germans to leave illegally in the next three days. This expression of "exit," in which citizens literally voted with their feet, spread to Czechoslovakia and beyond, until 343,854 had emigrated in 1989 alone, a level not seen since the crisis year of 1953.[1]

The old regime ended visa-free travel to Hungary, Czechoslovakia, and Poland, but only succeeded in bottling up the discontent. "What had begun as a flight from the GDR became a struggle to alter it from within."[2] Emboldened by these ever more successful expressions of exit, opposition movements led by the intelligentsia began organizing without waiting for legal recognition. They were small (New Forum had 2,000 members in September), but participation in the demonstrations they called mushroomed once it became clear that security forces would not shoot. Then the increase was exponential. The State Security Service secret police (Stasi) counted 140,000 demonstrators nationwide the week of October 16 and 1.35 million the week of October 30. A Berlin demonstration November 4 broke the one-half million mark, only to be matched the following week in the smaller city of Leipzig. The shift in demonstrators' chants from "we are *the* people" to "we are *one* people," which drove reunification so inexorably forward, illustrates the important role that "voice" played.

Strands of exit and voice mixed together in Dresden when an ailing Honecker, just back from gall bladder surgery and diagnosed with terminal cancer, decided to allow special night trains to carry aspiring emigres in Prague and Warsaw back across East German territory to the FRG. This impromptu policy, announced to the Politburo in an emergency session at the State Opera House in East Berlin, stimulated thousands of other aspiring emigres to converge on the Dresden train station, where the special trains made a technical stop. Simultaneously, the regime lost its will to continue employing force to stay in power.

The collapse of SED officials' will to use their legal monopoly on organized force to stay in power began among mid-level party-state officials in several regions outside Berlin.[3] Many citizens in Dresden and Leipzig believed an order to shoot at demonstrators had been issued. Whether or not it had, ominous bureaucratic language filled Stasi telegrams, which ordered contingency plans made to "arrest as well as liquidate . . . subversives," then warned regional commanders "the situation is serious" and "a question of power, nothing else."[4] In October, local newspapers featured a party Combat Group militia (*Kampfgruppe*) promise to act "if need be, with weapons in hand!"[5] Mielke's central intelligence analysis office (ZAIG) drew an explicit analogy to the 1953 uprising, concluding "enemy opposition and . . . rowdy forces . . . endanger the socialist state- and social-order."[6] Once an internationally embarrassing confrontation during Gorbachev's visit to Berlin for the regime's fortieth anniversary festivities October 6–7 had been avoided, the stage appeared to be set for showdowns in Leipzig and Dresden.

Krenz's claim to have single-handedly averted a bloody "Chinese solution" on the Tienanmen Square precedent as 70,000 gathered to march in Leipzig on October 9 is exaggerated. He did fly to Leipzig with his Politburo security issues specialist and a People's Police (VoPo) general, but only on October 13. At the crucial moment, it took him two hours to return the local party leadership's call on October 9 as the demonstration marched by local Stasi headquarters and completed a full circuit of the downtown "ring" road.[7] He did not sign the famous appeal for dialogue. Local SED secretary Jochen Pommert, who did, insists, "no one authorized us to act or provided us with cover . . . it was clear that under the circumstances, my party could well have held me accountable."[8]

Along with Pommert, internationally renowned Gewandhaus Orchestra conductor Kurt Masur, a cabaret star, a Protestant pastor, and two other SED local secretaries frantically broadcast their "appeal" by loudspeaker and radio:

Our common concern and responsibility have brought us together today . . . We all need the free exchange of opinions about the further development of Socialism in our country.[9]

Instead of a high-ranking official in Berlin, it was local mid-level party cadre who had joined with members of the intelligentsia and the church to prevent bloodshed.

The day before in Dresden, on October 8, while senior church leaders were approaching the mayor for the same reason, dialogue had developed from an even lower level of the state and church. When Catholic curate Frank Richter asked riot troops with whom he could negotiate, he found a plain clothes officer on the streets who agreed to accept twenty demonstrators as a representative delegation. The officer then ordered his riot troops to lay down their shields as a sign of good faith and a cheer went up from the protesters. "They're not going to believe us when we report this," the anti-terror unit officer's supervisor said that night.[10]

SED Mayor Wolfgang Berghofer agreed to receive the demonstrators' "Group of Twenty," which included five women and fifteen men from a wide range of professions, including at least one SED member, which was enough to prevent more showdowns with security forces. The next day 500 arrestees were freed. The Berlin leadership had not approved such a compromise in advance. Line security forces also had lost faith in the old regime. As the officer recalled:

We had been on alert 24 hours a day without sleep and from October 3 could not even go home . . . We were between a rock and a hard place . . . but what is a man to do? Orders are orders.[11]

Strikingly, his own actions showed how a disillusioned officer may subvert the spirit of his orders. In Leipzig and Dresden, many of the 10,000 part-time members of the party's militia resisted their orders. Even refugee train drivers exhibited signs of collapse. One, who had been driving too fast to stop for any protestors on the tracks, recalled:

I don't know if I had received the order if I could have driven into a crowd . . . Perhaps if they had put a pistol to my back.[12]

In Dresden, too, the repression first ended because regional and mid-level party officials finally talked to the growing number of nonviolent demonstrators on the streets.

The GDR was so dependent on the USSR – militarily, ideologically, diplomatically, and economically – that Gorbachev could trigger a succession crisis by issuing a warning during his visit October 6–7. Actually referring to perestroika in the Soviet Union, he said: "Life punishes those who come too late. That is what we have learned from our development,"[13] but the analogy to the GDR was clear enough. "He looked around the table, as if he wanted to see who *really* had understood him," Krenz recalls.[14] Honecker opponents inside the Politburo like Krenz and fellow plotter Günther Schabowski had. So had his party rival in Dresden, Hans Modrow, on whom the warning worked like "a signal."[15] And so had protesters in the streets, who began shouting "help us Gorby" when police continued to break up their protests. But Honecker continued to reject perestroika because it had led in the USSR to "demonstrations under the Czarist banner."[16] It took Krenz and Schabowski ten days to arrange the details. Then, at the Politburo showdown on October 17, Honecker would preserve the unity of the Socialist Unity Party for one last time by voting for his own removal. In hindsight, his successor Krenz concludes, "we acted too late and were therefore, as Gorbachev had warned, punished by life."[17]

LIBERALIZING A POST-TOTALITARIAN REGIME

After this belated succession, and faced with regime collapse, Krenz initiated a process of liberalization that stopped short of democratization.[18] His reluctant liberalizations eventually included granting: freedom to form political associations, reflected in New Forum's legalization on November 8; freedom of travel, even across the Berlin Wall beginning literally overnight on November 9; and, an end to television, press, and literary censorship by November 21. But his hand was being forced from below. When he reopened the GDR-Czech border in mid-October, another wave of "exit" eventually forced Czechoslovakia to open its border with Austria. Exit would peak as the Berlin Wall fell. One quarter of the entire population, 4.3 million East Germans, visited West Germany or West Berlin in the space of four days.[19]

Only in the confusion of a maneuver to purge Politburo hard-liners, by staging the Politburo's resignation and immediate reappointment, was the miscalculation made that led to the overnight opening of the Wall. Perhaps eager to beat his rival Modrow to the punch, Krenz presided over a hasty second revision meant to loosen existing travel restrictions beginning on November 10. The bureaucratic phrase "may request private trips abroad . . . without fulfilling the normal requirements" seemed to open radical new possibilities, which news reports emphasized. And Schabowski's off-hand press conference statement the night of November 9 that the changes would take effect "immediately," which seemed too good to last, created a last-minute panic (*Torschlusspanik*) among incredulous residents. Although border police expected requests to increase, the case can be made that the regime never intended to fully open the Wall.[20] Whatever was intended, the immediate run on the Wall that night came as a surprise. In its aftermath, several Politburo members rushed to claim they had ordered border guards to let the crowds through, but the guards had begun to act on their own when confronted with crowds of thousands quoting Schabowski's announcement. The first cable authorizing their spontaneous decisions came the afternoon of November 10. Gorbachev was informed after the fact, as well.[21]

In hindsight Krenz acknowledges he was a transitional figure, but his was not intended to be an interim government. Although he announced a policy "turnabout" (*Wende*),[22] he never made a credible promise to hold free and competitive elections in a reasonable period. As Schabowski recalls:

our thoughts were always based on the belief in an all-powerful party not the people's reactions . . . the words "free elections" were to come only with hesitation . . . only under pressure and against our will.[23]

Although the Politburo authorized a new electoral law during its tumultuous wall-opening November 8–10 session, actual drafting only began after Krenz had resigned. In his inaugural television address, Krenz conceded the old regime had made mistakes and explicitly rejected Honecker's callous phrase that one should "waste no tears" on emigres. But instead of free elections, Krenz promised only "renewal within continuity," which Schabowski now interprets as "a room full of continuity plus a thimble full of renewal."[24] And, as the Politburo member directly responsible for rigging the old regime's last undemocratic elections, when the municipal balloting on May 7 produced a 98.85 percent super majority for the SED's National Front list, Krenz lacked the credibility to promise any future election would be democratic.

Although he took symbolic actions, like moving out of the scandal-ridden leadership residential compound at Wandlitz, Krenz clung to the party's undemocratic constitutional "leading role" over all aspects of society. By the time he had agreed to end that neototalitarian aspiration, the tide of emigration, the continuing street protests and a grass roots rebellion inside the party itself had doomed his reform Communist regime. By year end, almost 850,000 of the SED's 2.3 million members would resign.[25] At the last minute, Krenz not only moved up the date of the next party congress to December 3, but also granted it unlimited powers as the GDR's first ever Special Congress. He and the last Politburo resigned the same day that Special Congress convened in Berlin. Krenz remained a reluctant post-totalitarian reformer who left democratization to another, self-consciously interim government.

MODROW I: A CARETAKER GOVERNMENT

As soon as he was named premier (chairman of the Council of State) the same weekend the Wall was opened, Dresden First Secretary and long-time perestroika advocate Hans Modrow began pursuing a strategy of backward legality and forward legitimacy. First, he breathed new life into the hollow shell of political institutions in which the SED had cloaked the "democratic centralization" of all political power in its own hands. Then he made a credible promise to hold free and competitive elections. Modrow's first interim government, which lasted from the Politburo's resignation on December 3 to the creation of a power-sharing government on January 22, was a caretaker. Unlike Krenz, he conceded the government's inherently temporary legitimacy and largely limited its role to arranging for free elections. Before Modrow could implement this caretaker government strategy, however, he had to overcome an unstable situation of dual rule by slowly expanding his power at the expense of Krenz's Politburo.[26]

Under legal cover of the communist constitution, Modrow began separating government ministries from party control. First, he positioned himself rhetorically above partisan politics, pledging his "intention as Premier to serve not just a party but the whole people."[27] Then he invigorated the People's Chamber (*Volkskammer*) and the puppet parties in the subservient National Front, both of which were particular German variations on the Stalinist "people's democracies" strategy originally inspired by the postwar Potsdam Accord commitment to political pluralism. Those nondemocratic institutions would prove particularly well-suited to a democratic transition. In the GDR's first democratic institutional proceeding, Modrow allowed the Front parties to elect one of their non-Communist colleagues the next People's Chamber chairman. The four parties – the Christian Democrats (CDU-East), the Democratic Farmers (BDB), the Liberals (LDPD), and the National Democrats (NDPD) – took on independent political significance for the first time. At the same time, Modrow used the People's Chamber to begin redressing the country's glaring rule of law deficit. In one early step, a legislative committee started reversing the infamously summary property confiscations along the Baltic Sea coastline in the 1950s known as "Operation Rose." Modrow started building a socialist *Rechtsstaat,* invoking the word Germans use for a state based on the rule of law.

In his November 17 inaugural address Modrow had promised a "democratic restructuring of socialism" without committing himself to a firm election date. The prospects for democratization remained open to question until the SED's constitutional "leading role" and institutional Politburo bulwark both ceased functioning. From early December, Modrow had consolidated enough control to begin implementing the promised democratization. An important tactic in this regard was the gamble that he could exploit a carefully managed flow of corruption revelations to discredit the legality of his hard-line rivals' behavior without simultaneously discrediting his own government's broader backward legality. Ultimately it was a tightrope he could not walk alone. He would only be able to continue ruling beyond January 1990 by sharing power with remarkably unorganized opposition movements in what would amount to a second interim government.

The People's Chamber special Abuse of Power and Corruption Committee began revealing the modest luxuries enjoyed by former Politburo members in their exclusive residential compound in the suburb of Wandlitz, northeast of Berlin. But, the West German news magazine *Der Spiegel* got in on the act in late November by revealing foreign trade secretary Schalck-Golodkowski's secret corporate empire and large-scale embezzlement. On December 2, East German reporters discovered a cache of arms his Coordinating Committee (KoKo) had prepared to export illegally. As an uncensored press revealed more signs of corruption, a Toquevillian dynamic took effect:

For the mere fact that certain abuses have been remedied draws attention to others and they now appear more galling; people may suffer less, but their sensibility is exacerbated.[28]

Modrow lost control of the corruption revelations even though he called in human rights lawyer Gregor Gysi to accelerate the party's own investigations. The revelations did help Modrow quickly consolidate his control of the SED, but they also condemned his caretaker government to a short life.

As Modrow finished consolidating his power during the Special Congress in early December and thousands of rebellious grass roots party members demonstrated outside the Central Committee headquarters building in Berlin known as "the big house," the powerful SED post of general secretary was abolished. Corruption investigator Gysi was elected to the new, less powerful post of chairman, which never posed a threat to Modrow's effective control of the interim government. In an awkward expression of the SED's slow transformation into a democratic party, the either redundant or contradictory hybrid name Socialist Unity Party of Germany-Party of Democratic Socialism (SED-PDS), was adopted. By election day, the echo of an undemocratic past in the first three letters would be jettisoned and the former SED became simply the PDS.

As a long-time economic reformer banished from Berlin to the southern city of Dresden to keep him out of the Politburo, Modrow had some of the credibility Krenz lacked as Honecker's hand-picked successor. Modrow committed himself at the Special Congress to creating "a multiparty country" and explicitly accepted the democratic possibility that the SED would someday be reduced to playing a minority role. In secret negotiations with a handful of relatively unorganized opposition groups, largest among them New Forum, Modrow orchestrated an invitation to church-mediated round table talks. He put free elections on the agenda at the first session on December 7 and accepted the immediate Round Table recommendation to schedule them for May 6, 1990.

At this Round Table, government representatives from the SED, the four National Front parties and two Communist corporative organizations[29] met eight opposition groups first in Berlin's Dietrich Bonhoeffer House then in the Niederschönhausen Castle salon where Gorbachev had issued his famous warning. Participants on the opposition side were: New Forum, Democracy Now, Democratic Awakening, the Greens, the Peace and Human Rights Initiative, United Left, Independent Women and the re-founded Social Democrats (SPD-East).[30] But the new quasi-parliamentary body convened only four times in the month of December as Modrow chose to rule through the still undemocratic if no longer rubber stamp People's Chamber, which finally began to draft a package of new electoral laws. The Round Table limited itself to making recommendations for the government's formal action, most of which were ignored. Modrow had rebuffed the opposition groups' initial demand for a broad government "oversight" function. The three church moderators stated their more modest compromise aspiration:

The Round Table cannot and will not become a parallel institution, cannot and will not be a substitute for the administration or the People's Chamber, for which it lacks all competence.[31]

In a formal "support decree," Modrow granted the opposition groups office space in the SED local headquarters building in downtown Berlin, renaming it "Democracy House." At the same time, however, he candidly considered the Round Table a "brake" on the accelerating pace of change.[32] For the first few weeks, as they were busily organizing for the first time, the opposition movements seemed to accept their advisory role. Soon though they reasserted their claim to a veto over government decisions. The test case was whether to dismantle the secret police.

Opposition groups at the Round Table demanded the complete dismantling of the old secret police (Stasi), but Modrow's caretaker government settled for firing 8,000 employees and renaming it the Agency for National Security (AfNS). Modrow's commitment to dismantling the Stasi internal repressive apparatus was conditioned on preserving a strong external security agency. He outraged the opposition with a proposal to put his friend and former espionage chief, Markus Wolf, in charge of the Stasi reforms. The Round Table opposition's assertiveness on this issue reflected the pace of the continuing "peaceful revolution" in the streets. When a Stasi/AfNS officer confirmed during a radio interview the rumor that documents were being destroyed, ad hoc "citizens' committees" stormed regional offices of the secret police in several cities. The Modrow government then issued secret authorization for regional Stasi offices to "destroy documents" and "hinder by appropriate means the exposure of state secrets to unauthorized persons."[33] In early January the Round Table opposition first demanded that Modrow turn over control of regional Stasi/AfNS buildings to the opposition-led citizens' committees. It set up its own Security Working Group, ironically under the leadership of SPD-East chairman and future prime minister candidate Ibrahim Böhme, who would be revealed after the elections as a Stasi informant.

The opposition issued an ultimatum to Modrow on January 8, demanding he dissolve the AfNS without preserving any successor organization and that he personally appear before the Round Table. Modrow's opinion that the Round Table lacked the requisite technical competence to help govern the increasingly ungovernable country was changing. On January 12 he conceded the AfNS would be dissolved without replacement, but only in an address before the People's Chamber. He finally appeared before the Round Table on January 15. That same day, however, New Forum had organized a march on Stasi/AfNS headquarters, the Normanenstrasse complex in Berlin-Lichtenberg. The crowd, carrying bricks with which to symbolically wall-up exits through which truckloads of documents were rumored to be passing, appeared ready to storm the building. Following the precedent of negotiated stormings already ordered in district offices, the Stasi allowed protesters to roam through many but not the most sensitive buildings.[34] The coincidence of this peak of mass action with Modrow's Round Table appearance inspired both opposition and government to start cooperating to fend off a revolutionary situation. During the Stasi occupation, the Round Table was abruptly adjourned. Modrow rushed to Stasi headquarters with several opposition leaders to help restore order. Together, Modrow and Round Table participants Böhme, Rainer Eppelmann, and Konrad Weiss addressed the crowd, calling for restraint and nonviolence.

MODROW II: A POWER-SHARING GOVERNMENT

In response to this peak of ungovernability, when the government and Round Table opposition groups risked ceding control of the transition to masses in the streets, Modrow proposed sharing power. "Only a new coalition . . . could stop the country's slide into chaos," he felt; "the government needs and seeks the counsel of those political parties and movements at the Round Table," he told the opposition.[35]

Inaugurating a second interim government, Modrow allowed the Round Table to participate directly in government by taking seats on the Council of Ministers and joining the diplomatic delegation then seeking to negotiate a confederation with West Germany. Eight ministers, nominally without portfolio but with specific issue areas of expertise and interest, formally joined the government, including one opposition leader who had addressed the crowd at Stasi headquarters. Modrow called this power-sharing arrangement, which formally began on January 28 and lasted until the March elections, a "Government of National Responsibility." This second interim government finally began dissolving the Stasi/AfNS.

Modrow conceded his loss of political control not only by sharing power, but also by moving up the first democratic elections, which were still scheduled for May. In a deal Modrow worked out with the SED-PDS and the SPD-East, neither of which shared the opposition movements' need for time to organize themselves into functioning political parties before the balloting, March 18 was chosen. Although the opposition movements disliked the early date, they still saw power-sharing as a way to retain influence and cooperate in preserving an independent GDR against the groundswell of popular sympathy for reunification.

The left-leaning opposition movements at the Round Table mostly advocated a "third way" model of democratic socialism meant to avoid the perceived shortcomings of "real existing socialism" and West German capitalism. They were easily coopted into Modrow's efforts to slow down or block altogether German reunification. Like the West German Left, the GDR intelligentsia shared with the SED "the notion that Germany's permanent division is one of the just costs exacted from the German people for Auschwitz."[36] Both Modrow interim governments shared some elements of this "third way" vision. They passed laws to limit foreign capital to minority shares in newly legalized joint ventures and set up the Trust Institution (*Treuhandanstalt*) to preserve existing state-owned firms by thoroughly restructuring them before risking privatization. Such laws were fundamentally rewritten, although the name *Treuhand* would survive, in both the democratic GDR and the reunified Germany. The Round Table codified its vision of democratic socialism in a complete draft constitution, which was ignored by the subsequent democratic government. It also sought in vain to ban West German politicians from campaigning in the GDR before March 18. The opposition movements at the Round Table formed a closed club from which later-developing, more conservative political groups were excluded. Despite the high voter turn out of 93.4 percent, the Round Table groups would lose the founding election on March 18 soundly (see Table 1).

The poor electoral performance of the PDS, and especially those opposition movements in Bündnis 90 that did not join the temporary CDU-led "Alliance for Germany," recorded the weak popular support for Modrow's second interim government and the Round Table opposition. "Where were the people" during all this predemocratic maneuvering, asks one observer?[37] Interestingly, most of the randomly selected Dresden Group of Twenty protesters voted for the Alliance, one even becoming the first democratic (and CDU) mayor.[38]

Opposing rapid reunification was one matter on which Modrow and the opposition groups at the Round Table could agree. Both calculated that their influence would be greater in a democratized but still independent GDR than in an expanded Federal Republic. The popular groundswell for rapid reunification sealed the electoral fate of these weak partners. Ultimately their power-sharing arrangement was built upon mutual weakness.

RAPID REUNIFICATION

However inevitable German reunification appears to have been in hindsight, its surprising rapidity was fueled in part by the GDR's accelerating collapse.[39] Once the diplomatic constellation had aligned favorably, not just in the Soviet Union but also in the United States, there may have

Table 1. *Elections to the People's Chamber,*
March 18, 1990

Party[40]	Vote (in %)	Seats (of 400)
CDU coalition	48.0	192
SPD	21.9	88
PDS	16.4	66
BFD	5.3	21
Bündnis 90	2.9	12
15 others	5.5	21

Source: Wolfgang Gibowski, "Dokumentation und Analyse der Wahl vom 18.März 1990," *Zeitschrift für Parlamentsfragen,* 21:1 (April 1990), pp. 8–9.

been no stopping reunification, but its mode and pace were under constant debate. The fast-track absorption of a democratized GDR into the existing West German system, consummated on October 3, 1990, ultimately was inspired by the fear that Soviet hard-liners would end Gorbachev's unprecedented flexibility (much as they would try to during the abortive coup of August 1991). Yet it was only possible to implement reunification so quickly because Modrow's interim governments grew ever weaker.

Before democratization began in earnest, while Krenz was announcing his "Turnabout" (*Wende*) without a specific election date, the SED resisted all talk of reunification. One of Modrow's first innovations as newly named premier of the liberalizing Communist regime was to carve out an independent line on inter-German relations in his November 17 inaugural by proposing a "treaty community" (*Vertragsgemeinschaft*). Whether such a German community would have been anything more than a customs union, its contracting partners would have been exercising their separate sovereignties. Two of the no-longer pliant block parties, the NDP and the CDU-East, issued the first calls for a broader German confederation. And Chancellor Helmut Kohl still used Modrow's more modest phrase when he successfully snatched back the domestic West German political initiative from his foreign minister and coalition partner Hans-Dietrich Genscher with his Ten-point Program for Overcoming the Division of Germany and Europe on November 28, 1989. He interpreted a "treaty community" as bilateral commissions plus "confederal structures" that would pave the way for federation with a democratized GDR after perhaps five years and "state unity" only in some unspecified future.[41] East German demonstrators were already waving emasculated East German flags with the GDR symbol cut out.

As Krenz' liberalizing regime collapsed and Modrow's first interim government met the most important precondition Kohl had laid down by declaring a date for free elections, both sides began to discuss the idea of a confederation more seriously. Modrow took the position that confederation would only be possible with a neutral FRG, that is, one that had withdrawn from the NATO alliance. He and the first democratic foreign minister of the GDR, Markus Meckel, held unswervingly to the idea of German neutrality, but ended up so weak that West German negotiators could afford to ignore them. Keeping an eventually reunified Germany inside NATO became the American precondition that Gorbachev would not be able to openly support, despite secret signs of flexibility, until he had purged hard-line rival Yegor Ligachev at a July party congress.

But it became evident much earlier that popular sentiment was strongly in favor of full-fledged reunification. Chants of "Germany, Germany" and "Helmut, Helmut" greeted Kohl at a public appearance in Dresden on December 19. That appearance was when Kohl began to drop the idea of mere confederation. In Dresden, Modrow asked for 15 billion Deutschmarks (DM) as well as foreign exchange guarantees for those East Germans wishing to exercise their new right to free travel. He called the lump sum payment "compensation" for the historically heavy war reparations burden the Soviet Union had inflicted on the GDR. Kohl said he preferred the term "Solidarity Contribution," then never mentioned the possibility again. The weakness of Modrow's interim government meant that instead of dictating terms he was soliciting financial aid.[42] Modrow admits the euphoric New Year's Eve celebration at the reopened Brandenburg Gate in Berlin made reunification sentiment clear to all participants. A certain wishful thinking nonetheless set in among GDR government and opposition circles. They both seemed to lose touch with mass sentiments.

The same accelerating collapse that helped inspire Modrow's power-sharing government, and its decision to move forward the election three months, inspired Kohl in January to revise his unofficial timetable for reunification down from five to two years. With the emigration rate doubling again, he envisaged unified elections in 1991 and on February 7 proposed monetary union before formal reunification, saying "if the DM doesn't come to Leipzig, then Leipzigers will come to the DM."[43] The introduction of the West German currency and the legal structure for its "social market economy" even before political reunification meant the democratic GDR would never exercise sovereignty over domestic economic policy. Democratic Finance Minister Romberg believed this was a concession not just of economic sovereignty but "consequently of political sovereignty" as well.[44]

The political campaign that winter was dominated by the question of how fast to reunify. The PDS position against reunification, shared by the Round Table opposition movements grouped together in Bündnis 90 was marginalized from the start. The decisive debate was whether to reunify as quickly as possible, by accession to the existing FRG through Article 23 of its constitution, or more slowly, by confederating and taking time to negotiate a new constitution for a unified Germany, as provided for in the overlapping Article 146. The CDU's Alliance for Germany advocated using Article 23, the SPD Article 146, although the CDU-West only convinced the CDU-East to drop its support for the slow track of Article 146 one week before the vote. After voters had endorsed the fast-track option on March 18, Prime Minister Lothar de Maizière accepted Kohl's offer of monetary union at the inflated exchange rate of 1:1 for wages and pensions (which would complicate economic recovery afterwards). Full reunification then faced only the diplomatic hurdle of "two plus four" talks incorporating Allies that had defeated Hitler in World War II. As de Maizière's CDU-SPD grand coalition government signed the monetary union treaty in May, it also proposed moving up the first unified elections from 1991 to December 1990, when the next West German elections already were scheduled. After Gorbachev finally accepted continued NATO membership during Kohl's trip to the Caucasus in July, the democratic People's Chamber voted for the early formal reunification date of October 3, 1990.

Under de Maizière, a lawyer who had already helped Modrow revise GDR legal codes, the short-lived democratic GDR became an interim state. Its life span was limited not by an electoral but a boundary deadline, not by regime change but by state change. As the chairperson of the newly elected People's Chamber, Sabine Bergmann-Pohl recalls, the Grand Coalition of CDU and SPD had "one common goal – to achieve German unity as soon and as well as possible."[45] One-third of all People's Chamber deputies became nonvoting members of the expanded transition Bundestag in session from October 3 to December 2. The wholesale importation of senior western administrative personnel and purging of lower-level state bureaucrats took place after reunification.[46]

"MASTERING THE PAST"

Because of the fast-track reunification permitted by accelerating collapse, the break with the authoritarian legal past seems complete. The radical break in legal continuity was too thorough, in the opinion of West German unification negotiator Wolfgang Schäuble, who had advocated preserving some of the GDR's simpler legal code instead of replacing it entirely with the FRG's more complicated legal system and exacerbating the shortage of qualified lawyers in eastern Germany today.[47] However, in a variation on the role of "old state legality" in democratic transitions, the Unification Treaty recognized the status of GDR law post hoc. It decreed that crimes committed during the old regime may be tried only under the defunct state's laws. This second birth of old state legality has complicated efforts to "even the score" for crimes committed in the name of the old regime.

The relentless revelations of prominent eastern German politicians' compromised pasts is a second legacy of the short East German democratic transition with its series of unstable transition governments. Partly by breaking socialist legal continuity and reestablishing *Rechtsstaat* traditions, the GDR's absorption into the FRG actually has slowed down this process that Germans refer to as mastering the past (*Vergangenheitsbewältigung*). A practical result of the old regime's accelerating collapse has been open access to its secret police documents. This openness has fueled a daily stream of press revelations about SED regime abuses. From Soviet Occupation Forces use of Nazi concentration camps to the Stasi paycheck of the East German lawyer who negotiated the ransom (*Freikauf*) of hundreds of political prisoners by the FRG, an endless flow of revelations has occurred.

After reunification the Bundestag ratified this unstructured, pluralistic approach to "evening the score" with the December 20, 1991, Law for the Documents of the State Security Service, or Stasi Documents Law, which waives the usual thirty-year restriction on access to official documents and grants all Stasi victims the right to see their files.[48] The first steps in opening the Stasi archives, however, were taken not by the Bundestag but by the democratic People's Chamber and by opposition movement veterans mounting pressure "from below" right before formal reunification. One of the most important People's Chamber decisions was to create the special Administrative Authority run by Joachim Gauck, the New Forum pastor from Rostock who had helped the Round Table dismantle the secret police, then went on to become Germany's first and only Stasi documents inquisitor.

We now know that Stasi operations were larger than suspected. The number of full-time personnel rose during the period 1973 to 1989 from 52,707 to 83,985. Six million files were kept, including files on at least 4 million East Germans out of a total population of 16 million.[49] The number of regular informers, or *Inoffizielle Mitarbeiter* (IM), doubled under Honecker to about 109,000. Three thousand deep cover domestic "moles," or Special Deployment Officers (OBiE) have been uncovered in government bureaus and state-run companies.[50] The "Gauck Authority" cannot actually fire anyone. "My job is to answer 15 questions on a form," Gauck has explained; "it is up to the requesting office to decide whether to exonerate or incriminate the person and to what degree."[51] Even the initiative for starting a background check lies elsewhere. The

Authority is so overworked that it cannot fully vet the names of mid-level public employees. In the first two months of 1992, as the Stasi Documents Law first went into effect, 500,000 citizens applied to read their files, but only 200 could be accommodated by the Authority's 1,500-man staff. By mid-1993, 651,701 of 1,768,784 applications had been processed by a staff of 2,975.[52]

The GDR's small opposition intelligentsia, including several Round Table veterans, has spearheaded efforts to purge old GDR officials – in striking contrast to the conciliatory line dissident Czech intellectuals have taken on Václav Havel's example.[53] It was also decisive when West Germans considered moving Stasi archives to the central federal archives in Koblenz. On September 4, 1990, one month before reunification, several prominent dissident intellectuals led by painter and New Forum founder Bärbel Bohley tried to occupy the central Stasi archives at the Normanenstrasse complex in Berlin. They accidentally occupied the wrong building, but the effect of their hunger strike was undiminished. Their demands included: lifting the FRG's thirty-year rule restricting access to documents in federal archives, putting Stasi leaders on trial, and revealing which members of the democratic People's Chamber had been Stasi IM's. Just five days before reunification negotiators signed an annex to the Unification Treaty allowing Stasi documents to remain in Berlin and committing the Bundestag to consider lifting the official secrets restrictions.

The absence of a comprehensive national lustration law, coupled with the legal right of access to documents and an under-manned agency for processing background checks on public officials, renders "overcoming the past" in eastern Germany somewhat capricious. To cite just one example, the radical West Berlin newspaper *TAZ* chose not to publish the Stasi employees' names and addresses it received anonymously on three computer diskettes in May 1990, but did print a list of OBiE moles leaked to it in March 1991.[54] During the March 1990 elections, charges of collaboration with the Stasi based on leaked documents and effectively "tried" in the daily press led to the resignation of three major party leaders (Democratic Awakening's Wolfgang Schnur, SPD-East's Ibrahim Böhme, and CDU-East's Martin Kirchner). Fifty-five of 400 democratic People's Chamber members had tainted pasts of one degree or another (CDU = 24, PDS = 12, FDP = 11, SPD = 6, Bündnis 90 = 2).

One result of the unstructured purge of collaborators with the old regime has been a shortage of political talent from eastern Germany today. The CDU imported its local party leaders in several of the newly reconstituted federal states, including Kurt Biedenkopf, now governor (*Präsident*) of Saxony, eastern Germany's most populous state. After persistent press charges of Stasi connections, Chancellor Kohl in late

1991 encouraged then CDU deputy national chairman de Maizière to resign. Only three of Kohl's nineteen ministers were easterners, as was only one of nine SPD vice-chairmen. Kohl first nominated an easterner, the CDU candidate to succeed federal President Richard von Weizsäcker, justice minister in Saxony, Steffen Heitman, a priest who had advised the Dresden Group of 20. But after a series of gaffes, Kohl dropped him for Constitutional Court chief justice Roman Herzog, a westerner who took office in 1994.

The Unification Treaty post hoc recognition of SED legality complicates legal proceedings.[55] Especially given the German *Rechtsstaat* tradition, which the GDR embraced at the same time it embraced democracy and capitalism, legal redress is slow even though it is not as obstructed by holdover justice officials as in many other new democracies. Legal proceedings have met no one's conception of justice. Although SED union boss Harry Tisch became one of the first regime veterans to stand trial, at first only lower-ranking officials were convicted. In 1992 the first in a series of border guards were sentenced to mostly suspended jail terms for having fired the shots that killed some of the 800 persons who died trying to leave the GDR. Several of the aging political leaders on whose orders the guards acted have escaped conviction. Once the Chilean embassy in Moscow had ousted him in 1992, by then seventy-nine-year-old Honecker was arrested and returned to a Berlin jail. Along with eighty-five-year-old former Stasi chief Erich Mielke, President Willi Stoph, Defense Minister Heinz Kessler, a defense ministry staffer, and a border district party chief, he was put on trial for approving the suspected "shoot order" during a National Defense Council meeting in 1974. A convoluted legal debate over his cancer, based on the German constitutional guarantee of "human dignity," resulted in his release and voluntary exile in Santiago, Chile, where he died in May 1994. Stoph was released after suffering a heart attack. In a reflection of prosecutors' haste, Mielke was excused to face trial on Nazi-era evidence for a prewar revenge killing during a skirmish between Communists and Weimar-era police in 1931. Eventually Kessler and the two lower-ranking officials were sentenced to modest jail terms, and pronounced "perpetrators" not just "accomplices" on appeal.[56] A follow-up trial of surviving Politburo members is planned.

Although the largely scandal-driven pace of revelations in reunified Germany seems to jeopardize any possibility for systematic "justice," it may in practice be more democratic than a rigid lustration law on the Czechoslovakian model, as the case of Manfred Stolpe illustrates. Stolpe has been able to survive as SPD governor (*Präsident*) of the reconstituted federal state of Brandenburg despite revelations about past collaboration with Stasi operatives only because of the broad support of the voting public. His is perhaps the most difficult case because it so fully blurs the always problematic distinction between victim and perpetrator under a post-totalitarian regime. As a high-ranking lay official in the GDR Lutheran Church hierarchy he successfully negotiated the release of many political prisoners held in the notorious Bautzen II jail and improved conditions for many others. He earned the respect of opposition dissidents, but that respect turned to outrage as evidence of his secret contacts with the Stasi multiplied. Unlike most IM's, Stolpe never signed a written statement of collaboration, but he concedes he met Stasi officials in secret and often neglected to inform his church superiors. He had a case officer and a cover name ("Secretary"), of which he claims to have been unaware. Stolpe argues that his go-between role was necessary "to give the people hope."[57] Opposition movement veterans, who were constant targets of Stasi spying and dirty tricks, consider Stolpe's a test case for Germany's second attempt to "master" an authoritarian past, but a state assembly investigative committee under sympathetic PDS chairmanship neither absolved nor condemned him.[58]

The largely unstructured process of evening the score in Germany today is a by-product of the clash between eastern German dissidents' search for moral justice, even at some cost to democratic procedures, and the traditional German allegiance to rule-of-law traditions, even at some cost to moral justice.[59] (The German word *Justiz* lacks the moral connotation *justice* has in English, for which the separate word *Gerechtigkeit* is used.) Some western intellectuals see a chance to make up for the truncated process of coping with the Nazi past during the Cold War by "doing it right this time," but compromises have been reached.

The result of these compromises between contending approaches to "overcoming the past" has been the unstructured and slow, but relentless pace of public revelations since reunification. The cumulative effect of this slow trickle has been to cast a shadow of suspicion over eastern Germany's most promising democratic politicians, most of whom emerged from previous experience in opposition movements that were thoroughly penetrated by the Stasi. The generational shortage of political talent thus created could restrict the representation of eastern concerns over how reunification is being implemented. At the same time, though, no rigid lustration law has preempted the democratic process. Voters and parties debate the difficult moral issues, such as just where the line between victim and perpetrator should be drawn. They have retained the possibility of deciding some individual politicians' fates themselves. This hybrid approach to "evening the score" illustrates more clearly than others the tension between moral justice and democratic procedures in the post-Communist democracies.[60] It is just one legacy of the accelerating collapse.

CONCLUSION

The rapid pace of reunification and a particular process of evening the score with collaborators make up the legacy of the GDR's short democratic transition under a succession of ever weaker interim regimes. I have called this transition, with its progression from reform authoritarian to caretaker interim and power-sharing interim regimes, a case of "accelerating collapse," in part to distinguish it from the simpler collapsed transition in Czechoslovakia with its single power-sharing interim government. The mutual weakness of the collapsing East German regime *and* the relatively unorganized opposition that made power-sharing necessary also made rapid reunification and a broad evening of scores possible. In spite of the Round Table, accelerating collapse meant the old regime could not protect its interest in preserving an independent GDR, much less its secret police and archives, by negotiating a transition pact with opposition leaders. At the same time, the opposition had so little mass support that it felt compelled both to sustain the last vestiges of the old regime by sharing power, then to seek its revenge later by purging as many regime collaborators as possible. Such is the ironic legacy of the East German road from liberalization to power-sharing.

10

Interim government and democratic consolidation: Argentina in comparative perspective

JAMES W. MCGUIRE

INTRODUCTION[1]

In July 1982, a few weeks after Argentina's defeat in the Falklands/ Malvinas conflict, the most repressive military government in Argentine history announced that elections leading to civilian rule would be held at an unspecified date no later than the end of 1983. For the next seventeen months, General Reynaldo Bignone's incumbent caretaker administration governed the country. This chapter examines the emergence, decisions, and impact of Bignone's caretaker government in the broader context of the Argentine transition from authoritarian rule. By comparing this interim government and transition to others in Latin America and Southern Europe, it will be possible to illuminate how, and to what extent, Argentina's interim government and transition shaped the quality and stability of its emergent democracy.

A transition from authoritarian rule is not always a transition to a consolidated democracy. The emergent regime may be a new kind of authoritarianism (e.g., Iran 1979) or a regime that falls short of full democracy (e.g., Brazil 1985). Even if a democracy emerges, it may not last. A brief democratic interlude may be terminated by a new military coup (e.g., Venezuela 1948), an elected leader who destroys the regime from within (e.g., Germany 1933), or a popular insurrection (no historical examples). These alternative outcomes suggest that emergent democratic regimes may vary along two dimensions: quality and stability. To evaluate the quality and stability of the democracy that emerges from a transition, democracy must be defined in a way that can be applied to actual regimes. Like most recent studies of transitions, this analysis will adopt a minimalist procedural definition. A democratic political regime is one in which (1) leaders are chosen in free and fair competitive elections in which virtually all adult citizens have the right to vote and to stand for office, (2) leaders so chosen make virtually all of the state's basic policy decisions, and (3) citizens are granted in principle, and not systematically denied in practice, basic civil rights like freedom from physical abuse by agents of the state, freedom of speech and the press, and freedom of association and assembly.[2]

Democracy may be viewed as consolidated when its quality exceeds the procedural minimum and when its stability is well-enough assured that few take seriously the possibility of a military coup, mass insurrection, or erosion from within by an incumbent leader.[3] Consolidated democracies are not perfect democracies. They may be improved in a variety of ways, for example, along the dimensions of breadth (with more people participating in a greater variety of ways), depth (with people participating in more well-informed, thoughtful, and autonomous fashion), and range (with the extension of democracy to a subnational and nonstate institution).[4] An adequate level and more equitable distribution of economic resources would certainly help to enlarge the breadth, depth, and range of democracy. It would be a mistake, however, to confuse democracy in the minimalist procedural sense with social justice. In addition to restricting, perhaps to zero, the number of democratic regimes available for analysis, writing social justice into the definition of democracy would guide attention away from critical questions about the causal relationships that may exist between social justice and democracy.[5]

An interim government administers the final phase of a transition, from the decision to hold unrestricted elections to the inauguration of the new regime. From one perspective, an interim government seems capable of exerting strong influence over the quality and stability of the new democracy. An interim government holds formal political power during the last stage of a transition, when constraints on political engineering are relatively loose.[6] More than periods of regime stability, transitions are intervals in which political actors are uncommonly free to forge new political identities, to invent new styles of political action, and to mold institutions that organize political activity. If a political regime is a set of rules for ruling, a transition is an interregnum when the rules are up for grabs. Because interim governments exercise formal political power during the last stage of this formative juncture, their composition and actions might well be expected to have powerful shaping and constraining effects on the subsequent regime. From another perspective, however, interim governments appear less potentially influential. An interim government comes into being precisely when it announces the certainty of its own demise. Why should anyone take seriously the preferences of political actors who are just marking time until more enduring rulers are chosen? Moreover, interim governments are not themselves elected, and usually come into being when the crisis that led to the authoritarian regime has long passed. Their decisions may therefore lack the weight of those made either by authoritarian incumbents at their height, or by elected officials with democratic legitimacy. More than anything else, it is the reservoir of legality that these interim governments usually enjoy, simply by virtue of their formal control over the state apparatus, that gives their decisions any weight at all.

Bignone's incumbent caretaker government enjoyed a modicum of legality simply by controlling the state apparatus. The preceding military incumbents (1976–82), however, had committed gross human rights violations that went beyond even their own repressive laws. They had also disregarded their own rules for presidential succession and violated the military chain of command. Because of these abuses, Bignone's reservoir of legality was much smaller than that enjoyed by other caretaker administrations. This depleted store of legality nonetheless proved sufficient to allow his government to exercise a degree of control over the transition – less control than the authoritarian incumbents in Brazil, Chile, or even Uruguay, but more than is usually recognized. A crucial nexus of such control involved an apparent pact between key army generals and a powerful faction of the Peronist union leadership. According to credible reports, the generals agreed to give the union leaders control of some unions under government trusteeship in exchange for the union leaders' promise that the new government, which most expected would be Peronist, would refrain from prosecuting military officers for human rights violations. Had the Peronists won the 1983 presidential election and delivered on their end of the reported bargain, Argentina's transition might well have been interpreted as a carefully staged, incumbent-controlled one along the lines of the ones in Brazil or Chile – not as a case of regime collapse along the lines of the ones in Greece or Portugal.

This reinterpretation of the Argentine case, and its comparison to other recent experiences in Latin America and Southern Europe, suggests a broad hypothesis about interim governments, transitions from authoritarian rule, and emergent democracies. The evidence in this chapter suggests that the caretaker model of interim government gives the outgoing authoritarian incumbents more control over the transition than does the power-sharing or provisional model. Greater control by the authoritarian incumbents tends, in turn, to diminish the quality, but increase the short-term stability, of the democracy that emerges from the transition (especially, it will be argued, if the authoritarian incumbents are military rather than civilian). Argentina is an exception to this generalization, for although it had a military-presided incumbent caretaker government, it got a democracy that was initially high in quality (fair initial election, maximum power to elected officials, respect for human rights and the rule of law) but low in stability (military rebellions in 1987 and 1988). To explain this exceptionality, it is crucial to recognize that the voters in October 1983 foiled what seems to have been a pact-in-the-making between the authoritarian incumbents and the Peronist union leadership. Had the Peronists won the election and abided by the terms of the alleged pact, Argentina's emergent democracy would have been low in quality (with no prosecutions for human rights violations and perhaps other concessions to the military) but high in short-term stability (such concessions would have made officers less inclined to rebel). Such a democracy would have resembled those which emerged from the military-controlled incumbent caretaker governments in Brazil, Chile, and Uruguay. The Argentine military regime's legality deficit played an important role in depriving the military self-amnesty of its capacity to evoke compliance in the event of a Peronist defeat.

THE ARGENTINE TRANSITION AND INTERIM GOVERNMENT: OVERVIEW

Between 1955, when populist leader Juan Perón was overthrown in a military coup, and 1973, when Perón was again elected president, conflict between Peronism and anti-Peronism mired Argentina in a spiral of weak civilian governments alternating with intervals of overt or covert military rule. In the late 1960s, the axis of conflict began to shift from Peronism versus anti-Peronism to left versus right. The reasons for this shift included the post-1966 military government's shutting down of political opposition, which helped push many, especially urban middle-class youth, to the left, and the impact of the global wave of radical thought and action on Argentina's cosmopolitan urban centers. A watershed in shifting the axis of conflict came in May 1969, when citizens occupied more than a hundred square blocks in the center of the city of Córdoba, fatally damaging a three-year-old military regime. After the Cordobazo, as the takeover came to be known, radicals began to organize guerrilla groups, the most important of which were the Montoneros (Peronist and mostly urban) and the Peoples' Revolutionary Army (Marxist and partly rural). The guerrillas began a campaign of bombings and assassinations aimed ostensibly at ushering in an ill-defined variant of socialism. After civilian rule returned in 1973, many erstwhile anti-Peronists were undoubtedly among those who elected Perón president, hoping that he could rein in the guerrillas. When Perón died in July 1974, leaving the presidency to his wife and vice-president Isabel Martínez de Perón, violence flared anew as the right-wing Argentine Anti-Communist Alliance outdid its leftist adversaries in assassinating perceived opponents. In March 1976, as violence and inflation spiraled out of control, the armed forces replaced the government with a military junta and announced the beginning of the "Proceso de Reorganización Nacional" (Proceso).

One of the first acts of the military government led by General Jorge Videla was to unleash a campaign of terror unprecedented in modern Argentine history. By the end of military rule in December 1983, at least 8,960 people had "disappeared."[7] The military rulers explained the kidnap and murder of thousands of Argentine citizens as the unavoidable cost of a "dirty war" against leftist subversion. But as the military itself recognized, only a small proportion of the victims actually belonged to terrorist groups. General Iberico St. Jean described the strategy succinctly: "first we'll kill the subversives, then their collaborators, then . . . their sympathizers, then . . . those who remain indifferent, and finally we'll kill the timid." In a war of this sort, errors were unavoidable. According to General Luciano Menéndez, "We are going to have to kill 50,000 people: 25,000 subversives, 20,000 sympathizers, and we will make 5,000 mistakes."[8] The junta's policy toward the press provides particularly telling insight into the use of state terror as a political weapon. Strict censorship was imposed on the day of the coup, but was lifted a month later. The repeal of censorship was among the most chilling decisions the military ever made. Between March 1976 and August 1980, sixty-eight journalists who (intentionally or not) put the regime in an unfavorable light "disappeared" and another thirty-six were killed outright. In the face of uncertainty about what was permitted and what was not, the press, with the partial exception of the English-language *Buenos Aires Herald,* was silenced more completely than it would have been had censorship existed.[9]

To make sure that subversion would never return, the new military government decided to eliminate once and for all the economic crises, social institutions, and ideological contamination to which subversion was attributed. It suspended political party activity, purged the universities, put the CGT (General Labor Confederation) under government trusteeship, outlawed strikes, and imprisoned hundreds of politicians and union leaders. The centerpiece of the Proceso was a long-term economic plan directed by civilian economy minister José A. Martínez de Hoz, which was aimed at replacing state spending, inefficient industry, and trade restrictions with a free-market economic model based in the short run on agricultural exports. The plan was designed not only to improve the fiscal and foreign exchange situation, but also to reduce the size and hence the power of the industrial working class, which was seen as a major source to the country's political and economic instability.[10] The economic plan would thus assure the long-term demobilization of a social sector whose short-term quiescence was assured by harsh repression. Despite the disruption entailed by these radical changes, the results of the economic model, measured by growth and inflation, were erratic but not at first altogether negative. GDP stagnated in 1976 and fell almost 4 percent in 1978, but rose 6 percent in 1977 and almost 7 percent in 1979. Meanwhile, inflation declined from 443 percent in 1976 to 160 percent in 1979. Wages, consumer goods production, hours worked in industry, and formal sector employment fell dramatically, but the government viewed this deterioration as the inevitable concomitant of rationalizing the country's productive structure.[11]

By 1979 the military government was rather pleased with itself. In a few short years it had won what it considered to be a "war" against subversion, rid the country of allegedly corrupt politicians, embarked on a radical transformation of the social and economic structure, and hosted a World Cup in soccer, which Argentina conveniently won. From this position of self-confidence, the military began to think about laying the groundwork for a return to civilian rule. In 1979 General Albano Harguindeguy, Videla's interior minister, began a series of interviews with "notable" Argentine citizens to sound out prospects for the creation of a civilian-led "Movement of National Opinion" (MON), whose mission would be to continue Martínez de Hoz's neoliberal economic policies and to anchor the future civilian-run polity in "the Christian conception of life and the traditions of our culture." The MON was to draw its leaders from conservative provincial parties and its votes from Peronist and Radical defectors. As a formula for a return to civilian rule, the MON was an aggressive, positive project initiated from a position of confidence. Even at this early stage, however, it also included defensive elements. The military recognized that its core problem would be to insulate itself from prosecution for human rights abuses. Accordingly, civilian politicians would have to refrain from questioning anything the military had done in the war against subversion. They would also have to let military officers participate in the cabinet and in a security council that would oversee all policies relating to matters of internal defense. Finally, electoral activity would not resume until 1984 or 1987 and would be carefully staged, with local and legislative elections preceding national and presidential contests.[12] Had the MON scheme come to fruition, Argentina's transition would have resembled the military-controlled ones in Brazil or Chile, both of which gave rise to civilian regimes constrained by military tutelage.

Prospects for the MON diminished, however, as the economy deteriorated. By the end of Videla's term in office (March 1981), it was clear that the economic plan would need serious revision. Wage cuts, reduced import tariffs, and an increasingly overvalued peso depressed demand for domestically produced goods, driving industries into bankruptcy and contributing to the collapse of dozens of financial institutions. In 1981, real per capita GDP declined 7.3 percent and industrial production dropped 15.2 percent.[13] Meanwhile, the overvalued peso led to a huge rise in imports and permitted middle-class Argentines to go on spending sprees abroad, where they acquired the nickname *los deme dos* ("give me two"). The need to finance the resulting balance of payments deficit, profligate weapons purchases, and gargantuan borrowing by state-owned corporations (which, far from being privatized, became military officers' private fiefdoms) caused the foreign debt to rise from $8.5 billion in December 1979 to $25.3 billion, or 42 percent of GDP, sixteen months later in March 1981.[14]

Combative union leaders began to protest Martínez de Hoz's economic policies as early as April 1979, when they called a partly successful general strike.[15] By March 1981, Argentina's major business organizations, the Rural Society and Industrial Union, had joined the unions in decrying an economic policy that benefited nobody except top-ranking military officers, financial speculators, a few coddled industrial conglomerates, and firms receiving contracts for the government's pharaonic construction projects.[16] Spearheading protest against human rights abuses were the Mothers of the Plaza de Mayo. On April 30, 1977, fourteen women whose children had been kidnapped assembled in front of the government house in downtown Buenos Aires, demanding to know where their children were. From that day forward the Mothers circulated in the same place every Thursday at 3:30 PM. They survived the disappearance of one of their leaders in December 1977, and their membership grew to 5,000 as additional women joined in search of relatives who had disappeared.[17] In the international arena, the Inter-American Commission for Human Rights, Amnesty International, and the United States government all demanded that the military government end human rights abuses and account for the disappeared.

Given the military's tight-lipped position that every aspect of the dirty war had been necessary to save the country from Marxist terrorists, national and international criticism of human rights abuses, even as it saved lives, promoted a siege mentality that reinforced the armed forces' internal cohesion. After 1980, however, military cohesion began to break down. The deepening economic crisis contributed to this erosion, but just as important was the "success" of the dirty war itself. By late 1977 the guerrilla groups had been largely demobilized, and recorded kidnappings in which the victims were presumed killed dropped from 3,485 in 1976 to 2,544 in 1977 to 830 in 1978 to 148 in 1979.[18] Without a war climate to submerge them, personal disputes, interservice rivalries, differences over economic policy, and conflicting views about how to structure a future civilian regime bubbled to the surface. The upwelling of internal differences raised the stakes of the presidential succession scheduled for March 1981. In September 1980, Videla indicated that he wanted General Roberto Viola, commander-in-chief of the army since May 1978, to succeed him as president. Viola supported a shift to more expansionary economic policies and was willing to hold a dialogue with pre-1976 party and union leaders. These positions put him at odds with navy officers, who had traditionally supported free-market economic policies and who felt that it was now an admiral's turn for the presidency. They also generated resentment from army hard-liners, who wanted no political opening and harbored deep hostility for the great majority of pre-1976 politicians, whom they regarded as self-interested hacks whose corrupt and demagogic practices had created a climate for Marxist subversion. Although Videla finally mustered enough army support to push through Viola's nomination, the new president began his term amidst the smoldering resentment of other officers.[19]

On taking office in March 1981, Viola began to lay the groundwork for a transition to civilian rule. On the crucial issue of impunity from prosecution for human rights violations, Viola stated categorically that "a victorious army is not investigated."[20] However, he did not share the hard-liners' maximalist goal of creating a brand-new political party to perpetuate free-market economic policies and a reactionary cultural climate under a future civilian regime. Viola made clear from the outset that he was willing to negotiate the terms of a transition with established politicians and union leaders, including Peronists. Although he never announced an electoral timetable, a plausible scenario involved Viola's transfer of the presidency when his term ended in 1984 to a civilian supported by both the armed forces and the leaders of the major political parties.[21] The shift in emphasis from the Videla/Harguindeguy dialogue with the minor conservative parties to the Viola dialogue with the Peronists and Radicals paralleled a similar shift in 1971, when General Levingston's dalliance with Oscar Alende, the leader of a small left-nationalist party, gave way to General Lanusse's "Great National Accord" with the major parties, which ultimately failed in its efforts to prevent Perón's return to the presidency and to halt the rise of the revolutionary left.[22]

Viola's negotiations with the main political parties and with a group of conciliatory union leaders antagonized military hard-liners and fueled rumors of an impending internal coup. At the same time, his incipient liberalization triggered a reactivation of civil society that would have been hard to reverse, even had it not been for the Falklands/Malvinas debacle.[23] In July 1981, combative union leaders, taking advantage of a let up of antilabor repression, called a general strike that idled 1.5 million workers.[24] In the same month, five political parties, including the Peronists and Radicals, formed a coalition to press for more expansionary economic policies and for a swift return to civilian rule. Recognizing that Viola's days might be numbered, the leaders of the Multipartidaria, as the party coalition was known, did not embrace his transition project wholeheartedly, but neither did they refuse to participate in a dialogue with him.

A key figure in the Multipartidaria was the long-standing leader of the Radical party, Ricardo Balbín. Unlike fellow Radical Raúl Alfonsín, who was one of the dictatorship's more outspoken opponents, Balbín was ready to agree to several of the military's conditions for a return to civilian rule. Crucially, he was willing drop the issue of human rights violations during the dirty war. Balbín also agreed that the reach of international terrorism required military participation in a future civilian cabinet and a military-led national security council to oversee matters of internal defense. Although he was never explicitly offered the chance to succeed Viola, Balbín's availability as a possible compromise candidate helped to keep Viola's transition project afloat. In 1981, however, Balbín fell ill, and in September of that year he died. His passing dealt a severe blow to the military's prospects for a negotiated transition. Viola's own illness, which also became apparent in September 1981, provided the excuse for hard-liners, led by General Leopoldo Galtieri and Admiral Jorge Anaya, to oust him from the presidency three months later.[25]

On assuming the presidency in December 1981, Galtieri broke off negotiations with the Multipartidaria and resurrected the maximalist strategy for a return to civilian rule. Like Videla and Harguindeguy, Galtieri hoped to use the tiny conservative provincial parties to build a new political force that would carry on the work of the Proceso after military rule ended. In contrast to his predecessors, however, Galtieri expected to lead the new party himself. Because of the economic collapse and the parties' recent resurgence, he had little chance of winning an open election. If his project was to succeed, the economy would have to improve (requiring the military to stay in power for several more years) and something would have to be done to shift popular support from the revitalized opposition to the military regime. Galtieri had plans for coping with both of these problems. His strategy in the economic sphere was to return to the Martínez de Hoz approach, which meant replacing Viola's relatively pragmatic economic team with a hard-line neoliberal group behind Roberto Alemann. His strategy for winning immediate popular support was more adventurous. Partly to assure navy support for Viola's ouster, Galtieri gave Admiral Jorge Anaya the green light for his pet military project: a military occupation of the Falkland/Malvinas islands, which were claimed by both Argentina and Great Britain.[26]

Although a large demonstration against military rule took place two days before the Argentines acted, the operation was not a last-ditch defensive measure aimed at saving the regime from an overpowering opposition. On the contrary, it was part of an offensive project aimed at achieving several related goals. Besides settling a long-standing international grievance, a successful occupation could help restore military cohesion and generate a "rally round the flag" effect that would move public opinion toward support for the regime and eventually behind a carefully groomed successor party led by Galtieri himself. Everything depended, of course, on the occupation's success. Defeat seems inevitable in retrospect, but Galtieri never expected that war would break out. He calculated that the British, which did not respond militarily when Argentina placed a token force on the nearby South Georgia islands in March 1982, would not resist when the main force moved onto the Falklands/Malvinas. He also calculated that the Reagan administration, which was relying on Argentine officers to train the Nicaraguan Contras, would not oppose the occupation.[27] Both of Galtieri's assumptions proved to be wrong. Britain went to war, the United States sided with its NATO ally, troops suffered and died, and Argentina surrendered on June 14, 1982.

Discredited by defeat, Galtieri resigned as president and was replaced as army commander-in-chief by General Cristino Nicolaides. As head of the most powerful service, Nicolaides named a retired army general, Reynaldo Bignone, to the presidency. Bignone's nomination angered the air force, which had performed better in the war than the ill-trained and frostbitten conscript army, and antagonized the navy, which had yet to place one of its own in the presidency.[28] In response to the army's unilateral act, the other services withdrew from the junta for what turned out to be three months. Nonetheless, Bignone formed an incumbent caretaker government on July 1, 1982, to administer what Nicolaides promised would be "an orderly, shared, and concerted transition to democracy."[29] In a bid to formalize the boundaries of such a transition, the junta in November 1982 published a fifteen-point document demanding military participation in the next government, rejecting any inquiry into the dirty war or military corruption, and prohibiting the dismissal of military-appointed judges. It also issued a veiled threat that hard-line officers might halt the transition if the parties refused these conditions. The Multipartidaria rejected the document and, disregarding the threat, called a huge rally to repudiate the military regime.[30]

In April 1983 the military made a less ambitious attempt to set terms for the transition by releasing a "Final Document of the Military Junta on the War Against Subversion and Terrorism." Read aloud on TV against a background of wistful guitar music, the "Final Document" admitted that the dirty war had included "errors" which, "as happens in all armed conflicts, may have sometimes exceeded the limits of respect for fundamental rights." But the document said pointedly that "God and history" would be "the only supreme tribunals for the acts committed." To discourage less exalted tribunals from disputing this jurisdiction, the military leadership appended to the document an institutional act stating that the dirty war had been authorized by the high command of each of the services. Such authorization would keep all charges in military courts, where the "just following orders" defense could be used.[31] The Multipartidaria, along with a broad spectrum of other civilian leaders, rejected the initiative. The military made a final attempt to safeguard its interests a few weeks before the October 1983 presidential election, when the army, without the full support of the navy or air force, had the government issue a "Law of National Pacification" that granted an amnesty for both subversive activities and "excesses of repression" committed between May 1973 and June 1983. By this time the economy was in a tailspin and gruesome stories of human rights violations were being aired daily. Even military-appointed judges declared the law unconstitutional, and one insisted that "there can be no amnesty for crimes against humanity."[32]

Until Raúl Alfonsín's unexpected victory, most people assumed that Peronism would win the October 1983 presidential election. Hence, the junta made a special effort to negotiate the transition with Peronist union leaders, who acted as king-makers in the Justicialist (Peronist) Party. In November 1982 press reports began to circulate that Nicolaides had cut a deal with Lorenzo Miguel, head of the powerful metalworkers' union, that would reportedly have given Miguel's allies control of unions under government trusteeship in exchange for a promise that a future Peronist government would take no legal action against military officers.[33] Both Miguel and Nicolaides denied these rumors, but Peronist political and union leaders at odds with Miguel stated that they thought a pact was in the making.[34] Radical Party presidential hopefuls Raúl Alfonsín and Fernando de la Rúa took up the issue in April 1983, insisting that Miguel and his allies, in exchange for control of unions under government trusteeship, had agreed to urge the next government to refrain from prosecuting military "excesses" and "illicit acts," from cutting the military budget or, at least during the first phase of civilian rule, from replacing the army high command.[35] After Alfonsín won his party's nomination lawyers for the Peronist union leaders initiated a libel suit against him, but the Radical candidate stood by his allegations and the suit came to naught. The charges of a military-union pact were viewed as credible by a significant sector of public opinion, and Peronist presidential candidate Italo Luder stated publicly that he would respect the amnesty that the military had granted to all who had committed crimes in the dirty war.[36] Had the Peronists won the elections, Argentina's transition would have been interpreted as a carefully staged, incumbent-controlled one on the Brazilian, Chilean, or Spanish model, not as a case of "regime collapse" as in Greece or Portugal. Defeat in external war is not favorable for an incumbent-controlled transition to a tutelary semidemocracy,[37] but the hypothetical scenario of Peronist electoral victory (which rumors of a pact actually helped to prevent) suggests that one may not preclude the other.

Although the military tried to negotiate immunity from prosecution, it made no serious effort to pursue its ends by rewriting the constitution or changing laws involving political parties or elections. In contrast to many other recent transitions,[38] amending the national constitution was not even discussed. When the military dropped a July 1983 proposal to alter provincial constitutions to provide for the indirect election of local authorities, journalists noted that officers had scrapped the plan because they thought "the time for constitutional tinkering is past."[39] No major party leader objected to the political party statute passed in August 1982, which simply required parties to reregister all members, stipulated a minimum membership for inclusion on the ballot, and outlawed parties that "deny human rights, seek the overthrow of the democratic system, use force illegally and systematically, or favor the personal concentration of power."[40] Nor did the June 1983 electoral law spark more than mild controversy. The previous electoral law, enacted in 1972, had provided for a direct presidential election in two rounds (as in present-day Brazil or France) and had stipulated that a party must obtain at least 8 percent of a province's vote before representing that province in the proportionally elected lower house of congress.[41] The 1983 law, by contrast, provided for the president to be chosen in a single round by an electoral college elected by popular vote, and reduced the threshold for a seat in the lower house from 8 to 3 percent of the province's national deputy vote. These changes made it easier for minor parties to win seats in congress and held out the possibility that they might even wind up with pivotal votes in the electoral college. Not surprisingly, the minor parties were happy with these arrangements while the Radicals and Peronists grumbled about them.[42] Skeptics might have viewed the new law as a sop to the tiny conservative provincial parties that had supported the military government or even as a technique for sowing chaos in the electoral college and legislature. In the end, however, not even the big parties objected strenuously to the new law.[43]

Seemingly in shock after surrender, citizens were largely quiescent during Bignone's first two months in office, but the opposition soon began to mobilize. Beginning in September 1982, the military faced in quick succession a demonstration in support of human rights groups, a tax revolt in the Buenos Aires metropolitan area, a general strike, and a large demonstration in support of democracy.[44] Moreover, the passage of the Statute of Political Parties in August 1982 triggered a surge of party activity. By March 1983 nearly a quarter of eligible voters had joined or rejoined political parties. The Justicialist Party alone claimed more than 3 million members, about 60 percent of whom were reported to have voted in the party's indirect primary elections in 1983. At the leadership level, however, both parties confronted major challenges. In the Justicialist Party, metalworkers' chief Lorenzo Miguel, filling the vacuum left by Juan Perón's death and Isabel Perón's retirement from Argentine politics, arranged the nomination of Italo Luder as the party's presidential candidate, chose many of the Peronist national deputy nominees, and was named to the party's top effective leadership post.[45] In the Radical Party, Balbín's death in 1981 set up a contest between Raúl Alfonsín (the heir apparent) and Fernando de la Rúa, a more conservative and traditional Radical politician. After a series of defeats in province-by-province direct primary elections, de la Rúa conceded defeat and Alfonsín became the Radical presidential candidate.

On October 30, 1983, Alfonsín defeated Luder by 52 to 40 percent, marking the first time in history that Peronism had lost a major national election.[46] Five factors help explain this outcome. Firstly, deindustrialization during the military dictatorship reduced the size of Peronism's traditional electoral base, the industrial working class – although the reduction was smaller than is commonly believed.[47] Many former industrial workers lost contact with the unions, and thus with peer pressure and active encouragement to vote Peronist. Secondly, Alfonsín made inroads into Peronism's working-class base, winning outright in a number of industrial suburbs of Buenos Aires, although not in the poorest ones. Thirdly, Alfonsín seems to have gotten decisive support from the center-right. The vote share of center-right parties was only 3 percent in 1983, down from 20 percent in 1973. It is likely that many center-right voters cast a strategic vote for Alfonsín as the candidate most likely to defeat the political movement that presided over the shattering 1973–6 experience.[48] Fourthly, the Radicals ran a better campaign than did the Peronists, whose image was tarred by the evident predominance in the party of widely disliked union leaders, by the back-room deals which resulted in Luder's nomination, by well-substantiated rumors of a union-military pact, and by an election-eve campaign rally at which Buenos Aires gubernatorial candidate Herminio Iglesias set fire to a coffin symbolizing Alfonsín's Radical Party. This ill-conceived gesture was carried on national television and did not sit well with a population exhausted by more than a decade of violence and intolerance. Finally, and perhaps most importantly, the Radicals, and Alfonsín in particular, presented the image of a tolerant party concerned with formal democracy and human rights, while Peronism continued to portray itself as an intransigent party preoccupied with nationalism and populism. In the wake of the devastating 1973–83 period, many Argentines not firmly committed to either party were simply more receptive to the Radicals' message.

THE ARGENTINE TRANSITION AND INTERIM GOVERNMENT: ANALYSIS

Argentina's 1982–3 transition has been categorized as one that (a) followed a military regime, (b) took place via "regime collapse" or "replacement," (c) was initiated by authoritarian incumbents who would have preferred a liberalized authoritarian regime but accepted democratization, (d) broke with the legality of the preceding regime, (e) was presided over by military rather than civilian actors, (f) was administered by an incumbent caretaker government, (g) escaped from the control of the authoritarian rulers, and (h) involved medium levels of compromise (Table 1).

A few examples will indicate the need to refine the criteria heretofore used to classify transitions. Firstly, features of the prior regime (column "a") certainly *shape* the transition process, but they do not constitute *aspects* of that process. Moreover, they shape the emergent democracy independently of the way in which they shape the transition process. Hence, conflating prior regime with type of transition will always exaggerate the degree to which the type of transition shapes the emergent democracy. Secondly, the degree of compromise involved in the transition (column "h") mingles compromise *among* the opposition parties with compromise *between* the opposition parties and the authoritarian incumbents. These dimensions vary independently, as Table 1 makes clear. Moreover, the cases sketched in Table 1 give no reason to believe that either dimension of compromise (or total amount of compromise) has any consistent effect on the quality or stability of the emergent democracy.[49] Thirdly, the transaction-extrication-collapse classification (column "b") is really a cluster of three analytically distinct dimensions: (1) the proximate cause of the transition, (2) the proactiveness of the decision that led to the transition, and (3) the degree to which the outgoing authoritarian elites were able to control the transition. These dimensions are neither logically commensurable nor empirically covariant. Dimension (1) is a cause of the transition, whereas dimensions (2) and (3) are characteristics of the transition. As Table 1 shows, moreover, the three dimensions vary independently of one another.

Writers using the transaction-extrication-collapse classification usually place Argentina, along with Greece and Portugal, in the "regime collapse" category. The proximate cause of each of these transitions indeed involved an actual or impending foreign war. But the Argentine dictatorship, unlike those in Greece and Portugal, did not "collapse" after its military misadventure. It initiated the transition by a deliberate decision, produced an incumbent caretaker government, generated new attempts to create a successor regime, delayed setting an election date for nine months, stayed in power for seventeen months, controlled the timing of elections, and made a secret pact with Peronist union leaders. Had the Peronists won the election, as most expected would happen, the Argentine military might also have retained prerogatives it was later denied: no prosecution for human rights violations, no immediate changeover in the high command, and no cuts in the military budget. The military in Argentina exercised less control over the transition than did authoritarian incumbents in Brazil, Chile, Spain, or Uruguay, but they exercised more control than did incumbents in Greece or Portugal. Moreover, the military in Argentina initiated the transition via a reactive decision (rather than a proactive one as in Brazil or Spain), but this mode of transition-initiation puts them in a class with the Chilean and Uruguayan incumbents (who reacted to the loss of a plebiscite rather than a war), not with the Greeks or Portuguese (who were simply overthrown). On the proximate cause of the transition Argentina looks like Greece or Portugal, but on the proactiveness of the decision to initiate the transition and on the degree to which the authoritarian incumbents controlled the transition process, Argentina looks more like Uruguay.

Whereas Greece and Portugal got provisional opposition governments, Argentina got an incumbent caretaker administration. These contrasting outcomes show that authoritarian regimes whose demise involves external war need not adopt a particular model of interim government. But if the proximate cause of the transition does not by itself determine the model of interim government, what other factors may be involved? It is important to specify these factors, for a caretaker government permits the incumbent authoritarian elites, by virtue of their control of the formal state apparatus, to exert considerable influence over the transition process, even if their rule is not considered to be legitimate and even if (as in the Argentine case) they have squandered a good part of their store of legality. The degree of control exercised by the authoritarian incumbents has, in turn, important effects on the quality and stability of the emergent democracy.

That Argentina, rather than Greece or Portugal, wound up with an incumbent caretaker government, is puzzling for a number of reasons. Firstly, external war dealt a more decisive defeat to the Argentine generals than to the Greek colonels or the Caetano administration. Argentina actually surrendered, whereas Greece withdrew before armed conflict broke out, and Portugal was still fighting a war of attrition when Caetano was deposed. Secondly, the Argentine military did more than either the

Table 1. *A Dimensionality of Transitions from Authoritarian Rule in Seven Latin American and Southern European Countries*

Dimension	Characteristics of prior regime		Mixed category	Characteristics of decision to initiate transition		Characteristics of transition process		
	Type of prior regime	Proximate cause of transition	Process by which transition takes place	Proactiveness of incumbent decision that begins transition	Outgoing authoritarian attitude to transition	Rules of authoritarian regime broken or intact?	Interim govt. actor	Interim govt. model
Country								
Argentina 1982–1983	Military	Lost war in Malvinas-Falklands	Regime collapse replacement	Reactive decision	Tolerant	Broken[2]	Military	Incumbent caretaker
Brazil 1974–1985	Military	Mil.-as-govt. wanted to rein in security app.	Transaction transformation	Proactive decision	Favorable	Intact	Military	Incumbent caretaker
Chile 1987–1990	Personal[1]	Lost referendum	Transformation	Reactive decision	Opposed	Intact	Military	Incumbent caretaker
Uruguay 1982–1985	Military	Lost referendum	Extrication transplacement	Reactive decision	Opposed	Broken[2]	Military	Incumbent caretaker
Greece 1974	Military	Mil.-as-instit. wanted to deter war in Cyprus	Regime collapse replacement	(Military coup)	Opposed	Broken	Civilian	Provisional opposition
Portugal 1974–1976	Personal	Coup by junior officers opposed to Africa war	Regime collapse replacement	(Military coup)	Opposed	Broken	Military	Provisional opposition
Spain 1975–1977	Personal	Death of personalistic leader (Franco)	Transaction transformation	Proactive decision	Favorable	Intact	Civilian	Incumbent caretaker
Reference in text	(a)		(b)	(c)		(d)	(e)	(f)
Dimension from	Huntington	Disaggregation of Share/Mainw, Huntington	Share/ Mainwaring, Huntington	Disaggregation of Share/Mainw, Huntington	Valenzuela	Linz, element of a Valenzuela dimension	Aguero	Linz/Shain
Coding from	Huntington	New	Share/ Mainwaring, Huntington	New	Valenzuela	Valenzuela	Aguero	New

Greek colonels or Portugal's Caetano government to earn the resentment of the population, in terms of both repression and economic mismanagement. To explain why Argentina got an incumbent caretaker government while Greece and Portugal did not requires a look at characteristics of both the authoritarian incumbents and the opposition.

At the time an external crisis dealt a fatal blow to the regime, Argentina's authoritarian incumbents were more strongly unified with the hierarchical military-as-institution than were the authoritarian incumbents in Greece or Portugal. In Argentina, the Galtieri coup actually restored a

Outgoing authoritarian control of transition	Compromise overall	Compromise among parties	Compromise between parties & authoritarian incumbents	Characteristics of emergent regime			
				Quality of initial election	Initial power of elected officials	Initial quality of civil liberties	Military rebellions after initial election
Very low[3]	Medium	High (Multipartidaria)	Medium (Secret pact with Peronist unionists)	High	High	High	4
High	Low	Medium (Some parties at some times)	Low	Low	Low	Low	0
High	Medium	High (Concertación)	Medium (During 1989 constitut. reforms)	Medium	Low	High	0
Medium	High	Medium (Some parties at some times)	High (Club Naval)	Medium	Medium	High	0
Very low	Low	Low	Low	High	High	High	1
Very low	Low	Low	Low (1975 pacts were with interim govt.)	High	Low	High	0
High	High	High (Plataforms, Coordinación)	High (Moncloa)	High	High	High	1[4]
(g)	(h)						
Aguero, disaggregation of many others	Karl/Schmitter	Disaggregation of Karl/Schmitter	Disaggregation of Karl/Schmitter	Similar to Valenzuela Category	Similar to Valenzuela Category	New	New
Aguero	Karl/Schmitter	New	New	New	New	New	New

[1] Others classify the Chilean regime as military.
[2] No clear criteria exist for deciding whether the rules of an authoritarian regime have been broken or remain intact. It seems particularly problematic to classify the Argentine and Uruguayan cases as ones in which the rules were broken.
[3] As argued in the text, the degree of authoritarian control in the Argentine case might better be classified as "low" or even "medium-to-low."
[4] In Spain, a second coup-in-the-making was nipped in the bud in 1982.

measure of military cohesion that had been lacking under Viola. In Greece and Portugal, the incumbent authoritarian government was overthrown by key segments of the military-as-institution – the Joint Chiefs of Staff in Greece and the junior officers in Portugal – from which it had become increasingly isolated.[50] Reinforcing military unity in Argentina was the breadth of responsibility for the dirty war. Some 300 to 400 high-ranking officers conceived of the antisubversive campaign, designed plans to implement it, and headed the detention centers that operated it. The kidnapping, interrogation, torture, sustained detention, and murder was carried out by another 300 to 400 lower-ranking officers, of whom about 50 are said to have engaged regularly in torture.[51] A commission charged with collecting information on disappearances implicated more than 1,300 officers in kidnapping, torture, and murder.[52] Direct involvement in the dirty war was expanded by the "Pact of Blood" system by which high-level officers were obliged personally to murder prisoners so that all levels of the chain of command would be implicated in illegal repression.[53] Given the breadth of responsibility for the dirty war, a transition like that in Greece, where the scale of repression was small enough that the military-as-institution could sacrifice the military-as-government,[54] or like Portugal's, where junior officers not implicated in domestic repression overthrew the authoritarian incumbents, was out of the question.

Also contributing to the formation of a caretaker government was the fact that some of Argentina's authoritarian incumbents, despite the military defeat, still aspired to perpetuate themselves in power or even create (and head) a successor movement. The day after General Menéndez surrendered to the British, Galtieri tried to contact the leaders of the main political parties to get their support for his continuation as president.[55] Galtieri was forced to resign, but that did not prevent two other top military figures from trying to create successor movements. Admiral Massera retained political ambitions after the Falklands/Malvinas dispute; his vehicle, first launched in 1981, was a would-be "Social Democratic Party" with Isabel Perón as his proposed vice-presidential candidate and, twistedly, surviving Montoneros as his top advisers.[56] Brigadier-General Basilio Lami Dozo, commander of the air force, tried in August 1982 to capitalize on his service's relatively good performance in the war by placing himself at the head of an "official party" that would carry on the work of the Proceso. The effort annoyed the army and navy, offended the political parties, antagonized junior officers (who wanted all the commanders to resign), and got Lami Dozo kicked out of the junta.[57]

Characteristics of the opposition also help explain why the authoritarian leaders in Argentina were able to form an incumbent caretaker government, whereas the authoritarian leaders in Portugal and Greece were replaced by a provisional government of the opposition. Strategic calculation by the parties was important in promoting the incumbent caretaker model. Now that Balbín and Perón had died and Isabel Perón had washed her hands of Argentine politics, both Radicals and Peronists were preoccupied with succession problems. The parties needed time to reorganize, and participation in either a provisional government or a power-sharing arrangement would have absorbed resources and energy. Moreover, some party leaders felt that the military should be responsible for getting the country out of the mess they had gotten it into. And in much the same way that the military put off the 1976 coup until Isabel Perón's government was completely discredited, other party leaders wanted to give the military time to play itself out before taking power themselves.[58] The military government may have been demoralized and discredited after its surrender to Britain, but in the absence of a reasonably cohesive military opposition of the type that overthrew the authoritarian regimes in Portugal and Greece, it still had control of force of arms. Another disincentive for the parties to form provisional or power-sharing interim governments was that there was always a danger, as Alfonsín would soon discover, that perceived responsibility for the economic crisis might shift away from those who produced it to those who had to administer it.

The availability of an opposition leader of suitable stature, acceptable to both the military-as-institution and much of the civilian population, is a supportive condition for the formation of a provisional government. Such leaders were available in Portugal and Greece, but not in Argentina. In Greece, Constantine Karamanlis, a former president and leader of the National Radical Union (renamed New Democracy in 1974), was acceptable to the military-as-institution because of his conservatism and to much of the population because he rejected the military regime.[59] In Portugal a half-century of authoritarian rule had left a vacuum of opposition politicians, but General Antonio Spinola, a flamboyant war hero whose 1973 book opposing the war in Africa had damaged the Caetano government, was able to take over the first provisional administration.[60] Argentina, by contrast, lacked an opposition leader of Karamanlis's or Spinola's stature and potential breadth of support. A military opposition like the one that produced Spinola did not exist in Argentina, and the Argentine parties failed to produce a figure who could lead a provisional government. A Peronist-led interim administration was out of the question, not just because the formal head of the Justicialist Party was Isabel Perón, whose disastrous leadership from 1974 to 1976 had accelerated the spiral of violence and economic crisis, but also because many officers, especially in the navy, retained strong anti-Peronist sentiments. A Radical-led provisional government was a more interesting proposition. Alfonsín, heir apparent to the late Balbín, was himself unacceptable to the military because of his human rights activism, but during the Falklands/Malvinas conflict he had proposed the formation of a provisional government under fellow Radical and former president (1963–6) Arturo

Illia. Foreseeing military defeat, Alfonsín reportedly felt that a civilian-
led government would be more stable than a military one and would
allow the British to be generous in victory.[61]

Alfonsín's proposal had at least one thing going for it: the climate of
the times had finally caught up with Illia's political style. While president,
Illia's pedestrian legalism had earned him the nickname "the turtle." So
out of step was Illia with the millenarian climate of the 1960s that when
the military overthrew him, eleven times as many survey respondents
backed the coup as opposed it. After Isabel Perón's deflated plebiscitari-
anism and Videla's state terror, however, pedestrian legalism clearly had
much to recommend it. In retrospect, according to a 1983 poll, three
times as many survey respondents approved of Illia's government as
disapproved of it.[62] Alfonsín's proposal got off to a good start, with
reporters making parallels between Illia and Karamanlis.[63] But the two
leaders were not really of comparable stature. Illia was a mild-mannered
country doctor who had spent his entire political career in the shadow of
Balbín. He had never expected to win the presidency in 1963, and had in
fact won only 25 percent of a fragmented vote in an election from which
Peronism was banned. The proposal to make Illia provisional president
did not even win backing from all sectors of the Radical Party, and did
not flourish.[64]

On the face of it, the Argentine transition was particularly propitious
for a power-sharing government. Linz and Shain argue that power-
sharing governments tend to emerge "when the incumbents' authority
has been severely undermined but is still sufficient to exercise control"
and when there is "a balance between the degeneration of the outgoing
government and the maturation and growth of the opposition."[65] Such
conditions were present in Argentina after the surrender to Britain. As
might have been expected in such a situation, at least one political actor
did propose a power-sharing arrangement. At about the same time that
Alfonsín suggested a provisional government headed by Illia, Peronist
first vice-president Deolindo Bittel proposed a power-sharing arrangement in which, for a minimum two-year period, the junta would retain
control of the executive branch. Meanwhile, a committee of generals and
politicians would choose a prime minister, with the junta retaining veto
power over the cabinet. Bittel's proposal had problems from the outset.
In the closing stages of the Falklands/Malvinas conflict, it is most unlikely that a military figure could have won civilian (or even military)
support for the prime ministership.[66] Moreover, any civilian politician
who accepted the post would be tarred with collaboration. Few wished
to replicate the experience of Arturo Mor Roig, the Radical Party leader
whose agreement to serve as interior minister in General Lanusse's
1971–3 incumbent caretaker government had probably cost his party

votes in the 1973 presidential election.[67] Bittel's proposal for a power-sharing arrangement met with no more support than Alfonsín's recommendation for a provisional government of the opposition.

It could be argued that Bignone's incumbent caretaker government conformed to a model of interim administration that Linz and Shain have termed "power-sharing from without." In this subtype of power-sharing government, opposition elites "use their influence to limit the freedom of action of the incumbent regime without joining in the government." The result of this influence is an interim administration which is "entirely dominated by the agenda" of the opposition.[68] The notion of "power-sharing from without" seems, however, to confuse the type of interim government with the degree of control that the authoritarian incumbents exercise over the transition. Argentina's interim administration, and other governments described as cases of power-sharing from without (e.g., Hungary 1989), might more clearly be conceptualized as incumbent caretaker governments whose capacity to control the transition is medium to very low.

As was argued earlier, the Argentine transition should not be grouped with Greece and Portugal as a case of "regime collapse." However, it was certainly one in which the authoritarian incumbents exercised less control than they would have liked. Each pre-1982 military president launched an offensive transition project, but Videla's aggressive one sputtered to a halt, Viola's conciliatory one cost him his presidency, and Galtieri's apocalyptic one failed spectacularly. The military's defensive projects fared no better than its offensive ones. Bignone's incumbent caretaker government failed on three separate occasions to get the parties to agree to a document prohibiting a future civilian government from prosecuting military officers for human rights violations. Moreover, unlike the outgoing authoritarian rulers in Uruguay, Brazil, and Chile (and, for that matter, Argentina in 1971–3), the Bignone government made no serious effort to alter the constitution, political party statute, or electoral laws to achieve its own ends. As incumbent caretaker governments sometimes do, Bignone's, perhaps hoping that the regime would recover, delayed for nine months setting an official election date, but the October 30, 1983 date, when announced, proved acceptable to the political parties, although some politicians criticized its lateness.[69] The military failed, however, to control the date for the transfer of the presidency, originally set for January 10, 1984, but ultimately advanced to December 10, 1983. Recalling the May 25, 1973, transfer-of-power ceremony, when outgoing military officials had been cornered and harassed by an angry public, a Peronist politician quipped in April 1983: "when this military regime hands the presidential sash to the winner of the election, it should hold the ceremony in the north near Bolivia – and preferably at night."[70]

The ceremony was held in Buenos Aires, but Bignone did not attend. He had slipped out of the Government House through the back door.[71]

One reason that the Bignone government did not retain more control over the transition was that its will was partly broken by defeat in war (but not so broken as to prevent it from forming a caretaker government) and its capacity was diminished by the opposition of virtually the entire society (with the partial exception of a faction of the Peronist leadership). Resentment toward the military regime came from three sources. First, like all authoritarian regimes in societies where democracy has at some point taken root (however precariously) and in which democratic values have been partly internalized, the military regime was perceived at the outset as a "regime of exception." Its main mission was to restore "order," that is, to suppress the activities of the guerrilla groups. But immediately upon achieving that goal, the regime had begun to overstay its welcome, even for many who had supported or acquiesced to its implantation. Secondly, the dirty war left the military with implacable domestic opponents, queasiness in the minds of some of its supporters, and a tarnished international reputation.[72] Both in absolute numbers and relative to population, the number killed or disappeared by the military in Argentina vastly exceeded that in Greece, Uruguay, or Brazil. Although per-capita disappearances were as high in Chile as in Argentina, most of those in Argentina took place closer in time to the installation of the interim government, making protest there especially intense. Thirdly, the Argentine military regime lacked performance legitimacy. Uniquely among the transitions led by military incumbents, Argentina actually fought and lost a major war with a foreign power. And whereas intermittently good economic performance helped to shore up the military governments in Brazil, Chile, Uruguay, and Greece, the Argentine military's economic policies wound up being an almost unmitigated disaster.

Authoritarian regimes deficient in legitimacy may nonetheless build an edifice of laws and routines that the public and its own officials get used to obeying. This legality may help permit the transition to be carried through to completion. If the decision to embark on a transition is anchored in the authoritarian regime's legality, lower-ranking officers and bureaucrats still sympathetic to the regime will be less likely to oppose the transition process. Linz cites Spain during the immediate post-Franco period as a case in which such legal continuity played this transition-smoothing role.[73] On the other hand, the old regime's legality also creates habits of obedience that may give the regime some staying power even if its legitimation deficit has become quite severe. If, as Linz argues, transitions anchored in the old regime's legality are less likely to be reversed from within, they are also likely to proceed more slowly. One reason that Argentina's transition was relatively short is that its caretaker government did not have this legality as a resource on which to draw. The problem was not that the Bignone government's decision to initiate the transition broke with the old regime's legality. Rather, the Bignone government could not draw on this resource because the Videla, Viola, and Galtieri governments had squandered much of the legality that accompanies formal control of the state apparatus, even when seized by force.

Ironically, Argentina's military rulers were preoccupied with legal forms. All told the military enacted more than 1,500 laws, more than any other government in modern Argentine history. Moreover, the military was careful to replace, according to an Americas' Watch report, more than 80 percent of the country's judges.[74] From the outset, however, the military began to violate not only the most elementary tenets of civilized existence, but also the very laws under which it claimed to be operating. In its antisubversive campaign, the military made use of two decrees inherited from the civilian government of Isabel Perón: a November 1974 state of siege declaration, which permitted the suspension of constitutional rights, and a February 1975 decree that ordered the army to conduct "whatever military operations may be necessary to neutralize or annihilate the action of the subversive elements acting in the province of Tucumán" (the decree was later extended to the rest of the country).[75] During the 1985 human rights trials a long debate emerged over the meaning of the word "annihilate," although strangely the prosecution failed to argue that to annihilate "the action of the subversive elements" is one thing and to annihilate the alleged subversives is another. Even if these decrees gave legal sanction for the physical repression of armed guerrillas, only a small proportion of those whom the military kidnapped and executed were in fact armed guerrillas, and none of them received the death penalty that the military were careful to institute in June 1976.[76] There was certainly no attempt to justify legally the torture of thousands of captives, the theft and ransacking of their property, the sale of children born in captivity, or the refusal to produce or divulge the whereabouts of the "disappeared." Moreover, in a particularly blatant violation of the principle of military hierarchy, the official armed forces spawned a secret antisubversive apparatus in which junior officers often gave orders to their nominal superiors.[77]

The regime's base of legality was further undermined by its failure to follow its own rules for presidential succession. According to these rules, to confer or revoke the presidency required the unanimous consent of the members of the military junta. But when it came time in 1978 to decide whether Videla, who had served as acting president since March 1976, should be designated to succeed himself for a formal three-year term, the navy opposed the decision. Videla's reappointment was finally secured by an ad-hoc procedure based on majority rule. The navy also reportedly opposed the nomination of Videla's successor, General Viola, who became president in March 1981. Viola served only the first few months of his term. In December 1981 he was ousted for "health reasons" in an episode bearing signs of an internal coup. The new president, General Galtieri, resigned after Argentina's June 1982 defeat in the Falklands/Malvinas conflict. Neither the navy nor the air force participated in the designation of Galtieri's successor, General Bignone, which was carried out unilaterally by army commander-in-chief Cristino Nicolaides. For the first three months of the Bignone presidency the navy and air force refused to participate in the junta.[78] Enrique Groisman has pointed out that the exclusion of two of the three junta members from the decision to appoint Bignone and the subsequent withdrawal of the army and navy from the junta constituted from a legal point of view "the nearest our country has come to anarchy in its entire history."[79]

The Argentine dictatorship suffered from a dearth of legality as well as of legitimacy, making it easier for the Alfonsín government to overturn the military's self-amnesty. In other areas, however, the legality deficit probably had only a small impact. Two hypothesized consequences of a big reservoir of legality are to slow the transition down and to reduce the likelihood that the regime's "standpatters" (to use Huntington's expression) will step in to reverse it. Among all of the factors that accelerated the pace of the Argentine transition – defeat in external war, internal military cleavages, the rise of opposition groups – the dearth of legality probably added little additional momentum. Moreover, the Bignone government's inability to draw upon legality did not pave the way for lower-ranking officers and bureaucrats to step in to halt the transition. Particularly because of the defeat in external war, but also because of abject economic failure, there were few lower-ranking officers or bureaucrats who considered restoring the authoritarian regime a feasible or desirable goal. The Argentine case suggests that legality plays an important role in sustaining the transition only if the old regime has a body of supporters inclined to restore authoritarianism.

THE NEW DEMOCRACY

A full discussion of the democratic regime that emerged from the Argentine transition is not possible here. What can be done is to evaluate briefly the quality and stability of Argentina's post-1983 democracy and to compare it to that of other recent cases of transition. This evaluation and comparison will lay the groundwork for a preliminary assessment of the extent to which Argentina's specific type of transition and interim government accounted for distinctive aspects of the quality and stability of its emergent democratic regime. Special attention will be given to a comparison between the first post-transition government in Argentina (1983–9 under Alfonsín) and its counterpart in Brazil (1985–90 under Sarney), although other cases will be brought in as appropriate. In evaluating the quality of democracy in Argentina and in comparable cases, this section will be concerned exclusively with whether the most important minimal conditions for procedural democracy have been met: fair elections, real power to elected officials, and protection of basic rights. The evidence presented below shows that Argentina met all three conditions, Uruguay met two, Chile met one, and Brazil met none.

Whereas Argentina's Alfonsín was elected in much the same way as presidents are elected in the United States, by an electoral college chosen by direct popular vote, Brazil's Sarney took office in 1985 because, as vice-president, he was next in the line when the indirectly elected president, Tancredo Neves, died before taking office. Neither the indirect character of the election nor the vice-presidential succession would have been objectionable had Brazil's 680-member electoral college been chosen fairly by popular vote, but it had not been. Instead, the electoral college comprised all senators and federal deputies plus six representatives appointed by each of twenty-two state legislatures. All of these electors had themselves been chosen after April 1977 electoral reforms deliberately and arbitrarily shifted voting clout toward the oligarchic northeastern states and toward municipal councils, in both of which the promilitary PDS (ARENA before 1979) party had a distinct advantage due partly to its control of patronage resources.[80] Moreover, up to and including the date of Sarney's election, Brazilian electoral law included a literacy clause that in effect excluded 23 percent of Brazilian adults from the suffrage (although it is far from clear that a majority of illiterates would have voted for the opposition).[81] Electoral engineering by the incumbent military government also took place in Uruguay, where the military prior to the 1984 elections banned two opposition leaders, Wilson Ferreira Aldunate of the Blancos and Liber Seregni of the Frente Amplio, who would otherwise have stood as presidential candidates. In similar fashion, the 1971–3 Lanusse government in Argentina passed a law that in effect barred Perón from running in the May 1973 presidential election. (A stand-in, Héctor Cámpora, took Perón's place and later resigned, paving the way for a new presidential election which Perón won.) In Chile, Pinochet and his allies reformed the constitution to allow them to appoint nine of thirty-eight senators, gerrymandered electoral districts to overrepresent the more proregime rural areas, and created a two-seat-per-district electoral system for the lower house in which a minority party (presumably of the right in most districts) could capture one of the two seats with as little as 33 percent of the vote. This manipulation did not work as well as Pinochet and his collaborators had hoped, but it did make parliamentary right strong enough after the 1989 elections to block proposals to reform the constitution enacted under military rule.[82]

Argentina exceeded Brazil and Chile not only in the freeness and fairness of the initial election that placed a civilian in the presidency, but also in the degree to which civilians exercised power after being elected. Argentina after 1983 was relatively free of what have been called military prerogatives or authoritarian enclaves.[83] Samuel Valenzuela has distinguished two types of institutions and practices that allow nonelected elites to hold sway over elected civilians.[84] The first type, which Valenzuela calls "tutelary powers," is diffuse and generic. Tutelary powers after military regimes have two main embodiments: constitutional clauses that grant the military the right to defend the fundamental interests of the nation (including at times when such "defense" sets the military at odds with the decisions of an elected government), and military-led National Security Councils that reserve the right to oversee all aspects of government policy (with an implicit threat of intervention should elected officials do anything the military deems harmful to national security). The military in post-1985 Brazil, post-1989 Chile, and post-1974 Portugal had both of these broad tutelary powers; the military in post-1983 Argentina had neither.

The second type of influence by nonelected elites, which Valenzuela calls "reserved domains," involves specific policy areas. Whereas Alfonsín took substantial control of military promotions, the military budget, and military-run industries, Brazil's president Sarney and Chile's president Aylwin were compelled to leave these matters in the hands of the armed forces. No military officer served in Alfonsín's cabinet, whereas six of Sarney's twenty-two ministers were members of the security forces. Using these sources of leverage, the army under Sarney exerted decisive influence over a wide variety of policy areas including the handling of strikes, the nuclear industry, economic integration with Argentina, agrarian reform, and the development of the Amazon.[85] Although military control over elected officials in Brazil and Chile never reached the height of more extreme military-fist-in-civilian-glove regimes like Guatemala's, it was high enough to call into question whether either of these countries in its initial postmilitary period surpassed the minimal threshold of democracy. Argentina definitely surpassed this threshold, although it was unable to expel all supporters of the previous authoritarian regime from the police, army intelligence, or SIDE, the state security agency attached to the presidency.[86]

Abuses of human and civil rights, similar in scale, severity, and systematic character to those that occur in the contemporary United States, were reported in Argentina, Chile, and Uruguay after the return to civilian rule. Such abuses compromised the quality of democracy in each of these countries, but they did not approach the scale, severity, or systematic character of human and civil rights abuses in Brazil. During the Sarney administration, criminal suspects were routinely tortured by Brazilian police. More than 1,000 prisoners were beaten at a São Paulo detention center in 1989, and eighteen prisoners suffocated to death at a São Paulo police station in February of that year. Since 1985 death squads, often composed of on-duty or off-duty police officers and operating with apparent impunity, have killed hundreds of street children and other suspects. Between 1985 and 1990, approximately 250 peasants, rural union leaders, or lawyers involved in land disputes were killed in the state of Pará alone, without a single assassin being brought to justice. A form of slavery involving confinement and forced unpaid labor (but not commodification) persisted in remote areas of the country, especially near the Peruvian border. In March 1991, Brazil's Supreme Court finally ruled unconstitutional a law by which men could kill spouses or lovers and win acquittal on the ground of "legitimate defense of honor." The magnitude of such killings is suggested by a study which reported that 722 men used the "honor killing" defense over a two-year period (1980–1) in the state of São Paulo alone. In August 1991, a local jury in Paraná ignored the Supreme Court's decision (as juries may do in Brazil) and acquitted the man whose case had sparked the earlier ruling.[87]

An area closely related to respect for human rights is respect for the principle that no category of persons should be exempt from laws that apply to everyone else. In Argentina, Brazil, Chile, and Uruguay, the military before leaving power gave itself an amnesty for human rights violations. As of April 1992, the amnesties in Brazil and Chile had not been challenged by the new civilian governments. In Uruguay more than 550,000 people (a quarter of the voting population) signed a petition to force a referendum on the military's self-amnesty, but when the votes were counted in April 1989, the amnesty was upheld by a 53 to 41 percent margin.[88] Argentina went farthest of the four countries in calling the military to account for human rights violations. The first act of the newly-seated legislature was to repeal the self-amnesty that the military had granted itself in September 1983. From the outset, however, Argentina's human rights trials were more limited than the ones in Greece. The Alfonsín government's initial legislation limited the prosecutions to two types of defendants: those accused of ordering their subordinates to commit crimes, and subordinates accused of exceeding orders. Officers who had simply followed orders were exempted, unless the crime included an "atrocious or aberrant act." Despite these exemptions, cases were initiated against an estimated 700 officers. Moreover, a December 1986 "full stop" law that set a sixty-day deadline for initiating further prosecutions did not prevent lawyers from bringing charges against an additional 130 officers before the period expired.[89] A more serious blow to the human rights prosecutions came a week after the 1987 Easter Week military rebellion, when the government, worried about the stability of the new democracy, introduced a bill exempting from prosecution for human rights violations all officers at or below the rank of lieutenant colonel, on the presumption (which no longer needed to be demonstrated) that they had been "just following orders." The bill passed and became known as the "due obedience" law.

Carlos Menem's election as president in May 1989 heralded the last stage in the unraveling of the prosecutions. In October 1989 Menem pardoned Galtieri, Anaya, and Lami Dozo, who were serving sentences for their part in the Falklands/Malvinas fiasco, and thirty-nine retired military officers awaiting trial for murder and torture during the dirty war. The latter pardons were of doubtful constitutionality. Under the Argentine constitution, only Congress has the right to declare general amnesties (Article 67, Section 17). The president is restricted to pardoning or commuting the sentences of those already convicted of crimes (Article 86, Section 6). The final denouement of the human rights trials came in December 1990, when Menem, in the interest of "national reconciliation," pardoned five top military officers (including Videla, Viola, and Massera) and two police chiefs serving prison sentences for their part in organizing the repression. Montonero leader Mario Firmenich was also pardoned, as was (in another act of dubious constitutionality) General Carlos Suárez Mason, who was awaiting trial on forty-three counts of murder and twenty-four of kidnapping/disappearance.[90]

Evaluated in terms of three key dimensions of democracy – electoral fairness, power of elected officials, and respect for basic rights and the rule of law – the quality of democracy under the first postmilitary government was thus highest in Argentina, next-highest in Uruguay, lower in Chile, and lowest in Brazil. The countries rank differently in terms of the short-term stability of democracy, however. Of the four Latin American cases considered in this comparison, Argentina alone experienced an armed military uprising in the post-transition period, although uprisings also took place in Greece (1975) and Spain (1981) after their respective transitions to democracy. Military rebellions took place in Argentina on four separate occasions: in April 1987, January 1988, December 1988, and December 1990. The main goal of the Argentine rebels on the first three occasions was not to destroy the democratic regime, but to secure the replacement of army commanders appointed by Alfonsín – who, in the rebel's eyes, had failed to defend the military against the human rights trials, budget cuts, and an overall loss of prestige.[91] The rebels expressed similar grievances during the December 1990 uprising, in which five civilians and sixteen soldiers died, but in this case there were reports that the rebellion was in fact aimed at deposing Menem and installing a military regime. Many of the grievances expressed by the Argentine rebels involved areas in which the Brazilian, Chilean, and/or Uruguayan militaries retained prerogatives: the appointment of military commanders, control of the military budget, and immunity from prosecution for human rights violations.

Apart from the short-term stability of democracy as indicated by the prevalence of military rebellions, it is also important to consider the long-term stability of democracy, which is affected by an enormous range of factors. Some such factors, like social structure, political culture, and international situation, are largely beyond the control of the political leadership. Others, like constitutional and legal structure (which in turn affects the capacity of the party system to organize and channel social conflict), are more amenable to political engineering. Interim governments which have made significant constitutional changes include those in Spain, Portugal, Greece, and Chile. In Argentina, by contrast, the previous constitution, which the military government had never replaced, was restored. Such restoration is, of course, a decision that may have important implications for democratic consolidation. As Linz and Stepan have argued, "when the old democratic arrangements have in fact contributed to democratic breakdown, restoration [of a prior constitution] precludes an historic opportunity to construct new and improved arrangements with different procedures and symbols."[92] It would be hard to dispute that Argentina's constitutional structure has created difficulties for democratic stability. In particular, presidentialism has weakened democracy. Of the aspects of presidentialism often cited as detrimental to democratic consolidation – the creation of an indivisible prize that gives politics a zero-sum character, the tendency to reinforce personalism, the conduciveness to executive-legislative deadlock, and the inflexibility generated by the fixed term of office – the latter has probably been the most important in Argentina.[93] Presidents Arturo Illia and Isabel Perón were largely discredited by the second year of a six-year presidential term. Had a parliamentary system existed, either could have been replaced at this point, eliminating the perceived leadership vacuum that contributed to the coups that overthrew each president. More debatable is whether all transitions are historic opportunities for constitutional change. In Argentina, the military was too discredited and the political parties too disorganized to have embarked on any sort of constitutional engineering.

CONCLUSION

This chapter is a case study of a single interim government and transition from authoritarian rule. It is informed by comparison with six other Latin American and Southern European cases, but given the myriad causal factors which may come into play, even seven cases are too few to do anything except generate hypotheses about the effects of types of interim government on broader transition processes and on the quality and stability of the emergent democracy. It will nonetheless be useful to summarize these hypotheses in the hope that future research may refine and test them.

A first hypothesis suggested by the comparison is that caretaker governments give authoritarian incumbents special opportunities to control the transition. In four of the five cases in which the caretaker model prevailed, the authoritarian incumbents exercised, according to Aguero's classification in Table 1, "high" or "medium" control of the transition. In the two cases in which the provisional model prevailed (Greece and Portugal), the authoritarian incumbents exercised "very low" control. In Argentina, which adopted the caretaker model, the authoritarian incumbents were also said to exercise "very low" control, making this case appear to contravene the hypothesis that caretaker governments give authoritarian incumbents a good deal of control over the transition. The evidence in this chapter suggests, however, that Argentina, properly considered, is really a case of "medium-to-low" control. If Argentina were reclassified from "very low" to "medium-to-low," the data would show that authoritarian incumbents exercised more control through each of the five caretaker governments than through either of the two provisional administrations. The association between the caretaker model and high authoritarian control is not trivial. It is an empirically observed association, not one that is true by construction. Under certain circumstances, the association may not hold. If the opposition is powerful, for example, the authoritarian incumbents may exercise little control over the transition even if they manage to create a caretaker government. (It is this situation that Linz and Shain term "power-sharing from without.") The evidence suggests that simply by retaining control of the formal machinery of the state – with or without legitimacy, and even with a depleted reservoir of legality – authoritarian incumbents gain an added resource with which to control the transition.

A second hypothesis generated by the comparison is that provisional governments produce higher-quality democracies than caretaker governments. Table 1 suggests that the fairness of the initial election is higher on average after provisional governments (two cases of high fairness) than after caretaker administrations (two cases of high, two of medium, and one of low fairness). On the other hand, the initial power of elected officials, as well as the initial level of civil liberties, seems to bear no systematic relationship to the type of interim government. But let us look more closely at the Spanish and Portuguese cases. Portugal (where the military exercised tutelary powers) wound up with less power to elected officials than was expected from a case of provisional government, whereas Spain wound up with more power to elected officials than was expected from a case of caretaker government. In explaining these anomalies, it may be relevant that military officers presided over the Portuguese transition whereas civilians presided over the Spanish one. Because they control the means of organized large-scale coercion, military officers, even if they were not the authoritarian incumbents beforehand (as in the case of Portugal), can threaten more dire consequences than can civilians if denied their preferred electoral arrangements or requested tutelary powers. It may therefore be that provisional governments, unless they are led by military officers, promote democracies in which the powers of elected officials are broad, whereas caretaker governments, unless they are led by civilians, promote democracies in which the powers of elected officials are constrained.

A third hypothesis to emerge from the comparison is that caretaker governments, by permitting authoritarian incumbents greater control over the transition, indirectly promote short-term democratic stability (as indicated by an absence of military coup attempts). It is clear from Table 1 that the type of interim government has no direct influence on short-term democratic stability: similar types of interim government are associated with varying levels of stability, and different types of interim government are associated with similar levels of stability. But as noted above, caretaker governments give authoritarian incumbents more control over the transition than do provisional governments, and the degree to which the authoritarian incumbents control the transition is indeed related systematically, and positively, to democratic stability. Of the four cases in which the authoritarian incumbents exercised "high" or "medium" control of the transition – Brazil, Chile, Spain, and Uruguay – a coup attempt occurred only in Spain. And of the three cases in which the authoritarian incumbents exercised "medium-to-low" or "very low" control of the transition – Argentina, Greece, and Portugal – a coup attempt was absent only in Portugal. Once again, the anomalous cases are Spain and Portugal. The actor (military versus civilian) that presides over the transition seems to specify the effect of the degree of authoritarian control of the transition not only on the quality of the emergent democracy, but also on its stability. High authoritarian control yields short-term democratic stability unless civilians preside over the transition, whereas low authoritarian control yields short-term democratic instability unless military officers preside.

Felipe Aguero's research corroborates the hypothesis that the nature of the actor (civilian versus military) that presides over the transition has an important and independent effect on the quality and stability of the emergent democracy. Aguero found that military-presided Portugal and Argentina had more trouble establishing "civilian supremacy over the military" than did civilian-presided Greece or Venezuela (1958), despite the fact that authoritarian incumbents were judged to have exercised "very low" control over the transition in each of the four cases (Aguero should probably have rated the authoritarian incumbents in Argentina as having exercised "medium-to-low" control). Conversely, Aguero found that military-presided Brazil and Chile had more trouble establishing civilian supremacy than did civilian-presided Spain, although the authoritarian incumbents were judged to have exercised "high" control over the transition in each case.[94]

A fourth hypothesis unites the first three. Where the military's specific interests are taken into account in the transition (Brazil, Chile, Uruguay, and Portugal), democracy initially is low in quality and high in stability; where they are not (Argentina, Greece, and Spain), democracy initially is high in quality and low in stability. This observed relationship holds across all seven cases, but additional empirical work will be required to test it. More conceptual work is also required. In particular, it will be important to devise ways to measure the goals and severity of military rebellions, to take into account rebellions that were nipped in the bud, and to measure democratic stability in ways that do not relate specifically to overt military rebellions, for example, factors that, in the long run, will make such rebellions more likely, or that may lead to popular insurrection or to the erosion of democracy from within. On further scrutiny, moreover, the degree to which authoritarian incumbents control the transition, and the type of actor that presides over the transition, may prove to be heavily shaped and constrained by prior factors like the nature of the antecedent authoritarian regime. If so, their causal status could be reduced to that of intervening factors. What seems more clear from this study of the Argentine case, and from the cases to which it has been compared, is that the quality and stability of a new democracy does depend on the type of interim government (incumbent caretaker, provisional opposition, or power-sharing), primarily because caretaker governments make it more likely that the incumbents of the outgoing authoritarian regime will be able to control the transition. Equally important in shaping the quality and stability of a new democracy is, however, the type of actor (civilian or military) that administers the transition.

11

The failure of an internationally sponsored interim government in Afghanistan

BARNETT R. RUBIN

On the evening of March 18, 1992, President Najibullah of Afghanistan interrupted normal radio and television broadcasts with a dramatic speech. "I agree," he announced, "that once an understanding is reached through the United Nations process for the establishment of an interim government in Kabul, all powers and executive authority will be transferred to the interim government as of the first day of the transition period."[1] By clearly announcing his intention to step aside, the former secret police chief who had headed the Soviet-backed regime since 1986 seemed to cleared the way for the implementation of a laboriously prepared international plan for resolving one of the last Cold War conflicts.

Less than a month later, President Najibullah was in hiding in the UN's office in Kabul. Rebels in his own military and party had allied with Islamic resistance fighters (mujahidin) to overthrow him during the night of April 15–16. Najibullah's Watan (Homeland) Party split on ethnic lines, with different factions allying with their coethnics among the mujahidin. The leading resistance commander, Ahmad Shah Massoud, spokesman for the alliance that overthrew Najibullah, told Benon Sevan, the UN Secretary General's representative for Afghanistan, that the now victorious mujahidin would form a provisional government themselves.

Before the end of April, fighting erupted in the streets of Kabul as guerrillas belonging to rival parties, factions, and ethnic groups battled for power. Tribal and ethnic coalitions took over the major regional garrisons. New power centers formed, paying scant if any allegiance to the interim government of the Islamic State of Afghanistan, which assumed authority on April 29, 1992.

Conflicts over power led to repeated battles in the capital itself. By August, according to the UN, over 1,800 civilian deaths had been reported, with several thousands injured and seeking treatment in hospitals that could not function. Food supplies in Kabul were becoming scarce, shops were closed, and over 500,000 people were fleeing the city in all directions.[2] By the end of 1994, the battle over the now-ruined city of Kabul was still continuing.

Afghanistan was one of those countries where the UN was trying to establish an internationally sponsored interim government. International involvement developed out of the same conditions that Shain and Berat argue made international interim governments imperative in other cases: "deep-seated historical rivalries [were] so profound, and so violent, and so seemingly irresolvable that the construction of an interim regime with the potential for creating real long-term stability [was] minimal"; the conflict was "exacerbated by the strong influence and sometimes actual physical presence of foreign powers"; "the political . . . rivalries among aspirants for power [were] so intense that they preclude[d] the possibility of the acceptance of an incumbent leading the transition as a caretaker . . . or the creation of power-sharing interim rule among the rivals for power"; "this impasse [was] reinforced by the very high level of accumulation of weapons which [were] dispersed widely without any faction having a clear-cut ability to exert monopoly over them."[3]

Berat and Shain originally mentioned eight components of the international interim government model, including the disarming of all factions, the participation by all factions in free elections, certification of the election as free and fair by international monitors, and the stationing of UN security forces in the country even for some time after the election of a permanent government, in order to act as a stabilizing influence. Such an interim government would be administered by the UN under a Security Council resolution, required for dispatching armed forces.[4]

Each aspect of the model is intended to solve one of the problems that makes the international interim government imperative. Disarming factions and dispatching UN security forces responds to the danger posed by the dispersal of large stockpiles of weapons. The international administration of at least the elections and perhaps other parts of the government substitutes for either a transitional government controlled by the incumbent, a provisional government of the opposition, or an impossible coalition. The imposition of international standards and law, combined with the upholding of domestic law (possibly fallen into desuetude) by international force compensates for the lack of state legality. The elections administered by the international community introduce a new principle of legitimacy, and the internationally supported armed forces enforce the new democratic, legal legitimacy.

The essential difficulty with this international interim government model is that the greater the extent to which the factors making it desirable are present, the less likely it is that the conditions of success are present. The harsher the conflict, the less likely it will be that the state has retained (or was ever run according to) the principle that Shain and

Linz find most essential for any form of interim government: legality of the state apparatus. Where conflicts are so severe that the state breaks down (or, more accurately, in many cases, where intense conflict results from competitive mobilization in response to state breakdown), an interim government leading to a change in regime must take upon itself the additional burden of rebuilding the state. Building state power in an environment characterized by widespread military organization among the population requires a level of force (and other resources) the international community has been unwilling and perhaps unable to mobilize in more than a few cases.

In Afghanistan, the forces required to implement such a model exceeded anything the international community was willing to attempt or even consider. Rather than invoke the powers of the Security Council, the international community, through the UN General Assembly, merely asked the Secretary General to use his good offices to promote a negotiated solution. The interim government that such negotiations would produce could either consist of a coalition among lower-tier leaders of both sides or a relatively neutral group of technocrats and dignitaries. No plan put forward by the UN ever addressed the key but apparently insuperable problem of the multiplicity of well-equipped, poorly disciplined armed forces. Furthermore, the intelligence agencies of key international sponsors of various antagonists never fully abandoned the goal of victory or predominance through military means.

Shain and Linz's contention that the decline of communism and the overthrow of bureaucratic authoritarian regimes "has left democracy almost unchallenged as the supreme principle of political legitimacy," while true (thanks to the qualifier "almost), implies more than it can deliver.[5] That in Afghanistan Islam rather than democracy was the rallying cry of the opposition was not a characteristic solely of one peculiarly backward state. Religious and national identities as well as criteria of economic performance are more prominent than democracy in the ideologies of political contenders in many areas of the world. Those who evaluate the legitimacy of government on the basis of its production of fixed policy outcomes – national, ethnic, religious, or economic – cannot accept the inherent uncertainty of democracy.[6] They may prefer to continue their struggle, armed or otherwise, rather than surrender to a process they cannot control. Such political forces may, indeed, call for elections as a means of choosing or legitimating a leader, as did Communist and other authoritarian regimes. But elections are democratic only when they are the means by which citizens periodically freely choose leaders who effectively control the state (and via the state, their own society) through an institutionalized, legal process that respects human rights.

Finally, political theories and belief systems (such as belief in democracy) can legitimate state power; they cannot create it. The disastrous sequels to the attempt to construct a limited-liability peace process in Afghanistan are among the events that led Shain and Berat to conclude that the international interim government model "is not a panacea for 'failed states' where no modern civil institutions remain functioning, where no contestant enjoys broadbased support, where main players are ideologically committed to a nondemocratic form of government, and where lawlessness, warlordism, and clientelism are pandemic."[7]

The listing of several negative factors, however, begs the question of which was more fundamental. In Somalia, for instance, none of the warlords is "ideologically committed to a nondemocratic form of government" or, apparently, to any particular form of government. One might imagine that if some were committed to an Islamic state or a Marxist-Leninist one-party state the problem would be even more insoluble, but the purely ideological component of the collapse of the state in Somalia appears to have been negligible. In Afghanistan too, despite the Islamic radicalism of some of the contenders, the principal obstacle has been the collapse of state institutions.

STATE AND SOCIETY IN AFGHANISTAN

The war in Afghanistan flared into a conflagration when local conflicts became linked to the Cold War. The international system provided competing elites in Afghanistan (and elsewhere) with access to ideologies, organizational models, and financial and coercive resources from the United States, the USSR, and the Islamic world. These ideologies and organizations coexisted with conceptions and modes of behavior derived from the local social structures. As international agreements decreased or ended the aid flows, the indigenous patterns reemerged, although in new organizational forms. Hence understanding the effects of the diplomacy on Afghanistan requires understanding both how the country was integrated into the modern state system and the social bases of political organizations there.

The old regime and the international system

Afghanistan entered the modern state system after the Second Anglo-Afghan War (1878–80) as a buffer between the British and Russian empires. Consolidation of a central state in this sparsely populated, largely tribal country depended on foreign aid.[8] During the 1950s, Prime Minister Daud, cousin of the king, Zahir Shah, played on the country's renewed status as a buffer – now between the USSR and the U.S.-sponsored

Baghdad Pact (later CENTO) – to build an expanded state apparatus with foreign aid from both the Cold War antagonists. The largest donor, the neighboring Soviet Union, supplied and trained the military and sponsored some state economic projects, while the United States engaged in teacher training, agriculture, and engineering. Islamic legal and educational officials were trained with the assistance of Egypt's al-Azhar University.

On global issues Afghanistan observed nonalignment between the United States and the USSR; it concentrated foreign policy on Afghanistan's claim to Pakistani territories inhabited by Pashtuns, the dominant ethnic group in Afghanistan (about 40–45 percent of the population).[9]

Ethnic stratification and the old regime

The structure of the Afghan state imposed a pattern of ethnic stratification on the diverse local societies. The head of state (king until 1973, president from 1973 to 1978) was a member of one clan of the Durrani confederation, one of the three major groups of Pashtun tribes. The state claimed to represent the national identity of Pashtuns. The official religion of the state was Sunni Islam. And the state's capital was the mainly Persian-speaking (Tajik) city of Kabul.

The royal clan topped the ethnic hierarchy. Below them came the other Pashtuns, with some preference for Durranis. The Shiʻa (about 15 percent of the population), most of them belonging to the Hazara ethnic group, occupied the bottom of the social hierarchy. Between the Pashtuns and Hazaras were the other predominantly Sunni ethnic groups. Of these, the Tajiks, Persian-speakers of the northeast, served as junior partners of the Pashtuns in ruling the country. Other groups of intermediate status included the Turki speakers of the north, mostly Uzbeks.

Since the 1920s various rulers had elaborated a legal basis for state administration in Afghanistan, but power itself was never constituted through law. Neither did the administration function according to impersonal norms when these contradicted the interests of the ruling dynasty or clan. Personal networks of clientelism based on tribal and marriage ties were dominant means of the exercise of power. In particular, the military and officer corps was always clearly dominated by the royal clan and members of a few tribal families closely linked to the rulers of the day.

ORIGINS OF THE CONFLICT

Between 1963 and 1973 Afghanistan enjoyed a form of constitutional rule known as "New Democracy." The government held two national elections to a consultative parliament. Although political parties were not permitted to compete in the elections, various factions of the intelligentsia began to organize politically. Few of these made procedural democracy or the rule of law a central concern of their program. Most were nationalist, Marxist, or Islamic.

Until the 1970s the United States and the USSR competed for influence over a regime they both supported rather than supporting political factions. In 1973, however, Daud overthrew his cousin Zahir Shah in a coup, abolished the monarchy, and proclaimed himself president. Both superpowers, as well as regional powers, feared a future succession crisis. The Brezhnev leadership considered that the correlation of forces in the world was favorable to the expansion of Soviet influence in the Third World.[10] Under the Nixon doctrine the United States encouraged the Shah of Iran to use his oil wealth to draw Afghanistan into a regional grouping under his leadership.[11] Both the USSR and Pakistan increased their support for political groups challenging the Afghan regime, the Communists and Islamists respectively.[12]

The formation of competing political elites

The principal Soviet-oriented Communist organization in Afghanistan was the People's Democratic Party of Afghanistan (PDPA), founded in 1965. In 1967 the party split into two factions: Khalq, led by Nur Muhammad Taraki and Hafizullah Amin, and Parcham, led by Babrak Karmal.[13] The Soviets pressured them into reunion in 1977.

Parcham and Khalq constituted (and still constitute) distinct political and social groups. Parcham recruited from the middle and upper ranks of the urban elite. Many were Tajiks, but the group also included some mainly urbanized Pashtuns. Khalq recruited from the newly educated of rural background, mainly tribal Pashtuns. Many of the leaders of both groups had studied or received military training in the USSR.

After 1965 an Islamic movement gained influence among students and professors at Kabul University. In 1973 the movement formed a leadership *shura* (council). Burhanuddin Rabbani, a lecturer at the shari'a (Islamic law) faculty of Kabul University, was chosen as chairman of the council, which selected the name Jamiat-i Islami (Islamic Society) for the movement.

In 1973, Daud repressed the Islamic movement, and its leaders fled to Peshawar, capital of the mainly Pashtun Northwest Frontier Province of Pakistan. This movement too split, into the Jamiat-i Islami, still led by Rabbani, and the Hizb-i Islami (Islamic Party), led by Gulbuddin Hikmatyar. Both of these groups recruited from the newly educated of rural background. Jamiat's leaders included Islamic scholars from different ethnic backgrounds, including several educated at al-Azhar, but its cadres largely consisted of Tajiks with secular educations from the northeast of Afghanistan. Rabbani, an Azhar-educated scholar from the Tajik heartland, linked the two groups. Hizb, the more radical of the two, mainly attracted Pashtuns with secular educations from outside the tribal social system, as exemplified by its leader, a former engineering student born in a Pashtun settlement in the north, outside the tribal homelands.

None of these factions was ethnically homogeneous, and all denied that ethnicity played any role in their politics. Nonetheless, Pashto was the main language within Hizb and Khalq, while Persian was the main language within Parcham and Jamiat. Members of several groups rarely joined these revolutionary organizations. Durrani Pashtuns tended to support the royal regime. Uzbeks participated little in national politics. Radical Hazara youth joined either Maoist or separate Shi'a Islamist organizations, most of which united into a single party, the Hizb-i Wahdat-i Islami (Islamic Unity Party) in 1990. Some Tajiks and Uzbeks also joined the Maoists, as the Soviets supported the Pashtun nationalist government.

Failed communist revolution, origins of resistance

In 1978 a shakily reunited PDPA seized power in a military coup in which Daud was killed. The PDPA established the Democratic Republic of Afghanistan, which became unilaterally dependent on Soviet aid. It began to arrest, torture, and execute real and suspected enemies. Within a few months the Khalqis expelled the more moderate Parchamis and announced a revolutionary program, which they attempted to impose by force. They undertook a radical purge of all state institutions. During this period the level of legality regulating the security apparatus was reduced to nil; the Khalqi leader Hafizullah Amin attempted to bring all security agencies under his personal control, in part by imprisoning and assassinating rivals.

In response to the Khalqis' policies, revolts broke out in parts of the country, usually without any link to national political groups. The Islamists declared jihad against the Communists from their Pakistani exile. They were soon joined by representatives of the conservative clergy and the elites of the old regime, although former high state officials generally made their way to the West rather than joining the struggle. The army and administration, weakened by mutinies and defections, seemed headed for collapse.

*Soviet intervention and response: Development of an
internationally supported resistance movement*

In December 1979 the Brezhnev Politburo feared that the United States
would exploit the disorder in Afghanistan to recoup its losses in the
previous February's Iranian Revolution by installing a pro-American
government in Kabul with Pakistani assistance.[14] The Soviets sent a
"limited contingent" of troops to seize the Afghan government from the
unreliable and brutal Khalqi leader, Hafizullah Amin, who was killed
when their original plan failed.[15] The Soviets forced the party to reunite
under Babrak Karmal, the leader of Parcham. By 1981 the Soviet troop
presence stabilized at about 105,000. The Soviet troops and the regime
they protected carried out massive, violent policies of repression, including systematic torture of thousands of detainees by the secret police,
headed by Najibullah, and indiscriminate bombing of rural areas.[16] In
contrast to the arbitrary terror of the Khalqi regime, the Soviets attempted to introduce "socialist legality." The aim of such legality was not
to increase the rights of the population against the state, but to make the
leadership's control of state organs more predictable and reliable. This
attempt had some apparent success as long as Soviet troops and advisers
were present to enforce it. After the Soviet withdrawal, however, it
foundered on endemic Afghan factionalism and clientelism, which penetrated the highest level of the party and security forces.

The Soviets soon found that, far from stabilizing the situation, their
troops provoked national resistance and worldwide condemnation. The
United States, Saudi Arabia, and China began programs of aid to the
mujahidin through Pakistan, whose Directorate of Inter-Services Intelligence (ISI) allocated the aid and attempted to direct the resistance movement.[17] In 1981 the Pakistani authorities recognized six mujahidin parties
out of dozens clamoring for aid. Later a seventh was added because of
the strong support it had in Saudi Arabia (though it had virtually none in
Afghanistan). Henceforth all refugees and resistance commanders had to
join one of these seven parties to receive aid. Three of the parties represented conservative and Islamic sectors of the old regime; four, including
Hizb and Jamiat, represented the new Islamist movement. While the
resistance harshly denounced the repressive and authoritarian – verging
on totalitarian – policies of the PDPA regime, Islam, not democracy, was
the symbol and value system that mobilized the movement. All of the
party organizations depended on personalist leaders who developed clienteles based on the redistribution of foreign aid, though the Islamist
parties had more of a formal organizational apparatus.

Within Afghanistan, the collapse of state administration and the arming
of all segments of the society created the political fragmentation which

became fully visible when the central government collapsed in 1992. Local power was in the hands of field commanders of the resistance or regime, who used aid from the parties to build local organizations based on ethnic or religious ties. While most commanded only a handful of followers, a few built up larger military organizations and even some civil administration. Not only did the state lose its monopoly over the means of violence; neither the state nor the resistance built up a single hierarchically coordinated force. Instead, dozens of armed forces linked by loose coalitions developed.

In the northeast, Ahmad Shah Massoud, a Tajik member of Jamiat, established a base area under his quasi-government, the Supervisory Council of the North. In the largely Uzbek areas of the north, government militia leader Gen. Abdul Rashid Dostum used Soviet aid to build up the most powerful military force of the Kabul regime. These forces ultimately became a base for Uzbek political claims. The Hazara areas in the center of Afghanistan became virtually independent with strong links to their fellow Shi'a in Iran. Mujahidin in the Persian-speaking West, around Herat, organized a *shura* led by Jamiat.

In the South, the Durrani Pashtuns around Qandahar built up a *shura* that resisted both the Kabul regime and, with less success, ISI interference. The Pashtun tribes of the East, between Kabul and Peshawar, were heavily armed but highly fragmented, both among resistance parties and between the resistance and the government. In the areas of Pakistan inhabited by Afghan refugees, Hikmatyar used the aid he received from ISI, the Pakistani Islamist party Jamaat-i Islami, and other sources to build up the most powerful of the Pakistan-based organizations. His forces ranged across the border from these sanctuaries.

Development of a stalemate: Background to attempts at conflict resolution

One of the conditions identified by Berat and Shain for the emergence of an international interim government is the development of a stalemate in which no side can win a military victory. To most international observers the war in Afghanistan appeared to have reached such a stage by the mid-1980s. The Soviet Union under Gorbachev could no longer tolerate an open-ended commitment to a regime that could not sustain itself independently, and by 1986 Moscow had begun the search for a way out. The Soviets replaced Babrak Karmal, symbol of the Soviet invasion, with Najibullah. This move created a split within the Parcham faction of the PDPA between Najibullah, who had mostly Pashtun support, and the non-Pashtun majority of Parcham. These resentments helped sabotage the UN plan in 1992.

Gorbachev sought to use the UN to forge a negotiated settlement that would enable him to withdraw his troops with some guarantees for the PDPA. He pressed Najibullah and the PDPA to share power with at least moderate mujahidin leaders and field commanders under a program called "national reconciliation." By late 1986, increased aid to the mujahidin confronted Soviet military planners with a stark choice of withdrawing or facing an unending war. The combination of Gorbachev's New Thinking and the obvious failure of old thinking in Afghanistan led to progress in the UN-sponsored Geneva Talks.

ATTEMPTS AT CONFLICT RESOLUTION

The Geneva Accords of April 14, 1988, provided the legal framework under which the Soviets withdrew their troops, who were gone by February 15, 1989.[18] Reflecting the political realities of the early 1980s, when the agenda had been set, these accords dealt only with "external" aspects of the conflict. They did not link the end of external involvement to a domestic political settlement based on the formation of an interim government or internationally monitored elections, as later agreements did in Cambodia, Nicaragua, Namibia, and elsewhere. The agenda included Soviet troop withdrawal, the end of aid to the resistance, refugee repatriation, and international guarantees.

Ultimately, the Accords amounted to little more than a UN cover for the Soviet decision to withdraw. Pakistan and the United States had agreed to link ending aid to the resistance to the withdrawal in the belief that the Soviets preferred keeping their troops in Afghanistan to withdrawing them without an end to aid to the resistance. By 1988, however, the preferences of the Soviet leaders had changed in a way that placed them at a disadvantage. In their quest for domestic reform and better relations with the United States, the Soviets now preferred to withdraw their troops whatever the United States and Pakistan did, and Washington knew it. The Soviets tried to dissemble, making threats as if their preferences had remained unchanged, but to no avail. At the end of the negotiations, Washington reserved the right to aid parties in Afghanistan as long as the Soviets did likewise. The State Department informed the USSR of this in a still-secret exchange of letters that the United States regards as part of the Accords. The Soviets and Kabul protested furiously, but in the end the withdrawal proceeded as required by the Accords without the United States and Pakistan fulfilling their original counterpart obligation to end aid to the resistance. As a result, the United States, Pakistan, Saudi Arabia, and private Arab sources continued to provide close to $1.5 billion per year in aid to the mujahidin in 1989–90, while Kabul received two to three times as much. These weapons transfers by and large went to the most intransigent groups, even as the aid donors claimed to be seeking a political settlement.

PROPOSALS FOR INTERIM GOVERNMENTS

After the Soviet decision to withdraw, various parties made proposals for interim governments, including incumbent-led, power-sharing, or provisional revolutionary governments. Another proposal was the installation of a government of "neutrals," sponsored by the UN, a variant of the international interim government model. In accord with the interim government model, all proposals, whether they claimed ultimate legitimacy from democracy, nationalism, or Islam, required that the interim government organize elections or some other procedure of national consultation in order to validate the assumption of permanent power by a successor government. Although some conservative clergy expressed ambivalence about or opposition to elections, the revolutionary Islamist parties always insisted on them, another illustration of their political modernity. Eventually a provisional government of the mujahidin assumed authority. Since military power is located in political groups, factional groups, and clienteles, rather than the state, the latter has been unable to control its territory and population or to hold elections.

The Soviets and at least some of their clients in Kabul realized early that no solution was possible without the participation of at least some of the forces supporting the mujahidin. Their proposal for "national reconciliation" included an interim government based on power-sharing between incumbents and opposition, which is the second form of interim government identified by Shain and Linz.[19] Najibullah invited the resistance leaders to join his cabinet and offered local power and military ranks to mujahidin field commanders. Still, the stigma attached to cooperating with the agents of the Soviet occupation, anti-Islamic forces, and especially the hated former secret police chief, Najibullah, prevented all significant resistance leaders from openly accepting his offers. This case conforms fully to hypotheses on "power-sharing interim governments" proposed by Shain and Linz:

[I]nterim governments based on power-sharing coalitions are more likely to be initiated when the period prior to their formation is not overshadowed by large-scale violence, and when the opposition is not controlled by a revolutionary elite or ideology. . . .

Power-sharing becomes a remote option when the outgoing elite, even when still in control, is directly implicated in violent suppression of the opposition, the perpetration of human rights violations, or in economic crimes and corruption.[20]

As the Soviet withdrawal approached and ended without an agreement on power-sharing, Najibullah proceeded with various unilateral reforms

designed at least to give the appearance of democratization. Both he and
his Soviet supporters at times advocated what they called "the Nicaraguan model," what Linz and Shain call an "incumbent caretaker" interim
government.[21] As in Nicaragua, where the Sandinistas organized the
internationally monitored election that defeated them, Najibullah, while
continuing as president, held elections where he offered participation to
all elements of the opposition.

In December 1987, Najibullah summoned a Loya Jirga, the traditional
Great Council of Afghanistan, to approve a new constitution providing
for an elected government and elect him as president with virtually
unlimited powers. The concentration of powers in the president nullified
any effect the elections might have had. During parliamentary elections
held the following April, immediately after the signing of the Geneva
Accords, Najibullah reserved seats in the National Assembly for the
resistance and invited seven field commanders of different parties and
ethnic groups to join his government. He appointed a nonparty prime
minister and unsuccessfully tried to persuade resistance commander Ahmad Shah Massoud to take the post of defense minister.

After the Soviet withdrawal, the development of perestroika in the
USSR, and the fall of Communist regimes in Eastern Europe, national
reconciliation developed into a broader program of reform. In May 1990
the PDPA renounced Marxism, embraced Islam, democracy, and market
economics, and changed its name to the Homeland (*Watan*) Party. It
modified the constitution in order to abolish all special status for the
party. None of these reforms attracted the participation of any of the
resistance organizations or major commanders. The failure of the incumbent caretaker model in Afghanistan is consistent with Shain and Linz's
proposition:

A transition led by incumbents as caretaker becomes a remote option when the
previous regime has disintegrated, [if] the incumbents cannot count on the loyalty
of the armed forces, and mass mobilization or the guerrilla activity against the
regime has undermined its authority in large parts of the country. The implication
of the incumbent elite in criminal human rights violations or in large-scale corruption further erodes its chances of successfully constituting a viable caretaker
government and its attempt to lead a democratic transition is more likely to be
viewed as a sham.[22]

The principal intelligence agencies of both the United States and Pakistan predicted that the DRA would not long outlast the Soviet withdrawal. Hence Washington and Islamabad concentrated their efforts on
promoting a military victory for the mujahidin rather than a political
solution. A military victory by the opposition over the incumbents generally gives rise to a "revolutionary provisional government."[23] Ultimately

this is what occurred, but only after the end of Soviet aid as well as the troop presence.

At the insistence of their foreign sponsors, the seven recognized Sunni mujahidin parties chose an "Interim Islamic Government of Afghanistan" (IIGA) at a *shura* (council) held in February 1989 as the last Soviet troops left Afghanistan. Of course a "provisional revolutionary government" can function only if its supporters have defeated the incumbents. Unfortunately for the IIGA's sponsors, however, the regime in Kabul had not yet been defeated, so the *shura* had to be held in Pakistan. This interim government, composed almost entirely of exiled leaders from the Pashtuns of Eastern Afghanistan, with few members of other ethnic groups, also excluded all participation by the Kabul regime, the officials of the old regime who had fled to the West, and the Shi'a parties. This government never succeeded in establishing itself in Afghanistan or organizing the elections it promised. In fact it was a government-in-exile rather than a provisional government.[24]

Besides these proposals, variants of an internationally sponsored interim government had been put forth by various actors since the beginning of the conflict. If the mujahidin and PDPA-Watan Party leaders could neither defeat each other nor agree to cooperate, the international community should help the Afghans form a transitional government of "neutrals," mostly officials and technocrats from the old regime. In such proposals the former king, Zahir Shah, exiled in Rome since 1973, played a central role as a compromise figure, though all, including Zahir Shah himself, agreed that restoration of the monarchy was out of the question. Such proposals appealed not only to the former officials but also to Pashtun tribal leaders and elders who had lost influence to new elites in the war. Such proposals also signaled support for partial restoration of the old order by calling for a Loya Jirga, the tribally based "Great Council" of Afghanistan, to legitimize the new government. Usually, the Loya Jirga was justified not by arguments against elections in principle, but by the rather convincing claim that without any state administration in most of the country's territory it would not be possible to hold elections. The far less demanding administrative requirements of a Loya Jirga, could be met under existing conditions. Unlike the Kabul regime and the mujahidin leaders, however, those who supported the latter proposal never received billions of dollars of weapons and cash from foreign supporters.

Such proposals envisaged a role for the UN and international community in supporting such a transition, but stopped well short of proposing a full "international interim government." No one advocated that the UN or any other international organization should actually administer the transition, or disarm the opposing sides. In December 1988, Gorbachev proposed a cease-fire in place monitored by a UN peacekeeping force as part of an interim arrangement leading to elections. The elections were to be organized by a power-sharing interim government to be set up under Kabul's program for "national reconciliation." Neither the United States nor the UN Secretariat ever seriously considered such a proposal. The resistance regarded such a proposal as an attempt to protect the Kabul regime, and no state would have been willing to send its troops to such a heavily armed, mountainous country where diverse armed forces functioned with no central control. Hence rather than use the Security Council to dispatch UN forces, the UN would only use the good offices of the secretary general to promote agreement on such a settlement among Afghans and their neighbors.

AFTER THE SOVIET WITHDRAWAL: REGIONAL RIVALRIES AND SUPERPOWER NEGOTIATIONS

Effect of troop withdrawal on Afghan society and politics

Proposals for a political settlement involving the establishment of a transition mechanism of some sort gained greater attention as a new military and political stalemate emerged after the Soviet withdrawal. The Soviet presence had galvanized the society into a certain unity of action, but for many fighters the withdrawal of Soviet troops meant the end of the jihad. Kabul too lost its ideological motivation. Hence the Soviet withdrawal as well as the decline of the Soviet empire, which became obvious in the fall of 1989, led to a loss of commitment and increased fragmentation of both government and resistance forces, while the continued bipolar flows of aid maintained a surface appearance of polarization.

Effect of Soviet withdrawal on superpower positions: The U. S.– Soviet dialogue of 1989–90

At the same time the Bush and Gorbachev administrations began discussions on the framework for a settlement in Afghanistan. A secret U. S. decision in the fall of 1989 defined the goal of U. S. policy after the Soviet withdrawal as "sidelining extremists" on all sides, including both Najibullah and Hikmatyar.[25] According to the new policy, no weapons paid for by U. S. funds would be given to Gulbuddin Hikmatyar. (Saudi funds took up the slack, so this policy made little if any difference on the ground.) The United States had also appointed Peter Tomsen as an ambassadorial-level special envoy to the Afghan resistance.

Tomsen traveled to the region frequently to consult with a large range of Afghan, Pakistani, and Saudi actors. He also maintained contact with the UN's Benon Sevan. The continuing UN effort and the U. S.–Soviet dialogue complemented each other. In the UN's view the external dependence of all political forces in Afghanistan was so great that they would never reach agreement until their sponsors developed an "international consensus" on means to bring peace to Afghanistan. The issues standing in the way of such a consensus were those on the agenda of the U. S.–Soviet discussions. These included the nature of a transitional authority and the cessation of military aid to Afghan parties to the conflict. Ending military aid was a weak proxy for a cease fire and disarmament.

In September 1989 during a meeting between U. S. Secretary of State Baker and Soviet Foreign Minister Shevardnadze in Wyoming both sides agreed that "a transition period is required, as well as an appropriate mechanism to establish a broad-based government."[26] Talks continued throughout 1990 in several venues. These discussions, like the parallel negotiations on Cambodia, increasingly focused on the holding of elections as a means to resolve the conflict.[27] The key issues were measures to assure that elections would be free and fair, and the relation of the termination of weapons supplies to the transition.

The United States initially insisted that a prerequisite for any transition was the departure of Najibullah.[28] Furthermore, Washington argued that in order to assure that the government could not use its control of the security forces and mass media to affect the outcome of an election, the "transition mechanism" should be an interim government with full powers replacing that of Najibullah.

The Soviets insisted that the "transition mechanism" should be either an election organized by the Najibullah government (the "Nicaraguan model") or an independent commission that would organize the election while the incumbent government remained in power. Negotiations between these two positions focused on the precise form of power-sharing between the existing government and such a "transition mechanism."[29]

Moscow insisted on both a cease-fire (which the United States could not deliver) and a simultaneous end to military aid by all parties – meaning Pakistan and Saudi Arabia as well as the two superpowers. On Tomsen's missions he tried to obtain various assurances from these governments, and the United States also advised the Soviets to open their own talks with them. By spring 1990 the United States came back to supporting a bilateral U. S.–Soviet agreement on ending aid that could later be expanded to include others. The United States began to insist on a "date certain" for such an agreement, known as "negative symmetry."

The United States and USSR appeared to have reached an agreement by December 11, 1990, when Shevardnadze met Baker in Houston. Both sides had agreed to support the establishment of a UN-sponsored transi-

tional organ that would replace the current government; to end all weapons supplies; and to leave the precise structure of the transition to UN
consultations with the Afghan parties. At the last minute, however, Shevardnadze, under apparent pressure from military and hardline officials,
refused to agree to a "date certain" for negative symmetry.[30] Upon his
return to Moscow he resigned, warning the public against "reaction-
aries."

EFFECTS OF THE PERSIAN GULF WAR

The rising power of the Soviet hard-liners in early 1991 stymied further
progress in the U. S.–Soviet dialogue, but the Persian Gulf war helped
settle some of the outstanding issues by leading both Pakistan and Saudi
Arabia to look more favorably on a political settlement. The radical
elements of the Afghan mujahidin, in particular Hikmatyar, as well as
their supporters in the Pakistani military and ISI, joined the international
Islamist opposition to the U. S.-led coalition operating from Saudi Arabia. Pakistan's conservative civilian leadership, along with the nationalists and moderates among the mujahidin, supported the U. S.–Saudi
position. The Saudis at least temporarily cut off funding to Hikmatyar
and some other groups. The United States also cut off funding for most
of the ministries of the IIGA in March. The rapid victory of the coalition
also discredited the Pakistani chief of army staff, who had opposed the
government's position, predicted failure for the U. S.–Saudi coalition,
and tried to block the departure of a mujahidin contingent to Saudi
Arabia.[31]

Immediately after the Gulf war, at the end of March 1991, the ISI
threw all its resources, including many Pakistani advisers on the ground,
into the battle for the Afghan garrison town of Khost. The garrison fell,
but the cost in Pakistani effort and the inability of the Pashtun tribal
mujahidin to establish a government even in this small town (instead they
pillaged it), only reinforced the loss of credibility of the military option,
one of the conditions for the abandonment of the provisional revolutionary government model. The president and prime minister of Pakistan
decided that it was time to promote a political settlement. The Saudi
government agreed as well.

The UN's five points of May 1991

As a result of the U. S.–Soviet dialogue in 1990 and the change in the
positions of Pakistan and Saudi Arabia after the Gulf War, in May 1991
the secretary general of the UN was able to issue a statement summariz-
ing an "international consensus" on Afghanistan in five very generally

worded points. According to these points, the political settlement would begin with the establishment of a "transition mechanism" in Afghanistan. In conjunction with the beginning of the transition, all external parties would stop supplying weapons to Afghanistan, and all internal parties should cease fire. The interim authority would organize "free and fair elections, in accord with Afghan traditions," to choose a "broad-based government."[32] "Afghan traditions" referred to the possibility of a Loya Jirga or to other forms of tribal representation which might replace elections in some areas. These principles, however, still said nothing about the composition of the "broad-based government."

Effects of the defeat of the Moscow coup: Agreement on a UN-mediated settlement plan

The remaining disagreements between Washington and Moscow were resolved after the August 1991 aborted coup. On September 13, 1991, Soviet Foreign Minister Boris Pankin and Secretary Baker agreed to the text that had been prepared for Houston the previous December, this time with a date certain for negative symmetry. The USSR agreed to the United States' proposal that the transitional authority should replace rather than operate alongside the government of President Najibullah. Both sides would cut off all weapons supplies at the end of the year. Pakistan and Saudi Arabia quietly indicated they would comply, without announcing the decision, which would have been difficult to justify to influential segments of public opinion in both countries. Soon after, Najibullah told the UN he would agree to resign at the beginning of the transitional period, and the secretary general of the UN stated in his October 1991 report on the situation in Afghanistan, "I have been given assurances that some of the controversial personalities concerned would not insist on their personal participation, either in the intra-Afghan dialogue or in the transition mechanism."[33]

This agreement advocated a limited-liability involvement by the international community in Afghanistan. The United States and the USSR agreed to try to remove sophisticated weapons and weapons of mass destruction from Afghanistan, but they made no provision for disarming or merging the various armed forces in the country. No one considered sending a peacekeeping force or setting up an international administration. Privately, UN officials also said they did not want to try to monitor elections in volatile, hyper-armed Afghanistan. The plan relied on the shift in aid flows that would accompany the change of government. External parties would cease providing arms and money to various parties and armed forces, which would all have to look to the internationally sponsored interim government for patronage.

In November the foreign ministers of the USSR, Russia, and Tajikistan met in Moscow with four of the seven Pakistan-based mujahidin parties (Jamiat and the three traditionalist parties) and the Iran-based Hizb-i Wahdat (Unity Party, the Shi'a Alliance). The three mainly Pashtun Islamist parties had refused to participate. The joint statement issued after the Moscow meeting supported the U. S.–Soviet agreement.

The UN prepares to install the transitional mechanism

Following the meetings in Moscow, UN Secretary General Pérez de Cuellar invited the permanent representatives of the United States, the USSR, Pakistan, Saudi Arabia, and Iran to a "tea party" in his office. Iran declined to attend a meeting with the United States, but those present, as well as Iran in absentia, affirmed support for the UN's initiative.

The UN accelerated its work on the transitional mechanism. Sevan set about concretizing plans which had been bruited about for years to use the forum of the UN to promote a dialogue among the various Afghan parties in order to create an interim government of "neutral" technocrats and lower-tier personnel of the contending parties. Such a government would have shared elements of a neutral caretaker and a power-sharing interim government.

In January the new secretary general, Boutros Boutros-Ghali, announced a plan under which all Afghan parties would submit to his office lists of candidates for an "Afghan gathering" (*ijlas*). The UN would negotiate agreement by all parties on about 150 representatives. The gathering would elect a committee of about 35 members. This committee would canvas the entire nation, and on the basis of these consultations summon a nationwide meeting to decide on an interim government and the holding of elections.

This cumbersome procedure was designed to overcome several obstacles. Direct power-sharing negotiations remained impossible, since the resistance parties still refused to meet or cooperate openly with Najibullah, the PDPA-Watan Party, or the existing government. Hence it was still not possible to organize a multiparty council as in Cambodia, where all four parties sat together and signed an agreement in Paris. Najibullah refused to hand over power to a resistance which had not defeated him, and the resistance refused to participate in a transition controlled by Najibullah. Furthermore, any Afghan who tried to convene a gathering, however prominent or "neutral," would be suspected of promoting his own power; any non-Afghan (including the UN secretary general) would lack legitimacy. Hence the UN settled on this complex procedure of using the secretary general's good offices to facilitate the formation of Afghan groups which would gain authority at every step. The procedure drew on certain Afghan traditions (in particular the "emergency Loya Jirga") propounded to the UN by exiled officials of the old regime, including the former king and his advisers.[34]

The three traditionalist-nationalist parties of the mujahidin submitted a joint list of proposed participants in the gathering, as did the Iran-based Hizb-i Wahdat. Zahir Shah and his advisers ultimately refused to submit a list to a gathering that gave such weight to the resistance parties. The Sunni Islamist parties also refused, suspecting that the UN effort was an effort to prevent an Islamist victory. Najibullah also postponed giving his list, which would have constituted a more decisive signal that he was prepared to depart than his previous confidential assurance.

By March Pakistan and the United States were telling Sevan that they needed an explicit, public commitment by Najibullah to depart to pressure the "rejectionists" in the resistance. After several long sessions in Kabul between Sevan and Najibullah, the latter presented his list and agreed to announce his intention to resign. On March 18, 1992, Najibullah addressed the nation on television and radio. In a speech drafted for him by Sevan, he stated that he would leave office as soon as a transitional authority was formed.

AFTER THE UN PLAN: FROM CONFLICT RESOLUTION TO ETHNIC FRAGMENTATION

With the end of aid from Washington and Moscow, and Najibullah's public statement that he would leave power, the ideological conflict was definitively over. Rather than moving toward collaboration, however, the movements the superpowers had supported, and whose leaders had been the UN's main interlocutors, were breaking up along largely (not exclusively) ethnic lines. The leaders involved in the political negotiations became less important compared to the military commanders who led organizations inside Afghanistan. Some had fought with the resistance, others with the government.

All leaders of the Watan party and the military had been seeking to assure their own survival by finding allies among the mujahidin. Given the structure of Afghan society, such alliances formed along ethnic or tribal lines. In March 1990 a Pashtun alliance formed when the Defense Minister Shahnawaz Tanai and other Khalqi officers allied with Gulbuddin Hikmatyar and nearly overthrew Najibullah in a coup supported by the ISI.

The anti-Najibullah Parchamis (mainly representing non-Pashtuns from

Kabul and northern Afghanistan) had also begun to negotiate with Shi'a, Tajik, and Uzbek mujahidin. After years in Moscow exile, Karmal had returned to Kabul in June 1991, shortly before the Moscow coup. Many Afghans believe both that he was the secret leader of a movement against his rival Najibullah and that the Iranians had promoted an alliance among the non-Pashtuns. The Iranians were seeking ways to balance the rise of Saudi and Pakistani influence among the Sunni mujahidin, especially Pashtuns.[35] For these reasons, since the Soviet withdrawal, Tehran had improved relations with Kabul and the Soviets. In 1991, Tehran had also sponsored an accord on cultural cooperation among Persian speakers, signed by Iran, Tajikistan, Hizb-i Wahdat (the alliance of Afghan Shi'a mujahidin), and Jamiat. This accord signaled Iran's intention to form a special relation with the northern, non-Pashtun, part of Afghanistan, which constituted a land bridge between Iran and the newly independent states of Uzbekistan and Tajikistan.

Najibullah had faced open revolt from his own forces in northern Afghanistan since January 1992, shortly after the end of both Soviet aid and the Soviet Union itself. The rebels were led by the Uzbek general, Abdul Rashid Dostum, who had long feuded with the Pashtun generals to whom he supposedly had to report. The revolt enjoyed the support of the mainly non-Pashtun pro-Karmal forces in Parcham. These factional and ethnic revolts within the armed forces and party were the means through which the lack of institutionalization of the Afghan state rendered the transition impossible.

As the transition approached, both Parchamis and Khalqis attempted to engage in what Shain and Linz have called "power-sharing from without." Under adverse circumstances the incumbents may transfer power to a weak opposition in the hope of exercising control through political pressure or other means:

A . . . version of "power-sharing from without" may occur when the incumbent leaders realize that their dictatorship cannot survive a deep political crisis. To forestall a total collapse, they may choose to transfer power to a broadly acceptable interim rule, which they hope to dominate, even from without.[36]

The Parchami rebels (predominantly Dostum's forces) had formed an alliance with commanders of the Shi'a Hizb-i Wahdat, Jamiat, and other northern resistance groups. The day after Najibullah announced he would depart, this coalition seized control of the northern capital of Mazar-i Sharif, cutting off Kabul from its main supply lines. Massoud, an acknowledged national hero of the resistance, emerged as political spokesman for the alliance, whose most powerful military force consisted of Dostum's troops.

The UN plan blocked

As the revolt threatened to topple the government before the completion of the lengthy transition process, the UN streamlined its plan. On April 10, Sevan met in Geneva with Boutros-Ghali, who approved a new version. A "pre-transition council composed of impartial personalities" chosen from the lists submitted to the UN would take over "all powers and executive authority" from the current government.[37] This council would then convene a *shura* (presumably in Kabul) to choose the interim government.

The UN hurriedly canvased support for the plan, and under severe pressure from the United States and Pakistan the major leaders on all sides accepted it. Those members of the proposed interim authority who were outside Afghanistan assembled in Pakistan. Both sides agreed that on the night of April 15–16 a UN plane would fly the members of the interim government into Kabul, where Najibullah would transfer power to them at the airport and leave on the same plane. During the day of April 15, however, at a meeting of over eight hours at the Islamabad residence of the Prime Minister of Pakistan, two of the mujahidin parties expressed misgivings about the pre-transition council. Rabbani, whose forces seemed on the verge of taking Kabul with the support of the northern rebels, wavered. The son of another leader, Mujaddidi, who harbored ill-concealed ambitions to serve as president of the country, suggested a mujahidin government instead. The UN asked them to submit a list of members of such a government; Najibullah and his remaining followers had indicated they would transfer power to such a government. When the mujahidin leaders were unable to agree on a list that day, Sevan flew to Kabul in the early hours of April 16.

There, however, Najibullah had tried to leave the country in secret despite the failure to form a transitional government, and the northern rebels allied with Massoud had prevented him from escaping. In an operation coordinated by Karmal's brother, Mahmud Baryalai, they had seized control of the airport with 750–1,000 troops flown from northern military bases.[38] When they refused to let Najibullah into the airport, he fled to the office of the UN, which found itself in the awkward situation of granting asylum in his own country to a deposed head of state accused of serious human rights violations.

Establishment of the Islamic state of Afghanistan

Led by Karmal's second cousin, Foreign Minister Abdul Wakil, the Parchami rebels who now controlled Kabul denounced Najibullah as a hated dictator and secretly asked Massoud to enter the capital as head of

state. In a form of power-sharing from without, the Parchamis intended
to use Massoud as a figurehead who would continue to depend on them.[39]

Massoud rejected this offer and asked the leaders in Peshawar to
accelerate their efforts to form an interim government of mujahidin.
Under intense Pakistani pressure, the leaders in Peshawar argued for ten
days over arrangements for a transitional government.

Meanwhile Pashtuns in the Afghan military – mainly Khalqis, but also
some Parchamis close to Najibullah – reacted to the threatened takeover
of Kabul by the northerners. These officers infiltrated unarmed fighters
of Hizb-i Islami into the city, where they received arms from their coethnics in the Interior Ministry. Hikmatyar's conventional military force
also crossed over the border from Pakistan and camped south of Kabul.
Despite Pakistan's official neutrality, Hikmatyar was able to continue
to recruit fighters and transfer weapons from Pakistan. Jamaat-i Islami
continued to support him, as did a sector of the intelligence apparatus. It
is unclear to what extent they enjoyed official support and to what extent
part of the ISI had become a virtual law unto itself, operating with Arab
funds and drug money.[40] Some Afghans speculate that Pakistan and
Saudi Arabia wanted to strengthen Hikmatyar to counter Iranian influence in the coalition that was assembling north of Kabul.

On April 26, before the Peshawar leaders had reached agreement,
Massoud's and Dostum's forces, already in control of the airport, entered
the rest of the city to preempt the coup by Hizb. The non-Pashtun
Parchamis, assisted by the Iranian embassy, had also armed the Shi'a of
Kabul city.[41] After violent battles at the Interior Ministry and the Presidential Palace, Massoud and Dostum's forces expelled the Khalqi-Hizbi
Pashtun forces. The latter, however, had breached the security cordon
around the city, and other mujahidin also started to flow into Kabul, set
up check points, and engage in looting. These guerrillas included Arab
Islamists, who had flocked to Afghanistan from the Middle East to train
for jihad.

In Peshawar, the leaders finally reached agreement on a transitional
arrangement, known as the Peshawar Accords, which claimed to establish, in effect, a provisional revolutionary government of mujahidin. An
interim government arrived in Kabul from Peshawar on April 29. Massoud became minister of defense. For two months, Sibghatullah Mujaddidi, a moderate but weak leader, would be acting president; he would be
followed by Rabbani for four months. After the six-month interim period
the government was to hold a *shura* to choose an interim government for
eighteen months, at the end of which elections would be held. The acting
president answered to a "leadership council," composed of the leaders of
mujahidin parties. As is typical of provisional revolutionary governments, the new powerholders were unable to resist introducing elements

of their program before establishing a more legitimate basis for their power.[42] Under pressure from the more extreme Islamist and fundamentalist elements, the government banned women news readers from television, imposed an Islamic dress code on the largely Westernized women of Kabul city, and established summary Islamic courts, which executed men found guilty of killings, rape, and pillage.[43] The first two measures were deeply unpopular in Kabul, while the third seemed partly to relieve the anxieties of the remaining city dwellers.

Fragmentation and new civil wars

In the rest of the country, mujahidin negotiated the surrender of the government garrisons with whom they had been dealing. Regional councils, some including commanders formerly on opposite sides, formed on the basis of ethnic and tribal ties. Two linked conflicts took thousands of lives in Kabul: these were sectarian (Sunni–Shi'a) and ethnic (Pashtun–non-Pashtun). Shi'a mujahidin who controlled about one fourth of Kabul city repeatedly clashed with Saudi-supported militantly anti-Shi'a Pashtun mujahidin aided by Arab volunteers. By October hundreds of civilian hostages taken in these clashes in June were still missing.[44]

Even more serious, however, the longstanding rivalry between Hikmatyar and Massoud, between Hizb and Jamiat, now overlaid with the feud between Khalq and Parcham, took on the dimensions of a battle for the control of Afghanistan between Pashtuns and non-Pashtuns or even between Iran and the Pakistan–Saudi alliance. Hikmatyar charged that, since the new government relied in large part on Dostum's Uzbek forces and some Parchami Tajik officers who had joined Massoud, it was not a genuine mujahidin government at all, but a form of power-sharing with Communists. (Of course, he was still allied with many Khalqis, and his personal bodyguard consisted of members of a former progovernment Pashtun tribal militia.)

Hikmatyar periodically bombarded the city with rockets. In August his attacks destroyed both the electrical grid and the water system of the city, shutting down hospitals and killing thousands. The UN and many diplomatic missions withdrew all non-Afghan personnel.

Iran continued to support the Shi'a and also developed direct relations with both Herat in the West and Dostum's administration in the north. Tehran even established a consulate in Dostum's capital of Mazar-i Sharif without informing Kabul. Dostum visited Uzbekistan, Turkey, and Pakistan, where he was received at the highest levels. A bizarre coalition, partly ethnic and partly ideological, supported Hikmatyar. His supporters included Pakistani Islamists, leftist Pakistani Pashtun nationalists (who were sheltering some of Najibullah's associates), and former ISI officers, backed by Middle Eastern money (some from the Muslim Brotherhood, some reportedly from al-Qaddafi and Saddam Hussein).

Other elements of the population maneuvered between the two power centers. The Pashtun tribes of Eastern Afghanistan opposed Hikmatyar's attacks on Kabul, but they supported his demand for the removal of "Communists" from the government. A weak government suited them, as they were occupied with the trade in the profitable opium crop, planted right up to the roadside around Jalalabad in the spring of 1992.[45]

The Durrani Pashtuns of southwest Afghanistan, while they had some presence inside the government, opposed its dominance by "fundamentalist" and non-Pashtun elements. They firmly opposed Hikmatyar. They organized a *shura* of eight predominantly Durrani provinces that opposed the "nondemocratic" rule of the leadership council. Their area too had become a major center for the cultivation of opium.

No one had any reason to "secede" from such an impotent state, and all the regional states, most aggressively Pakistan, let the various Afghan commanders know that they would not countenance any formal division of Afghanistan. In fact, however, the regionally based ethnic coalitions became autonomous, with their own armed forces and sources of revenue. All major customs posts, the government's principal source of revenue, were under the control of regional *shuras* who kept the income for themselves. Tens of thousands of barely controlled armed men occupied the streets of the capital. The government, with neither tax revenue nor foreign aid, paid its armed forces by distributing freshly printed banknotes which continued to arrive by plane from Russia. (Hikmatyar demanded that Russia stop printing the banknotes.) The government was forced to default on promised aid to the regional *shuras*. Kabul city had been fed for the past few winters only by massive shipments of wheat from the defunct Soviet Union, and by October the silos were empty. Hikmatyar's forces and other disgruntled Pashtuns controlled the roads from Pakistan by which traders could bring food to the capital.

Six months after assuming authority, on October 28 the leadership council (composed of leaders of the resistance parties or their representatives) voted to extend Rabbani's mandate for forty-five days. After that period the government would summon a nationwide *shura-yi hal o 'aqd* (council of those who loose and bind, an Islamic legal term unfamiliar to most Afghans). The *shura* would elect a president for the next eighteen months. Somewhat belatedly, Rabbani managed to convoke a shura of 1,335 men at the end of December. Over a tenth of the members were drawn from Dostum's organization; Jamiat predominated among the rest. Most areas of the country had some representation, but most of the parties boycotted it, charging it was manipulated by Rabbani, whom, to no one's surprise, it elected as president.

This election led to a fresh outbreak of fighting and a realignment of forces. Hikmatyar reached an agreement with the Shi'a of Hizb-i Wahdat, who now switched sides. After several more months of war, Pakistan and Saudi Arabia, with some participation by Iran, persuaded eight of the mujahidin leaders to sign a new agreement on the transition in Islamabad on March 7, 1993.[46]

This accord now aimed at setting up not so much a provisional revolutionary government of the mujahidin, as a power-sharing interim government to end the conflict between Hizb and Jamiat. Jamiat's leader, Rabbani, would remain president for eighteen months, while Hikmatyar or his nominee would be prime minister. An election commission was to start work immediately in order to convene a "Grand Constituent Assembly" in eight months. This assembly would draft a constitution under which elections of the president and prime minister would be held at the end of the eighteen-month interim period.

Unlike the UN plan, this one specifically addressed the problem of the multiplicity of armed forces. It provided for a joint defense council to oversee disarmament and merging of armed forces. It contained within it, however, a fatal vagueness which was essential to obtaining agreement. The prime minister was to appoint a cabinet "in consultations with the president." He would thus appoint the minister of defense. The president, however, was supreme commander of the armed forces. Hikmatyar immediately let it be known that he intended to sack his rival Massoud. The president and supreme commander of the armed forces announced his intention to resist that decision. Hikmatyar, the putative prime minister, continued to wage war on his own president and defense minister, who continued to prevent him from entering the capital. By January 1994, this agreement broke down completely. In a new round of battles, Dostum now sided with Hikmatyar against Rabbani and Massoud. House-to-house fighting combined with aerial bombardment by both sides destroyed much of what was left of Kabul, and tens of thousands of the remaining population streamed bare-handed out of the city in all directions. Afghanistan now lacked not only a state and a government, but even, for all intents and purposes, a capital city.

INTERIM GOVERNMENTS WITHOUT A STATE

The failure of the UN plan attracted much international attention, because of the way in which it approached success and collapsed dramatically, but in fact virtually every known variety (and some hitherto unknown varieties) of interim government have been proposed in Afghanistan, and all of them have thus far failed to reestablish political order, to say nothing of democracy. The interim governments formed under the Peshawar and Islamabad agreements may ultimately evolve into a forum within which new power-sharing arrangements are worked out among the various centers of power in the country. The process through which this will occur will involve a mixture of warfare and negotiation; ballots alone will not transfer power to anyone for a long time.

Afghanistan does not necessarily show the failure of the "international interim government" model, since the UN-supported transition council in Afghanistan lacked many features of that model. What it does show is that while an international interim government has many attractive features, its requirements for success seem to be so stringent that they will rarely be present. Afghanistan fell far short of these criteria, and I would hazard a guess that most intractable conflicts will do so as well, as in Angola.

Many in Afghanistan found the UN's plan mystifying or, in the words of a former PDPA Central Committee member, a "joke." He asked, "How could these people, outsiders, rule Afghanistan, when they did not command any military forces?"[47] In a state where the duties of office are separate from the identity of those who occupy them, such a question does not arise. But in Afghanistan – and in any state not conforming to the Weberian model of rational bureaucracy – it does.

For some states, at least, the end of the Cold War means an unraveling of institutions previously funded by foreign aid. Their locations no longer strategic, they can no longer extract the resources they once did. When state institutions unravel, and armed factions emerge as the main form of collective action, interim governments offer no quick solution to the problem of political order. No government can compensate for the dissolution of the state.

12

Electoral transitions in Yugoslavia[1]

PAULA FRANKLIN LYTLE

The devastating war in the republics of the former Yugoslavia has over-shadowed the electoral transitions of 1990. Yet just as the decentralized politics of Yugoslavia through the 1960s to the 1980s laid the groundwork for separate, republic-level transitions, the results of the 1990 elections were crucial to the process of the state's demise. The issue on the agenda of the republic elections was the future of the Yugoslav state, although the final electoral playing-out of that issue was to await the plebiscites. The punctuated nature of the electoral transitions extended the process over the course of 1990, creating multiple transitions at the level of each republic.

Placing the Yugoslav transitions (with emphasis on the punctuated and plural nature of those transitions) in context of the framework developed here by Shain and Linz, it is evident that in all the cases the interim governments were incumbent caretaker governments. However, the interim governments conducting the elections were the variously renamed Communist party organizations of the republics, not the League of Communists of Yugoslavia (SKJ). Indeed after the Fourteenth Congress in January 1990, the SKJ no longer existed. Thus the determination of the transition variables of timing and electoral rules were at the discretion of the republic parties.

The dissolution of the SKJ meant that effectively there was no central arena in which the question of democratization and the future political order of the state was being discussed, elections were not called by a central state organization nor were voters choosing simultaneously for the same slate of candidates. The transition was handled separately on the republic levels by the different republic party organizations. Yugoslav Prime Minister Ante Marković's reform package was an economic reform, designed to address the inflation. It was not a political reform, and the breakup of the SKJ demonstrated how volatile the question of political reform was to prove.

The question of stateness and the future of the Yugoslav state were thus being answered through the series of republic elections which occurred over the course of 1990. The answers given offered competing interpretations of what the state should look like, dominated by the struggle over centralism versus confederalism. These interpretations were not neutral, but represented national ideologies with potentially oppositional constructions of the ideal political order of the state.

This devolution of transitions to republic parties created a dichotomy with respect to transition variables. The transition variables of timing, rulemaking, and political environment operated in two spheres. The first sphere was the internal dynamic of each republic's elections in which the incumbent caretaker government declared that elections will be held and established the electoral rules (subject to pressure from the various oppositions). The second sphere is the interrelationships between the elections in the different republics of what then still constituted one country.

Therefore, the raising of the question of the integration of the Yugoslav state versus the possibility of secession (even in early and tentative formulations) in the first elections, held in Slovenia in April 1990, placed that issue on the agenda of the elections of the other republics. The form of the democratic transition process as punctuated and devolved transitions also underscored the open nature of the question of the state. Furthermore, the declaration of and subsequent holding of multiparty, competitive elections in and of itself placed pressure on the other republic Communist party organizations to follow suit. Much as regime challenge in Eastern Europe can be seen in terms of demonstration effects, electoral transitions in the republics involved a similar process.

The separate transitions also illustrate different responses to the pre-1990 form of Yugoslavia and the different possibilities of response by interim governments to both this challenge and the prospect of electoral competition. An electoral competition in a previously noncompetitive system which raises the possibility of secession from the existing state simultaneously introduces the use of voice and the potential for exit.[2] The internal barriers to expression of preference about the organization of the Yugoslav state were being lifted, and through that process the physical boundaries (which had been maintained through the limiting of the voice option) were subject to challenge.

As Shain and Linz observe, interim governments operate in a "volatile and vulnerable period for the polity marked by the deflation of power, uncertainty, anxiety, and high expectations concerning the future distribution of power and loyalties."[3] This volatility was heightened in the Yugoslav transitions by the extended period over which elections took place – from April 1990 to December 1990. For although the collective presidency remained in place, negotiation and attempted redefinition of Yugoslavia awaited the results of all elections. The transitions in former Yugolavia also confirm their observations on the conditions under which electoral transitions are initiated. In the case of Yugoslavia, several of these conditions were present. Economic deterioration over the course of the 1980s had culminated in an annual inflation rate of 1,950 percent by the end of 1989. Furthermore, there had been a severe rupture in the ruling elite, culminating in the Slovenian walkout of the Fourteenth Congress. Finally, the collapse of Communist rule elsewhere in Eastern Europe created a climate of expectation of change, heightened by ongoing criticisms between and within republics.

PREELECTION DEVOLUTION: REPUBLIC AUTONOMY

With the death of Tito in 1980, the death knell for Yugoslavia began to toll. His role as the "one Yugoslav"[4] was widely eulogized while his political legacy of the collective presidency was subjected to intense scrutiny. The apparent initial ease of the succession on one level belied the cleavages elsewhere. Yet processes that preceded Tito's death were crucial for the devolution of power to the republic level, rather than the institutional framework created for the succession.

Since the 1960s, decentralization of party authority to republic-level parties has characterized Yugoslav politics. The republics had considerable control over the political, economic, and administrative matters.[5] Decision making had gradually devolved to the republic-level parties, leaving the republics as the primary locus of political and economic activity, pursuing independent development policies. Party control over resources at the republic level thus reinforced the tendency for individuals to seek political careers in the republic arena.[6] Tito had acted to limit the extent to which republic actors mobilized national identity by cracking down on such expressions.[7]

In the absence of Tito, the mechanism of the presidency represented each of the republics and the autonomous provinces in collective power-sharing with each representative to the presidency selected by and a member of a republic-level Communist party. The constitution of 1974 had raised the expectation of consensus of separate republics to a principle of governance. The federal budget required unanimous consent of all republics and the provinces. Although considerable coordination and cooperation occurred, interrepublican and federal interaction relied on an assumption of united interests.

The Twelfth Party Congress in 1982 further reinforced the growing inefficacy of the federal party organizations despite the increased appeals to the contrary. The growing tendency for party members in federal party organizations to view themselves as "representatives of their respective federal units" was condemned,[8] but it was apparent that SKJ had become a forum in which the various positions were contested and not an independent actor.

This decentralization of power to the republic level was at times mistaken for a "new pluralism," with emphasis on diffusion and decentralization in contrast to conventional Communist centralized authority.[9] In effect, what had occurred was the enshrinement of each republic as the arena for politics. Republic-level debates and politics were the ones that mattered and the federal party had relatively little authority. The federal party met as representatives of the constituent republics, and competition among republic interests dominated politics. In addition, the absence of lateral transfers between republics reinforced the separation of party apparatus.[10]

The consolidation of authority by republic level elites took different forms among republics. Although the variation in the level of economic development has been widely discussed,[11] the different republics also contained distinctive political patterns. The complex relationship between nation and republic ensured that politics would not proceed in a similar fashion in all republics.[12] Slovenia and Serbia are more nationally homogeneous while other republics contained varying percentages of different nations and nationalities. Bosnia-Hercegovina is divided among Serbs, Croats, and Muslims and these participated in power-sharing arrangement. Croatia contains a Serb minority of less than 12 percent. Of the two autonomous provinces, Kosovo is mainly Albanian, but the presence of the Serb minority remains a crucial aspect of that area. Hungarians are over one-fifth the population of Vojvodina. Montenegro and Macedonia pose additional delicate questions. Montenegro has been divided into two factions, one maintaining the separateness of the Montenegrins, the other advocating Serb unity. It also contains Muslim and Albanian minorities. Macedonia too has an Albanian minority, and Macedonian as a nationality has been contested by the republic's neighbors, most vociferously by Greece.

With his rise to power as the president of the League of Communists of Serbia (SKS), Slobodan Milošević began to challenge the principles of republican autonomy and decentralization. Claiming to speak for all Serbs (not only those within the republic of Serbia), Milošević invoked the need for increased federal power and increased centralism while championing Serb interests.[13] He thus linked the constitutional principle with mobilization of one nation within Yugoslavia, a construction which worked to exacerbate the growing crisis of the state. Meanwhile, within Slovenia, oppositional pressure had grown for increased democratization and liberalization of politics. These competing formulations were headed for conflict.

Prior to the elections, the political autonomy to Kosovo and Vojvodina granted under the 1974 constitution was unilaterally revoked through Serbia's amendment of its own constitution in March 1989. The effect of aggregating Kosovo and Vojvodina under the rules of the collective presidency was to gain two more seats on the presidency for Serbia. With the subsequent removal of the party leadership in Montenegro, Milošević had effective control over four of the eight party apparatus.

In Slovenia criticism had intensified of the role of the Yugoslav National Army (JNA), especially in Kosovo. The youth journal *Mladina* had been active in this respect. In June 1988 three journalists associated with *Mladina* and one Slovene in the JNA were tried for disclosure of secret military documents by attempting to publish the JNA's plans to suppress the growing oppositional movement in Slovenia through military intervention. The arrests themselves were seen as a beginning of this process.[14] The trial triggered large-scale public protests in Slovenia and served as an impetus for the formation of several political parties.[15]

The Fourteenth (Extraordinary) Congress of the League of Communists of Yugoslavia was held in Belgrade in January 1990. The dimensions of the conflict were apparent in the gulf between the positions advocated by Slovenia and Serbia. The Slovene delegation proposed a new federal party structure with eight freely associated (Kosovo and Vojvodina included) parties independently proceeding with democratic reforms and with free elections. The relationship between the demonstration effect of events elsewhere in Eastern Europe was apparent in references to democratic changes in debate by Ciril Ribičić (president of the Central Committee of the League of Communists of Slovenia) and the more negative example of Romania invoked by Milan Kučan in an interview.[16] Serbia had countered the Slovene proposals with a renewed call for strengthening and centralizing the role of the Communist party. On January 22, the Congress voted to abolish the leading role of the SKJ in society, but the Slovene proposals to restructure the party were rejected. Following the rejection of their proposal, the Slovene delegation walked out of the Congress. Attempts to continue the Congress broke down. The Slovene walkout resulted in a de facto adoption of multiparty elections as they proceeded with their election plans and other republics followed suit.

SLOVENIA

Following the walkout from the SKJ Congress, the Slovenia Communist party voted to end its membership in the SKJ and to change its name to the League of Communists of Slovenia-Party of Democratic Renewal (later Reform) (ZKS-SDP). The prominent role of the Communists in pushing for reform gave a certain advantage to their candidate for president, Milan Kučan. The primary opposition to the renamed Communist party came from an alliance of parties known as DEMOS.

Coalition politics played an important role in shaping the dimensions of the political contest. Part of this was due to the adoption of modified proportional representation voting rules. Multimember electoral districts were established with deputies seated on the basis of percentage of vote within each district. This contrasted with direct election for the president on a two ballot system. The formation of a coalition also allowed member parties to campaign more effectively against the better-organized re-named Communist party, yet still maintain the individual platforms and identities of their parties. DEMOS (Democratic Opposition of Slovenia, later amended to Democratic United Opposition of Slovenia) was founded in December of 1989. It expanded to eventually comprise six political parties.[17] Seventeen political groups registered for the campaign, of which only thirteen were parties. The others were citizens' lists or independent candidates. DEMOS therefore represented a substantial proportion of the contenders for political office.

The elections were held for a three chamber National Assembly (comprising the Socio-Political Chamber, the Chamber of Municipalities, and the Chamber of Associated Labor[18]) and for the office of president and four seats in the collective presidency. Amendments to the constitution had established the electoral laws as well as dropping the term "socialist" from the republic's name prior to the elections.

The fear of potential intervention by federal authorities to prevent the election was heightened by the visit of the Secretary of National Defense Colonel General Veljko Kadijević to Ljubljana on April 5.[19] Following the elections, the military charged presidential candidate Joze Pučnik with violations of provisions of the Federal Criminal Code pertaining to attacks on the Socialist Federal Republic of Yugoslavia. Despite the concerns raised on the eve of the elections, turnout was still high, with over 80 percent of the eligible voters participating in the elections.

The first round of elections for president did not produce the simple majority required and forced a runoff between Kučan and Pučnik of DEMOS (and the Social Democratic Alliance). The separate direct election for president facilitated Kučan's ability to translate personal popularity as an architect of the transition into elected office. His win contrasted with the stronger showing of DEMOS in parliament,[20] thus creating a party division between parliament and the president. The results with the other seats in the presidency gave two seats to DE-MOS,[21] two to the ZKS-SDP[22] and the final seat was won by Ciril Zlobec of the Alliance of Socialists.

The Slovenes had set the agenda of possible secession of Slovenia (thus raising the issue for other republics) prior to the elections and indeed, prior to the breakup of the SKJ Congress. On January 9, 1990, the issue had been debated in an unprecedented public forum by representatives of some of the political opposition. Although DEMOS was seen as standing for the possibility of eventual secession, Kučan was perceived as more moderate on this issue. Furthermore, the mixed results of the elections made it less of a complete rejection of Communist rule than anticipated by the opposition. The potential also existed for divisions between the president and the parliament on the issue of sovereignty. Still, Kučan's election in a direct vote translated into the ability to claim popular mandate. The gradual and ongoing process of democratization had raised the expectations for the electoral transition. The realization of the elections, however, did not complete the transition.

CROATIA

The elections in Croatia (April 22 and 29) were marked by greater volatility of national identity as an issue than in the Slovene elections. The issue of relations between the Serb minority in Croatia and Croats was an explosive one, rendered more so by rhetoric and events preceding the elections. Campaign rallies held by the Croatian Democratic Union (HDZ) stressed Croat national identity. A mass rally in Croatia in March attended by Serbs from Croatia and from other republics protested meetings of the HDZ. The Serbian Democratic Party (SDS) competed in the elections as a Serb alternative to the other parties organized.

The ease with which parties could be registered produced a wider political field in Croatia than in Slovenia. Of the thirty-three political groups registered, many joined with other parties and three main coalitions emerged. Numerous other parties remained outside of the coalitions, including the renamed League of Communists of Croatia. The League of Communists of Croatia-Party for Democratic Changes (SKH-SDP) campaigned on similar themes of reform communism and European Community orientation as their Slovene counterparts. Like them, they also stressed the political inexperience of their opponents and sought to take credit for initiating the electoral transition.

Of the coalitions that were established, a significant pre-election role was played by the Coalition of National Accord which comprised eight political groups or parties.[23] Its main characteristic was the presence in the coalition of former Communists who had been purged from the party as nationalists by Tito for their participation in the Croat reform movement of 1971. One of the most prominent of these, Miko Tripalo, emphasized the continuities with the earlier movement in his interviews. Their personal appeal and references to their role in the earlier movement did not translate into significant electoral success, contrasting with the ascendance of another purged member of the same movement, Franjo Tudjman.

The Croatian Democratic Union (HDZ) had been founded in 1989, and it later joined with five other parties to form the Croatian Democratic Bloc immediately before the elections.[24] The HDZ was by far the most significant party of this coalition with well-developed regional branches and a substantial following outside the country. The HDZ emphasized the sovereignty of Croatia and Tudjman incorporated appeals to Croat identity in his campaigning.[25] Like DEMOS, however, it pushed for a confederal solution to Yugoslavia without ruling out the possibility of eventual secession.

A noticeable difference in the elections in Croatia from those in the other republics was the role of Croats from overseas returning to campaign and to vote in the elections. These were not limited to *gastarbeiter* in Germany and Austria, but included substantial numbers from North America. The HDZ received substantial financial and technical support from the diaspora.

The Yugoslav level of competition in the transitions was particularly noticeable in the Croatian elections, but also present in the Slovenian. Electoral opposition was taking place in two arenas simultaneously. Opposition was not only directed towards the other parties in the republic's elections, but towards political actors in other republics, especially, (but not only) Milošević. At the same time, opposition outside the republic denounced both the HDZ and the electoral process.

The electoral laws in Croatia provided for the selection of the president from the party which won a majority in parliament (the Sabor), thus eliminating the possibility of the division between a directly elected president and the parliament as in Slovenia. Anticipating popular support, the League of Communists of Croatia-Party of Democratic Changes was caught off guard by the results of the elections. The electoral law created single-member districts, a system in which the Communists assumed they could dominate through their better developed organizational structure. The HDZ, however, ran candidates in all parts of the republic, in contrast to other parties which concentrated their efforts on the capital. The electoral law thus translated 40 percent of the vote for the HDZ into two-thirds of the seats in the most powerful chamber and 205 seats of the 356 available.[26] Run off elections were held if candidates did not achieve a 50 percent-plus-one majority on the first ballot. Many of the seats in the Sabor were decided on the second round of voting. After the second round, the HDZ had a majority in all chambers, with the SKH-SDP a distant second. Voter turnout was somewhat less than in Slovenia, about 76 percent of the electorate. The electoral victory of the HDZ allowed for Tudjman to be elected president in the Sabor and represented a decision for the confederal alternative of Yugoslavia over a federal solution.

MACEDONIA

Macedonia had in February 1990 announced its plan to delay holding of elections until April 1991, the parliament claiming that additional time was necessary for multiparty elections to be held. Pressure increased with the progress of the Croat and Slovene elections, and the date finally set for the elections by the government was for November 11. The League for Democracy and the Movement for All Macedonian Action (MAAK) were the earliest organized opposition to the Communist party in that republic. The incarnation of the League of Communists of Macedonia was as the party of Democratic Transformation.

Macedonia had one of the lowest thresholds for party registration, requiring only twenty members for a group to register as a party. Of the twenty parties organized (a high number given the relatively small population of the republic), six emerged as contenders. Macedonia also marked the electoral debut of Yugoslav Prime Minister Ante Marković's Alliance of Reform Forces. Organized following the Croatian and Slovenian elections, the Alliance of Reform Forces sought to provide an all-Yugoslav party as an alternative to national or republic-based parties.

Other dominant parties included: the Party for Democratic Prosperity (Albanian), the Socialist Party-Socialist Alliance of the Working People of Macedonia, and the evocatively named Internal Macedonian Revolutionary Organization-Democratic Party for Macedonian National Unity (VMRO-DPMNE).[27]

The debate over Macedonia's role in the future Yugoslavia resembled aspects of the discussion in Bosnia-Hercegovina. In both republics, the debate recognized the extent to which decisions made in Croatia and Slovenia would affect the changed balance of the new state. MAAK and VMRO both advocated a confederal arrangement, but indicated that their positions would change if Croatia and Slovenia were to secede. Also on the agenda were issues of Macedonian nationality. Prior to the elections, the constitution had been amended to omit specific references to Albanian and Turkish minorities. The republic was balanced between increased appeals to Macedonian nationalism as a counter to growing Serb nationalism and a tendency to support the Serbian concerns over Albanian nationalism.

Unlike the tricameral arrangements in Croatia and Slovenia, elections in Macedonia were to a unicameral National Assembly. The National

Assembly then selected the president and the government. As in Croatia, voting was on the basis of districts with similar rules for proceeding to the second ballot.

The first round of voting failed to produce significant results with only 11 seats of the 120 decided in that round. Elections proceeded to a second round, and then to a third round in December without producing a clear majority in parliament. VMRO won thirty-eight seats, followed by the Communists with thirty and twenty-three seats for the Albanian Party of Democratic Prosperity and the Independent Democratic Party. Kiro Gligorov was elected president through parliamentary vote and formed a coalition government. Rejecting the incorporation of Macedonia into a Yugoslavia without Croatia and Slovenia, he argued for a modified version of the confederalist plan.

BOSNIA-HERCEGOVINA

Reacting to the pressure of the initial elections, Bosnia-Hercegovina announced August 1 that it constituted a sovereign and democratic state and that its elections would be held in November. Multiparty elections were not legalized until July 31 with amendments to the republic's constitution, although registration of political parties was permitted under a law passed in February. Over forty-one parties or political groups registered for the elections.

In contrast to the electoral rules in other republics, Bosnia-Hercegovina had established specific electoral rules to deal with the national composition of the republic. Elections were held for a bicameral National Assembly and a state presidency. Voting for the Chamber of Citizens was on a proportional representation and for the Chamber of Municipalities on majority vote. Electoral rules recognized concern over one nationality's dominance by limiting representation of nation-based (or ethnic) parties. Furthermore, the presidency was established as a seven member body with two representatives from each of the principal nations (Croat, Serb and Muslim) and one from a minority nationality group. The president of the presidency was not a directly elected position as in Slovenia, but selected among those who were elected to the seven member body.

As elsewhere, the League of Communists ran under a new name, the League of Communists of Bosnia-Hercegovina-Socialist Democratic Party (SKBH-SDP). The other major non-national party was the party organized by Yugoslav Prime Minister Ante Marković, the Alliance of Reform Forces of Yugoslavia for Bosnia-Hercegovina (SRSJ-BH). The other major parties were based on nationality. The Party for Democratic Action (SDA) ran as a Muslim party, the HDZ sought Croat support, and the Serbian Democratic Party (SDS) targeted Serb voters. Prior to the holding of elections, party activists from Croatia and Serbia had been involved in setting up Bosnian branches of their parties. The success of the Croat HDZ in the neighboring republic facilitated its organizing ability in Bosnia-Hercegovina. However, meetings of the HDZ in Bosnia-Hercegovina were twice banned during the Croatian elections.

The political future of Yugoslavia as confederation or federation was also on the agenda in Bosnia-Hercegovina. The Muslim Party for Democratic Action advocated a confederal solution with Bosnia-Hercegovina as a sovereign state within Yugoslavia. The Serb parties rejected a confederal solution, and the Croats advocated one. The debate over Yugoslavia's future did not only mirror the overall cleavages, but reflected the sense of Bosnia-Hercegovina as poised between the two alternatives and trying to mediate them.

Despite preelection polling which gave an edge to the Communists and Marković's Alliance of Reform Forces, the actual voting closely mirrored the national composition of the republic. In the Chamber of Citizens, the SDA (Muslim) won forty-one seats, the SDS (Serb) won thirty-four seats, and the HDZ (Croat) twenty. The remaining seats were divided among eight other parties with the Communists and Marković's party making the strongest showing. In the Chamber of Municipalities, many of the seats were decided in a second round of voting with similar results. The bicameral legislature was therefore dominated by the three parties organized on the basis of nationality, dividing 201 of 240 seats among them.

Alija Izetbegović of the Muslim Party for Democratic Action was chosen president of the collective presidency.[28] The prime minister was Jure Pelivan, a Croat, and the president of the parliament, Momčilo Krajišnik, a Serb. This formal power-sharing served only to mask the different, and ultimately irreconcilable, notions of the future role of Bosnia-Hercegovina which were now represented in the elected bodies.

SERBIA

The electoral transitions in Serbia demonstrates the risk to transition if old political elites remain strong. Although all republics were marked by discussions of the control of Communist party elites over information and various accusations of unfairness, the difficulty for opposition groups in Serbia to win concessions over election rules influenced electoral politics. The strength of Milošević's appeals to Serb nationalism also defined the terms in which opposition leaders could challenge him. The reorganized Communist (as Socialist) party was not vulnerable to challenges from nation-based parties as in other republics, because the ruling party had already mobilized support on the basis of national identification.

Fifty-three parties and political groups were registered in Serbia. The League of Communists of Serbia merged with the Socialist Alliance in July, Milošević retaining control over the reorganized party. Milošević faced two other contenders who sought to transform the Serb national movement into their own basis for power. The first of these, the Serb Movement of Renewal, was led by the writer and mystic Vuk Drašković. The territorial program of this party eschewed the federation/confederation debate that had shaped electoral discussions of the future of Yugoslavia. Rather, the party sought a restoration of the monarchy and a redrawing of republic boundaries to incorporate all Serbs within an expanded Serbia. Some of meetings of the Serb Movement of Renewal had been banned in March 1990, and Drašković was perceived as the major rival for Milošević's support. The other significant party in the Serb elections was the Democratic Party. Like the Serb Movement of Renewal, this party had been established in January 1990.

The electoral rules were established under continuing threats of boycotts of the election by the opposition parties. The presidency first managed to extend presidential power through a referendum on adoption of a new constitution prior to the election despite campaigns by the opposition against this. By as late as November, aspects of the electoral laws were still under discussion. Although discussions about the rules of the elections existed in other republics, in Serbia the opposition then threatened to boycott the election if demands for participation in the electoral commissions overseeing the elections were not met. The conflict was only resolved by the end of November with the election set for December 9. Albanians maintained the call for a boycott of the elections, however.

As in Macedonia, the National Assembly was organized as unicameral. However, the election for presidency was a separate, direct election. This was in line with the strengthening of the powers of the presidency in the constitutional changes made in September which also extended the powers of the state.[29] As in Croatia, representation was on the basis of districts which tended to distort the extent of popular support for the winners when translated into actual seats.

The election results reflected the ability of the interim government to remain in power. Milošević defeated Drašković in the direct elections for president by with over 65 percent of the vote to Drašković's 20 percent. After the first round, the Socialist party was headed for a clear victory with over 60 percent of the seats in the Serbian National Assembly. The relative failure of coalitional politics in Serbia was countered after the first round of elections with the formation of the United Serbian Opposition by the main oppositional parties for the second round elections held on December 23. The damage had already been done by that point, and the final allocation of seats gave the Socialists 194 of the 250 possible seats, and the Serbian Movement of Renewal only 19. These results were not received with equilibrium, and the opposition parties accused the ruling Socialist party of electoral fraud, particularly when it was discovered that the votes cast for presidential candidates totaled 104 percent.[30] The challenges did not hamper Milošević's claim to have received a mandate.

MONTENEGRO

The first proposals for elections in Montenegro were made in January 1990 amid open discussion of the effects of events elsewhere in Europe on politics in Yugoslavia. The initial proposal was for elections to be held in October. Several parties were founded early in the year, but the law legalizing multiparty elections was not passed until October 3, and the elections were held on December 9. Eleven parties or political groups competed in the elections.

Of the parties in Montenegro, Marković's Alliance of Reform Forces presented the strongest opposition to the League of Communists of Montenegro (SKM). Unlike other republic party organizations, the SKM did not bother to rename itself, as it represented younger party members who had only recently come to power after the removal of the previous party leadership. Three opposition parties representing national minorities organized themselves as the Democratic Coalition.[31]

Elections in Montenegro were held for a unicameral National Assembly (previously tricameral) with a separate race for the president and the four member presidency. Most parties emphasized a federal and united Yugoslavia, yet additional pressure existed in the form of the Movement for the Unification of Serbia and Montenegro. That organization agitated for the submission of the question of annexation of Montenegro by Serbia to a referendum within Montenegro. Although the referendum was not introduced, the old question of Montenegrin Greens versus Whites was thus raised again in the context of multiparty elections.

The sitting president, Momir Bulatović, was elected president, although not on the first ballot as expected. The SKM seated the majority of the delegates in the 125 member National Assembly, with some seats won by the Alliance of Reform Forces and the Democratic Coalition. The election results were overshadowed to some extent by the Serbian elections taking place at the same time. The strong showing of the LCM as the incumbent caretaker government holding the elections thus also indirectly supported the results of those elections as well.

TIMING AND SEPARATE REPUBLIC TRANSITIONS

Once the issue of the future arrangement of Yugoslavia had been raised in one republic election, it was inevitably on the agenda in all of the others. Yet the results of the elections produced clearer mandates in some republics over others, therefore complicating further the process of negotiation. The demands of other actors within republics seeking separate resolution of their claims exacerbated the situation.

In terms of the interrelations between republics, the direct effect of a party such as the Muslim SDA or the Croat HDZ organizing in more than one republic created the framework of demands and recognizable political profile for those parties (especially given the intense scrutiny the early elections received from other republics). Other interaction between parties in one republic extended beyond the organizing of national-based parties from Serbia and Croatia described in the electoral contest in Bosnia-Hercegovina. Once the pattern of successful party activity by opposition parties was established in one republic, other would-be party organizers from another attended their conventions and organizational meetings. The relative failure of Marković's Alliance of Reform Forces (when compared to projected support in preelection polls) derives from its later founding (after the first two republic elections) in contrast to its political program as an all-Yugoslavia reform party. Its failure to participate in the initial elections negated the effectiveness of that claim. If it had won a majority in Bosnia-Hercegovina or Macedonia, it still would have remained without any voice or seats in the Slovene or Croat parliaments. Its stated objective of multiparty federal elections never materialized.

Each republic Communist party organization demonstrates possible sequences for incumbent caretaker governments. Kučan was able to translate his role in encouraging reform into the presidency, presenting himself both as a reformer and as an advocate for Slovene national interests. In Croatia the electoral rules established by the party based on their perceptions of support translated into electoral success for the HDZ. Although in Bosnia-Hercegovina, the incumbent caretaker government initially tried to block national parties from forming, the framework established for the election worked to channel national percentages of the population into parliamentary representation. In Serbia consolidation of the power of the president prior to the election hampered the ability of the opposition to challenge the incumbent government.

The electoral transitions also exhibit one typical pattern for transitions from authoritarian rule, the inevitably large number of parties competing in the elections. One alternative available to parties was that of coalition building to present a united opposition to the ruling Communist governments and to aid in the process of negotiating over electoral rules. The dynamics of the campaign process tended to force smaller parties to join with major coalitions in Croatia and Slovenia. In Montenegro, a coalition was formed of the minority national parties under a similar logic. The formation of the United Serbian Opposition only came after losses in the first round of elections by the opposition. Despite the logic encouraging coalition formation, results were more in support of parties with clear-cut identities (except in Slovenia) rather than for coalitions.

The political environment of the ongoing debate over the future of Yugoslavia also tended to favor parties with clear-cut positions on the role of the republic or nation in potential negotiations over the structure. The two levels of the transitions were particularly salient in this regard. Candidates for republic presidencies were thus presenting themselves as capable of representing the republic in negotiations as well as seeking support within the republic. In these dual arenas, leaders were legitimated through the electoral process in the republics, but the unresolved state questions on the federal level meant that they filled the existing roles in federal interactions.

Certain features of the earlier elections were repeated in the other electoral transitions. Some form of threshold voting rules were established in the republics, generally requiring a turnout of at least a third of the electorate for the results of the election to be considered valid. Other common features included rules against campaigning the day of and forty-eight hours before the elections. One result of the separate timing of elections was that Zagreb Radio and Television requested that Yugoslav Radio and Television refrain from broadcasting any political messages during that time frame and to avoid coverage that would constitute involvement in the preelection activities by groups outside the republic.

The fear of military intervention for subsequent elections lessened slightly after the successful completion of the Croatian and Slovenian elections. The juxtaposition of those elections was also perceived as lessening the threat of intervention, by raising the costs for the military. With the condemnation of multiparty elections by the federal President Borislav Jović in the middle of May, concerns were raised as to whether other elections would take place, and the actual announcements of some of the dates for other republic elections did not occur until later. Still, once successful multiparty elections had been held in Slovenia and Croatia, the opposition in other republics had readily available for imitation possible transitions (including elements to avoid).

Finally, the elections constituted an assertion of the voice option within the existing Yugoslav system as to voter preference for a renegotiated Yugoslavia. This use of voice in the earlier elections increased pressure for the exercise of voice elsewhere. The timing of the elections also represented a partial exit from the existing Yugoslav state system in which Slovenia and Croatia successfully challenged the principles of one-party rule and indicated their intention to challenge other principles of the Yugoslav state organization.

GOVERNABILITY AND THE PUNCTUATED TRANSITION

Once the issue of the future of Yugoslavia was on the agenda in the electoral transitions, it could not be resolved until all elections had been held. Thus the punctuated transition produced a crisis of governability. Federal authority had collapsed with the implosion of the KPJ, and Jović's accession to the federal presidency and his advocacy of accelera-tion of centralization only reinforced the sense of dissonance between existing structures and the changes on the republic levels. The process of a democratic transition could not be completed until the new framework was in place. Holding of elections within the republics and transfer of power on that level was not sufficient; the institutions that comprised Yugoslavia needed to be addressed. Assertion of centralization by the Serb representative to the Federal presidency was not therefore a neutral statement of a principle of governance; it was linked to one of the competing national interpretations of Yugoslavia. The question of state-ness which had been raised by the elections could not be deferred.

The earlier discussion of the shape of a new Yugoslavia reopened in early 1991 with all of the actors in place. This does not imply that it had not been ongoing between republics over the course of 1990, but posi-tions had crystallized through the elections. The process and the results of the elections themselves had moved the debates about centralization/decentralization of Yugoslavia from within and between republic Com-munist elites to the public sphere, and the competing formulations were submitted to democratic tests. The ongoing destabilization of Yugosla-via[32] thus had been brought into focus by the electoral transitions.

Yet events in the intervening months had exacerbated the crisis. The debate in Croatia about the extent of autonomy for the Serbs there had remained unresolved.[33] In mid-September, delegates of the dissolved Kosovo national assembly had met secretly and proclaimed a consti-tution, following their earlier declaration of Kosovo as a republic. In addition, other confrontations formed a backdrop to the political debates. In connection with the referendum in August, Serbs in Knin (Croatia) blockaded roads and bombed railway lines. In Foča (Bosnia-Hercegovina), Serbs had demonstrated over the dismissal of Serb em-ployees at a bus company; in Novi Pazar (in the Sandžak within Serbia) Muslims had demonstrated against a rally by the Serb Movement for

Renewal. In the last two cases, police dispersed demonstrators with tear gas. In the first, the newly formed Croatian territorial defense came into conflict with the Yugoslav National Army (JNA).

The crisis at this point was also marked by a lack of clear legal norms for the continuing functioning of the state. The republics had amended their constitutions to permit multiparty elections, but the Federal Constitution of 1974 had not been amended and the elections were in violation of its provisions. Invoked in the discussion of the future of Yugoslavia was the guarantee of the right of secession in that constitution. As other institutions of the federation ceased to function, the federal collective presidency retained some role as an arena in which republic positions were represented. The rotation of Croatia's Stipe Mesić to the chair of the presidency was blocked by Serbia's Jović in May 1991, heightening the contrast between formal legality of the decaying state and the actual practice of politics.

In October 1990, Croatia and Slovenia proposed a plan for a confederal Yugoslavia, to some degree modeled on the European Community. Serbia and Montenegro rejected this proposal, arguing against the lack of powers for the state. In January of 1991, following the last elections, several rounds of negotiations commenced with both federal and republican presidents and prime ministers participating. The federal officials, however, were also representing republic interests. Macedonia supported the confederal proposal, and Bosnia-Hercegovina demonstrated willingness to accept it with some compromises towards preserving aspects of the existing structure. Serbia and Montenegro reiterated their earlier statements that, failing a federal Yugoslavia, the borders of the republics would have to be redrawn to incorporate all Serbs in one state.

The issue of secession was clearly on the table with Slovenia clearly stating its intention to secede if agreement was not reached by June. Croatia and Bosnia-Hercegovina also made clear similar intentions as part of the process of negotiation. Despite repeated rounds of negotiations with modified proposals discussed, no agreement was reached among the republics on the institutional structure of a future Yugoslav state.

With the discussions deadlocked at basically the same point at which they had been initiated, Slovenia and Croatia withdrew further from federal institutions and prepared for secession. The Slovene referendum on independence held on December 1990 resulted in 88 percent of the population supporting secession and a sovereign Slovenia. Croats voted for independence with similar results.

Slovenia and Croatia declared their independence on June 25, 1991. The war which has ravaged much of Croatia and Bosnia-Hercegovina began with the attack by the Yugoslav National Army (JNA) on Slovenia, and then on Croatia. The military embarked on the path it had warned it would take,[34] supported and encouraged by Serbia and Montenegro. The separate transitions which had begun with the optimism of democratization were plunged into the cauldron of war.

13

Democratization and the international system: The foreign policies of interim governments

ALLISON K. STANGER

> As to whether it is just or unjust to fulfill or not to fulfill [agreements] when the city undergoes revolution into another regime, that is another argument.
>
> Aristotle, *The Politics,*
> Book 3, chapter 3

INTRODUCTION*

While the other essays in this volume focus on the domestic challenges that interim regimes face, all twentieth-century democratic transitions are also inescapably international phenomena. The collapse of any dictatorship elicits a reaction from foreign powers – one whose content has converged over time – to which interim governments must somehow respond. As global consensus on the desirability of liberal democracy has grown,[1] the role of this pressure from without has only become an all the more critical force in any transition dynamic. The aim of this chapter is to advance our understanding of both the international impact of democratic transitions and the role of international factors in enhancing or undermining the prospects for democratic consolidation.

Considerable scholarly attention has been focused on the domestic policies that can impede or advance democratization,[2] but comparatively little work has been done to date on either the foreign policies that can contribute to or detract from the task of building democracy or the interaction between the domestic and international agendas of fledgling democracies.

In many ways, the relative neglect of the foreign policies of postauthoritarian regimes is understandable.[3] After all, in the immediate aftermath of revolutionary upheaval, the task of reestablishing domestic order

* The author is indebted to Michael Kraus, Russell Leng, Juan Linz, Yossi Shain and the Olin Institute's National Security Seminar, Harvard University, for valuable comments on earlier versions of this chapter, and to Janine Hetherington and Brendan Murphy for research assistance.

would seem to overwhelm any concerns about building new international identities. Elites themselves are preoccupied with the reconsolidation of domestic political authority, and hence scholarly focus is similarly oriented. Given that attention and time are limited, conventional wisdom goes, foreign policy of necessity must take a back seat to domestic concerns, since domestic problems overwhelm international objectives in elite agendas.[4] Foreign policy may be harnessed to the cause of soliciting international support and aid, but the foreign policy of choice when one's domestic house needs to be put in order is one that eschews active international engagement.

Yet when we look at the agendas that governments actually pursue in the aftermath of authoritarianism's demise, the reality is much more complicated. Some states do turn inward, others immediately seek international engagement, striving to redefine themselves on the world stage, just as they do on the domestic one. Indeed, the first move of many newborn governments, from Kerensky's Russia to Havel's Czechoslovakia, is to issue a foreign policy statement. This presents a puzzle, one which is at the heart of this inquiry: Why do some new regimes pursue activist foreign policies while they attempt to forge new political orders, while others embrace a tactical isolationism? Why do some postauthoritarian governments break with the external orientation of the *ancien régime,* while others choose the path of continuity? How do these choices impede or promote democratization? How does the goal of democratization circumscribe the realm of state choice in international affiliation?

To address these questions, this essay examines the changing alliance patterns and international economic relationships of a wide range of interim governments in the twentieth century.[5] By interim government, I refer to the administration that rules "in the hiatus between the breakdown of the authoritarian regime and the selection of a new government as a result of free and contested elections."[6] If any process of democratization involves three basic stages: "(1) the end of an authoritarian regime; (2) the installation of a democratic regime; and (3) the consolidation of the democratic regime,"[7] then interim governments are the temporary authorities that preside over the second stage. Interim regimes are always governments whose legitimacy, however tentative, is by definition only conditional, because it is based on a promise to deliver a new political order, democratic or otherwise.[8]

All sovereign interim governments – those not supervised by an occupying power or the United Nations – immediately face two critical choices with respect to their external orientation. First, they must decide whether to uphold the international security agreements forged by the *ancien régime.* Second, they must evaluate the state's international economic relationships. Each constellation of decisions involves a fundamental choice for the postrevolutionary governing elite: to what extent should the new regime distinguish itself from the old in the realm of its international relations?

Just as for any new government, the game of transition politics must be played on two levels.[9] The interim leadership has to present its departure from the past for both a domestic and an international audience, and the policies it pursues to please the latter inevitably influence those pitched to the former – and vice versa. Yet for interim regimes, the stakes in this two-level game are always the highest possible. Outcomes at either level potentially represent more than mere political setbacks; the interaction between the internal and external strategies that transitional elites pursue ultimately can either advance or impede democratization. As the case studies that follow amply illustrate, the way in which interim governments choose to play their domestic and international cards is shaped significantly by the form interim government takes.

PROVISIONAL REVOLUTIONARY GOVERNMENTS AND THE INTERNATIONAL SYSTEM

Provisional revolutionary governments typically seize power at a time when the authoritarian regime has steered the ship of state into profound international crisis. Often the nation is at war at the time of revolution, and systemic factors serve as a catalyst for revolutionary change. The interim governments of the opposition that I examine below were united in their pursuit of a radical reorientation of the *ancien régime*'s foreign policy. For the Ebert provisional government in Germany, this required befriending the wartime enemies of the imperial order. For Portugal, the break with the old policies further strengthened the interim government's ties with the West. For Iran, distancing the new government from the international policies of the Shah meant weakening the new administration's relationship with the West. The Kerensky provisional government of Russia, however, while promising a democratic revolution within, adhered to rather than renounced the tsar's war aims, with fateful consequences for Russian political development.

Woodrow Wilson and the birth of the Weimar Republic

The circumstances of the Weimar Republic's birth highlight the role that forces from without can play in democratic institution building. In the fall of 1918, with Germany on the brink of complete military defeat and the imperial regime still tentatively in place, the German foreign office began to cast about for some way to extract the country from its present predicament without compromising Germany's territorial integrity.

Two radically different policy proposals emerged from the cabinet and the foreign office's deliberations. The first – the European alternative – recommended that Germany pursue the war, while building the peace through alliance with leftist forces in the Allied countries. The second – the American alternative – urged Germany to appeal to the United States for a peace along the lines of the Fourteen Points, while undertaking "a revolution from above" that would transfer powers to the Reichstag. A monarchy was not well positioned to pursue either strategy with much credibility. Yet to simply continue without adopting one or the other only threatened to ensure ever greater losses.[10]

The new chancellor and foreign minister, Prince Max of Baden, chose the American alternative. Upon assuming power, he promptly appealed to President Wilson for an armistice consistent with the goals of the Fourteen Points.[11] Suspecting that Wilson was unlikely to entertain a proposal for peace that did not at least have the appearance of the backing of the masses, Prince Max promised publicly that "the German Empire [had] undergone a fundamental change of its political course, that the Reichstag had been granted genuine powers, marking "the beginning of a new epoch in Germany's internal history."[12]

How was the German appeal received in Washington? The Wilson administration viewed the proposal as a tactical maneuver, insincere in its alleged interest to democratize Germany, since Prince Max was promising only a reshuffling of personnel rather than a change of regime. Wilson informed the German cabinet – in notes on October 8 and 14 – that the proposal, while interesting had a fundamental flaw: it came from the old imperial order, not from the German people. Without real democratic reform, there could be no peace.[13]

In their response dispatched on October 20, the German cabinet protested that by empowering the Reichstag, they were embarked on real constitutional reform.[14] Wilson, however, was unwavering in his demands for genuine democratization. It was an election year, and he faced a Republican opposition whose calls for unconditional surrender were growing ever louder.[15] Wilson's third note of October 23 spelled his conditions out clearly: for peace negotiations to take place, Germany must have a new democratic constitution and free elections, not just mere promises:

... the Government of the United States cannot deal with any but the veritable representatives of the German people who have been assured of a genuine constitutional standing as the rulers of Germany. If it must deal with the military masters and the monarchical autocrats of Germany now, or, if it is likely to have to deal with them later in regard to the international obligations of the German

Empire; it must demand, not peace negotiations, but surrender. Nothing can be gained by leaving this essential thing unsaid.[16]

Wilson's third note, a not so veiled call for the Kaiser's abdication, enraged both the Kaiser and the Supreme Command, who jointly called for Germany to break off negotiations and fight to the bitter end. In the discussions that ensued, Foreign Minister Solf argued that the Americans were not insisting on abdication but instead on more radical constitutional reform. Though the cabinet at first believed that if the Reichstag were presented with legislation to transform the regime into a constitutional monarchy, the king would not have to abdicate, subsequent discussions led them to the reluctant conclusion that the Kaiser had to relinquish the throne to save his dynasty.[17]

Reports of mutinies in the German navy and calls from the leadership of the SPD for the Kaiser's abdication led Max of Baden to dispense with cautious overtures. To demonstrate to the Americans that a new Germany was in the making, Prince Max's government broke off relations with Bolshevik Russia on November 5, just as Wilson himself had done just three months prior. Four days later, the Kaiser had abdicated and was enroute to Holland. After announcing that the Kaiser had abdicated, Prince Max handed over the government to the president of the German Social Democratic Party, Friedrich Ebert, and the German Republic was, shortly thereafter, proclaimed from a window at the Chancellery. With these moves, the path to an armistice had been cleared. Europe would address its reparations demands to Ebert, not the Kaiser.[18]

The Ebert provisional government immediately recast German foreign policy. One of Ebert's first moves – after publicly declaring himself a Wilsonian and proclaiming the end of German imperialism – was to request food aid from the United States. Simultaneously, he asked for membership for "the largest republic in the world after the United States" in the League of Nations. In his first communication with President Wilson as foreign minister of the German Republic, Solf extolled the democratic ideals which Germany and the United States allegedly held in common.[19]

The Americans, for their part, were now interested in seeing elections held as soon as possible. Two weeks into Ebert's provisional rule, representatives from the German states met in Berlin and agreed on a date for elections to a Constituent Assembly. With the Spartacist uprising as a backdrop, those elections were held as promised, on the January 18, at the same time that the Army and the SPD were forcing the German Communists to acquiesce in bourgeois democracy. Thus, the time between the collapse of the imperial system and the Weimar Republic's first elections was notably short.

The Ebert provisional government in Germany based its mandate to rule in the transition on both a radical break with imperial Germany's domestic political structures and its foreign policy. It delivered quickly on both promises. The trajectory of the imperial order's collapse and the provisional government's subsequent policies were shaped by both Germany's imminent defeat and Wilson's refusal to negotiate a peace with anything less than a government of the opposition that had scheduled elections for a Constituent Assembly.

The remaking of Portugal's foreign policy

The six provisional governments that followed the military coup of April 25, 1974, that initiated Portugal's transition to democracy pursued a similar strategy in the interim period. As the makers of the coup were united in opposition to Portugal's ongoing colonial wars, foreign policy was a prominent issue in transition politics.[20] Consequently, despite the transient nature of each interim coalition, the transitional period was one of radical reforms within (nationalization and land redistribution) and a break with the Salazar dictatorship's colonial policies without.[21] Indeed, Mario Soares, who was appointed prime minister by Portugal's first democratically elected president (Eanes) in July 1976, often described the aims of the military coup as the three Ds: Decolonization, Democratization, and Development.

By the time of Eanes's election, despite the brief tenure in power of each governing coalition, the provisional governments had terminated the old regime's colonial wars, and secured Soares's first "D", granting independence to Guineau-Bissau (September 1974), Mozambique (June 1975), and Angola (September 1975). Overtures to the EEC and Council of Europe were also made in the interim period. Throughout, NATO and the Western powers threatened economic sanctions if elections did not take place as scheduled, a threat that seems to have had a positive effect on the outcome of provisional rule.[22]

Ruptura and the provisional government of Iran

After the fall of the Shah, the short-lived and ill-fated interim government of Iran also took immediate concrete steps to distance itself from the external policies of the outgoing order. One of the first priorities of the Bazargan provisional government was to restore "equilibrium" to Iran's foreign policy by terminating Iran's special relationship with the United States. Whereas Mossadegh's external policy had sought to maintain Iranian independence by breaking with Britain, Bazargan, through the policy of "negative equilibrium," sought to restore Iran's international freedom of action by undoing the Shah's close relationship with the

United States. Thus, the Bazargan provisional government withdrew Iran from CENTO in March, and in November, one day prior to the seizure of the American hostages, cancelled the Iranian-U.S. defense agreement of 1959. On that same day, Iran also abrogated the country's 1921 treaty with the Soviet Union.[23]

Because of the negative legacy of U. S. intervention in Iran's internal affairs and pressure from the theocratic opposition, the Bazargan interim government had little choice but to attempt to build democracy without the direct support of the West. Bazargan, an anticlerical Islamist, had strong liberal credentials, but he owed his position to Khomeini, and transforming Iran's relations with the world was one of the few areas on which the two could agree.[24] And of course, the anti-Western thrust of the revolution itself only further restricted the range of viable foreign policy options.[25]

The Kerensky anomaly

The struggle to consolidate domestic political authority in Russia after the March 1917 revolution was from the start bound inextricably with foreign policy questions. Like the other provisional revolutionary governments we have examined, the newly formed Russian provisional government promptly issued a foreign policy statement. Rather than charting a new course, however, Prince Lvov's government pledged "to strictly observe the international obligations contracted by the fallen regime."[26] Thus, the Kadet-led interim administration, while pledging devotion to democratization, not only did not break with the tsar's foreign policies; it continued to prosecute Nicholas II's war, whose destruction and perceived lack of purpose had played a large role in catalyzing the forces that had brought down the imperial order. It did not, however, do this with the unanimous support of the forces that had made the revolution. The Petrograd Soviet simultaneously issued a foreign policy statement of its own, which urged proletarians of all countries, Russia included, to renounce imperial war aims.[27]

Not surprisingly, the West promptly recognized the Lvov government, which had also called for elections by universal male suffrage to a Constituent Assembly. Viewed from abroad, the March revolution seemed to enhance Russia's ability to pursue the war; with a democratic government, it was thought that Russia was only now capable of mobilizing the full strength of its people.[28]

From the perspective of the liberal interim government, the war had to be pursued to the end, for democracy could not take root in Russia under the shadow of the German empire. Further, the Western Allies were willing to provide financial support for rebuilding a democratic Russia – if and only if Russia stayed in the war.[29] Finally, since the United States was not yet in the war, a separate peace with Germany held little appeal, especially since the Bolsheviks would have attempted to turn any bargains struck with German imperialists to their domestic political advantage.

In the eyes of the liberal forces in Russia, the path to democracy clearly seemed to lie through winning the war that the *ancien régime* had begun. The decision to uphold tsarist war aims, however, had a host of unanticipated negative consequences, for it also meant that the Kadet-dominated first interim government failed to make a symbolic break with the authoritarian order. Over time, the inescapable appearance of continuity with the past undermined the legitimacy and power of the liberals in the critical interim period.

The assault from the left on the foreign policy agenda of the liberals was immediate and palpable, both reflecting and further loosening the tenuous Kadet grip on the reins of power. A mere five days after the foreign policy proclamation that had won the provisional government international recognition was promulgated, the Lvov government compromised with the Bolsheviks and issued a second declaration of war aims for domestic consumption, one which called for "a stable peace based on self-determination of all peoples."[30] Though the Kadet cabinet refused the Bolshevik request that the new statement become an official diplomatic document, the compromise statement alarmed the Allies, who understandably feared that Russia had reversed course and was now angling for a separate peace.[31]

It was Foreign Minister Miliukov's attempt to undo the damage that he perceived the compromise statement to have wrought that was the catalyst for the collapse of the Lvov liberal cabinet. Concerned about the Allied reaction to the second statement, Miliukov sent a note reassuring the Allies that Russia intended to abide by the commitments that the tsar had made, the tone of the government's last foreign policy statement notwithstanding.[32] Though this pleased the Allies, it enraged the Petrograd Soviet, particularly since Miliukov had earlier on fought publicly to preserve the monarchy, making him a suspect custodian of change in the eyes of the left.[33] They demanded that the Lvov cabinet make clear that it had renounced imperialist aspirations.[34]

The controversy forced Miliukov to resign his position, and ultimately brought down the first provisional government. Though Lvov would remain prime minister, the new coalition cabinet, announced on May 18, was noteworthy for the number of Socialist Revolutionaries (SRs) holding prominent positions. Kerensky had been the only SR in the original cabinet. The controversy over war aims, that is, played a significant role in transforming what had been a nonsocialist government into a coalition of socialists and liberals with Kerensky as its new minister of war.

The new government's first official statement on foreign policy aimed to please everyone. To the Allies, the foreign ministry pledged its unwavering commitment to the Allied cause. To cover its left flank, it simultaneously insisted that revolutionary Russia was fighting the war to secure a democratic peace.[35] With Russian morale at the front faltering, the latter strand quickly grew to dominate the provisional government's external policy.[36] By mid-June, the Lvov government's earlier promise to adhere to the tsar's secret territorial agreements had been indisputably broken by the foreign ministry's call for an Allied conference on the revision of war aims.[37]

Although he refrained from formally approaching the Allies with this proposition, Foreign Minister Tereschenko released the proposal to the Russian press.[38] Needless to say, the unofficial announcement had equivalent impact. As we have seen, this schizophrenic approach to diplomacy – publishing radical statements for domestic consumption while insisting through formal diplomatic channels that the Russian commitment to the war was unwavering – was a pattern of Russian external policy throughout the provisional government's tenure in power.

Although its position on tsarist secret agreements for divvying up the territory of the former Ottoman Empire grew increasingly ambiguous, the Kerensky government's position on territorial questions within the Russian Empire, such as the Ukraine's and Finland's requests for autonomy remained unwaveringly clear. No territorial changes could be made, Kerensky insisted, until elections had been held and the Constituent Assembly had approved of them; the provisional government simply did not have the authority to decide constitutional issues of this sort.[39] Yet as the war dragged on and the influence of the left in the formulation of Russian policy rose, the provisional government's position on this point also wavered. In July, Kerensky approved a resolution granting the Ukraine considerable autonomy.[40] In response, the Kadets in the cabinet tendered their resignations; a provisional government, in their view, did not have the authority to break up the Russian state.[41] From that point forward, the argument that all matters of constitutional import should be tabled until elections had been held and a Constituent Assembly convened would no longer be voiced by members of the provisional government.

Because the Bolsheviks would lay the foundation for consolidating their revolutionary power by negotiating a separate peace with Germany, the question arises: might democracy have been saved had the liberals only done the same in the immediate aftermath of the March revolution? Instead of announcing that the new regime would pursue the wartime objectives of the old, that is, what if the Lvov provisional government had, instead, called for free elections and renounced the tsar's war simultaneously? Might not the task of democratic refounding have been more readily accomplished under these circumstances?

These are, of course, the sorts of questions that Kerensky spent much of his exile life in the West attempting to answer. While it is true that building democracy in Russia required some sort of radical break with the past, and that a fundamental transformation of the state's external orientation is one way of accomplishing such, this path was not really so inviting to the democrats, as it might, in the realm of theoretical speculation, appear to be. The bind for the liberals in Russia was that renouncing the war aims of the *ancien régime* meant betraying the cause of the Western European democracies. Removing Russia from the war might well have solidified the gains of the March revolution, thereby furthering the cause of Russian democracy, but that same move would have provoked Britain and France. As long as the German empire held sway in Central Europe, this was a chance that the liberals in Russia felt they could not take – particularly if the democratization of Russia was their ultimate aim.

What was a fundamental bind for the liberals dissolved in the shadow of Bolshevik aspirations for Russia's future. Holding bourgeois democracy in utter contempt, Lenin had little interest in maintaining healthy relations with Europe's bourgeois democracies. To the contrary, Lenin exploited every opportunity to provoke and belittle both the war aims of the Allies and the Kadet blueprint for post-tsarist Russia. His was the indisputable party of change, the party that promised an end to both tsarist imperialism and imperial tyranny. Precisely because he was not a democrat, Lenin could turn the liberals' wartime predicament into an opportunity to consolidate Soviet power.

POWER-SHARING INTERIM GOVERNMENTS AND FOREIGN POLICY

Power-sharing interim governments must walk a precarious line in their efforts to remake the political system. Since movement toward democracy in this type of transition depends on the maintenance of an uneasy alliance between the opponents of the outgoing order and the representatives of the system that had once tormented them, power-sharing interim governments typically avoid blanket condemnations of the policies of the *ancien régime*. Instead, they are likely to postpone consideration of the most controversial issues whenever possible, and this is the case for external as well as internal policy. Policymaking in the transition is constrained by the overarching imperative of preserving the governing coalition until it is possible to hold free and fair elections. Often this results in foreign policy that at face value looks like more of the same rather than the bridge to a new order.

The restoration of Polish sovereignty

The foreign policy of the power-sharing interim government in Poland[42] was constrained by the nature of the transition, as well as Poland's long-standing unfortunate geopolitical position. The first foreign policy statements from the new government, rather than proclaiming a bold new course for Poland's relations with the outside world, instead pledged to uphold Communist Poland's international commitments, from membership in the Warsaw pact to obligations that followed from Polish participation in the CMEA. Both Mazowiecki and the new foreign minister Krysztof Skubiszewcki promised Warsaw Pact reforms; the new government would work to transform the Warsaw Pact into an alliance of equals. The alliance commitments of Communist Poland, however, would continue to be upheld.[43] Several months later, the government elaborated further, releasing a new national defense doctrine that asserted an end to Poland's satellite status within the Warsaw Pact. For many Solidarity members, the new doctrine was more noteworthy for what it did not do than for what it did do, and consequently met with considerable public criticism.[44]

On the controversial topic of Soviet troops on Polish soil, the interim administration delayed raising this issue for diplomatic discussion until after Czechoslovakia and Hungary had negotiated agreements for the departure of Soviet forces, focusing instead on securing guarantees from Germany on the legitimacy of Poland's western border. Unlike its two Visegrad partners, the Mazowiecki government, while insisting that the Soviet troops would one day depart, proposed no timetables for their departure and made no demands until September 1990. For their perceived foot-dragging on the troop withdrawal issue, the coalition government was criticized extensively, particularly by Solidarity's leader, Lech Walesa. Indeed, the government's decision to finally put pressure on the Soviets may well have been influenced by the prospect of presidential elections in December, in which Mazowiecki would challenge Walesa for the presidency.[45]

Though its approach to revising Poland's relations with its former protector to the East was cautious, the coalition government enthusiastically broke with the external orientation of the old order in other areas. The interim administration established diplomatic relations with Chile, Israel, and South Korea and set up a new section in South Africa. It also forged new cooperative relationships with a number of West European international institutions, including the establishment of a liaison office with NATO in 1990.[46] At the same time, the foreign ministry worked to strengthen Poland's ties to the East, both with the Soviet Union and its at that time constituent republics.[47]

The careful modification of Poland's security arrangements can be explained, in part, by the demands of preserving the transitional coalition. The balance of power in the power-sharing arrangement – particularly prior to General Jaruzelski's graceful exit – precluded a radical break with the foreign policies of the outgoing order.[48] In emphasizing the constraints that power-sharing arrangements placed on the international strategies of the Mazowiecki interim regime, however, I do not mean to suggest that geostrategic factors are not important for understanding Polish foreign policy. Rather, it is instead to point out that geopolitical factors are rarely purely independent variables. That Poland is sandwiched between two countries with long-standing traditions of intervention in Poland's internal affairs may have shaped elite perceptions of their foreign policy options, but at the same time, Poland's strategic location made a power-sharing arrangement while communism imploded elsewhere all the more likely. In short, the form the transition took in Poland was, in important ways, a child of geopolitics.

The Czechoslovak exception

In contrast to the cautious evolution of the Polish interim authority's external strategies, and, as we shall see below, those of the Hungarian caretaker government, the interim government of Czechoslovakia broke openly and immediately with long-standing patterns of international interaction. Four days after his appointment, Czechoslovakia's new dissident foreign minister, Jiři Dienstbier, announced that Czechoslovakia would resume diplomatic relations with Israel; Havel affirmed this change of course in his 1990 New Year's speech.[49] In the months that followed, the Havel government also established relations with South Korea and the Vatican and placed the country's relations with the Western democracies on an entirely new footing. Despite the enormous task of building democracy at home, Havel himself took an active role in the effort to infuse Czechoslovakia's foreign policy with what he called "a new spirit," visiting no less than eight foreign countries and receiving numerous foreign dignitaries in Prague during his first two months as Czechoslovakia's interim president.[50] He also offered to play a mediating role in the Arab-Israeli conflict, as well as to host a U. S.-Soviet summit in Prague.[51]

The flurry of diplomatic activity in the interim period was part of a larger effort to redefine Czechoslovakia's "international political identity" in a post-Communist Europe.[52] After the events of November 1989, the new government lost little time in proposing a timetable for the departure of Soviet troops from Czechoslovak soil.[53] Concurrently, Foreign Minister Dienstbier had announced the country's intention to curb its profitable involvement in international arms trade.[54] In the short period between the revolution and its first elections, Czechoslovakia also applied for IMF membership, petitioned the Council of Europe for special observer status (a precondition for membership), and expressed its intent to apply for EC membership. While pursuing these unilateral initiatives, Havel and Dienstbier simultaneously sought to promote regional cooperation among the countries of Central Europe, which they saw as the foundation for Czechoslovakia's "return to Europe."[55]

That returning to Europe required a transformation of existing European security arrangements was clear, but the Havel government's perceptions of what changes were optimal evolved over time. Initially, Havel and Dienstbier saw the dissolution of both NATO and the Warsaw Pact, as well as German neutrality, as a necessary condition for securing the country's new found independence. After Havel's visit to Washington in February 1990, however, the interim government backed away from its original radical position, and argued instead that U. S. forces in Europe could play a stabilizing role in the transition to a new European security system.[56] NATO, Havel argued, unlike the Warsaw Pact, had the potential to serve as the foundation for a new security order, provided the organization's name was changed and its mission transformed.[57]

Attempting to accelerate movement toward a supplementary pan-European security system more appropriate for the post-Cold War world, the Dienstbier foreign ministry simultaneously circulated its own framework for ensuring Europe's security after the Cold War. Dienstbier's "Memorandum on the European Security Commission," which was delivered to the ambassadors of the thirty-five countries participating in the Helsinki process in April 1990, outlined a new post-Cold War security system for Europe founded on a restructured CSCE.[58] Though these proposals were largely ignored by both East and West, that they were enunciated by an interim government, occupied with a host of unresolved domestic questions, is itself noteworthy.[59]

In contrast to the strategies of its Visegrad partners, who operated under similar systemic constraints, the Havel interim government broke markedly and immediately with the Communist legacy in Czechoslovak foreign affairs. Moreover, while formally remaining in the Warsaw Pact, it felt no compulsion to consult with Czechoslovakia's allies before announcing its latest policy innovations.[60] How might we begin to account for these differences?

One reason that Havel and Dienstbier, unlike their Polish and Hungarian counterparts, pursued such an activist foreign policy course in the months following the collapse of communism was that the dissident community in Czechoslovakia had concerned itself with foreign policy issues prior to the revolution. The opposition in Czechoslovakia had articulated (quite idealistic) foreign policy positions, in addition to the better known criticisms of the old regime's domestic abuses.[61] As a result, an alternative tack for the nation's foreign relations did not have to be formulated by the Havel interim government; instead, it could simply implement previously formulated ideas. That the new foreign minister happened to be one of the principal architects of the opposition's foreign policy framework and the interim president to be the darling of the West only made bold action all the easier.[62]

Explaining the Czechoslovak anomaly by referring to the opposition's control of foreign policy during the transition, of course, begs the question of how such a state of affairs arose in Czechoslovakia, but did not in Poland and Hungary. The answer to this more fundamental question is found in the character of the transition itself.

While the interim government of national understanding formed by Marian Čalfa on December 10 looked like a power-sharing arrangement on paper, because of Václav Adamec's prior attempt to stack the first interim government (which forced his resignation), in practice, it was not. The Czechoslovak transition, unlike the transitions in Poland and Hungary, began as a power-sharing arrangement and ended with the opposition in de facto control of both internal and external policy.[63] Consequently, in the interim period, opposition to the new regime's foreign policies did not develop in Czechoslovakia, as it did in Poland and Hungary, where representatives of the old order still had a strong grip on the transitional reins of power, particularly in the realm of security affairs.

The international impact of redemocratization in Greece

As in Czechoslovakia, the road to redemocratization in Greece involved an initial power-sharing arrangement that rapidly unraveled.[64] Prior to its demise, the ruling Greek junta had staged an ill-fated foreign adventure in Cyprus, to which Turkey had responded by seizing most of the island. Here the political regime was faced with a dilemma: it could retreat and suffer enormous humiliation or escalate. That it chose the latter course was the catalyst for its removal from power. The leadership of the military's main branches, citing fear of full-scale war with Turkey if the ruling junta's external policies continued to be pursued,[65] reasserted its hierarchical control over the dictatorship and then handed the reins of power over to a yet to be formed civilian government of national unity – a body which the military thought it could control.[66] In this, much like the Communists in Czechoslovakia, it was ultimately mistaken.

In the negotiations that ensued, the military first attempted to extract a promise from the civilian opposition (mostly representatives of the conservative right) that elections would not be called immediately, and the military would retain control of the ministries of defense, security, and the interior. When the opposition threatened to walk out of the negotiations, the old order backed down, and eventually settled on calling Karamanlis, in exile in Paris, to form a government.[67]

Once installed, Karamanlis did not hesitate in initiating a series of sweeping decrees to undo the domestic excesses of the military dictatorship. In this sense, the transitional government made a symbolic break with the past.[68] In the realm of the state's external policies, however, Karamanlis had to tread more cautiously. Rather than renouncing the military adventurism of the political order he had replaced and breaking with the legacy of the past in Greece's external relations with equivalent force, the interim government essentially pursued the middle course: it did not retreat and it did not escalate, but instead worked to negotiate a cease-fire agreement that would hold.[69]

Renouncing the dictatorship's military venture and refounding Greece's international orientation was not an option for the Karamanlis regime for at least two reasons. First, the interim government's position on the Cyprus crisis was influenced by the force of Greek public opinion. While jubilant over the prospect of restoring democracy, the general public still viewed the Greek claim to Cyprus as legitimate and the threat from Turkey as real and compelling. Second, while the civilian government did not officially share power with the military in the period prior to the first elections (held just four months after the collapse of the dictatorship), it had to operate in the omnipresent shadow of the military, precluding a preelection purge of the junta's principal henchmen, as well as a radical renunciation of the dictatorship's crisis in Cyprus. Viewed in this light, it is not surprising that the Karamanlis interim government's response to U. S. criticism of the Cyprus venture was to withdraw Greece from NATO's military command structure and threaten to close down American military bases on Greek soil.[70] In this sense, especially in the realm of foreign policy, the nature of the Greek transition "imposed severe restraints on undoing the machinery of the dictatorship."[71]

CARETAKER INTERIM GOVERNMENTS AND THE LEGACY OF THE PAST

Caretaker governments of transition face a unique dilemma in formulating an international agenda for the interim period. The external policies of the outgoing authoritarian order are, for all practical purposes, creatures of the caretakers' creation. Though renouncing those policies might further the task of consolidating democracy, *ruptura* in the state's international relations would also undermine the legitimacy of the interim arrangement. Consequently, as the case studies that follow elucidate, caretaker interim governments were unlikely to undertake major foreign policy initiatives prior to the first elections, especially when the military either administered the transition or was a powerful independent force in transition politics.

When caretakers are generals: Argentina

As was the case in Greece's redemocratization, discussed above, the catalyst for democratic change in Argentina was also an ill-fated military venture, designed to rally support for the failing authoritarian order in a time of economic crisis. Unlike the Greek colonels, however, Argentina's generals did not cut their losses by attempting to share power (and the blame) when it became clear that the outcome was unlikely to be as intended. Instead, the Galtieri junta stood behind its attempt to seize the Falkland Islands. Argentina's armed forces – who had never before been defeated in battle – fought on until the country was forced to surrender to the British at Port Stanley in June 1982.[72]

While the original move to seize the islands from the British met with strong public support, Argentina's unprecedented defeat in the Falklands war provoked an enormous public backlash against the junta that would be its undoing. The circumstances of the country's defeat deprived the ruling authorities of a scapegoat; there was no "knife in the back" type excuse available to a military dictatorship. Galtieri was forced to resign, and the air force and navy withdrew from the junta. The army, the last branch united enough to attempt to govern, named a new president, who shortly thereafter called for elections.[73]

Drained of the last remnants of legitimacy by the Falklands fiasco, the military regime had essentially collapsed, but curiously continued to govern in the transition, albeit with decreasing authority. Though opposition to the regime had grown more vocal, the rump junta's call for elections was less a response to mounting public pressure than an expression of sheer exhaustion; the Army, abandoned by its ruling partners, had simply run out of ideas.[74]

The result was a de facto power vacuum, but it was not one that the opposition rushed to fill. Instead, democracy's proponents focused their attention on organizing for the upcoming elections, rather than on attempting to negotiate an interim power-sharing arrangement, or declaring a provisional government and appealing to the international community for recognition.

The opposition refrained from more radical action for at least two reasons. First, because there had been no real opposition to the war effort, when the defeat brought the military regime crashing down, there was no organized opposition to step into the resultant power vacuum and claim the reins of power. Second, even though the military's political authority was virtually nonexistent, calling elections gave the interim government considerable leverage over the transition process, for the threat of a coup which would turn back the clock was a compelling constraint on opposition demands. Thus, the authoritarian elite may have been unable to mold the transition to its liking, but "it would be a mistake to exaggerate the regime's loss of control over the transition."[75]

Given the character of the Argentine transition, it should come as no surprise to the reader that the state's external policy in this period was not a central concern of the interim government. Since the military regime had controlled Argentina's foreign policy, its paralysis led to the same in Argentina's international relations. To the best of my knowledge, no major foreign policy announcements were made and no new initiatives were taken in the period between the Falklands defeat and the October 1983 elections. The interim government turned inward in a way that conventional wisdom might deem predictable, but that this study has shown is rarely the case. The new president, Raul Alfonsin, would quickly reverse this state of affairs and reorient the external posture of the reborn democratic state.[76]

Spanish foreign policy after Franco

In the aftermath of the Second World War, the Allies were first united in their resolve to isolate Franco's Spain. The institutionalization of the Cold War, however, caused Western Europe and the United States to part ways on the question of how to deal with Franco, with the Americans persuaded that NATO membership for Spain would serve the ends of containment, and most of Western Europe united in opposition to the inclusion of nondemocratic members. In some ways, the debate was largely beside the point; the bilateral defense agreements that the United States and Spain eventually initialed in 1953 were arguably more to Franco's liking, since they bolstered the international security of his dictatorship while making no demands for domestic liberalization. Franco did, however, apply for EC membership in 1962 and was summarily rejected. Thus, while Francoist Spain's relative isolationism may have been in part a strategic choice, it was also dictated by the understandably hostile attitudes of the West.[77]

By the time of Franco's death, a consensus had emerged in Spain's business and political circles that EC membership was the key to restoring Spain to economic health, but that membership would only be a possibility if Spain's domestic political order was transformed.[78] Reflecting this consensus, the Adolfo Suárez interim government expressed open support for Spain's return to Europe via EC membership, "with all that this implies."[79] His newly elected centrist government officially reapplied for membership just six weeks after the first elections.[80] The topic of NATO membership, in contrast to that of EC membership, however, was more divisive, and was studiously avoided until Suárez's second term of office.

In the interim period, Franco's bilateral ties with the United States were preserved, while new relationships with democratic Europe were pursued – relationships, again, that Franco himself had paradoxically sought. Two months after Franco's death, Spain renewed its bilateral treaty of cooperation with the United States, thereby endorsing the security arrangements forged by the outgoing order. Though Franco's death was the catalyst for what would eventually be a complete makeover of both Western attitudes toward Spain and of Spain's international identity, this reorientation took place neither abruptly nor immediately.[81]

That authoritarian Spain had had a long standing special relationship with the United States complicated the question of how post-Franco foreign policy might promote Spain's continued democratization. For some, the Socialist party in particular, NATO membership only institutionalized the very ties that had propped up the Franco dictatorship and restricted Spanish sovereignty. For Suarez's UCD (*Unión de Centro Democrático*), in contrast, NATO membership was a necessary condition for Spain's acceptance to the European Community.[82] Since Franco himself had pursued EC membership, a radical break with the authoritarian past on this issue would have required the perpetuation of Spain's isolation. The paradoxical aspects of Franco's foreign policy fueled divisions over democratic Spain's external orientation that would linger long after the first elections had been held.

The evolutionary transformation of Spain's international relations was also a product of the character of Spain's transition to democracy. Spain's democratization was orchestrated – under considerable opposition pressure – by the minions of the Franco dictatorship; Suárez himself was a former minister under Franco. In this sense, the *ancien régime* was never rejected symbolically, as it had been in both the Portuguese and Greek transition to democracy.[83] Moreover, since the armed forces had answered to Franco rather than the *Movimiento,* their allegiances in the post-Franco era were something of an open question.[84] Hence, the Suárez caretaker government, in attempting to reconstitute post-Franco political legitimacy while maintaining Francoist legality, had to proceed with considerable caution to avoid alienating those segments of the military loyal to Franco's controversial legacy, rather than to Franco's heirs.[85]

The ghosts of Kadar

In contrast to Poland and Czechoslovakia, the process of democratization in Hungary was both initiated and supervised by the old order under the watchful eye of the democratic forces.[86] Indeed, Hungarian foreign policy was already under reconstruction prior to Kadar's fall. Though troop withdrawals began in April 1989, Kadar's regime had initiated the movement for a reduction of Soviet troops stationed in Hungary. Thus, Kadar's heirs continued a process already begun by the communist regime, yet could claim it as a symbol of their commitment to democratic change.[87]

Disagreement between members of the old and emerging orders on the demands Hungary should make with respect to the pace of the Soviet departure, however, was quick to surface. As in Poland, the democratic opposition (the Alliance of Free Democrats or the opposition round table) immediately criticized what it perceived to be the reform communist interim government's moderation on the issue of Soviet troop withdrawal, demanding an immediate and complete withdrawal. The Hungarian parliament was surrounded by crowds chanting "Russians go home!" on the very day that the interim National Assembly voted to proclaim the Hungarian Republic, dropping the word *Socialist* from the country's official title. As in Poland, too, foreign policy issues divided those who had brought the old regime crashing down and those who had been members of the outgoing political system – and were now struggling for political survival – well before campaign positions had to be articulated.[88]

In contrast to Poland, however, the form the transition took in Hungary facilitated rather than impeded the eventual convergence of interests between representatives of the old and new orders. The turning point in Hungary was the scheduling of national elections in December 1989. Shortly thereafter, the caretaker interim government, now comprised of former Communists after the party's October self-liquidation, adopted the opposition's position as its own, announcing the commencement of bilateral negotiations with the Soviet Union to accelerate the timetable for the complete departure of Soviet forces. With calls for Hungary's withdrawal from the Warsaw Pact mounting, the caretaker regime also began to call for the transformation of the Warsaw Pact, even hinting that Hungary might one day conceivably be a member of NATO.[89]

With both tactical moves, the ex-Communists distanced themselves from their more moderate previous positions, each of which would have been an election liability. As a caretaker administration, the old order's participation in interim foreign policymaking was indisputable; the tactical shifts after the date had been set for elections were predictable, since to do otherwise would have only confirmed existing suspicions that the caretakers were the principal impediment to the restoration of Hungarian sovereignty.[90]

The preelection dynamic just described had lasting postelection ramifications. Before the new government had been formed, the Alliance of Free Democrats moved in Parliament to reaffirm the 1956 declaration of unilateral withdrawal from the Warsaw Pact and Hungarian neutrality. The opposition's radical proposal was rejected by the Parliament at the time, but one of the new Democratic Forum-led government's first actions was to announce Hungary's intention to negotiate a complete withdrawal from the Warsaw Pact and to rejoin Europe, while maintaining friendly relations with the Pact's former hegemon.[91] In so doing, the government partially adopted the opposition's position and furthered the task of redefining Hungary's international identity. The pattern of logrolling on foreign policy issues, established prior to the first elections, however, would outlive the transition period.

The interim government of Hungary was largely comprised of reconstructed Communists – those who had been responsible for commanding the armed forces prior to the transition. Because the military had been subordinated to the party under communism, Hungary's caretaker political elite had the unusual luxury of presiding over a transition where the threat of a military challenge to their interim authority was minimal. This may well be the only positive legacy of Communist rule.

CONCLUSION

The preliminary investigations presented in these pages suggest that the task of forging democratic consensus out of authoritarian institutions and attitudes involves an oft overlooked international component.[92] Just as democratizers must render new modes and order legitimate in the eyes of former subjects who would be citizens, in similar fashion they must seek the affirmation of those efforts in the international arena. I have argued that elites use foreign policy as a tool to further the task of reconstituting political authority in the wake of authoritarianism's demise. In turn, the way in which states attempt to redefine themselves in the eyes of the world has consequences for transition politics. Put another way, an interim government's foreign policy agenda reflects the character of the transition, and the external actions of democratizing states can either advance or impede democratization.

If the metaphor of a two-level game sheds light on the international actions and inactions of stable polities, it is especially compelling for states whose political systems are in the process of being reborn. This study has revealed some general patterns in the ways in which aspiring democracies approach their national and international constituencies.

First, the character of the transition was a critical factor in the formulation of postrevolutionary state preferences. Provisional revolutionary governments were most likely to break abruptly and radically with the external policies of the outgoing order. An exception to this rule was the case of the Kerensky provisional government, where Russia's democratic allies pressured Kerensky to pursue the tsar's war, ultimately a burden too heavy for the liberal forces in Russia to bear.

Interim governments based on a power-sharing arrangement, whether explicit or implicit, recast the state's external orientation in more cautious fashion, the resultant policies embracing elements of both continuity and change between past and present. The case of Czechoslovakia was a noteworthy exception to this rule. The Havel interim government pursued an immediate and radical break with the foreign policies of the Communist regime, and did so prior to the collapse of the Soviet Union. Because the de facto power of the Communists in the interim governing coalition was limited, what was a power-sharing arrangement on paper conducted itself in the international arena as an interim government of the opposition.

Caretaker interim regimes, where the independent power of the military was often a factor, were more likely to defer major foreign policy decisions until after the first elections had been successfully held. In Hungary's transition to democracy, however, where the military was not an independent actor, the interim regime was able to break with the past in striking ways.

The second pattern that emerges from this study is that interim governments that renounced the external policies of the dying authoritarian order in such a way that relations with other democracies were concurrently improved seemed to be more likely to avoid authoritarian retrenchment and consolidate democracy. Similarly, interim governments that severed the international ties of the outgoing order in such a way that relations with the West were worsened were more likely to lose control of the transition and find their democratic goals threatened by rising antidemocratic public sentiment. When the relative power of anti-Western forces in the opposition coalition was high (as in Kerensky's Russia or Bazargan's Iran), the road to integration with the West, both political and economic, was at least temporarily foreclosed, with momentous consequences.

What these patterns suggest is that even when the path to internal *ruptura* is foreclosed, external *ruptura* (in the realm of the state's international obligations) that strengthens the nascent democratic regime's ties to other democracies can enhance the prospects for democratic consolidation for at least two reasons. First, if democratic development relies on a "revolutionary break with the past," as Barrington Moore persuasively argues, yet the road to breaking decisively with the legacy of the past in the state's domestic political structures is always paved with violence, breaking instead with the old regime's international commitments is one potential means by which the link with the past might be symbolically severed with a minimum of violence.[93]

Second, a radical reorientation of the state's external posture – one that embeds the fledgling democracy in a web of new international commitments that established democracies have already made – creates additional incentives for staying the democratic course, as well as enhancing the prospects for continued international cooperation. For example, the promise of EC membership can provide ammunition for democratic forces in the countries of Central Europe in their struggle with the powerful remnants of the Communist order.[94]

My focus on interim governments is not meant to downplay the role that systemic variables can play in democratization. In many of the cases examined in these pages, the authoritarian regime's impending defeat in war served as a catalyst for democratic change. Systemic factors shaped the transition, just as the form of transition constrained the international repercussions of revolutionary change.

What this study suggests, however, is that systemic theories of international relations may be ill-suited for the task of understanding state behavior when the state's very identity is undergoing transformation because of the core assumption of fixed state preferences they must make to promote parsimony. Precisely because their penetrating insights follow from the assumption of enduring state interests, such theories are mute on the question of how and under what circumstances state preferences may change.

What this investigation of the international policies of interim governments has shown is that while the dynamics of the process are anything but uniform, democratization inevitably involves a reconceptualization of state interests. States that consolidated democracy, regardless of the transition dynamic, eventually moved to fundamentally alter the alliances and economic relationships of the *ancien régime,* though the pace and scope of that change varied. Under these circumstances, theories that abstract away this possibility are unlikely to be illuminating.

The investigations herein, in their attempt to explain international behavior when state preferences are in flux, might be thought of as a preliminary inquiry into the dynamics of preference formation. To account for the variance in foreign policy outcomes that this chapter examines, I argue that we must understand foreign policy as the product of an elite struggle at the domestic level to remake the identity of the *ancien régime,* both in the eyes of the nation and in the eyes of the world. We can best understand foreign policy outcomes while that struggle is ongoing as a reflection of what might be thought of as the domestic balance of threats, as well as the systemic balance of threats.

This chapter has only examined cases where the legitimacy of the political order alone was undergoing redefinition. The next daunting task for those interested in the dynamics of preference reformation would be to examine those cases where the legitimacy of both state and regime are simultaneously challenged.[95] Introducing this additional dimension, which renders the very notion of the international system an ambiguous concept, only makes the standard systemic paradigms for explaining state behavior seem all the more inadequate.

The collapse of the Cold War order has challenged political scientists to ask new questions, to look at old problems in new ways. Answering those questions will require unprecedented forms of collaboration between the subfields of comparative politics and international relations. Though it in the end raises more questions than it answers, this study is an attempt to explore that largely uncharted territory.

Notes to Part Two

7. The provisional government and the transition from monarchy to Islamic republic in Iran

1 Henceforth the abbreviations "Ay." and "Ho." are used for "Ayatollah" and "Hojjatoleslam," the highest and second highest ranks in the Shi'ite hierarchy.

2 Abdol-Ali Bazargan, ed., *Masa'el va moshkelat-e nakhostin sal-e enqelab az zaban-e ra'is-e dowlat-e movaqqat* (The Problems of the Revolution's First Year, as Told by the Head of the Provisional Government) (Teheran: Nehzat-e azadi, 1983), p. 1.

3 On the Iranian revolution see Said Amir Arjomand, *The Turban for the Crown: The Islamic Revolution in Iran* (New York: Oxford University Press, 1988) or Mohsen Milani, *The Making of Iran's Revolution: From Monarchy to Islamic Republic* (Boulder, Col.: Westview Press, 1988). On events since the revolution see Shaul Bakhash, *The Reign of the Ayatollahs: Iran and the Islamic Revolution* (New York: Basic Books, 1984) or David Menashri, *Iran: A Decade of War and Revolution* (New York: Holmes & Meier, 1990). On Mehdi Bazargan and his role in Iranian politics prior to the revolution see H. E. Chehabi, *Iranian Politics and Religious Modernism: The Liberation Movement of Iran under the Shah and Khomeini* (Ithaca, N.Y.: Cornell University Press, 1990).

4 For an interesting comparative study that subsumes violent revolution in the phenomenon of regime transition see Leonardo Morlino, *Come cambiano i regimi politici: strumenti di analisi* (Milan: Franco Angeli, 1980), especially pp. 86–107.

5 On the revolutionary tendency in Portugal's transition see Thomas Bruneau's chapter in this volume; on the Philippines see Mark Thompson, *The Anti-Marcos Struggle: Personalistic Rule and Democratic Transition in the Philippines* (New Haven: Yale University Press, forthcoming).

6 For a good political history of the Shah's rule see Richard W. Cottam, *Iran and the United States: A Cold War Case Study* (Pittsburgh: University of Pittsburgh Press, 1988), pp. 55–188.

7 Guillermo O'Donnell and Philippe Schmitter, *Transitions from Authoritarian Rule: Tentative Conclusions about Uncertain Democracies* (Baltimore, Md.: Johns Hopkins University Press, 1986), p. 6.

8 See Samuel P. Huntington, *The Third Wave: Democratization in the Late Twentieth Century* (Norman: University of Oklahoma Press, 1991).

9 On this point see Ahmad Ashraf and Ali Banuazizi, "The State, Classes and Modes of Mobilization in the Iranian Revolution," *State, Culture, and Society* 1 (Spring 1985).

10 Robert Fishman, "Rethinking State and Regime: Southern Europe's Transition to Democracy," *World Politics* 42 (April 1990).

11 See Khosrow Fatemi, "Leadership by Distrust: The Shah's *Modus Operandi*," *The Middle East Journal* 36 (Winter 1982).

12 See Joel Podolny, "The Role of Juan Carlos I in the Consolidation of the Parliamentary Monarchy," in Richard Gunther, ed., *Politics, Society, and Democracy: The Case of Spain* (Boulder, Col.: Westview Press, 1993), pp. 88–112.

13 Khomeini began catching the imagination of the Iranians after the Shah ended his first liberalization of 1960–2. In January 1963 all leaders of the constitutionalist opposition were jailed, which led many in the opposition to conclude that parliamentary methods were inadequate.

14 Ebrahim Yazdi, *Akharin talash-ha dar akharin ruz-ha* (The Last Efforts in the Last Days) (Teheran: Qalam, 1984), p. 160.

15 Juan J. Linz, "Il fattore tempo nei mutamenti di regime," *Teoria Politica* 2 (1986):10.

16 For an English translation see Ay. Ruhollah Khomeini, "Islamic Government," in *Islam and Revolution: Writings and Declarations of Imam Khomeini*, translated and annotated by Hamid Algar (Berkeley, Cal.: Mizan, 1981).

17 See Otto Kirchheimer, "Confining Conditions and Revolutionary Breakthroughs," *The American Political Science Review* 59 (December 1965).

18 A. Bazargan, ed., *Masa'el*, p. 75.

19 For background information on the major ministers see Ahmad Mahrad: *Iran nach dem Sturz des Schahs: Die provisorische Revolutionsregierung Bazargans* (Frankfurt: Campus, 1983), pp. 68–86. For a complete list of the cabinets see D. Menashri, *Iran*, p. 80.

20 *Showra-ye enqelab va dowlat-e movaqqat* (The Council of the Revolution and the Provisional Government) (Tehran: Nezat-e azadi, 1983).

21 Hassan Nazih, personal interview, Paris, June 1982.

22 For details see Vahe Petrossian, "Dilemmas of the Iranian Revolution" *World Today* 36 (1980): 19–25.

23 On his political and economic philosophy see H. E. Chehabi, *Iranian Politics*, pp. 52–60 and 62–4.

24 For an account of the economic problems facing the provisional government see Joseph Vernoux, *L'Iran des mollah: la révolution introuvable* (Paris: Anthropos, 1981), pp. 71–8.

25 On the listening post at Kabkan see James Bamford, *The Puzzle Palace* (Boston: Houghton Mifflin, 1982), p. 200. On the CIA see James A. Bill, *The Eagle and the Lion: The Tragedy of American-Iranian Relations* (New Haven: Yale University Press).

26 The only person who seems to have predicted this was Karim Sanjabi, who turned down an invitation to join the Council for this reason. See his book *Omid-ha va na-omidi-ha: Khaterat-e siasi-ye doktor Karim-e Sanjabi* (Hopes and Despair: The Political Memoirs of Dr. Karim Sanjabi) (London: Jebhe, 1989), pp. 314–15.

27 Ibid., p. 318.

28 For details about the revolutionary tribunals' activities see *Law and Human*

Rights in the Islamic Republic of Iran (London: Amnesty International, 1980).

29 For details see K. Sanjabi, *Omid-ha*, pp. 352–5.
30 For a detailed account of Nazih's travails see A. Mahrad, *Iran nach dem Sturz des Schahs*, pp. 126–80.
31 Assef Bayat, *Workers and Revolution: A Third World Experience in Workers' Control* (London: Zed Books, 1987).
32 K. Sanjabi, *Omid-ha*, pp. 294–5.
33 Interview with Oriana Fallaci, *The New York Times Magazine*, October 28, 1979, p. 64.
34 K. Sanjabi, *Omid-ha*, p. 324.
35 For the context see A. Mahrad, *Iran nach dem Sturz des Schahs*, pp. 141–2.
36 One might add that unlike Portugal, the democratic parties in Iran did not benefit from any foreign help. In any event, the strongly antiimperialist, not to say anti-Western, thrust of the revolution would have delegitimized any party that accepted Western help. In October, Sanjabi was invited to address the meeting of the Socialist International in Vancouver, but cancelled his trip when Great Britain's Labour foreign secretary publicly supported the Shah. See K. Sanjabi, *Omid-ha*, p. 292.
37 Sa'id Ahmadi, "Darbareh-ye enhelal-e hezb-e jomhuri-ye eslami-ye Iran" (About the Dissolution of the IRP), *Aghazi now*, nos. 5–6 (Summer–Autumn 1987):28.
38 H. E. Chehabi, "Religion and Politics in Iran: How Theocratic is the Islamic Republic?," *Daedalus* 120 (Summer 1991).
39 Cheryl Benard and Zalmay Khalilzad, *"The Government of God": Iran's Islamic Republic* (New York: Columbia University Press, 1984), p. 109.
40 *The New York Times Magazine*, October 28, 1979, p. 65.
41 *Keesing's Contemporary Archives*, March 21, 1980, p. 30143.
42 See Said Amir Arjomand, *The Shadow of God and the Hidden Imam: Religion, Political Order and Societal Change in Shi'ite Iran from the Beginning to 1890* (Chicago: The University of Chicago Press, 1984).
43 For a discussion see Hamid Enayat, "Iran: Khumayni's Concept of the Guardianship of the Jurisconsult," in James Piscatori, ed., *Islam in the Political Process* (Cambridge University Press, 1983).
44 See David Menashri, "Shi'ite Leadership: In the Shadow of Conflicting Ideologies," *Iranian Studies* 13 (1980).
45 For the discussions in the Assembly of Experts see Said Saffari, "The Legitimation of the Clergy's Right to Rule in the Iranian Constitution of 1979," *British Journal of Middle Eastern Studies* 20 (Spring 1993).
46 These are exhaustively treated in Asghar Shirazi, *Die Widersprüche in der Verfassung der Islamischen Republik vor dem Hintergrund der politischen Auseinandersetzungen im nachrevolutionären Iran* (Berlin: Das arabische Buch, 1992).
47 There was genuine fear in Iran that the United States might try to put the Shah back on his throne, as they had done in 1953.
48 For a discussion of the hostage crisis and its political background see R. W. Cottam, *Iran and the United States*, pp. 210–22.
49 K. Sanjabi, *Omid-ha*, pp. 338–9.
50 For details on the elections see H. E. Chehabi, *Iranian Politics*, pp. 281–6.
51 See Werner Kaltefleiter, *Die Funktionen des Staatsoberhauptes in der parlamentarischen Demokratie* (Cologne and Opladen: Westdeutscher Verlag,

1970), pp. 185–7; and Juan J. Linz and Arturo Valenzuela, eds., *The Failure of Presidential Democracy* (Baltimore, Md.: Johns Hopkins University Press, 1993).

52 For details on the power struggle see D. Menashri, *Iran*, pp. 168–83.

53 Concentrating on the political dynamics of the regime transition, this essay has deliberately shied away from providing a detailed account of Iranian politics in this period. For a history see Sh. Bakhash, *The Reign of the Ayatollahs*, pp. 52–70. For an account centered on the provisional government see H. E. Chehabi, *Iranian Politics*, pp. 253–77.

54 Crane Brinton, *Anatomy of Revolution* (New York: Random House, 1965).

55 See Mohsen Milani, "The Evolution of the Iranian Presidency: From Bani Sadr to Rafsanjani," *British Journal of Middle Eastern Studies* 20 (Spring 1993).

8. From revolution to democracy in Portugal: The roles and stages of the provisional governments

1 I have provided a short overview of the Portuguese transition in "Portugal's Unexpected Transition," in Kenneth Maxwell and Michael Haltzel, eds., *Portugal: Ancient Country, Young Democracy* (Washington, D.C.: The Wilson Center Press, 1990).

2 The lack of preparation and vague goals is obvious from a reading of the description of the coup and its aftermath by one of its leading planners. See Otelo Saraiva de Carvalho, *Alvorada em Abril* (Amadora: Livraria Bertrand, 1977).

3 I have dealt with the background and immediate results of the revolution in my *Politics and Nationhood: Post-Revolutionary Portugal* (New York: Praeger, 1984). See also the extensive bibliography cited there. In addition to those references see also the very good chapters in the two edited volumes resulting from conferences of the International Conference Group on Modern Portugal. Lawrence Graham and Harry Makler, eds., *Contemporary Portugal: The Revolution and its Antecedents* (Austin: University of Texas Press, 1979) and Lawrence Graham and Douglas Wheeler, eds., *In Search of Modern Portugal: The Revolution and its Consequences* (Madison: University of Wisconsin Press, 1983).

4 On the initial phases of party formation see in particular Albertino Antunes, et al., *A Opção do Voto* (Lisbon: Intervoz, 1975).

5 Senator George McGovern, "Revolution into Democracy: Portugal After the Coup." A Report to the Committee on Foreign Relations of the United States Senate, 94th. Congress 2nd. Session. GPO, Washington, 1976, p. 29.

6 See my discussion in Bruneau, 1984, pp. 47–52. There is much good literature on the topic of the PCP. See for example Eusebio Mujal-Leon, "The PCP and the Portuguese Revolution," *Problems of Communism* 26 (Jan–Feb 1977):21–41.

7 The best books on the armed forces in this period are written by Avelino Rodrigues, Cesario Borga, and Mario Cardoso. They are *O Movimento dos Capitaes e o 25 de Abril: 229 Dias para Derrubar O Fasciscmo* (Lisbon: Moraes, 1974), *Portugal Depois de Abril* (Lisbon: Intervoz, 1976), and *Abril nos Quarteis de Novembro* (Lisbon: Bertrand, 1979).

8 See for example Marcelo Rebelo de Sousa, *Os Partidos Politicos no Direito*

Constitucional Portugues (Braga: Livraria Cruz, 1983). A good discussion on the contribution of political parties is Ken Gaddish, "Portugal: an open verdict," in Geoffrey Pridham, ed., *Securing Democracy: Political parties and democratic consolidation in Southern Europe* (London and New York: Routledge, 1990).

9 Our book gives particular attention to the formation and roles of the political parties. See Thomas Bruneau and Alex Macleod, *Politics in Contemporary Portugal: Parties and the Consolidation of Democracy* (Boulder, Col.: Lynne Rienner, 1986). A very useful discussion of the PS, PSD, and CDS, which is based on good data, is Maria Jose Stock, *Os Partidos do Poder Dez Anos Depois do "25 de Abril"* (Evora: Universidade de Evora, 1986).

10 On this topic see the material by the single most important individual in defining the legal space of the armed forces, Diogo Freitas do Amaral, "A Constituicao e as Forcas Armadas," in Mario Baptista Coelho, ed., *Portugal: O Sistema Politico e Constitucional 1974–87.* (Lisbon: Instituto de Ciencias Sociais, 1989), pp. 647–62. See also his *A Lei de Defesa National e Das Forcas Armadas* (Coimbra: Coimbra Editora, 1983). See also Chapter 2 in Bruneau and MacLeod as well as Maria Carilho, *Forcas Armadas e Mudanca Politica em Portugal no Sec. XX: Para uma explicacao sociologica do papel dos militares* (Lisbon: Imprensa Nacional-Casa de Moeda, 1985).

11 Alvaro Vasconcelos, "Portuguese Defence Policy: Internal Politics and Defence Commitments," in John Chipman, ed., *NATO's Southern Allies: Internal and External Challenges* (London: Routledge, 1988), p. 123–4.

12 I have dealt with this topic in "Defense Modernization and the Armed Forces in Portugal," *Portuguese Studies Review* Vol I, no. 2, (1991–2):27–43. See also Maxwell, ed., "Portuguese Defense and Foreign Policy Since Democratization" Camoes Center Special Report No. 3. Columbia University, 1991.

13 For a very good background study see U.S. Government, *US Military Installations in NATO's Southern Region,* Congressional Research Service, Washington, D.C. 1986.

14 See chapter 6 of Bruneau and MacLeod for this topic. For an excellent and updated discussion see Kenneth Maxwell and Scott Monje, "Portugal: The Constitution and the Consolidation of Democracy, 1976–1989," Camoes Center Special Report No. 2. Columbia University, 1991.

15 On the revision see also Francisco Pinto Balsemao, "The Constitution and Politics: Options for the Future," in Kenneth Maxwell, ed., *Portugal in the 1980's: Dilemmas of Democratic Consolidation* (New York: Greenwood, 1986), pp. 197–232.

16 On this general topic see Jose Calvet de Magalhaes, Alvaro Vasconcelos, and Joaquim Ramos Silva, *Portugal – The Atlantic Paradox: Portuguese/U.S. Relations after the EC Enlargement* (Lisbon: Institute for Strategic and International Studies, 1990).

9. Accelerating collapse: The East German road from liberalization to power-sharing and its legacy

1 Both *exit* and *voice* are defined in Albert O. Hirschman, "Exit, Voice, and the Fate of the GDR: an Essay in Conceptual History," *World Politics* (January, 1993):175–6, 179.

2 Henry A. Turner, *Germany from Partition to Reunification* (New Haven: Yale, 1992), p. 229.

3 See the author's "Regime Collapse in the Peaceful East German Revolution: the Role of Middle-level Officials," *German Politics*, 2:1 (April 1993):97–112.

4 Jochen von Lang, *Erich Mielke, eine deutsche Karriere* (Berlin: Rohwolt, 1991), pp. 151, 158.

5 *Leipziger Volkszeitung* article (Oct. 6), reprinted in Manfred Behrend and Herbert Meier, eds., *Der schwere Weg der Erneuerung* (Berlin: Dietz, 1991), p. 93.

6 Armin Mitter and Stefan Wolle, eds., *Ich liebe euch doch alle!* (Berlin: Basis, 1990), p. 201.

7 Interviews with SED secretary Roland Wötzel, Leipzig (December 13, 1993) and VoPo chief, Major General Gerhard Strassenburg, Leipzig (February 24, 1994). Also see journalist Ekkehard Kuhn's *Der Tag der Entscheidung, Leipzig, 9. Okt. 1989* (Berlin: Ullstein, 1992), pp. 48–51.

8 Letter published in the SED newspaper *Neues Deutschland* (November 21, 1989), p. 3.

9 Volker Gransow and Konrad H. Jarausch, eds., *Die deutsche Vereinigung: Dokumente zu Bürgerbewegung, Annäherung, und Beitritt* (Köln: Wissenschaft und Politik, 1991), pp. 76–7.

10 Eckhard Bahr, *Sieben Tage im Oktober* (Leipzig: Forum Verlag, 1990), p. 134. This account draws on interviews with Chaplain Frank Richter, Dresden (May 11, 1994), Lieutenant Detlef Pappermann, Dresden (June 23, 1994), and Mayor Wolfgang Berghofer, Berlin (February 19, 1994).

11 Bahr, ibid., pp. 134–5.

12 Ibid., p. 156.

13 Frank Sieren and Ludwig Köhne, eds., *Das Politbüro: Ende eines Mythos,* (Hamburg: Rohwolt, 1991), p. 74. See also the transcript "Stenografische Neiderschrift" (7 Oct. 1989) SAPMO: IV 2/1/704, pp. 83–4.

14 Egon Krenz, *Wenn Mauern Fallen* (Wien: Paul Neff, 1990), p. 87.

15 See Hans Modrow, *Aufbruch und Ende* (Hamburg: Konkret, 1991), p. 11.

16 Reinhold Andert and Wolfgang Herzberg, *Der Sturz: Honecker im Kreuzverhör* (Berlin: Weimar, 1990), p. 71.

17 Krenz, op. cit., p. 22.

18 On the distinction between liberalization and democratization, see Guillermo O'Donnell and Philippe Schmitter, *Transitions from Authoritarian Rule: Tentative Conclusions* (Baltimore, Md.: Johns Hopkins University Press, 1986), p. 9.

19 Turner, op. cit., p. 235.

20 M. E. Sarotte, "Elite Intransigence and the End of the Berlin Wall," *German Politics*, 2:2 (August 1993): 270–87. Interior Minister Dickel warned district police chiefs on November 2 to expect requests to increase (Fernschreiben 166, Bundesarchiv-Dahlwitz/Hoppegarten, DO1/8.0/54462).

21 See Deputy Interior Minister Arendt's November 10 cable (Fernschreiben 484), ibid. Krenz' cable to Gorbachev that morning is in SAPMO: IV 2/1/704, pp. 83–4.

22 The modest label that Germans have unaccountably adopted for their first successful revolution.

23 Sieren and Köhne, op. cit., pp. 104, 110.

24 *Der Absturz* (Berlin: Rohwolt, 1991), p. 273.
25 Patrick Moreau, *PDS, Anatomie einer postkommunistischen Partei* (Bonn: Bouvier, 1992), p. 332.
26 Although Gorbachev's role in inciting the palace coup is clear, Honecker suspected that his preference as successor was not Krenz but Modrow. See Erich Honecker, *Moabiter Notizen* (Berlin: edition ost, 1994): pp. 14, 34. Modrow had secret "back channel" ties to the Soviet embassy in Berlin. Modrow interview, Berlin (August 1, 1994).
27 Modrow, *Aufbruch*, p. 39.
28 Alexis de Toqueville, *The Old Regime and the French Revolution (1856)*, Gilbert Stuart trans. (New York: Doubleday, 1955), p. 177.
29 The single trade union (FDGB) and the farmers collective. The Sorbian ethnic minority was also represented.
30 Originally called the SDP in distinction from the FRG's party.
31 As quoted in Modrow, *Aufbruch*, p. 66.
32 Ibid. p. 130.
33 Anne Worst, *Das Ende eines Geheimdienstes* (Berlin: Links Druck, 1991), p. 26.
34 See Deputy Chief Schwanitz' December 6, 1989 cable in the Gauck Authority Archives, Berlin (BdL 353/89).
35 Modrow, *Aufbruch,* pp. 73, 79.
36 Andrei Markovits, "The West German Left in a Changing Europe," in Christiane Lemke and Gary Marks, eds., *The Crisis of Socialism in Europe* (Durham, N.C.: Duke University Press, 1992), pp. 171–90.
37 The subtitle of Uwe Thaysen, *Der Runde Tisch* (Opladen: Westdeutscher Verlag, 1990).
38 Mitteldeutsche Rundfunk (MDR), "Helden a. D.: die Dresdner Gruppe der 20 drei Jahre danach" broadcast (Dec. 16, 1992).
39 See the reasonable "alternative scenario" A. James McAdams sketches in *Germany Divided: From the Wall to Reunification* (Princeton, N.J.: Princeton University), p. 194.
40 The PDS (Party of Democratic Socialism) was the rechristened SED. The CDU, BFD (Free Democrats) and SPD had become West German sister parties.
41 Full text in Gert-Joachim Glaessner, *The Unification Process in Germany* (London: Pinter, 1992), pp. 160–3. See Elizabeth Pond, *Beyond the Wall: Germany's Road to Unification* (Washington, D.C.: The Brookings Institution, 1993), pp. 137–8.
42 U.S. Secretary of State James Baker visited Modrow to help boost his flagging authority; Pond, op. cit., p. 169.
43 Pond, op. cit., p. 172. His chief negotiator had advocated making the proposal in December; Ibid, p. 148.
44 As quoted in Glaessner, op. cit., p. 97.
45 *Abschied ohne Träne: Rückblick auf das Jahr der Einheit* (Frankfurt: Ullstein, 1991), p. 40.
46 By 1991, 27 percent of all employees in eastern ministry offices were from western Germany; Klaus König, "Bureaucratic Integration by Elite Transfer," *Governance* 6:3 (July 1993): 391.
47 See Pond, op. cit., p. 226.
48 Text in Klaus-Dietmar Henke, ed., *Die Debatte über die Stasi-Akten* (München: DTV, 1993), pp. 183–222.

49 Gauck, op. cit., p. 11.
50 See David Gill and Ulrich Schröter, *Das Ministerium für Staatssicherheit: Anatomie des Mielke-Imperiums* (Berlin: Rohwolt, 1991), p. 119.
51 *Financial Times,* February 4, 1992.
52 *Erster Tätigkeitsbericht des Bundesbeauftragten für die Unterlagen des Staatssicherheitsdienstes* (Berlin, 1993): pp. 6, 79.
53 See Claus Offe, "Rechtswege der 'Vergangenheitspolitik:' Disqualifizierung, Bestrafung, Restitution," in his *Der Tunnel am Ende des Lichtes* (Frankfurt am Main: Campus, 1994), p. 204n.
54 March 30, 1991, pp. 9–11.
55 See Klaus Lüderssen *Der Staat geht unter, das Unrecht bleibt?* (Frankfurt: Suhrkamp, 1992): pp. 71, 148.
56 A surprisingly readable account by a law professor is Uwe Wesel, *Ein Staat vor Gericht. Der Honecker Prozess* (Frankfurt am Main: Eichhorn, 1994).
57 See his collected speeches, *Den Menschen Hoffnung geben* (Berlin: Wichern, 1991); and his memoirs, *Schwieriger Aufbruch* (Berlin: Siedler, 1992).
58 See *Bericht des Untersuchungsausschusses 1/3,* Drucksache 1/3009 (Potsdam: Landtag Brandenburg, 1994). For the case against Stolpe, see Ralf Georg Reuth, *IM Sekretär* (Frankfurt: Ullstein, 1992). For a PDS rebuttal, see Ulla Jelpke, et al., *Die Eroberung der Akten* (Mainz: Podium Progressiv, 1992).
59 Josef Isensee, ed., *Vergangenheitsbewältigung durch Recht* (Berlin: Dunker & Humblot, 1992).
60 A comparative overview of the German, Czech, Hungarian, Polish, and Russian approaches may be found in the proceedings of the Bündnis 90/Die Grünen colloquium in Berlin, May 22–4, 1992, "Dicker Schlusstrich oder Durchleuchtung? über den Umgang mit der kommunistischen Vergangenheit in Osteuropa" (Bonn: Bundeshaus, 1992).

10. Interim government and democratic consolidation: Argentina in comparative perspective

1 I acknowledge the helpful comments of Giuseppe Di Palma, Scott Mainwaring, María José Moyano, Pierre Ostiguy, Yossi Shain, and J. Samuel Valenzuela. I take responsibility for any errors of fact or interpretation.
2 This definition is consistent with Dahl's seven-point definition of polyarchy but puts more emphasis on the ability of elected officials actually to make basic policy decisions. See Robert Dahl, *Polyarchy* (New Haven: Yale University Press, 1971), esp. chap. 1, and *Democracy and Its Critics* (New Haven: Yale University Press, 1989), esp. chaps. 15–17. Some of the advantages of using a minimalist conception of democracy are discussed in Guillermo O'Donnell and Philippe C. Schmitter, *Transitions from Authoritarian Rule: Tentative Conclusions About Uncertain Democracies* (Baltimore, Md.: Johns Hopkins University Press, 1986), p. 8; and in Terry Lynn Karl and Philippe C. Schmitter, "Modes of Transition in Latin America, Southern and Eastern Europe," *International Social Science Journal* 128 (May 1991):272. Condition (2) is designed to rule out regimes in which elected officials cannot make collectively binding decisions without the approval of actors outside their territorial domain or nonelected actors (e.g., the military) within that domain (Karl and Schmitter, "Modes of Transition," p. 4). Another condition that might be added, particularly in light of the Spanish and post-Communist

cases, is that no significant set of people wants to secede from the country. See Juan J. Linz and Alfred Stepan, "Political Crafting of Democratic Consolidation or Destruction: European and South American Comparisons," in Robert A. Pastor, ed., *Democracy in the Americas: Stopping the Pendulum* (New York: Holmes and Meier, 1992).

3 A more extensive and more explicitly theoretically grounded treatment of the notion of democratic consolidation may be found in J. Samuel Valenzuela, "Democratic Consolidation in Post-Transitional Settings: Notion, Process, and Facilitating Conditions," in Scott Mainwaring, Guillermo O'Donnell, and J. Samuel Valenzuela, eds., *Issues in Democratic Consolidation* (Notre Dame, Ind.: University of Notre Dame Press, 1992).

4 Carl Cohen, *Democracy* (New York: Free Press, 1971).

5 Terry Lynn Karl and Philippe C. Schmitter, "Modes of Transition in Latin America, Southern and Eastern Europe," p. 5. For a forceful argument that adversarial politics and an active press promote social justice, see Jean Drèze and Amartya Sen, *Hunger and Public Action* (Oxford: Clarendon, 1989).

6 Guillermo O'Donnell and Philippe C. Schmitter define regime as "the ensemble of patterns, explicit or not, that determines the forms and channels of access to principal governmental positions, the characteristics of the actors who are admitted and excluded from such access, and the resources or strategies that they can use to gain access" (*Transitions from Authoritarian Rule: Tentative Conclusions About Uncertain Democracies,* p. 73 n. 1). Significantly, two important studies of transitions include the word "craft" or "crafting" in their titles. See Giuseppe Di Palma, *To Craft Democracies: An Essay on Democratic Transitions* (Berkeley, Cal.: University of California Press, 1990), and Juan J. Linz and Alfred Stepan, "Political Crafting of Democratic Consolidation or Destruction."

7 The figure for number of disappearances, which is from Comisión Nacional Sobre la Desaparación de las Personas, *Nunca Más* (Buenos Aires: CONADEP, 1985), p. 16, includes about 600 cases from before the March 1976 coup, but excludes cases of abductions whose victims later reappeared. The authors of this study note that the actual number of disappearances is higher because many cases went unreported (ibid., p. 479).

8 St. Jean quote from Carlos H. Acuña and Catalina Smulovitz, "¿Ni olvido, ni perdón? Derechos humanos y tensiones cívico-militares en la transición argentina," paper prepared for the 16th International Congress of the Latin American Studies Association, Washington, D.C., April 4–6, 1991, pp. 8–9. Menéndez quote from William C. Smith, *Authoritarianism and the Crisis of the Argentine Political Economy* (Stanford, Cal.: Stanford University Press, 1989), p. 232. An early report on human rights abuses in Argentina estimated that less than 20 percent of the disappeared were members of guerrilla groups. *Latin America Political Report,* January 6, 1978, cited in David Rock, *Argentina 1516–1982: From Spanish Colonization to the Falklands War* (Berkeley: University of California Press, 1985), p. 367.

9 Robert Cox, "The Sound of One Hand Clapping: A Preliminary Study of the Argentine Press in a Time of Terror," Working Paper 83, Latin American Program, The Woodrow Wilson International Center for Scholars, Washington, D.C., 1980. Figures on killings of journalists from p. 9.

10 This interpretation of the goals of the government's economic policies is drawn from Adolfo Canitrot, "Discipline as the Central Objective of Eco-

nomic Policy: An Essay on the Economic Programme of the Argentine Government Since 1976," *World Development* 8:11 (November 1980):917–18.

11 Figures on GDP and inflation from William C. Smith, *Authoritarianism and the Crisis of the Argentine Political Economy*, p. 248.

12 Quotation from p. 27 of Inés González Bombal, "El diálogo político: La transición que no fue." Buenos Aires: Centro de Estudios de Estado y Sociedad, Documento CEDES/61, 1991. Other information from ibid., pp. 21–3, 40–4, 69–82.

13 Figures on real per capita GDP and industrial production from William C. Smith, *Authoritarianism and the Crisis of the Argentine Political Economy*, p. 248.

14 David Rock, *Argentina 1516–1982: From Spanish Colonization to the Falklands War* (Berkeley: University of California Press, 1985), p. 373. According to the Stockholm International Peace Research Institute, Argentina spent up to $14.3 billion on arms purchases between 1976 and 1982. Jimmy Burns, *The Land That Lost Its Heroes: The Falklands, The Post-War, and Alfonsín* (London: Bloomsbury, 1987), p. 18. The sales pitches of international banks, which found themselves awash in petrodollars after the oil price hikes of 1979, also helped boost the foreign debt to $43.5 billion by the time the military left office.

15 Alvaro Abós, *Los organizaciones sindicales y el poder militar (1976–1983)* (Buenos Aires: Centro Editor de América Latina, 1984), pp. 54–5; Pablo A. Pozzi, "Argentina 1976–1982: Labour Leadership and Military Government," *Journal of Latin American Studies* 20:1 (May 1988):127–8. Belying the image of a society immobilized by repression, individual strikes began almost immediately after the 1976 coup. Impressively, given the risk of engaging in (or even reporting) overt protest, the newspapers recorded at least ninety strikes and stoppages during Videla's presidency. Ricardo Falcón, "Conflicto Social y Régimen Militar. La Resistencia Obrera en Argentina (marzo 1976–marzo 1981)," in Bernardo Gallitelli and Andrés A. Thompson, eds., *Sindicalismo y regimenes militares en Argentina y Chile* (Amsterdam: Centrum voor Studie en Documentatie van Latijns Amerika, 1982), p. 115.

16 Alejandro Dabat and Luis Lorenzano, *Conflicto malvinense y crisis nacional.* (Mexico D.F.: Teoria y Política, A.C, 1982), pp. 112–16. On the construction projects see John Simpson and Jana Bennett, *The Disappeared: Voices From a Secret War* (London: Robson Books, 1985), pp. 198–203.

17 Maryssa Navarro, "The Personal is Political: Las Madres de Plaza de Mayo," in Susan Eckstein, ed., *Power and Popular Protest* (Berkeley: University of California Press, 1989). Membership figure from Iain Guest, *Behind the Disappearances: Argentina's Dirty War Against Human Rights and the United Nations* (Philadelphia: University of Pennsylvania Press, 1990), p. 210.

18 Yearly figures for recorded disappearances from María José Moyano, "The 'Dirty War' in Argentina: Was It a War and How Dirty Was It?," in Hans Werner Tobler and Peter Waldmann, eds., *Staatliche und parastaatliche Gewalt in Lateinamerika* (Frankfurt: Vervuert Verlag, 1991), p. 53.

19 David Pion-Berlin, "The Fall of Military Rule in Argentina: 1976–1983," *Journal of Interamerican Studies and World Affairs* 27:2 (1985):64–5.

20 Quoted in Iain Guest, *Behind the Disappearances*, p. 271.

21 Inés González Bombal, "El diálogo político: La transición que no fue," pp. 83–4.

22 Guillermo O'Donnell, *Bureaucratic Authoritarianism: Argentina, 1966–1973, in Comparative Perspective* (Berkeley: University of California Press, 1988), pp. 238–41; William C. Smith, *Authoritarianism and the Crisis of the Argentine Political Economy*, pp. 178–9, 190–4.

23 On the difficulty of reversing the "resurrection of civil society" during transitions from authoritarian rule see Guillermo O'Donnell and Philippe C. Schmitter, *Transitions from Authoritarian Rule: Tentative Conclusions About Uncertain Democracies*, pp. 48–56.

24 Federal Police figures given in Alejandro Dabat and Luis Lorenzano, *Conflicto malvinense y crisis nacional*, p. 122.

25 Inés González Bombal, "El diálogo político: La transición que no fue," pp. 40–4, 99–102, 112–13.

26 Andrés Fontana, "De la crisis de Malvinas a la subordinación condicionada: Conflictos intramilitares y transición política en Argentina," paper prepared for the International Seminar on Autonomizacón Castrense y Democracia en América Latina, Santiago de Chile, May 22–25, 1985, pp. 6–7; Inés González Bombal, "El diálogo político: La transición que no fue," pp. 114–16; Aldo Vacs, "Authoritarian Breakdown and Redemocratization in Argentina," in James M. Malloy and Mitchell A. Seligson, eds., *Authoritarians and Democrats: Regime Transition in Latin America* (Pittsburgh, Pa.: University of Pittsburgh Press, 1987), p. 28.

27 Iain Guest, *Behind the Disappearances*, pp. 337–40. Galtieri had impressed the Reagan administration on a tour of the United States shortly before taking office. National Security Adviser Richard Allen remarked that he possessed "a majestic personality" and Defense Secretary Caspar Weinberger was "very impressed" by Galtieri (Oscar Raúl Cardoso, Ricardo Kirschbaum, and Eduardo van der Kooy, *Malvinas, la trama secreta*. Buenos Aires: Sudamericana-Planeta, 1983, p. 29). These remarks, publicized in the press, were not lost on Galtieri. In an April 1983 interview with the newspaper *Clarín*, Galtieri said that he had thought of himself "as the pampered child of the North Americans," and added "if I had known the Americans would take the position they finally adopted, we would never have invaded." Elizabeth Fox and Stanley Meisler, "Buenos Aires: The Weight of the Past," *Atlantic Monthly* 253:1 (January 1983):14.

28 Andrés Fontana, "De la crisis de Malvinas a la subordinación condicionada," p. 16.

29 *Latin America Weekly Report* 23 July, 1982:7.

30 Horacio Verbitsky, *Civiles y militares. Memoria secreta de la transición* (Buenos Aires: Editorial Contrapunto, 1987), p. 33; Andrés Fontana, "De la crisis de Malvinas a la subordinación condicionada," pp. 22–3.

31 María Laura San Martino de Dromi, *Historia Política argentina (1955–1988)*. Vol. II (Buenos Aires: Astrea, 1988), p. 361; Horacio Verbitsky, *Civiles y militares*, pp. 34–5. It was in fact not until March 1985 that the human rights trials passed from military to civilian jurisdiction.

32 Andrés Fontana, "De la crisis de Malvinas a la subordinación condicionada," pp. 27–31.

33 *Latin America Weekly Report* 5 November 1982:2–3.

34 Centro de Estudios Sobre el Estado y la Administración, *Argentina 1983* (Buenos Aires: Centro Editor de América Latina, 1984), pp. 102–3.

35 Gustavo Beliz, *CGT, El otro poder* (Buenos Aires: Planeta, 1989), pp. 168–9;

Alvaro Abós, *Los organizaciones sindicales y el poder militar (1976–1983)*, p. 148.

36 Mark Osiel, "The Making of Human Rights Policy in Argentina: the Impact of Ideas and Interests on a Legal Conflict," *Journal of Latin American Studies* 18:1 (May 1986):143.

37 Eduardo Viola and Scott Mainwaring, "Transitions to Democracy: Brazil and Argentina in the 1980s," *Journal of International Affairs* 38:2 (Winter 1985):193–219; Alfred Stepan, "Paths toward Redemocratization: Theoretical and Comparative Considerations," in Guillermo O'Donnell, Philippe C. Schmitter, and Laurence Whitehead, eds., *Transitions From Authoritarian Rule: Comparative Perspectives* (Baltimore, Md.: Johns Hopkins University Press, 1986).

38 On constitutional change in transitions to democracy see Juan J. Linz and Alfred Stepan, "Democratic Transition and Consolidation in Southern Europe (With Reflections on Latin America and Eastern Europe)," draft of paper prepared for the conference on "Problems of Democratic Consolidation: Spain and the New Southern Europe," Madrid, July 6–8, 1990; and Andrea Bonime-Blanc, *Spain's Transition to Democracy: The Politics of Constitution-Making* (Boulder, Col.: Westview, 1987).

39 *Latin America Weekly Report* 16 July 1983:6.

40 *Latin America Regional Report – Southern Cone* 10 September 1982:2.

41 These features of the 1972 statute had been aimed at preventing the Peronists from winning the presidency. The idea was that the Peronists would win a plurality in the first round against a divided opposition – but not too divided, owing to the 8 percent minimum threshold – which would then coalesce to keep the Peronists from winning in the second round. But partly in the hope that a Peronist government could rein in the Montoneros, many more than the government anticipated voted for Peronism in the first round. Peronist candidate Héctor Cámpora won 49.6 percent of the vote, and runner-up Balbín conceded the second round before it took place.

42 Julio Nosiglia, "La nueva ley electoral," in Emiliana López de Saavedra et al., eds., *Formación política para la democracia* (Buenos Aires: Editorial Redacción, 1983), p. 715.

43 *Latin America Regional Report – Southern Cone* 11 March 1983:1.

44 Eduardo Viola and Scott Mainwaring, "Transitions to Democracy: Brazil and Argentina in the 1980s," p. 207.

45 Mora Cordeu, Silvia Mercado, and Nancy Sosa, *Peronismo: La mayoría perdida* (Buenos Aires: Sudamericana/Planeta, 1985), pp. 19–41; Vicente Palermo, *Democracia Interna en los Partidos* (Buenos Aires: Ediciones del Instituto de Desarrollo Económico y Social, 1986), pp. 90–1.

46 Analysis of the reasons for the Radical victory in the 1983 elections may be found in Jorge Raúl Jorrat, "Las elecciones de 1983: ¿Desviación o realineamiento?," *Desarrollo Económico* 26:101 (April–June 1986):89–120; Leticia Maronese, Ana Cafiero de Nazar, and Victor Waisman, *El voto peronista '83* (Buenos Aires: El Cid, 1985); and Manuel Mora y Araujo, "The Nature of the Alfonsín Coalition," in Paul Drake and Eduardo Silva, eds., *Elections and Democratization in Latin America* (San Diego: Center for Iberian and Latin American Studies, University of California at San Diego, 1986).

47 A labor ministry study recorded a 30 percent drop in manufacturing employment between 1974 and 1981. Similarly, data in the National Statistical Insti-

tute's quarterly bulletin gave evidence of a 34 percent drop between 1974 and 1983 (Ministerio de Trabajo de la Nación, "Ocupación y producto en la industria manufacturera argentina, 1976–1983," Argentina, Ministerio de Trabajo de la Nación, Dirección Nacional de Recursos Humanos y Empleo, 1983, p. 31; William C. Smith, "Democracy, Distributional Conflicts, and Macroeconomic Policymaking in Argentina, 1983–89," *Journal of Interamerican Studies and World Affairs* 32:2 (Summer 1990):31). The more definitive 1985 economic census showed, however, a 4 percent increase in manufacturing employment between 1973 and 1984, although employment in factories with more than 500 workers – the bastion of industrial unionism – dropped from 341,816 to 244,438 (Instituto Nacional de Estadística y Censos, *Censo Nacional Económico 1985, Industria Manufacturera, Resultos Definitivos, Primera Etapa.* Buenos Aires: INDEC, 1988, p. 15).

48 A 1983 survey of Argentina's major urban centers showed that only 6 percent of upper-class respondents approved of the 1973–6 Peronist government, whereas 82 percent disapproved. On the other hand, 64 percent of upper-class respondents approved of the 1963–6 Illia government (the last time the Radicals had held the presidency), whereas only 15 percent disapproved (Edgardo Catterberg, *Argentina Confronts Politics: Political Culture and Public Opinion in the Argentine Transition to Democracy,* Boulder, Col.: Lynne Rienner, 1991, p. 80).

49 Philippe Schmitter and Terry Lynn Karl point to an interesting association between total amount of compromise and the type of democracy that ultimately emerges. Low levels of compromise are correlated with what Schmitter and Karl classify as populist or electoralist democracies, and high levels with corporatist or consociational democracies. Whether this correlation includes a causal component will have to be demonstrated by identifying the mechanisms by which, in individual cases, specific amounts of compromise cleared or obstructed the paths toward certain types of democracy. Disaggregating the two types of compromise would probably be helpful in identifying such mechanisms. Philippe C. Schmitter and Terry Lynn Karl, "What Kind of Democracies are Emerging in South America, Central America, Southern Europe, and Eastern Europe?" Paper prepared for the Coloquio Internacional sobre "Transiciones a la democracia en Europa y América Latina," Universidad de Guadalajara y FLACSO, Mexico, 21–5 January 1991, Guadalajara, Jalisco, Mexico.

50 On Greece see P. Nikiforos Diamandouros, "Regime Change and the Prospects for Democracy in Greece: 1974–1983," in Guillermo O'Donnell, Philippe C. Schmitter, and Laurence Whitehead, eds., *Transitions From Authoritarian Rule: Southern Europe* (Baltimore, Md.: Johns Hopkins University Press, 1986), p. 157. On Portugal see Kenneth Maxwell, "Regime Overthrow and the Prospects for Democratic Transition in Portugal," in Guillermo O'Donnell, Philippe C. Schmitter, and Laurence Whitehead, eds., *Transitions From Authoritarian Rule: Southern Europe* (Baltimore, Md: Johns Hopkins University Press, 1986), pp. 109–15.

51 Mark Osiel, "The Making of Human Rights Policy in Argentina," p. 141.

52 Elizabeth Fox, "Argentina: A Prosecution in Trouble," *Atlantic Monthly* 255:3 (March 1985):42.

53 María José Moyano, "The Dirty War in Argentina," p. 64.

54 On the distinction between military-as-government and military-as-institution

see Alfred Stepan, *Rethinking Military Politics: Brazil and the Southern Cone* (Princeton, N.J.: Princeton University Press, 1988), pp. 30–2.
55 Jimmy Burns, *The Land That Lost Its Heroes*, p. 104.
56 Iain Guest, *Behind the Disappearances*, pp. 71–2, 346.
57 *Latin America Weekly Report* 13 August 1982:6; 27 August 1982:1.
58 Andrés Fontana, "De la crisis de Malvinas a la subordinación condicionada," p. 15.
59 P. Nikiforos Diamandouros, "Regime Change and the Prospects for Democracy in Greece," p. 158.
60 Kenneth Maxwell, "Regime Overthrow and the Prospects for Democratic Transition in Portugal," pp. 236–7; Walter C. Opello Jr., *Portugal's Political Development: A Comparative Approach* (Boulder, Col.: Westview), p. 69.
61 Jimmy Burns, *The Land That Lost Its Heroes*, pp. 124–5.
62 For the 1966 poll see Guillermo O'Donnell, *Bureaucratic Authoritarianism*, p. 39n; for the 1983 survey see Edgardo Catterberg, *Argentina Confronts Politics*, p. 80.
63 Oscar Raúl Cardoso, Ricardo Kirschbaum, and Eduardo van der Kooy, *Malvinas, la trama secreta*, pp. 312–13.
64 Jimmy Burns, *The Land That Lost Its Heroes*, p. 125.
65 Yossi Shain and Juan J. Linz, "The Role of Interim Governments in Transition to Democracy," paper prepared for the Annual Meeting of the American Political Science Association, Washington, D.C., August 30–September 2, 1991, p. 15.
66 Jimmy Burns, *The Land That Lost Its Heroes*, p. 125.
67 Wayne S. Smith, "The Return of Peronism," in Frederick C. Turner and José Enrique Miguens, eds., *Juan Perón and the Reshaping of Argentina* (Pittsburgh, Pa.: University of Pittsburgh Press, 1983), pp. 125, 140.
68 Yossi Shain and Juan J. Linz, "The Role of Interim Governments in Transition to Democracy," p. 18.
69 On the manipulation of electoral dates by incumbent caretaker governments see Yossi Shain and Juan J. Linz, "The Role of Interim Governments in Transition to Democracy," pp. 25–32; on the parties' reaction to the March announcement of the election date see *Latin America Weekly Report* 4 March 1983:12.
70 *Latin America Weekly Report* 29 April 1983:3.
71 Jimmy Burns, *The Land That Lost Its Heroes*, p. 172.
72 Except in the USSR, whose leaders were willing to overlook human rights abuses in return for wheat imports, and in the United States, where the Reagan administration, at a time when Congress had partially blocked its adventures in Central America, invited Argentine military officers to train the Salvadoran security forces and Nicaraguan Contras.
73 Juan J. Linz, "Some Comparative Thoughts on the Transition to Democracy in Portugal and Spain," in Jorge Braga de Macedo and Simon Serfaty, eds., *Portugal Since the Revolution: Economic and Political Perspectives* (Boulder, Col.: Westview, 1981), pp. 26–7.
74 Carlos H. Acuña and Catalina Smulovitz, "¿Ni olvido, ni perdón?," p. 7 n. 11; p. 9 n. 18.
75 Gerardo López Alonso, *1930–1980: Cincuenta años de historia argentina* (Buenos Aires: Editorial de Belgrano, 1982), p. 315. Neither the Argentine constitution nor any international covenant on human, civil, or political rights

gives a government unlimited powers during a state of siege. Article 23 of the Argentine constitution gives those detained during such periods the option of leaving the country, but this option was legally suspended during the 1976–83 dictatorship. See Enrique I. Groisman, "El 'Proceso de Reorganización Nacional' y el sistema juridico," in Oscar Oszlak, ed., *"Proceso," crisis y transición democrática* (Buenos Aires: Centro Editor de América Latina, 1984), pp. 63–4.
76 Carlos H. Acuña and Catalina Smulovitz, "¿Ni olvido, ni perdón?," p. 9 n. 18.
77 Mark Osiel, "The Making of Human Rights Policy in Argentina," p. 141.
78 Andrés Fontana, "De la crisis de Malvinas a la subordinación condicionada," pp. 16, 37 n. 5; Inés González Bombal, "El diálogo político: La transición que no fue," pp. 85–6.
79 Enrique I. Groisman, *Poder y derecho en el "Proceso de Reorganización Nacional"* (Buenos Aires: Centro de Investigaciones Sobre el Estado y la Administración, 1983), p. 19.
80 David V. Fleischer, "Constitutional and Electoral Engineering in Brazil: A Double-Edged Sword 1964–1982," *Interamerican Economic Affairs* 37:4 (Spring 1984):20–30.
81 Literacy figure from World Bank, *World Development Report 1990* (New York: Oxford University Press), Table 1. On popular attitudes toward the Brazilian military regime, see Youssef Cohen, *The Manipulation of Consent: The State and Working-Class Consciousness in Brazil* (Pittsburgh, Pa.: University of Pittsburgh Press, 1989), and Barbara Geddes and John Zaller, "Sources of Popular Support for Authoritarian Regimes," *American Journal of Political Science* 33:2 (May 1989):319–47.
82 Pamela Constable and Arturo Valenzuela, "Chile's Return to Democracy," *Foreign Affairs* 68:5 (Winter 1989):175–6.
83 See respectively Alfred Stepan, *Rethinking Military Politics,* and Manuel Antonio Garretón, "La transición chilena: Una evaluación provisoria," Documento de Trabajo, FLACSO – Programa Chile, Serie Estudios Políticos No. 8, Santiago de Chile, January 1991.
84 J. Samuel Valenzuela, "Democratic Consolidation in Post-Transitional Settings," pp. 62–70.
85 On Brazil see Alfred Stepan, *Rethinking Military Politics,* pp. 103–16, and Wendy A. Hunter, "Military Control in a Civilian Regime: The Armed Forces' Political Role in Post-1985 Brazil," unpublished paper, Department of Political Science, University of California at Berkeley, 1990, pp. 14–27. On Chile see J. Samuel Valenzuela, "Democratic Consolidation in Post-Transitional Settings," pp. 62–70.
86 Retired major Raúl Guglielminetti served until June 1985 as the chief of Alfonsín's personal security staff, a branch of SIDE. In that month he was identified as a former torturer and as a current member of a right-wing group engaged in kidnapping and plotting to overthrow the government (Mark Osiel, "The Making of Human Rights Policy in Argentina," p. 142 n. 16; Jimmy Burns, *The Land That Lost Its Heroes,* pp. 178–9). As late as November 1991, high-ranking members of the Buenos Aires municipal police and former members of the secret service (including Guglielminetti) were arrested and charged with membership in a kidnap-for-profit ring which had operated since 1978 (*Clarín Edición Internacional* 19–25 November 1991:1; January 14–20, 1992:3).
87 On the "honor killings" of women in Brazil see *The New York Times* 29

March 1991:B-16 and *The Washington Post National Weekly Edition* 14–24 November 1991:16. On the other human rights abuses see *Amnesty International Report 1991*:46–9 and *The New York Times* 15 May 1989; 19 June 1990:3; 1 August 1990:6; 6 September 1990:9; 13 November 1990:17.

88 On the Uruguayan referendum see Lawrence Weschler, *A Miracle, A Universe: Settling Accounts With Torturers* (New York: Penguin, 1990), pp. 173–236.

89 Mark Osiel, "The Making of Human Rights Policy in Argentina," pp. 147–8; David Pion-Berlin, "Between Confrontationa and Accommodation: Military and Government Policy in Democratic Argentina," *Journal of Latin American Studies* 23:2 (1991):563.

90 On the human rights trials in Argentina see Carlos H. Acuña and Catalina Smulovitz, "¿Ni olvido, ni perdón?"; Mark Osiel, "The Making of Human Rights Policy in Argentina," and Kathryn Lee Crawford, "Due Obedience and the Rights of Victims: Argentina's Transition to Democracy," *Human Rights Quarterly* 12:1 (February 1990):17–52.

91 Deborah L. Norden, "Rebels With A Cause?: The Argentine Carapintadas," paper prepared for the Annual Meeting of the Midwest Political Science Association, Chicago, Ill., April 5–7, 1990, p. 10.

92 Juan J. Linz and Alfred Stepan, "Democratic Transition and Consolidation in Southern Europe (With Reflections on Latin America and Eastern Europe)," draft of paper prepared for the conference on "Problems of Democratic Consolidation: Spain and the New Southern Europe," Madrid, July 6–8, 1990, pp. 14–15.

93 Juan J. Linz, "The Perils of Presidentialism," *Journal of Democracy* 1:1 (Winter 1990):51–69; Scott Mainwaring, "Presidentialism in Latin America," *Latin American Research Review* 25:1 (1990):157–79.

94 Felipe Aguero, "Democratic Consolidation and the Military in Southern Europe and Latin America." Paper prepared for the Social Science Research Council Conference on Democratic Consolidation in Southern Europe, Rome, December 14–15, 1990, pp. 12, 29. Aguero's analysis might have been even more useful had he disaggregated the absence of civilian supremacy into military prerogatives (which reduce the quality of democracy) and military contestation (which reduces the short-term stability of democracy, albeit with indirect effects on its quality). (For an exposition of these terms, see Alfred Stepan, *Rethinking Military Politics*.) The present analysis suggests, in fact, that the amount of military contestation is inversely proportional to the amount of military prerogatives. Aguero demonstrates convincingly, however, that the actor that presides over the transition has important and independent effects on the subsequent democracy.

11. The failure of an internationally sponsored interim government in Afghanistan

1 *New York Times,* March 19, 1992.

2 United Nations Office for the Co-ordination of Humanitarian and Economic Assistance Programmes relating to Afghanistan (UNOCA), Press Release, "Immediate Humanitarian Needs in Afghanistan Resulting from the Current Hostilities," August 23, 1992; United Nations Department of Humanitarian Affairs, "Note on Winter Emergency Needs in Afghanistan," November 1, 1992, p. 2.

3 See page 63, Part One of this volume. An additional condition mentioned by Shain and Berat was that "a complete victory of an opposition group that installs a provisional government" was also impossible. The collapse of the Soviet Union convinced mujahidin that they might be able to achieve such a complete victory, as they eventually did – or would have, had they been able to form a coherent provisional government.

4 Lynn Berat and Yossi Shain, "Provisional Governments in Democratization: The 'International Interim Government' Model and the Case of Namibia," *Coexistence* 29 (1992):34.

5 An earlier version omitted the word "almost." See Yossi Shain and Juan J. Linz, "The Role of Interim Governments," *Journal of Democracy* 3 (January 1992):75.

6 Adam Przeworski, "Democracy as a Contingent Outcome of Conflicts," in *Constitutionalism and Democracy*, Jon Elster and Rune Slagstad, eds. (Cambridge University Press, 1988), p. 61.

7 See page 64, Part One of this volume.

8 For overviews of state formation in Afghanistan, see M. Nazif Shahrani, "State Building and Social Fragmentation in Afghanistan: A Historical Perspective," in *The State, Religion, and Ethnic Politics: Afghanistan, Iran, and Pakistan*, Ali Banuazizi and Myron Weiner, eds. (Syracuse, N.Y., 1986), pp. 23–74; Ashraf Ghani, "Afghanistan xi. Administration," in *Encyclopedia Iranica*, vol. 1, Ehsan Yarshater, ed. (London, 1982), pp. 558–64; and Barnett R. Rubin, *The Fragmentation of Afghanistan: State Collapse in the International System* (New Haven, and London: Yale University Press, 1995).

9 There has never been a complete census of Afghanistan, let alone a count of competing ethnic groups.

10 Henry S. Bradsher, *Afghanistan and the Soviet Union* (Durham, N.C.: Duke University Press, 1983).

11 Selig S. Harrison, "Dateline Afghanistan: Exit through Finland?" *Foreign Policy* (Winter 1980–1):163–87.

12 On these groups see Olivier Roy, *Islam and Resistance in Afghanistan* (Cambridge University Press, 1986); Anthony Arnold, *Afghanistan's Two-Party Communism: Parcham and Khalq* (Stanford, Cal.: Hoover Institution, 1983); and Barnett R. Rubin, "Political Elites in Afghanistan: Rentier State Building, Rentier State Wrecking," *International Journal of Middle East Studies* 24 (1992):77–99. I follow Roy in using the term "Islamist" for those groups often described as "fundamentalist." These Islamic revolutionaries treat Islam as the political ideology of a movement to seize state power and reshape society. Religious leaders who preach a return to the Islamic law (*shariʿa*) and religious observance would more properly be called "fundamentalists."

13 *Khalq* (the masses) and *Parcham* (the flag) were the names of the factions' newspapers.

14 Interviews with officials of the UN, Iran, and USSR.

15 See the account in Raja Anwar, *The Tragedy of Afghanistan: A First-hand Account* (London: Verso, 1988).

16 Jeri Laber and Barnett R. Rubin, *"A Nation is Dying": Afghanistan under the Soviets, 1979–1988* (Evanston, Ill.: Northwestern University Press, 1988).

17 Brigadier Mohammad Yousaf and Major Mark Adkin, *The Bear Trap: Afghanistan's Untold Story* (London: Leo Cooper, 1992).

18 On the negotiations see Riaz M. Khan, *Untying the Afghan Knot: Negotiating*

Soviet Withdrawal (Durham, N.C.: Duke University Press, 1991); Selig S. Harrison, "Inside the Afghan Talks," *Foreign Policy* 72 (Fall 1988):31–60; and Barnett R. Rubin, "Afghanistan: The Next Round," *Orbis* 33 (Winter 1989):57–72. The account below draws as well on numerous interviews with officials of the UN and all concerned governments since 1985.

19 See page 41, Part One of this volume.
20 See pages 41 and 48 of this volume.
21 See page 53 of this volume.
22 See page 57 of this volume.
23 See page 28 of this volume.
24 Barnett R. Rubin, "Afghanistan: Political Exiles in Search of A State," *Journal of Political Science* 18 (Spring 1990):63–93.
25 Interviews with US diplomats.
26 "Communique of U.S. Secretary of State James Baker and Soviet Foreign Minister Eduard Shevardnadze," Jackson Hole, Wyoming, September 1989.
27 Speech by Under Secretary of State Robert Kimmitt, Asia Society (Washington, D. C., April 18, 1990).
28 As Kimmitt stated: "A stable political settlement is not achievable so long as the Najib regime remains in power. This is not a U.S. demand; it is a statement of Afghan reality." Ibid., p. 8.
29 See the rather circumspect discussion of this by Baker and Shevardnadze at their press conference in Irkutsk, August 2, 1990.
30 At his joint press conference with Secretary Baker on December 11, Shevardnadze stated that the two sides had agreed on "the idea of free elections and the formation of a transitional body that would supervise those free elections. We also support cease-fire and a cutoff in arms deliveries. As to exact date, that is still a subject of further consideration."
31 Interviews with State Department officials.
32 "Statement by Secretary-General Javier Pérez de Cuellar," U.N. Department of Public Information, May 21, 1992.
33 "The Situation in Afghanistan and its Implications for International Peace and Security: Report of the Secretary-General, U.N. General Assembly and Security Council," U.N. Doc. A/46/577, S/23146 (New York: United Nations, 12 October 1992), p. 12.
34 Interviews with Afghan exiles.
35 Interview with Afghan diplomat.
36 See page 50, Part One of this volume.
37 "Statement by the Secretary-General on Afghanistan," April 10, 1992.
38 Interviews with UN and Afghan diplomats.
39 Interviews with Parchami former Watan Party Executive Committee members exiled in the United States and Central Asia.
40 These reports come from interviews with Afghans and Pakistanis who were on the ground at the time.
41 Interview with exiled Parchami Central Committee member and U.S. diplomat.
42 See p. 30, Part One, of this volume.
43 Amnesty International, "Afghanistan: New Forms of Cruel, Inhuman, and Degrading Punishment," ASA 11/02/92, September 1992.
44 *Guardian,* October 14, 1992.
45 Interview with journalist who traveled from Peshawar to Kabul by road with Mujaddidi.

46 I have a copy of an untitled telex giving the text of the accord in English. I received it from an Afghan diplomatic mission.
47 Interviewed in his place of exile in Central Asia.

12. Electoral transitions in Yugoslavia

1 I would like to thank the Joint Committee on Eastern Europe of the ACLS/ SSRC and the International Research and Exchanges Board for their support. During my 1990 stay at the Institut za suvremenu povijest in Zagreb, Dr. Ivo Jelić guided my research, and we enjoyed many long conversations about contemporary politics. This article is dedicated to his memory.
2 See Albert O. Hirschman, " 'Exit, Voice and Loyalty': Some Reflections and a Survey of Recent Contributions," *Social Science Information* 13 (1974):7– 26 and the articles which follow. I am grateful to Yossi Shain for drawing my attention to this argument.
3 Yossi Shain and Juan J. Linz, "The Role of Interim Governments in the Transitions to Democracy," paper prepared for the Annual Meeting of the American Political Science Association, Washington, D.C., August 30–September 2, 1991, p. 4.
4 The reference is the joke (now relegated to the status of historical curiosity) that Yugoslavia was a country with six republics, five nations, four languages, three religions, two alphabets and one Yugoslav – Tito.
5 Sabrina Ramet lists the following areas over which republics had exclusive jurisdiction by 1977: agriculture, mining, transport, forestry, urban planning, education, environmental protection, and public safety. *Nationalism and Federalism in Yugoslavia, 1962–1991,* (Bloomington: Indiana University Press, 1992), p. 73.
6 Sabrina Ramet has analyzed Yugoslavia as a balance-of-power system, stressing the extent to which politics resembled that among states rather than within one.
7 Christopher Cviic, "Background of the Domestic Scene in Yugoslavia," in Paul Shoup, ed., *Problems of Balkan Security: Southeastern Europe in 1990s* (Washington, D.C.: Wilson Center Press, 1990), pp. 91–2.
8 Wolfgang Hopken, "Party Monopoly and Political Change: The League of Communists Since Tito's Death," in Pedro Ramet, ed., *Yugoslavia in the 1980s* (Boulder, Col.: Westview Press, 1985), p. 36.
9 Dennison Rusinow, "After Tito," American Universities Field Staff Reports 1980/no. 34 (Hanover, N.H.), p. 12.
10 Sabrina Ramet, *Nationalism and Federalism in Yugoslavia, 1962–1991,* p. 73.
11 See Sabrina Ramet, *Nationalism and Federalism in Yugoslavia, 1962–1991,* Chapter 8; Mark Cichok, "Reevaluating a Development Strategy: Policy Implications for Yugoslavia," *Comparative Politics* 17 (January 1985):211–28.; Joseph T. Bombelles, "Federal Aid to the Less Developed Areas of Yugoslavia," *East European Politics and Societies* 5:3 (Fall 1991):439–65 and Dijana Pleština, *Regional Development in Communist Yugoslavia,* (Boulder, Col.: Westview Press, 1992).
12 Postwar federal Yugoslavia was structured around the dominant role of the KPJ simultaneous with recognition of the multinational nature of the country and attempts by the party to control the expression of nationalism. The issue of republic boundaries cannot be adequately discussed here. See Ivo Banac,

With Stalin Against Tito (Ithaca, N.Y.: Cornell University Press, 1988), pp. 99–111.

13 Dennison Rusinow, "Yugoslavia: Balkan Breakup?," *Foreign Policy* (Summer 1991), pp. 150–1.

14 Tomaž Mastnak, "The Night of Long Knives," *Across Frontiers* 4:4 (1989), p. 5.

15 Sabria Ramet, *Balkan Babel,* (Boulder, Col.: Westview Press, 1992), pp. 24–5 and 67–70.

16 Jelena Lovrić, "Zašto smo otišli- Intervju: Milan Kučan," in *Danas,* 30 January 1990, pp. 11–12.

17 These were: the Slovenian Democratic Alliance, the Social Democratic Party of Slovenia, the Slovenian Christian Democrats (SKD), the Greens of Slovenia (ZS), the Slovenian Peasant Alliance, and the Slovenian Craftsmen Party.

18 The Socio-Political Chamber is the most powerful of the three; the Associated Labor has very circumscribed powers and was not elected on a party basis.

19 The fear of potential military intervention should not be forgotten. Rumors that the JNA would intervene to prevent the elections were circulating in Zagreb in the month prior to the elections. At the same time, events in Lithuania fueled fears of a similar crackdown. See, for example, Dubravko Jelčić, *Dnevnik: Od rujna do rujna 1989–1990* (Zagreb: Grafički zavod Hrvatske, 1991), pp. 162–3, 175; compare Ivica Vrkić, "Kradljivci vremena" *Danas* no. 425 (10 April 1990):31.

20 DEMOS won 55 percent of the vote which translated into 47 of the 80 seats in the Socio-Political Chamber. The ZKS-SDP gained only 17 percent of the vote and 14 seats, but as a single party outperformed all the others.

21 Ivan Oman – President of the Slovene Peasant Alliance and Dušan Plut – President of the Green Alliance.

22 Kučan as the President of the presidency held one and the other was won by Matjaž Kmecl.

23 These were: the Croatian Democratic Party (HDS), the Croatian Christian Democratic Party (HKDS), the Democratic Alliance of Albanians of Croatia (DSAH), the Croatian Peace Movement (HMP), the Muslim Democratic Party (MDS), the Croatian Social Liberal Party (HSLS), the Social-Democratic Party of Croatia (SDSH), and the Croatian Peasant Party (HSS). D. Durić, B. Munjin and S. Španović, *Stranke u Hrvatskoj* (Zagreb: Radničke novine, 1990), pp. 111–240.

24 Those were: the Croat Peasant Party (HSS), the Croatian Party (HS), the Croat Party of Rights (HSP), Democratic Action of Croatia (DAH), and the Democratic Christian Party.

25 The campaign was not without incident. At a meeting in Benkovac, Tudjman's speech was interrupted by a Serb brandishing a pistol, Sava Čubrilović. The man was subdued by Tudjman's bodyguards. The incident provoked further controversy over the lack of police protection, the bodyguards' use of force, the authenticity of the threat, and a videotape made of the event. Jasna Babić, 'Žrtvama raste cijena," *Danas* 423 (27 March 1990):12–13.

26 Ivan Grdešić, Mirjana Kasapović, Ivan Šiber and Nenad Zakošek, *Hrvatska u izborima '90* (Zagreb: Naprijed, 1991), p. 82.

27 VMRO was not the only party named resurrected from the Yugoslav past. In Croatia, the Party of Rights and the Croat Peasant Party were historical parties.

28 Other members elected were: Fikret Abdić (Muslim), Biljana Plavšić and

Nikola Koljević (Serbs), Stjepan Kljuić and Franjo Boraš (Croats), and Ejup Ganić.
29 Under the new constitution, the president had the right to propose the republic's prime minister and to dissolve the parliament.
30 Sabrina Ramet, "The Breakup of Yugoslavia," *Global Affairs* 6:3 (Spring 1991):104.
31 These included: the Party for Democratic Action (the Muslim party successful in Bosnia-Hercegovina), the Muslim Party for Equality, and Albanian Democratic Alliance.
32 It is outside of the scope of this article to discuss the origins of the war itself. See Ivo Banac, "Yugoslavia: The Fearful Asymmetry of War," *Daedalus* 121:2 (Spring 1992), pp. 141–74.
33 The referendum organized by Serb activists in parts of Croatia between August 19 and September 2 consisted of ballot slips marked "For Serbian Autonomy – Yes or No." This did not indicate whether it was political, cultural, or territorial autonomy subjected to vote.
34 An excellent source on the military role is James Gow, *Legitimacy and the Military: The Yugoslav Crisis,* (New York: St. Martin's Press, 1992). The leadership of the JNA revamped itself as the League of Communists-Movement for Yugoslavia (SK-PJ) which became known as the Generals' Party.

13. Democratization and the international system: The foreign policies of interim governments

1 Francis Fukuyama sees this unanimity as a sign that we have reached the end of history, as Hegel understood it. See Francis Fukuyama, "The End of History," and responding comments by Allan Bloom, Pierre Hassner, Gertrude Himmelfarb, Irving Kristol, Daniel Patrick Moynihan and Stephan Sestanovich in *The National Interest* no. 16 (Summer 1989):3–35.
2 In the last few years, the already vast literature on transitions has grown exponentially. See, for example, Samuel P. Huntington, *The Third Wave* (Norman: University of Oklahoma Press, 1991); Guiseppe Di Palma, *To Craft Democracies* (Berkeley: University of California Press, 1990); Nancy Bermeo, ed., *Liberalization and Democratization: Change in the Soviet Union and Eastern Europe* (Baltimore, Md.: Johns Hopkins University Press, 1991); special issue of *Daedalus* on "The Exit From Communism" 121:2 (Spring 1992).
3 Stephen Walt's work on the foreign policies of revolutionary states is a notable exception, but his research focuses exclusively on the international consequences of social revolutions, revolutions that, in his words, "create new states." The revolutions he examines are consolidated through dictatorship. As such, cases of democratic transition fall beyond the scope of his analysis. See Walt, "Revolution and War," *World Politics* 44:3 (April 1992):321–68.
4 Here I refer to variants of the "turning inward" argument, all of which stress the triumph of economic over political factors.
5 The cases were selected to maximize the variance in foreign policy outcomes for each type of sovereign interim government: provisional revolutionary government (opposition governs in the interim period), power-sharing government (opposition and representatives of the *ancien régime* govern), and care-

taker interim government (representatives of the old order supervise the transition).

6 Yossi Shain and Juan J. Linz, "The Role of Interim Governments in Transitions to Democracy," paper delivered at the APSA annual meetings, Washington, D.C., August 30–September 2, 1991, p. 4. For a full elaboration of this concept, see ibid., pp. 4ff. For a shorter, less amply documented version of this paper, see Shain and Linz, "The Role of Interim Governments," *Journal of Democracy* 3:7 (January, 1992):73–89.

7 Huntington, *The Third Wave*, p. 35.

8 Regardless of the aims of the transitional authority, clear signs of movement toward that promised end must quickly make themselves manifest, or the revolution arrested by the interim government's claim to power will begin anew, sweeping aside those who did not deliver on their promises. See Shain and Linz, APSA paper, p. 5.

9 On the dynamics of two-level games, see Robert Putnam, "Diplomacy and Domestic Politics: The Logic of Two-Level Games," *International Organization* 42:3 (Summer 1988):427–60.

10 Klaus Schwabe, *Woodrow Wilson, Revolutionary Germany, and Peacemaking, 1918–19* (Chapel Hill: University of North Carolina Press, 1985), pp. 30–7.

11 For a text of the note from the new German imperial chancellor to President Wilson, transmitted by the Swiss charge, Oederlin, see U.S. State Department, *Papers Relating to the Foreign Relations of the United States, 1918*, supplement 1 (the World War), vol. I (Washington: U.S. Government Printing Office, 1933), p. 338.

12 For the text of Prince Max's speech, published in the *North German Gazette* on October 6, see ibid., pp. 346–51.

13 Klaus Schwabe, op. cit., pp. 43–5; 50–5.

14 For the text of Solf's note, see U. S. State Department, *Papers Relating to the Foreign Relations of the United States, 1918*, op. cit., pp. 380–1.

15 See Arno J. Mayer, *Politics and Diplomacy of Peacemaking, 1918–1919* (New York: Knopf, 1967), pp. 55ff.

16 For the text of Wilson's third note, see U. S. State Department, *Papers Relating to the Foreign Relations of the United States, 1918*, op. cit., pp. 381–3.

17 Klaus Schwabe, op. cit., pp. 95–104.

18 Ibid., pp. 108, 105, 120, 126.

19 Ibid., pp. 121–2, 124.

20 M. Porto, "Portugal: Twenty Years of Change," in Allan Williams, *Southern Europe Transformed: Political and Economic Change in Greece, Italy, Portugal and Spain* (London: Harper and Row, 1984), pp. 97–8.

21 Di Palma, *To Craft Democracies*, pp. 71–3.

22 George W. Grayson, "Portugal's Crisis," *Current History* 73:431 (November 1977):173ff.

23 R. K. Ramazani, "Iran's Foreign Policy: Contending Orientations," in R. K. Ramazani, ed., op. cit., pp. 50–2. See also Shireen T. Hunter, *Iran and the World* (Bloomington: Indiana University Press, 1990), pp. 54–9.

24 See Richard Cottam, "Inside Revolutionary Iran," in R. K. Ramazani, ed., *Iran's Revolution: The Search for Concensus* (Bloomington: Indiana University Press, 1990), pp. 3–8.

25 For a penetrating analysis of the struggle between liberal and radical Islamists

during the provisional government period, see H. E. Chehabi, "The Provisional Government and the Transition from Monarchy to Islamic Republic in Iran," in this volume.

26 For the text of the Government's initial statement on foreign policy, see Robert Browder and Alexander Kerensky, eds., *The Russian Provisional Government 1917: Documents* (Stanford: Stanford University Press, 1961), vol. II, pp. 1042–3.

27 Ibid., pp. 1077–8.

28 Adam B. Ulam, *Expansion and Coexistence* (New York: Praeger, 1974), pp. 34 and 37.

29 Theda Skocpol, *States and Social Revolutions* (New York: Cambridge University Press, 1979), p. 209.

30 For a text of the second document, reluctantly drafted by the Kadet foreign minister Miliukov, see Frank Alfred Golder, ed., *Documents of Russian History, 1914–17* (New York: The Century Company, 1927), pp. 329–31.

31 See, for example, the British and American responses in Robert Browder and Alexander Kerensky, eds., *Documents,* vol II, pp. 1050, 1053.

32 Ibid., pp. 1058, 1098, 1106–10.

33 See Golder, ed., *Documents,* pp. 295–6. Miliukov later wrote a history of the Russian revolution, which has been translated into English in three volumes. See Paul N. Miliukov, *The Russian Revolution* (Gulf Breeze: Academic International Press, 1978).

34 Browder and Kerensky, eds., *Documents,* vol. II, pp. 1100–1. See also Kerensky's account in Alexander Kerensky, *The Catastrophe* (New York: D. Appleton and Company, 1927), pp. 129–35. Kerensky insists Miliukov was acting unilaterally. For a Kadet perspective on these and subsequent events, see Virgil D. Medlin and Steven L. Parsons, eds. *V. D. Nabokov and the Russian Provisional Government, 1917* (New Haven: Yale University Press, 1976), pp. 33–140.

35 Browder and Kerensky, eds., *Documents,* vol. II, pp. 1103–5. Lenin, of course, in evaluating the intentions of the coalition government would focus on the pledge of continuity and ignore the elements of substantive change in the government's official position. See ibid., pp. 1105–6.

36 For an account of the rhetoric Kerensky used in his attempts to rally Russian forces at the front, see Paul N. Miliukov, *The Russian Revolution* (Gulf Breeze: Academic International Press, 1978), vol. 1 (The Revolution Divided), pp. 97–8.

37 Robert Browder and Alexander Kerensky, eds., *Documents,* vol. II, pp. 1120–1.

38 See ibid., p. 1123.

39 Frank Alfred Golder, ed., *Documents,* pp. 366–8.

40 For a text of the declaration of the provisional government on the Ukrainian question, see ibid., pp. 439–40.

41 Ibid., pp. 440–3.

42 When I speak of Poland's power-sharing interim government, I am actually referring to two governments, the Mazowiecki government, which was the first Solidarity-led administration (formed in September 1989) and the Bielecki government, which was formed after Mazowiecki's defeat in the November 1990 presidential elections and presided over the period leading up to the first National Assembly elections in October 1991. Roger East, *Revolutions in Eastern Europe* (London: Pinter Publishers, 1992), p. 126.

43 Jan B. de Weydenthal, "Poland and the Soviet Alliance System," *Report on Eastern Europe*, June 29, 1990, pp. 30–2.

44 Michael Sadykiewicz and Douglas L. Clarke, "The New Polish Defense Doctrine: A Further Step Toward Sovereignty," *Report on Eastern Europe*, May 4, 1990, pp. 21 and 22–3. The new doctrine was drafted by a Communist-dominated National Defense Committee.

45 Louisa Vinton, "Soviet Union Begins Withdrawing Troops – But on Its Own Terms," *Report on Eastern Europe*, April 26, 1991, p. 21; Vladimir S. Kusin, "Security Concerns in Central Europe," *Report on Eastern Europe*, March 8, 1991, p. 31; Jan B. de Weydenthal, "Finding a Place in Europe," *Report on Eastern Europe*, December 28, 1990, p. 22; Anna Sabbat-Swidlicka, "The Signing of the Polish-German Border Treaty," *Report on Eastern Europe*, December 7, 1990, pp. 16–19.

46 Jan B. de Weydenthal, "Finding a place in Europe" and "Rapprochement with the West Continues," in *Report on Eastern Europe*, December 28, 1990, p. 23 and December 20, 1991, pp. 22–6.

47 Anna Sabbat-Swidlicka, "Friendship Declaration Signed With Ukraine and Russia," *Report on Eastern Europe*, November 2, 1990, pp. 24–7; Roman Stefanowski, "Polish-Soviet Trade Relations," *Report on Eastern Europe*, May 18, 1990, pp. 32–3.

48 In addition to electing General Jaruzelski president, the round table agreements of March and April 1989 also provided for Communist control of the Ministries of Defense, Foreign Relations, and the Interior. See Paul Lewis, "Non-Competitive Elections and Regime Change: Poland 1989," *Parliamentary Affairs*, January 1990, pp. 90–107.

49 Jiri Pehe, "Diplomatic Relations with Israel to be Resumed," *Report on Eastern Europe*, February 2, 1990, pp. 6–8, and Havel's first New Year's Address, reprinted in Paul Wilson, ed., *Open Letters: Selected Writings, 1965–1990* (New York: Knopf, 1991), pp. 390–6. Shimon Peres was an honored guest in Prague less than a month after the commencement of the Velvet revolution.

50 Jiri Pehe, "Vaclav Havel's First Two Months in Office," *Report on Eastern Europe*, March 16, 1990, pp. 11–15; Peter Martin, "Czechoslovakia and the Vatican Restoring Relations," *Report on Eastern Europe*, March 23, 1990, pp. 8–10. On Havel's conception of the new spirit of Czechoslovak foreign policy, see Václav Havel, *Summer Meditations* (New York: Knopf, 1992), pp. 97–101.

51 Peter Martin, "Czechoslovakia's New Foreign Policy," *Report on Eastern Europe*, March 9, 1990, p. 19. The latter proposal was something of an embarrassment, since both superpowers politely ignored Havel's offer. Havel also offered to mediate the conflict between Moscow and the Baltics.

52 The choice of words is Havel's. See Václav Havel, *Summer Meditations* (New York: Knopf, 1992), p. 82.

53 The Red Army's timely apology for the 1968 invasion made this all the easier. For the text of the apology, see *Krasnaia Zvezda*, December 5, 1989, p. 3.

54 Jan Obrman, "Czechoslovakia and the Arms Trade," *Report on Eastern Europe*, April 20, 1990, pp. 21–2.

55 Peter Martin, "Czechoslovakia's New Foreign Policy," March 9, 1990, *Report on Eastern Europe*, pp. 17–19.

56 Richard Weitz, "International Security Institutions and Eastern Europe,"

paper delivered at the APSA annual meetings, Chicago, September 3–6, 1992, pp. 30–3.
57 Jan Obrman, "Putting the Country Back on the Map," *Report on Eastern Europe,* December 28, 1990, p. 11. Later in the year, Havel would express an interest in joining NATO. See ibid., p. 12.
58 Jan Obrman, "Foreign Policy: Sources, Concepts, Problems," *Report on Eastern Europe,* September 14, 1990, pp. 12–13. Since Havel's Washington visit, Czechoslovakia has been a vocal supporter of maintaining a strong American presence in Europe's new security structures. See, for example, speeches by Havel and Dienstbier in Federalní Ministerstvo Zahraničních Věcí, *Československá Zahraniční Politika: Dokumenty,* 3/1991, pp. 179–86, 4/ 1991, pp. 285–92, and 8–9/91, pp. 849–51 and 897–906.
59 The Paris CSCE summit meeting in November 1990, which resulted in the Charter of Paris for a New Europe, adopted many aspects of Dienstbier's proposal, including the call for the creation of a Council of Security and Cooperation. The Council held its second meeting in Prague in January 1992. For the texts of the Prague Document and the Summary of Conclusions that resulted, see Federalní Ministerstvo Zahraničních Věcí, *Československá Zahraniční Politika: Dokumenty,* 1/1992, pp. 68–80 and 91–100. For documents from the first meeting of the Council in Berlin in June 1991, see Federalní Ministerstvo Zahraničních Věcí, *Československá Zahraniční Politika: Dokumenty,* 6/1991/b, pp. 576–89.
60 Remarks by Foreign Minister Dienstbier, Center for European Studies, Harvard University, May 1990.
61 See, for example, Civic Forum's letter (11/21/89) to Bush and Gorbachev, demanding a condemnation of the '68 Soviet invasion, as well as the movement's seven point program of 11/26/89, which included a call for the integration of Czechoslovakia into the "Common European Home." RFE Research, *Situation Report: Czechoslovakia* 14:51 (December 22, 1989):4–5.
62 While a dissident, Dienstbier wrote an entire book on Czechoslovak foreign policy, *Snění o Evropě* (Dreaming of Europe), which was published in samizdat. The manuscript was published in Czechoslovakia after the revolution. See Jiří Dienstbier, *Snění o Evropě: Politický esej* (Praha: Lidové noviny, 1990).
63 Michael Kraus, "Settling Accounts: Post-Communist Czechoslovakia," Paper delivered at the APSA annual meetings, Chicago, September 3–6, 1992, pp. 4–6. That the Czechoslovak Communists had minimal actual power in the interim government is one of the reasons they did not find it necessary to immediately rename their party, as their counterparts in Poland and Hungary, whose role in shaping the transition was more substantive, were compelled to do, if they were to present themselves as agents of change.
64 Shain and Linz characterize Greece's transition as a case of attempted (but failed) "power-sharing from without." See Shain and Linz, APSA paper, pp. 18–19.
65 Nikiforos Diamandouros, "Regime Change and the Prospects for Democracy in Greece, 1974–83," in Guillermo O'Donnell, Philippe C. Schmitter and Laurence Whitehead, eds., *Transitions from Authoritarian Rule: Southern Europe* (Baltimore, Md.: Johns Hopkins University Press, 1986), p. 157.
66 Harry J. Psomiades, "Greece: From the Colonels' Rule to Democracy," in John Herz, ed., *From Dictatorship to Democracy: Coping with the Legacies of Authoritarianism and Totalitarianism* (Westport, Conn.: Greenwood Press,

1982), pp. 252–3; Robert Fishman, "Rethinking State and Regime: Southern Europe's Transition to Democracy," *World Politics*, 42:3 (April 1990):440.
67 Harry J. Psomiades in Herz, op. cit. (1982), pp. 253–5.
68 Robert Fishman, op. cit., p. 432.
69 Harry J. Psomiades in Herz, op. cit. (1982), pp. 255–7.
70 Laurence Whitehead, "International Aspects of Democratization," in Guillermo O'Donnell, Philippe C. Schmitter, and Laurence Whitehead, eds., *Transitions from Authoritarian Rule: Comparative Perspectives* (Baltimore, Md.: Johns Hopkins University Press, 1986), pp. 33–4; Harry J. Psomiades in Hertz, op. cit. (1982), p. 260.
71 Ibid., p. 256.
72 Virgilio Beltran, "Political Transition in Argentina: 1982 to 1985," *Armed Forces and Society* 13:2 (Winter 1987):217.
73 Aldo C. Vacs, "Authoritarian Breakdown and Redemocratization in Argentina," in James M. Malloy and Mitchell A. Seligson, eds., *Authoritarians and Democrats: Regime Transitions in Latin America* (Pittsburgh, Pa.: University of Pittsburgh Press, 1987), pp. 28–9; Phillip Mauceri, "Nine Cases of Transitions and Consolidations: Argentina," in Robert A. Pastor, ed., *Democracy in the Americas: Stopping the Pendulum* (New York: Holmes and Meier, 1989), pp. 241–2.
74 Ibid., p. 242.
75 Eduardo Viola and Scott Mainwaring, "Transitions to Democracy: Brazil and Argentina in the 1980s," *Journal of International Affairs* 38 (Winter 1985):206–10 (quoted segment from p. 209).
76 Ibid., pp. 214–16; Edward Schumacher, "Argentina and Democracy," *Foreign Affairs* 62 (Summer 1984):1084–5; Daniel Poneman, *Argentina: Democracy on Trial* (New York: Paragon, 1987), pp. 57–8.
77 Laurence Whitehead, "International Aspects of Democratization," in Guillermo O'Donnell, Philippe C. Schmitter and Laurence Whitehead, eds., *Transitions from Authoritarian Rule: Comparative Perspectives* (Baltimore, Md.: Johns Hopkins University Press, 1986), p. 20; Benny Pollack, *The Paradoxes of Spanish Foreign Policy* (New York: St. Martin's Press, 1987), pp. 134–5, 150–1; Edward Malefakis, "Spain and Its Francoist Heritage," in John Herz, ed., *From Dictatorship to Democracy* (Westport, Conn.: Greenwood Press, 1982), pp. 220–1.
78 Kenneth Medhurst, "Spain's Evolutionary Pathway from Dictatorship to Democracy," in Geoffrey Pridham, ed., *The New Mediterranean Democracies* (London: Frank Cass and Company, 1984), p. 32.
79 Quoted in Guy de Carmoy and Jonathan Story, *Western Europe in World Affairs: Continuity, Change, and Challenge* (New York: Praeger, 1986), pp. 68–9.
80 Benny Pollack, op. cit. (1987), p. 138.
81 Ibid., pp. 1 and 152–6. For a complete history of the debates and events leading up to Spain's eventual NATO membership, see ibid., pp. 149–74.
82 On the formation of the UCD, see Paul Preston, *The Triumph of Democracy in Spain* (London: Methuen, 1986), pp. 108–13.
83 Robert Fishman, "Rethinking State and Regime: Southern Europe's Transition to Democracy," *World Politics* 42:3 (April 1990):440. As I point out above, what this symbolic break would have entailed in the realm of Spain's external relations, in light of the paradoxes of Francoist foreign policy, is an open question.

84 Donald Share, *The Making of Spanish Democracy* (New York: Praeger, 1986), pp. 19–20.
85 On the attitudes and actions of the armed forces during the transition, see Stanley G. Payne, "The Role of the Armed Forces in the Spanish Transition," in Robert P. Clark and Michael Haltzel, eds., *Spain in the 1980s: The Democratic Transition and a New International Role* (Cambridge: Ballinger, 1987), pp. 79–95.
86 For a concise and lucid summary of the lines of political division in Hungary's transition, see Judy Batt, *East Central Europe: From Reform to Transformation* (London: Royal Institute of International Affairs, 1991), pp. 34–8.
87 Alfred Reisch, "New Foreign Policy Emphasis on Opening Up and National Interests," *Report on Eastern Europe,* January 12, 1990, p. 15; Alfred Reisch, "Primary Foreign Policy Objective to Rejoin Europe," *Report on Eastern Europe,* December 28, 1990, pp. 15–16; Alfred Reisch, "The Hard Task of Setting Relations with the USSR on a New Footing," *Report on Eastern Europe,* May 24, 1991, pp. 6–7.
88 See Zoltan D. Barany and Alfred Reisch, "Withdrawal of All Soviet Troops by End of 1990 Demanded," *Report on Eastern Europe,* February 9, 1990, pp. 22–5.
89 Alfred Reisch, "The Hungarian Dilemma: After the Warsaw Pact, Neutrality or NATO?," *Report on Eastern Europe,* April 13, 1990, pp. 17–19.
90 That the Soviet and Hungarian authorities reached an agreement on a timetable for accelerated withdrawal just two weeks prior to the elections, likewise, is not surprising. The Soviet troop withdrawal was completed in June of 1991.
91 Alfred Reisch, "Government wants Negotiated Withdrawal from the Warsaw Pact," *Report on Eastern Europe,* June 8, 1990, pp. 25–34 and "Interview with Foreign Minister Geza Jeszenszky," *Report on Eastern Europe,* July 27, 1990, pp. 17–18.
92 Exceptions include Laurence Whitehead, who has examined the influence of international factors on democratization and Miles Kahler, who has explored the consequences for domestic politics of British and French decolonization. See Laurence Whitehead, "International Aspects of Democratization," in Guillermo O'Donnell, Philippe C. Schmitter, and Laurence Whitehead, eds., *Transitions from Authoritarian Rule: Comparative Perspectives* (Baltimore, Md.: Johns Hopkins University Press, 1986), and Miles Kahler, *Decolonization in Britain and France* (Princeton, N.J.: Princeton University Press, 1984), especially pp. 3–58 and 354–88. Like Kahler, I am also interested in the domestic ramifications of the foreign policy choices states must make.
93 See Barrington Moore, Jr., *Social Origins of Dictatorship and Democracy* (Boston: Beacon Press, 1966), especially pp. 426–31.
94 Samuel P. Huntington, *The Third Wave* (Norman: University of Oklahoma Press, 1991), p. 274.
95 Linz and Stepan refer to this challenge as a "stateness problem." See Juan J. Linz and Alfred Stepan, "Political Identities and Electoral Sequences: Spain, the Soviet Union, and Yugoslavia," *Daedalus* 121:2 (Spring 1992):123.

Index